John Locke

Philosopher
Of
American Liberty

Praise for *John Locke: Philosopher of American Liberty*

Mary-Elaine Swanson's book on John Locke is a masterpiece of scholarship, made interesting and readable for the twenty-first century. Was Locke a founder of the unbelieving "Enlightenment"? Or was he a Christian apologist who promoted a Biblical view of government and society? Mary-Elaine's fine book gives an authoritative defense of Locke and his Christianity.

Marshall Foster, DD
Author, Speaker, and President, World History Institute, Thousand Oaks, California
Author, *The American Covenant: The Untold Story*, co-authored by Mary-Elaine Swanson

In *John Locke: Philosopher of American Liberty,* **Mary-Elaine Swanson** shows how modern academia gets it wrong again. The founding fathers of America are often presented as atheists, or at best a bunch of deists, along with all those political philosophers who influenced them—Locke being chief among them. Unfortunately, many Christian thinkers have been influenced by these views, writing that Locke exalted reason above revelation and saw the laws of nature as more valuable than the laws of nature's God. Swanson clearly shows that Locke was no deist, rationalist, or secularist, but Christian in his profession and Biblical in his worldview. According to Locke, "the holy Scripture is to me... the constant guide of my belief; and I shall always hearken to it, as containing infallible truth relating to things of the highest concernment."

Swanson does an excellent job in clarifying ideas of Locke that are misunderstood, including *tabula rasa* (the mind as a blank slate) and the laws of nature. She clearly traces the influence of Locke upon the founding of America and shows how the founding fathers and founding clergy looked to Locke as the source of many of their ideas. Jefferson considered Locke as one of the three greatest men that ever lived. Swanson's book is the best way you can get to know this important man.

Stephen McDowell
President, The Providence Foundation and Biblical Worldview University
Charlottesville, Virginia

Free men, especially in America, have recognized a minimum of six kinds of liberty. Christians the world over, no matter what form of civil government prevails, can enjoy the first two kinds of internal, God-given liberty: Spiritual or Christian liberty (Romans 2:8; 2 Cor. 3:17; Gal. 5:1) and its correlative, liberty of conscience (Acts 16:24). But in God's Providence, Americans studied and appropriated much of John Locke's view of God, man, and government and subsequently enjoyed the fullest expression of the four "external" liberties once secured by our Constitutional Federal Republic: economic, religious, civil, and political liberty.

In this compelling and timely volume, Mary-Elaine Swanson affirms John Locke's Christian character and convictions, and documents how he inspired the American clergy and our founding statesmen, far in advance of others, to elucidate the Biblical and reasonable ground or foundation of American Liberty. Read and be refreshed with the historic path of Biblical reasoning which helped to establish and advance the greatest expression of individual liberty in the history of the world.

James B. Rose
Author, Educator, and President of the American Christian History Institute
Palo Cedro, California

Praise for John Locke: Philosopher of American Liberty

Swanson's excellent groundbreaking book *John Locke: Philosopher of American Liberty* is a much-needed antidote to current misinformation about Locke. In Part I, using his essay *The Reasonableness of Christianity* and other writings, Swanson demonstrates clearly and unmistakably that Locke was a Bible-believing, Trinitarian Christian, and that he based his political theories on his Biblical convictions. In Part II she demonstrates that the colonial American religious and political leaders based their case for independence upon Lockean theory, while the radicals who engineered the French Revolution ignored Locke and followed Rousseau—with tragic results. Finally, she demonstrates that modern American jurists have discarded the Lockean principles of the U.S. Constitution in favor of a "living Constitution" that can be stretched to mean whatever a liberal judge wants it to mean.

At last, someone has understood Locke's thinking and its importance for American constitutionalism today.

John A. Eidsmoe, JD, DMin
Colonel, Alabama State Defense Force; Legal Counsel, Foundation for Moral Law
Author, *Christianity and the Constitution: The Faith of Our Founding Fathers*

Mary-Elaine Swanson's work gives irrefutable, primary-source evidence that Locke's ideas are rooted deeply in Christian doctrine. "Why is it important to us today that a seventeenth century philosopher has been misunderstood?" she asks. When John Locke's ideas are characterized as being rooted in godless rationalism, American liberty is <u>mis</u>characterized because John Locke's ideas formed the Declaration and the U.S. Constitution. Mrs. Swanson's *John Locke* gives strength to the link between Christ and American liberty which is of considerable importance to the future of the United States. Because Americans generally are disconnected from their true national identity, this book should be in every home and every schoolroom.

Carole Adams, PhD
President, Foundation for American Christian Education
Founder, StoneBridge School, Chesapeake, Virginia

What a blessing to have a new book showing the Christian contributions of the great English philosopher John Locke, whose political writings were an enormous influence on America's founders in the establishment of representative government. Often ignored today is the importance of his Biblical faith. This book sets the record straight.

Jerry Newcombe, DMin
Spokesman, Truth in Action Ministries (formerly Coral Ridge)
Author, *The Book that Made America: How the Bible Formed Our Nation*

This book makes clear the impact of "The Great Mr. Locke" upon America's founding clergy. Their studied sermons and teachings are apparent in the words and reasoning of America's founding fathers. The intellectual quality with which Mrs. Swanson reveals distortions of Locke's positions is impressive.

This book ranks among the ten most significant books of the decade. It should be read by every American pastor and activist patriot! "Ignorant activism is more dangerous than apathy!"

Ben Gilmore
Founder and Director, ACH Study Groups, Citrus Heights, California

Praise for John Locke: Philosopher of American Liberty

Government today is on steroids, taking rights from the people at an exponential rate. This is exactly why Mary-Elaine Swanson's timely book, *John Locke — Philosopher of American Liberty*, is so vitally needed. If Americans are not aware of where our liberties came from, they will slip through our fingers like sand. The most common form of government in all of the 6,000 years of recorded human history has been dictatorship. Whether called Pharaohs, Caesars, Emperors, Sultans, Rajas, Kings, Khans, Kaisers, or Czars, power always concentrates into the hands of one individual—the dictator. Equality is relative, based on how close a relationship you can get to this dictator. If you are his friend, you are more equal, if you are not his friend, you are less equal, and if you are his enemy, you are dead—it's called treason. In America, we take for granted ideas such as inalienable natural rights, private property, right to resist unlawful authority, parental authority, separation of powers, and social compact—where governments "derive their just powers from the consent of the governed." Our liberties did not occur by accident. They are the result of centuries of sacrifice and brilliant minds, such as John Locke. We are greatly indebted to Mary-Elaine Swanson for helping to preserve our liberties by reminding us of their origins through her classic book.

William J. Federer
Best-selling author of *America's God and Country Encyclopedia of Quotations,*
Change to Chains — the 6,000 Year Quest for Control.
Nationally-known speaker, host of Faith in History on TV, and
AmericanMinute.com daily radio feature

God's Hand of Providence brings into this hour of history no more timely a volume of work than *John Locke: Philosopher of American Liberty*, by Mary-Elaine Swanson. Mrs. Swanson's masterful research of primary sources, patient pursuit of truth, intellectual acuteness, intense labors, and ease in articulating philosophical reasoning with her customarily dignified writing style will be appreciated by all students and lovers of liberty for decades to come. She substantively and convincingly recovers the Christian reputation of an individual so much maligned by modernists of the past two hundred years, of a man counted guilty of denying Christianity by his associations, rather than judged by his intrinsic character and practices. To separate John Locke—the principal philosopher of the American Revolution—from his Christianity is simply to separate America from Christianity. That would attribute the greatest individual liberty known to mankind to the wit and wiles of human reason alone, without the guidance of Divine Revelation; which also is to say man, not God, is the creator of man and is the author of his own liberty. The Constitution of the United States derives its purpose and political principles from The Declaration of Independence. The Declaration is born of the extensively studied and widely taught *Treatises On Civil Government* by John Locke. Without the Biblical scholarship of a John Locke, American liberty could hardly have ever come to exist in the world. *John Locke: Philosopher of American Liberty* affirms the fact, "There would be no America if there were no Christianity," an idea likely to disturb the mind of a modernist intellectual, but a truth welcomed by every true free thinker.

Katherine Dang
President and Founder, Philomath Foundation
Author, *Universal History*, Volumes I and II

Praise for John Locke: Philosopher of American Liberty

The deep Biblical roots of America's liberty are largely unknown to Americans today. John Calvin's role as a theological father of American liberty and John Robinson's role as Shepherd of the Pilgrim Fathers who helped to plant the theory of Ecclesiastical liberty in Plymouth through the hearts and minds of the Mayflower Pilgrims are slowly being recovered.

However, there has remained a deep chasm in the minds of many as to the origin of the civil liberties argued and defended during the time of the war for American Independence. That the Clergy were deeply involved is obvious, but did they derive their ideas of civil liberty from foreign, pagan sources, or did they derive them from the Bible? When using phrases such as the "law of nature," "liberty," "toleration," and a "state of nature," some believers today assume the definitions according to pagan thought and thus they remain isolated from impacting their culture, finding no historic Biblical link for righteous civil action in the history of their nation.

What Mary-Elaine Swanson has done in her masterful book is to connect the missing link between the Biblical ideas of church government found among the Pilgrims and Puritans prior to the Great Awakening and the powerful sermons that inspired the American Colonies to stand "as one man" in the face of British tyranny. That link was John Locke. He was not a deist, and he was not a pagan, but he was a Puritan in the Reformed tradition of authentic Christianity, and theologically linked the church government among God's people as a model for the civil liberties of a nation.

I highly recommend this book, for it will help you to know the real meaning of the "law of nature" as it was embraced in Colonial America and the true jurisdictional separation of church and state under God embraced in the Constitution. It will demonstrate Locke's role of taking ideas from the Bible, applying them to the civil realm, and theologically leading many of the Colonial Clergy for more than half a century prior to the birth of American civil liberty. John Locke, as Swanson demonstrates, is truly the philosopher of American liberty.

Paul Jehle, MDiv, EdD
Senior Pastor, New Testament Church
Executive Director, Plymouth Rock Foundation
Plymouth, Massachusetts

If there ever was a right time for the people of the United States to become knowledgeable about the philosophical underpinnings of our country, this is it. The great bulk of our population is woefully ignorant of the fundamental principles of our nation's founding. Mary-Elaine Swanson's scholarly work is the antidote for our history-deficient population. Arming our people with the information in *John Locke* will equip them to become involved in the restoration of America's solid, founding principles of liberty and fervent Christianity. This should be read by anyone who is deeply troubled about the direction in which America is headed.

Robert M. Damir, MBA, JD
Founder, Bridgemont Christian High School
San Francisco, California

Praise for John Locke: Philosopher of American Liberty

Late in life the author assumed the hugely difficult task of writing about John Locke's life work, influence, and impact. The book is a worthy accomplishment. Her valuable insights, everyday language, and rich documentation from original sources make understanding John Locke disarmingly simple. For anyone newly interested in John Locke, this book provides an excellent foundation for learning the broad sweep of his life and thought, and it gently corrects a number of misconceptions generally received about him. This book will be a particularly helpful starting point for one who chooses to dig deeper into the details of Locke's life and thought.

Gary Amos
Author, *Defending the Declaration:*
How the Bible and Christianity Influenced the Writing of the Declaration of Independence

I often tell my students that it is vital that they actually read what the Founding Fathers wrote. But equally vital is to read what the Founding Fathers read. In this important work, Mary-Elaine Swanson reminds us all just why. In many respects, Locke was the fountainhead of American liberty and, as this book shows, he may yet prove to be the harbinger of a new day of freedom ahead. Highly recommended.

George Grant, PhD
Author, Educator, and Pastor of Parish Presbyterian Church, Franklin, Tennessee

Swanson's scholarly work on John Locke is an essential read for anyone interested in discovering America's success formula. She corrects the record on Locke, which has been grossly distorted by those wishing to downplay the influence of the Bible on America. Every state and national legislator in America needs to read this book and rediscover the true meaning of the Laws of Nature and of Nature's God.

Rick Green, JD
Founder, Torch of Freedom Foundation and Patriot Academy
Co-host of WallBuilders Live with David Barton, Aledo, Texas

John Locke was the premier philosopher to guide our founders in their writings which produced the Declaration and the Constitution. This book should be read by anyone who wants to know how our founders were guided by Biblical truth to form the first Christian republic in history. Of the many sources for the thinking of those who helped create our nation, John Locke's contribution was most important. Almost every pastor and every college student in colonial times studied the principles of government proposed by John Locke.

This book will help pastors, educators, and elected officials understand the principles upon which our form of government is based. In order for our nation to return to governing by our Constitution, we must be willing to study the works of those men who understood the Laws of Nature and of Nature's God. This book on John Locke is an excellent place to begin.

Rev. David R. Brown
Educator, author, Pastor of Danville (California) Presbyterian Church (PCA)

John Locke

PHILOSOPHER
OF
AMERICAN LIBERTY

Why Our Founders Fought for
"Life, Liberty, and Property"

Mary-Elaine Swanson

Ventura, California

2012

John Locke
Philosopher of American Liberty
by Mary-Elaine Swanson

Copyright © 2011 by Mary-Elaine Swanson

Second Printing 2013

International Standard Book Number: 978-0-9831957-3-3

Library of Congress Control Number: 2012936346

James B. Rose
Representative of the Author and Special Consultant to the Publisher

Theology Editor: Ronald W. Kirk

Editor and Design: Desta Garrett

Copy Editor: Mary Malcolm

Original Cover Painting by Rich Brimer, Camarillo, California
Inspired by the 1697 painting from life by Sir Godfrey Kneller (1646–1723)
and other historical images of John Locke.

As publisher I chose to commission a new painting instead of using one of the few classic portraits from life painted in Locke's latter years. In this book, you will get to know the colorful, engaging, and friendly man who maintained deep, lifelong friendships. Mr. Locke was a brilliant and serious student of Holy Scripture, who reasoned theologically and systematically from the Bible to develop its application in the arena of civil government. He was not a cloistered scholar but an active participant and influence in the great events of his day, including the Glorious Revolution in England. His governmental reasoning from the Bible also profoundly influenced the quest for American liberty. He befriended, corresponded with, and served men and women, churchmen, nobles and kings, and scholars such as Isaac Newton, as well as gardeners and tradesmen. He practiced as physician to many and as a playful friend and educational Christian tutor and mentor to their children. This is the John Locke we desire to be revealed in the hand-painted cover. – GCN

EDITOR'S NOTE: Some British and antiquated spellings and unusual initial capitalizations used by custom or for emphasis in the quoted material from old original sources have been retained.

Printed in the United States of America
by Versa Press

Published 2012 by

 Nordskog Publishing Inc.

Nordskog Publishing, Inc.
2716 Sailor Avenue, Ventura, California 93001, USA
1-805-642-2070 • 1-805-276-5129
www.NordskogPublishing.com

Member
Christian Small
Publishers Association

IN MEMORIAM

VERNA M. HALL

1912–1987

ACKNOWLEDGMENTS

THE author wishes to acknowledge the great debt of gratitude she owes to Verna M. Hall, historian of the Christian history of the United States Constitution which Miss Hall made come to life in her many historical compilations of the Founding period. Seeing my interest in John Locke and my growing conviction that he had been greatly misunderstood by many modern writers, she encouraged me to write a book about him. I was startled by her suggestion, since I was then a young and inexperienced writer. I benefited greatly from her wise counsels, particularly her advice to "begin with primary documentation. Later you can include secondary sources that you know are reliable." These words should be engraved on the consciousness of every budding author of biography. After years of writing other books and articles in the field of America's Christian history and lecturing on the subject, the book on Locke was finally written. It was put aside, however, for a long time because of other writing demands. Now here it is at last thanks to Nordskog Publishing Inc., which took a keen interest in its completion.

As is often the case, many people contributed helpful suggestions to the writing of this book.

Among them is Sylvia Vrabec, who read every page, chapter by chapter, and was a constant encouragement and support to me. James B. Rose, my colleague at the American Christian History Institute, is a very wise critic whose counsels were invaluable. Mrs. Bobbie Ames, who published my book *The Education of James Madison*, has also been tireless in spreading the word about my Locke book. When my energy has been low, it has been quickly revived by the insistent question, "When is the Locke book coming out?" posed by Ruth Smith of the Pilgrim Institute. Maria Washington has urged me on and made several helpful suggestions.

Finally, I must not neglect to thank my editors at NPI, Ron Kirk and Desta Garrett. Their patience and meticulous attention to detail are much appreciated.

TABLE OF CONTENTS

FOREWORD

by David Barton

FOUNDER AND PRESIDENT
WALLBUILDERS

JOHN LOCKE (1632-1704) is one of the most important, but largely unknown names in American history today. A celebrated English philosopher, educator, government official, and theologian, it is not an exaggeration to say that without his substantial influence on American thinking, there might well be no United States of America today—or at the very least, America certainly would not exist with the same level of rights, stability of government, and quality of life that we have enjoyed for well over two centuries.

Historians—especially of previous generations—were understandably effusive in their praise of Locke. For example:

➤ In 1833, Justice Joseph Story, author of the famed *Commentaries on the Constitution,* described Locke as "a most strenuous asserter of liberty"[1] who helped establish in this country the sovereignty of the people over the government,[2] majority rule with minority protection,[3] and the rights of conscience.[4]

➤ In 1834, George Bancroft, called the "Father of American History," described Locke as "the rival of 'the ancient philosophers' to whom the world had 'erected statues',"[5] and noted that Locke esteemed "the pursuit of truth the first object of life and...never sacrificed a conviction to an interest."[6]

➤ In 1872, historian Richard Frothingham said that Locke's principles—principles that he said were "inspired and imbued with the Christian

---

* See Endnotes to the Foreword on pages xxiv-xxvi.

idea of man"—produced the "leading principle [of] republicanism" that was "summed up in the Declaration of Independence and became the American theory of government."[7]

➤ In the 1890s, John Fiske, the celebrated nineteenth-century historian, affirmed that Locke brought to America "the idea of complete liberty of conscience in matters of religion" allowing persons with "any sort of notion about God" to be protected "against all interference or molestation,"[8] and that Locke should "be ranked in the same order with Aristotle."[9]

Such acknowledgments continued across the generations; and even over the past half century, U.S. presidents have also regularly acknowledged America's debt to John Locke:

➤ President Richard Nixon affirmed that "John Locke's concept of 'life, liberty, and property'" was the basis of "the inalienable rights of man" in the Declaration of Independence.[10]

➤ President Gerald Ford avowed that "Our revolutionary leaders heeded John Locke's teaching 'Where there is no law, there is no freedom'."[11]

➤ President Ronald Reagan confirmed that much in America "testif[ies] to the power and the vision of free men inspired by the ideals and dedication to liberty of John Locke...."[12]

➤ President Bill Clinton reminded the British Prime Minister that "Throughout our history, our peoples have reinforced each other in the living classroom of democracy. It is difficult to imagine Jefferson, for example, without John Locke before him."[13]

➤ President George W. Bush confessed that "We're sometimes faulted for a naive faith that liberty can change the world. [But] [i]f that's an error, it began with reading too much John Locke...."[14]

The influence of Locke on America was truly profound; he was what we now consider to be a renaissance man—an individual skilled in numerous areas and diverse subjects. He had been well-educated and received multiple degrees from some of the best institutions of his day, but he also pursued extensive self-education in the fields of religion, philosophy, education, law, and government—subjects on which he authored numerous substantial works, most of which still remain in print today more than three centuries after he published them.

One of Locke's earliest writings was his 1660 "First Tract of Government" followed by his 1662 "Second Tract of Government." Neither was published at that time, but they later appeared in 1689 as his famous *Two Treatises of Government*. The first treatise (i.e., a thorough examination) was a brilliant Biblical refutation of Sir Robert Filmer's *Patriarcha* in which Filmer had attempted to produce Biblical support for the errant "Divine Right of Kings" doctrine. Locke's second treatise set forth the fundamental principles defining the proper role, function, and operation of a sound government. Significantly, Locke had ample opportunity to assert such principles, for he spent time under some of England's worst monarchs, including Charles I, Charles II, and James II; but he also saw many of his principles enacted into policy during the rule of Lord Cromwell and then William and Mary.

In 1664, Locke penned "Questions Concerning the Law of Nature" in which he asserted that human reason and Divine revelation were fully compatible and were not enemies—that the Law of Nature actually came from God Himself. (This work was not published, but many of its concepts appeared in his subsequent writings.)

In 1667, he privately penned his "Essay Concerning Toleration," first published in 1689 as *A Letter Concerning Toleration*. This work, like his *Two Treatises*, was published anonymously, for it had placed his very life in danger by directly criticizing and challenging the frequent brutal oppression of the government-established and government-run Church of England. (Under English law, the Anglican Church and its 39 Doctrinal Articles were the measure for all religious faith in England; every citizen was required to attend an Anglican Church. Dissenters who opposed those Anglican requirements were regularly persecuted or even killed. Locke objected to the government establishing specific church doctrines by law, argued for a separation of the state from the church, and urged religious toleration for those who did not adhere to Anglican doctrines.) When Locke's position on religious toleration was attacked by defenders of the government-run church, he responded with *A Second Letter Concerning Toleration* (1690), and then *A Third Letter for Toleration* (1692)—both also published anonymously.

In 1690, Locke published his famous *Essay Concerning Human Understanding*. This work resulted in him being called the "Father of Empiricism," which is the doctrine that knowledge is derived primarily from experience. Rationalism, on the other hand, places reason above experience; and while Locke definitely did not oppose reason, his approach to learning was more focused on the practical, whereas rationalism was more focused on the theoretical.

In 1693, Locke published *Some Thoughts Concerning Education*. Originally a series of letters written to his friend concerning the education of a son, in them Locke suggested the best ways to educate children. He proposed a three-pronged holistic approach to education that included (1) a regimen of bodily exercise and maintenance of physical health (that there should be "a sound mind in a sound body"[15]), (2) the development of a virtuous character (which he considered to be the most important element of education), and (3) the training of the mind through practical and useful academic curriculum (also encouraging students to learn a practical trade). Locke believed that education made the individual—that "of all the men we meet with, nine parts of ten are what they are, good or evil, useful or not, by their education."[16] This book became a runaway best-seller, being printed in nearly every European language and going through 53 editions over the next century.

Locke's latter writings focused primarily on theological subjects, including *The Reasonableness of Christianity as Delivered in the Scriptures* (1695), *A Vindication of the Reasonableness of Christianity* (1695), *A Second Vindication of the Reasonableness of Christianity* (1697), *A Common-Place-Book to the Holy Bible* (1697), which was a re-publication of what he called *Graphautarkeia, or, The Scriptures Sufficiency Practically Demonstrated* (1676), and finally *A Paraphrase and Notes on the Epistles of St. Paul to the Galatians, 1 and 2 Corinthians, Romans, Ephesians* (published posthumously in 1707).

In his *Reasonableness of Christianity*, Locke urged the Church of England to reform itself so as to allow inclusion of members from other Christian denominations—i.e., the Dissenters. He recommended that the Church place its emphasis on the major things of Christianity (such as an individual's relationship with Jesus Christ) rather than on lesser things (such as liturgy, church hierarchy and structure, and form of discipline). That work also defended Christianity against the attacks of skeptics and secularists, who had argued that Divine revelation must be rejected because truth could be established only through reason. Locke's defense evoked strong criticism from rationalists, thus causing him to pen two additional works defending the reasonableness of Christianity.

(While these are some of Locke's better known works, he also wrote on many other subjects, including poetry and literature, medicine, commerce and economics, and even agriculture.)

The impact of Locke's writings had a direct and substantial influence on American thinking and behavior in both the religious and the civil realms—an influence especially visible in the years leading up to America's separation from Great Britain. In fact, the Founding Fathers openly acknowledged their debt to Locke:

➤ John Adams praised Locke's *Essay on Human Understanding,* openly acknowledging that "Mr. Locke…has steered his course into the unenlightened regions of the human mind, and like Columbus, has discovered a new world." [17]

➤ Declaration signer Benjamin Rush said that Locke was not only "an oracle as to the principles…of government" [18] (an "oracle" is a wise authority whose opinions are not questioned) but that in philosophy, he was also a "justly celebrated oracle, who first unfolded to us a map of the intellectual world," [19] having "cleared this sublime science of its technical rubbish and rendered it both intelligible and useful." [20]

➤ Benjamin Franklin said that Locke was one of "the best English authors" for the study of "history, rhetoric, logic, moral and natural philosophy." [21]

➤ Noah Webster, a Founding Father called the "Schoolmaster to America," directly acknowledged Locke's influence in establishing sound principles of education. [22]

➤ James Wilson (a signer of the Declaration and the Constitution, and an original Justice on the U.S. Supreme Court) declared that "The doctrine of toleration in matters of religion…has not been long known or acknowledged. For its reception and establishment (where it has been received and established), the world has been thought to owe much to the inestimable writings of the celebrated Locke…." [23]

➤ James Monroe, a Founding Father who became the fifth President of the United States, attributed much of our constitutional philosophy to Locke, including our belief that "the division of the powers of a government . . . into three branches (the legislative, executive, and judiciary) is absolutely necessary for the preservation of liberty." [24]

➤ Thomas Jefferson said that Locke was among his "trinity of the three greatest men the world had ever produced." [25]

And just as the Founding Fathers regularly praised and invoked John Locke, so, too, did numerous famous American ministers in their writings and sermons. [26] Locke's influence was substantial; and significantly, the closer came the American Revolution, the more frequently he was invoked.

For example, in 1775, Alexander Hamilton recommended that anyone wanting to understand the thinking in favor of American independence should "apply yourself without delay to the study of the law of nature. I would recommend to your perusal...Locke."[27]

And James Otis—the mentor of both Samuel Adams and John Hancock —affirmed that: "The authority of Mr. Locke has...been preferred to all others."[28]

Locke's specific writing that most influenced the American philosophy of government was his *Two Treatises of Government*. In fact, signer of the Declaration Richard Henry Lee saw the Declaration of Independence as being "copied from Locke's *Treatise on Government*"[29] —and modern researchers agree, having authoritatively documented that not only was John Locke one of three most-cited political philosophers during the Founding Era,[30] but that he was by far the single most frequently-cited source in the years from 1760-1776 (the period leading up to the Declaration of Independence).[31]

Among the many ideas articulated by Locke that subsequently appeared in the Declaration was the theory of social compact, which, according to Locke, was when:

> Men...join and unite into a community for their comfortable, safe, and peaceable living one amongst another in a secure enjoyment of their properties and a greater security against any that are not of it.[32]

Of that theory, William Findley, a Revolutionary soldier and a U.S. Congressman, explained:

> Men must first associate together before they can form rules for their civil government. When those rules are formed and put in operation, they have become a civil society, or organized government. For this purpose, some rights of individuals must have been given up to the society but repaid many fold by the protection of life, liberty, and property afforded by the strong arm of civil government. This progress to human happiness being agreeable to the will of God, Who loves and commands order, is the ordinance of God mentioned by the Apostle Paul and...the Apostle Peter.[33]

Locke's theory of social compact is seen in the Declaration's phrase that governments "derive their just powers from the consent of the governed."

Locke also taught that government must be built firmly upon the transcendent, unchanging principles of natural law that were merely a subset of God's greater law:

> [T]he Law of Nature stands as an eternal rule to all men, legislators as well as others. The rules that they make for other men's actions must...be conformable to the Law of Nature, i.e., to the will of God.[34]

> [L]aws human must be made according to the general laws of Nature, and without contradiction to any positive law of Scripture, otherwise they are ill made.[35]

The Declaration therefore acknowledges "the laws of nature and of nature's God," thus not separating the two but rather affirming their interdependent relationship—the dual connection between reason and revelation which Locke so often asserted.

Locke also proclaimed that certain fundamental rights should be protected by society and government, including especially those of life, liberty, and property[36]—three rights specifically listed as God-given inalienable rights in the Declaration. As Samuel Adams (the "Father of the American Revolution" and a signer of the Declaration) affirmed, man's inalienable rights included "first, a right to life; secondly, to liberty; thirdly, to property"[37]—a repeat of Locke's list.

Locke had also asserted that:

> [T]he first and fundamental positive law of all commonwealths is the establishing of the Legislative power.... [and no] edict of anybody else...[can] have the force and obligation of a law which has not its sanction [approval] from that Legislative which the public has chosen.[38]

The Founders thus placed a heavy emphasis on preserving legislative powers above all others. In fact, of the 27 grievances set forth in the Declaration of Independence, 11 dealt with the abuse of legislative powers—no other topic in the Declaration received nearly as much attention. The Founders' conviction that the Legislative Branch was above both the Executive and Judicial branches was also readily evident in the U.S. Constitution, with the *Federalist Papers* affirming that "the legislative authority necessarily predominates"[39] and "the judiciary is beyond comparison the weakest of the three departments of power."[40]

Locke also advocated the removal of a leader who failed to fulfill the basic functions of government so eloquently set forth in his *Two Treatises*;[41] the Declaration thus declares that "whenever any form of government becomes destructive of these ends, it is the right of the people to alter or to abolish it and to institute new government."

In short, when one studies Locke's writings and then reads the Declaration of Independence, they will agree with John Quincy Adams' pronouncement that:

> The Declaration of Independence [was]...founded upon one and the same theory of government...expounded in the writings of Locke.[42]

But despite Locke's substantial influence on America, today he is largely unknown; and his *Two Treatises* are no longer intimately studied in America history and government classes. Perhaps the reason for the modern dismissal of this classic work is because it was so thoroughly religious: Locke invoked the Bible in at least 1,349 references in the first treatise, and 157 times in the second[43]—a fact not lost on the Founders. As John Adams openly acknowledged:

> The general principles on which the Fathers achieved independence. . . . were the general principles of Christianity.... Now I will avow that I then believed (and now believe) that those general principles of Christianity are as eternal and immutable as the existence and attributes of God.... In favor of these general principles in philosophy, religion, and government, I [c]ould fill sheets of quotations from...[philosophers including] Locke—not to mention thousands of divines and philosophers of inferior fame.[44]

Given the fact that previous generations so quickly recognized the Christian principles that permeated all of Locke's diverse writings, it is not surprising that they considered him a theologian.[45] Ironically, however, many of today's writers and so-called professors and scholars specifically call Locke a deist or a forerunner of Deism.[46] But since Locke included repeated references to God and the Scriptures throughout his writings, and since he wrote many works specifically in defense of religious topics, then why is he currently portrayed as being antireligious? It is because in the past fifty-years, American education has become thoroughly infused with the dual historical malpractices of Deconstructionism and Academic Collectivism.

Deconstructionism is a philosophy that "tends to de-emphasize or even efface [i.e., malign and smear] the subject" by posing "a continuous critique" to "lay low what was once high"[47] and "tear down the ancient certainties upon which Western Culture is founded."[48] In other words, it is a steady flow of belittling and negative portrayals about the heroes, institutions, and values of Western civilization, especially if they reflect religious beliefs. The two regular means by which Deconstructionists accomplish this goal are (1) to make a negative exception appear to be the rule, and (2) deliberate omission.

These harmful practices of Deconstructionists are exacerbated by the malpractice of Academic Collectivism, whereby scholars quote each other and those from their group rather than original sources. Too many writers today simply repeat what other modern writers say, and this "peer review" becomes the standard for historical truth rather than an examination of actual original documents and sources.

Reflecting these dual negative influences of Deconstructionism and Academic Collectivism in their treatment of John Locke, many of today's "scholars" simply lift a few short excerpts from his hundreds of thousands of written words and then present those carefully selected extracts in such a way as to misconstrue his faith and make it seem that he was irreligious. Or more frequently, Locke's works are simply omitted from academic studies, being replaced only with a professor's often inaccurate characterization of Locke's beliefs and writings.

But in this work, Mary-Elaine Swanson has returned to the sound historical practices of previous generations, thereby reprinting and quoting extensively from the actual writings of John Locke. As a result, it will become obvious to every reader that Locke was not an irreligious freethinker (as claimed by so many of today's so-called scholarly writers) but instead was a dedicated Christian philosopher whose substantial influence on American faith and government cannot be overemphasized.

Significantly, the charge that Locke is a deist and a freethinker is not new; it has been raised against him for over three centuries. It first originated when Locke advocated major reforms in the Church of England (such as the separation of the state from the church and the extension of religious toleration to other Christian denominations); Anglican apologists who stung from his biting criticism sought to malign him and minimize his influence; they thus accused him of irreligion and deism. As affirmed by early English theologian Richard Price:

> [W]hen . . . Mr. Locke's *Essay on Human Understanding* was first published in Britain, the persons readiest to attend to it and to receive it were those who have never been trained in colleges, and whose minds, therefore, had never been perverted by an instruction in the jargon of the schools. [But t]o the deep professors [i.e., clergy

and scholars] of the times, it appeared (like the doctrine taught in his book, on the *Reasonableness of Christianity*) to be a dangerous novelty and heresy; and the University of Oxford in particular [which trained only Anglicans] condemned and reprobated the author.[49]

The Founding Fathers were fully aware of the bigoted motives behind the attacks on Locke's Christian beliefs, and they vigorously defended him from those false charges. For example, James Wilson (signer of the Declaration and Constitution) asserted:

> I am equally far from believing that Mr. Locke was a friend to infidelity [a disbelief in the Bible and in Christianity[50]].... The high reputation which he deservedly acquired for his enlightened attachment to the mild and tolerating doctrines of Christianity secured to him the esteem and confidence of those who were its friends. The same high and deserved reputation inspired others of very different views and characters...to diffuse a fascinating kind of lustre over their own tenets of a dark and sable hue. The consequence has been that the writings of Mr. Locke, one of the most able, most sincere, and most amiable assertors of Christianity and true philosophy, have been perverted to purposes which he would have deprecated and prevented [disapproved and opposed] had he discovered or foreseen them.[51]

Thomas Jefferson agreed. He had personally studied not only Locke's governmental and legal writings but also his theological ones; and his summary of Locke's views of Christianity clearly affirmed that Locke was not a deist. According to Jefferson:

> Locke's system of Christianity is this: Adam was created happy and immortal.... By *sin* he lost this so that he became subject to total death (like that of brutes [animals])—to the crosses and unhappiness of this life. At the intercession, however, of the Son of God, this sentence was in part remitted.... And moreover to them who *believed*, their *faith* was to be counted for righteousness [Romans 4:3, 5]. Not that faith without works was to save them; St. James, chapter 2 says expressly the contrary [James 2:14-26].... So that a reformation of life (included under *repentance*) was essential, and defects in this would be made up by their *faith*; i.e., their faith should be counted for righteousness [Romans 4:3, 5].... The Gentiles; St. Paul says, Romans 2:13: "the Gentiles have the law written in their hearts," [A]dding a *faith* in God and His attributes

that on their repentance, He would pardon them; (1 John 1:9) they also would be justified (Romans 3:24). This then explains the text "there is no other *name* under heaven by which a man may be saved" [Acts 4:12], i.e., the defects in good works shall not be supplied by a faith in Mahomet, Fo [Buddha], or any other except Christ.[52]

In short, Locke was not the deist thinker that today's shallow and often lazy academics so frequently claim him to be; and although Locke is largely ignored today, his influence both on American religious and political thinking was substantial, directly shaping key beliefs upon which America was established and under which she continues to operate and prosper.

Mary-Elaine Swanson has done an invaluable service for this and subsequent generations by resurrecting not only an awareness but also an accurate knowledge of John Locke and his writings. She has literally rescued him from the effects of Deconstructionism and Academic Collectivism by presenting an uncensored view of his life, writings, and incalculable influence on America.

Swanson has an excellent record in recovering such lost knowledge, for not only has she produced short biographies of over sixty American historians, but she has also authored several full-length works, including her award-winning book, *The Education of James Madison: A Model for Today*; *The American Covenant: The Untold Story* co-authored with Marshall Foster; and now the third of her trilogy: *John Locke: Philosopher of American Liberty*.

It is regrettable that Mary-Elaine did not live long enough to see this last work make it into print, but by reviving for all of us a general knowledge of John Locke and his specific ideas that helped produce American Exceptionalism, she has given us the means to preserve and continue the blessings of prosperity, stability, and liberty that we have enjoyed for the past several centuries.

[See **Foreword Endnotes**
on the following page.]

FOREWORD ENDNOTES

1 Joseph Story, *Commentaries on the Constitution of the United States* (Boston: Hilliard, Gray, and Company 1833), Vol. I, 299, n2.

2 Joseph Story, *Commentaries on the Constitution of the United States* (Boston: Hilliard, Gray, and Company 1833), Vol. II, 57, n2.

3 Joseph Story, *Commentaries on the Constitution of the United States* (Boston: Hilliard, Gray, and Company 1833), Vol. I, 293, n2; 299, n2; 305-306.

4 Joseph Story, *Commentaries on the Constitution of the United States* (Boston: Hilliard, Gray, and Company 1833), Vol. III, 727.

5 George Bancroft, *History of the United States of America* (Boston: Little, Brown, and Company, 1858; first edition Boston: Charles Bowen, 1834), Vol. II, 150.

6 George Bancroft, *History of the United States of America* (Boston: Little, Brown, and Company, 1858; first edition Boston: Charles Bowen, 1834), Vol. II, 144.

7 Richard Frothingham, *The Rise of the Republic of the United States* (Boston: Little, Brown, and Company, 1872), 165.

8 John Fiske, *Old Virginia and Her Neighbors* (New York: Houghton, Mifflin and Company, 1897), Vol. II, 274.

9 John Fiske, *Critical Period of American History: 1783-1789* (New York: Mifflin and Company, 1896), 225.

10 Richard Nixon, "Message to the Congress Transmitting the Report of the American Revolution Bicentennial Commission," *The American Presidency Project*, September *11, 1970* (at: http://www.presidency.ucsb.edu/ws/index.php?pid=2658&st=John+Locke&st1=#ixzz1Vm7XvNfc).

11 Gerald Ford, "Address at the Yale University Law School Sesquicentennial Convocation Dinner," *The American Presidency Project*, April 25, 1975 (at: http://www.presidency.ucsb.edu/ws/index.php?pid=4869&st=John+Locke&st1=#ixzz1Vm8RSZbl).

12 Ronald Reagan, "Toasts of the President and Queen Elizabeth II of the United Kingdom at a Dinner Honoring the Queen in San Francisco, California," *The American Presidency Project*, March 3, 1983 (at: http://www.presidency.ucsb. edu/ws/index.php?pid=40996&st=John+Locke&st1=#ixzz1VmAxJTEw).

13 William Clinton, "Remarks at the State Dinner Honoring Prime Minister Tony Blair of the United Kingdom," *The American Presidency Project*, February 5, 1998 (at: http://www.presidency.ucsb.edu/ws/index.php?pid=55226&st=John+Locke&st1=#ixzz1VmCqe1mq).

14 George W. Bush, "Remarks at Whitehall Palace in London, United Kingdom," *The American Presidency Project*, November 19, 2003 (at: http://www.presidency.ucsb.edu/ws/index.php?pid=812&st=John+Locke&st1=#ixzz1VmDpUlFV).

15 John Locke, *The Works of John Locke* (London: Arthur Bettesworth, John Pemberton, and Edward Simon, 1722), Vol. III, 1, "Some Thoughts Concerning Education."

16 John Locke, *The Works of John Locke* (London: Arthur Bettesworth, John Pemberton, and Edward Simon, 1722), Vol. III, 1, "Some Thoughts Concerning Education."

17 John Adams, *The Works of John Adams*, Charles Francis Adams, editor (Boston: Little, Brown and Company, 1856), Vol. I, 53, to Jonathan Sewall on February 1760.

18 Benjamin Rush, *The Selected Writings of Benjamin Rush*, Dagobert D. Runes, editor (New York: The Philosophical Library, Inc., 1947), 78, "Observations on the Government of Pennsylvania."

19 Benjamin Rush, *Medical Inquiries and Observations* (Philadelphia: T. Dobson, 1793), Vol. II, 17, "An Inquiry into the Influence of Physical Causes upon the Moral Faculty."

20 Benjamin Rush, *Medical Inquiries and Observations* (Philadelphia: Thomas Dobson, 1794), Vol. I, 332, "Duties of a Physician."

21 Benjamin Franklin, *The Works of Benjamin Franklin*, Jared Sparks, editor (Boston: Tappan & Whittemore, 1836), Vol. II, 131, "Sketch of an English School."

22 Noah Webster, *A Collection of Papers on Political, Literary and Moral Subjects* (New York: Webster & Clark, 1843), 308, "Modes of Teaching the English Language."

23 James Wilson, *The Works of the Honourable James Wilson*, Bird Wilson, editor (Philadelphia:

Lorenzo Press, 1804), Vol. 1, 6-7, "Of the Study of the Law in the United States."

24　James Monroe, *The Writings of James Monroe*, Stanislaus Murray Hamilton, editor (New York: G. P. Putnam's Sons, 1898), Vol. I, 325, "Some Observations on the Constitution, &c."

25　Thomas Jefferson, *The Writings of Thomas Jefferson*, Henry Augustine Washington, editor (Washington, D.C.: Taylor & Maury, 1853), Vol. V, 559, to Dr. Benjamin Rush on January 16, 1811.

26　See, for example, REV. JARED ELIOT IN 1738 Jared Eliot, *Give Caesar His Due. Or, Obligation that Subjects are Under to Their Civil Rulers* (London: T. Green, 1738), 7, Evans #4241. REV. ELISHA WILLIAMS IN 1744 Elisha Williams, *The Essential Rights and Liberties of Protestants. A Seasonable Plea for the Liberty of Conscience, and the Right of Private Judgment, in Matters of Religion* (Boston: S. Kneeland and T. Gaben, 1744), 4, Evans #5520. REV. JONATHAN EDWARDS IN 1754 Jonathan Edwards, *A Careful and Strict Inquiry into the Modern Prevailing Notions of That Freedom of Will, which is Supposed to be Essential to Moral Agency, Virtue and Vice, Reward and Punishment, Praise and Blame* (Boston: S. Kneeland, 1754), 38-140, 143, 164, 171-172, 353-354 (available online at: http://edwards.yale.edu/chive?path=aHRocDovL2V kd2FyZHMueWFsZS5lZHUvY2dpLWJpbi9uZ XdwaGlssby9uYXZpZz2FoFsS5wbD93amVvLjA=). REV. WILLIAM PATTEN, 1766 William Patten, *A Discourse Delivered at Hallifax in the County of Plymouth, July 24th, 1766* (Boston: D. Kneeland, 1766), 17-18n, Evans #10440. REV. STEPHEN JOHNSON, 1766 Stephen Johnson, *Some Important Observations, Occasioned by, and Adapted to, the Publick Fast, Ordered by Authority, December 18th, A.D. 1765. On Account of the Peculiar Circumstances of the Present Day* (Newport: Samuel Hall, 1766), 22n-23n, Evans #10364. REV. JOHN TUCKER, 1771 John Tucker, *A Sermon Preached at Cambridge Before His Excellency Thomas Hutchinson, Esq., Governor; His Honor Andrew Oliver, Esq., Lieutenant-Governor; the Honorable His Majesty's Council; and the Honorable House of Representatives of the Province of the Massachusetts-Bay in New England, May 29th, 1771* (Boston: Richard Draper, 1771), 19, Evans #12256. REV. SAMUEL STILLMAN, 1779 Samuel Stillman, *A Sermon Preached before the Honourable Council and*

the Honourable House of Representatives of the State of Massachusetts-Bay, in New-England at Boston, May 26, 1779. Being the Anniversary for the Election of the Honorable Council (Boston: T. and J. Fleet, 1779), 22-25, and many others.

27　Alexander Hamilton, *The Papers of Alexander Hamilton*, Harold C. Syrett, editor (New York: Columbia University Press, 1961), Vol. I, 86, from "The Farmer Refuted," February 23, 1775.

28　James Otis, *A Vindication of the Conduct of the House of Representatives of the Province on the Massachusetts-Bay: Most Particularly in the Last Session of the General Assembly* (Boston: Edes & Gill, 1762), 20n.

29　Thomas Jefferson, *The Writings of Thomas Jefferson*, Andrew A. Lipscomb, editor (Washington, D.C.: The Thomas Jefferson Memorial Association, 1904), Vol. XV, 462, to James Madison on August 30, 1823.

30　Donald S. Lutz, *The Origins of American Constitutionalism* (Baton Rouge: Louisiana State University Press, 1988), 143.

31　Donald S. Lutz, *The Origins of American Constitutionalism* (Baton Rouge: Louisiana State University Press, 1988), 143.

32　John Locke, *Two Treatises of Government* (London: A. Bettesworth, 1728), Book II, 206-207, Ch. VIII, §95.

33　William Findley, *Observations on "The Two Sons of Oil"* (Pittsburgh: Patterson and Hopkins 1812), 35.

34　John Locke, *Two Treatises of Government* (London: A. Bettesworth, 1728), Book II, 233, Ch. XI, §135.

35　John Locke, *Two Treatises of Government* (London: A. Bettesworth, 1728), Book II, 234, Ch. XI, §135 n., quoting Hooker's *Eccl. Pol.* 1. iii, sect. 9.

36　See, for example, *John Locke, The Works of John Locke* (London: T. Davison, 1824), Vol. V, 10, "A Letter Concerning Toleration"; John Locke, *Two Treatises of Government* (London: A. Bettesworth, 1728), Book II, 146, 188, 199, 232-233, *passim*; etc.

37　Samuel Adams, *The Writings of Samuel Adams*, Harry Alonzo Cushing, editor (New York: G. P. Putnam's Sons, 1906), Vol. II, 351, from "The Rights Of The Colonists, A List of Violations Of Rights And A Letter Of Correspondence,

Adopted by the Town of Boston, November 20, 1772," originally published in the *Boston Record Commissioners' Report*, Vol. XVIII, 94-108.

38 John Locke, *Two Treatises of Government* (London: A. Bettesworth, 1728), Book II, 231, Ch. XI, §134.

39 Alexander Hamilton, John Jay, and James Madison, *The Federalist, or the New Constitution Written in 1788* (Philadelphia: Benjamin Warner, 1818), 281, Federalist #51 by Alexander Hamilton.

40 Alexander Hamilton, John Jay, and James Madison, *The Federalist, or the New Constitution Written in 1788* (Philadelphia: Benjamin Warner, 1818), 420, Federalist #78 by Alexander Hamilton.

41 John Locke, *Two Treatises of Government* (London: A. Bettesworth, 1728), Book II, 271, Ch. XVI, §192.

42 John Quincy Adams, *The Jubilee of the Constitution. A Discourse Delivered at the Request of the New York Historical Society, in the City of New York, on Tuesday, the 30th of April, 1839; Being the Fiftieth Anniversary of the Inauguration of George Washington as President of the United States, on Thursday, the 30th of April, 1789* (New York: Samuel Colman, 1839), 40.

43 John Locke, *Two Treatises of Government* (London: A. Bettesworth, 1728), passim.

44 John Adams, *The Works of John Adams*, Charles Francis Adams, editor (Boston: Little, Brown and Company, 1856), Vol. X, 45-46, to Thomas Jefferson on June 28, 1813.

45 See, for example, Richard Watson, *Theological Institutes: Or a View of the Evidences, Doctrines, Morals, and Institutions of Christianity* (New York: Carlton and Porter, 1857), Vol. I, 5, where Watson includes John Locke as a theologian.

46 See, for example, *Concise Oxford Dictionary of World Religions*, John Bowker, editor (Oxford: Oxford University Press, 2000), 151; Franklin L. Baumer, *Religion and the Use of Skepticism* (New York: Harcourt, Brace, & Company), 57-59; James A. Herrick, *The Radical Rhetoric of the English Deists: The Discourse of Skepticism, 1680-1750* (Columbia, SC: University of South Carolina Press, 1997), 15; Kerry S. Walters, *Rational Infidels: The American Deists* (Durango, CO: Longwood Academic, 1992), 24, 210; Kerry S. Walters, *The American Deists: Voices of Reason and Dissent in the Early Republic* (Lawrence: University Press of Kansas, 1992), 6-7; John W. Yolton, *John Locke and the Way of Ideas* (Oxford: Oxford University Press, 1956), 25, 115.

47 Jack M. Balkin, "Tradition, Betrayal, and the Politics of Deconstruction–Part II," *Yale University*, 1998 (at: http://www.yale.edu/lawweb/jbalkin/articles/trad2.htm).

48 Kyle-Anne Shiver, "Deconstructing Obama," *AmericanThinker.com*, July 28, 2008 (at: http://www.americanthinker.com/2008/07/deconstructing_obama.html).

49 Richard Price, *Observations on the Importance of the American Revolution and the Means of Making it a Benefit to the World* (Boston: True and Weston, 1818), 24.

50 Noah Webster, *An American Dictionary of the English Language* (New York: S. Converse, 1828), s.v. "infidel."

51 James Wilson, *The Works of the Honourable James Wilson*, Bird Wilson, editor (Philadelphia: Lorenzo Press, 1804), Vol. I, 67-68, "Of the General Principles of Law and Obligation."

52 Thomas Jefferson, *The Works of Thomas Jefferson*, Paul Leicester Ford, editor (New York: G. P. Putnam's Sons, 1904), Vol. II, 253-254, "Notes on Religion," October, 1776.

John Locke
The Philosopher of American Liberty

Why Our Founders Fought for "Life, Liberty, and Property"

INTRODUCTION

JOHN LOCKE has the unique distinction of being a philosopher whose political ideas were important to three revolutions: England's "Glorious Revolution" of 1688; our own American Revolution of 1776; and the early days of the French Revolution of 1789. This book shows how England adapted Lockean ideas to its monarchical system and how the French Revolution, while starting off well with Lafayette's presentation of Lockean ideas in his Declaration of Rights, finally degenerated into a Reign of Terror and completely abandoned Locke. It was only the revolution of the American Founding Fathers which truly adopted Lockean views of government and civil and religious liberty. Hence the title of this book: *John Locke: Philosopher of American Liberty.*

Historians, biographers, and professors of political science generally agree that the writings of John Locke, particularly his *Second Treatise Of Civil Government*, exerted considerable influence on American political ideas during our founding period. Numerous books and essays have been written analyzing Locke's political philosophy. It would seem, indeed, that more than enough has been written on this subject. Why, then, another book concerning John Locke's ideas on civil government?

It is needed, I believe, in order to correct a widespread misunderstanding of Lockean political philosophy that claims it was rooted in a godless rationalism. Particularly persistent has been the notion that Locke was in reality a non-Christian rationalist who merely used the language of religion to conceal his real ideas which relied entirely on reason, not

1

Revelation. This view has been advanced by the late Dr. Leo Strauss of the University of Chicago and his followers. The distinguished Professor Forrest MacDonald and others have also followed the notion that Locke "secularized" Natural Law. Many believe that he was a rationalist and perhaps even a closet atheist. These sweeping assertions ignore certain important facts: that Locke always insisted that reason was the gift of God and that it was always subordinate to the Revelation revealed in the Scriptures. There is no evidence that he disbelieved in what he wrote and much evidence to the contrary. So it is most troubling that the critiques of Locke written by the followers of Strauss do not rely on textual analysis of Locke's work so much as upon reading between the lines and asserting that there is a hidden sub-text to Locke's writings. This seems an extraordinarily unfair way to analyze an author's works. They also show little knowledge of John Locke's life or the testimony of those who knew him personally and attested to his Christian character and convictions.

To provide a corrective, it has been necessary to go back to primary sources, i.e., the writings of those who knew Locke personally and to a thoughtful consideration of his own words without attempting to read into them views which would have been entirely alien to him. In Locke's own writings and in the writings of those who knew him intimately, a very different person emerges from the one so often described as only a nominal Christian.

Most helpful in determining Locke's actual character and the record of that character in action are Locke's many letters written to his friends. Particularly useful are his letters contained in *The Correspondence of John Locke and Edward Clarke*, an extensive collection edited by Benjamin Rand. These letters range over many subjects, including Locke's ideas on how Clarke should educate his children (later published as *Some Thoughts Concerning Education*). Most useful to me were their letters on political matters. Edward Clarke was first elected to Parliament in 1690 and served there for twenty years. It was through him that many of Locke's political ideas left the realm of theory and took shape in parliamentary legislation.

Also particularly helpful was the earliest biography of Locke written by his friend Jean Le Clerc and titled *The Life and Character of Mr. John Locke*, (published in 1687 and reprinted in a 1905 edition). This work also contains a lengthy appraisal of his Christian character by Lady Masham, one of Locke's closest friends.

Finally, there is *The Character of Mr. Locke*, by Pierre Coste, the translator of his works into French and his secretary for the last seven years of

Locke's life. First published in 1705 in *Les Nouvelles de la Republique des Lettres*, it details Locke's last days and his acknowledgment of Jesus Christ as his Saviour, which Locke gave to the circle of friends around his bed-side the day before his death. This was no sudden death-bed confession, however. Locke's faith had deep roots in his upbringing in a devout Puritan home. Here he acquired his life-long love of the Scriptures.

Locke lived through turbulent times that saw the overthrow and ex-ecution of Charles I, the restoration of the monarchy under the reigns of Charles II, and James II, and finally what Englishmen called "the Glorious Revolution" of 1688 that placed William and Mary on the throne as con-stitutional sovereigns. This was Locke's revolution in a far more personal sense than has generally been recognized. Locke was not a mere passive spectator of the stirring events surrounding the writing of the English Declaration of Rights. Rather, he was an active advisor to Lord Mordaunt and Sir Williams Somers, the key statesmen involved in planning William and Mary's accession to the throne and the drafting of the English Declaration of Rights that began the slow but steady shift in power from the throne to Parliament.

While writing this book it soon became clear to me that it must begin with a thorough biographical treatment that would clear away the many misconceptions about Locke's life, character, and contribution to his own nation's constitutional and political development. It may well be asked, though, why is it important to us today that a seventeenth-century English philosopher has been misunderstood? Is this not merely a matter for schol-ars to thrash out among themselves? I believe this is not so, because how Americans understand Locke and his political writings affects how they understand our nation's political origins, which is a subject of considerable importance to the future of the United States. It is worth remembering that Locke's political ideas appear in the Declaration of Independence (almost verbatim) and in our Federal Constitution, particularly in the Bill of Rights. They also appear in our early State Declarations of Rights.

During my research, it became evident to me that the Declaration of Independence and the Constitution of the United States were neither of them the products of deists nor of godless rationalists, nor was Locke one of those. Locke's philosophical and political ideas actually came from the English Puritan tradition in which he was raised. While in exile in Holland, these ideas were broadened by his contacts with Dutch Arminian theologians whose emphasis on religious toleration greatly impressed him. It was because of Locke's grounding in Christian theology and his expression of it in his writings that the American Founders—and what I call the Founding Clergy—recognized that Locke's views were in harmony with Christian doctrine.

Samuel Adams of Massachusetts and George Mason of Virginia were particularly acute Lockean thinkers, Adams in educating the people in Lockean political principles prior to the American Revolution, and Mason in enunciating these ideas in Virginia's great Declaration of Rights which became a model for the Declarations of the other fledgling states.

Locke's views on religious toleration also were of great interest to Congregationalist and Presbyterian dissenters from the Anglican Church during the period leading up to the American Revolution. Even more interesting to them was Locke's espousal of full religious liberty, which he had so clearly expressed in the early Constitution of Carolina that he helped to draft. This little-known episode shows how much individual liberty of conscience meant to Locke. Although he championed religious liberty in this document, he did not champion here (or anywhere in his writings) freedom from religion. It should also be noted that when Locke used the term "religion," he was usually referring to Christianity which had brought individual liberty of conscience to light.

The New England pastors in particular expounded Locke's political ideas approvingly, often referring to him in their sermons, as "the great Mr. Locke." These sermons were widely distributed throughout the colonies and became highly influential in developing public consciousness regarding the urgent political issues facing the colonists.

Were these learned ministers deluded in their acceptance of Lockean ideas? I believe not. It seems clear that they discerned his views correctly as being within the Christian tradition. Were they uncomfortable with his definition of the Law of Nature? Clearly, they were not. Like him they viewed the Law of Nature as the Law of God. Like him, they believed that man was guided by God-given reason which had to be consonant, however, with the Divine Revelation found in the Holy Scriptures.

The Founding Fathers and the Founding Clergy certainly approved of Locke's writings on human rights as springing from the Creator's Law of Nature. Locke saw property as essentially three-fold, as the individual's right to "life, liberty, and possessions." Locke's expanded view of property as comprised of an individual's life, liberty, and estate was something new in the field of natural law theory and involved men's responsibilities to their Maker because men are, in turn, God's property. Locke contended that government had no right to take away a man's life, liberty, or possessions unless to punish him for invading another man's rights.

Some scholars have asserted that Locke's views constituted a break with classic natural law. I believe this is true. I am convinced, however, that the break was not because Locke "secularized" the older natural law tradition based on Thomas Aquinas and the ideas of Aristotle and Plato. Rather, the break in this tradition was the result of the Protestant Reformation which emphasized the importance of the individual and his liberty of conscience.

Where then did the notion come from that Locke was a godless rationalist philosopher? It is my contention that it came from Voltaire and other irreligious French *philosophes* of the eighteenth century who affected to adopt Lockean philosophy while deleting its critical religious underpinnings. They changed the way later scholars came to think of Locke. This was not lost on Founding Father James Wilson who wrote "that the writings of Mr. Locke, one of the most able, most sincere, and most amiable asserters of Christianity and true philosophy have been perverted to purposes which he would have deprecated and prevented, had he discovered or foreseen them."

The French Revolution was in sharp contrast with our American Revolution. Locke's philosophical ideas were indeed perverted by the prevailing materialist, anti-Christian views its leaders had inherited from Voltaire. The voice of Lafayette, who had learned Lockean ideas of government while in America, was silenced by the strident demands of the radicals. It was Rousseau, rather than Locke, whom the radicals followed. Of these, Robespierre was perhaps the most ardent disciple of Rousseau's authoritarian ideas of government outlined in the *Social Contract*. Robespierre's Reign of Terror eventually claimed his own life. Other radicals who followed him tried to strip all religion from France, massacred priests, and turned churches into "Temples of Reason." The Revolution, which men like Lafayette had hoped would bring liberty to Frenchmen, resulted instead in a disaster which took France many years to overcome as it oscillated between monarchy and republican government, always seeking an elusive "equality" rather than liberty.

The final section of this book deals with why I have concluded that the United States is now following, at its peril, many of the absolutist political ideas of Rousseau rather than the truly liberating ones of John Locke. It shows how important Locke's political ideas were—and still are—to a free people. It is also my contention that when American law schools threw out natural law and natural right, they threw out absolutes necessary to the perpetuation of liberty and justice. They did this in favor of a relativism that has become deeply destructive of our political institutions, built as these institutions were on the idea that certain absolutes exist and are essential to the perpetuation of a free society. There are signs, however, that Americans are awakening from their long sleep on these issues and may be ready once again to become Lockean political thinkers.

Mary-Elaine Swanson
Asheville, North Carolina, 2011

PART ONE

The Life and Times of John Locke

*"I had no sooner perceived myself in the world but
I found myself in a storm which has lasted almost hitherto."*

JOHN LOCKE
(1660[1])

---

1 Cited in Thomas Fowler, *Locke*, London, 1888, New York: AMS Press, Inc., 1968, 2.

BIRTHPLACE OF JOHN LOCKE
1632–1704

CHAPTER ONE

Puritan Beginnings

JOHN LOCKE's birth and childhood coincided with a period of intense religious and political ferment in England. It was a time when Englishmen, under the leadership of Puritan politicians and divines, were calling into question the right of a king to force religious conformity upon his people or to tax them without the concurrence of their representatives in Parliament. Resistance to royal assertions of the Divine Right of Kings to absolute rule had occurred during the reign of James I, but it was the stubborn, short-sighted and duplicitous actions of his son, Charles I, which finally caused open rebellion.

It was in 1642 that a young and prosperous country attorney living in the village of Pensford, Somersetshire, decided to risk his all in the war which had broken out between King and Parliament. Leaving his wife and two young sons behind, he rode off as captain of a troop of cavalry to support the parliamentary cause. The actions of this obscure country lawyer doubtless were repeated many times over by other equally obscure young men who remained only nameless participants in the great struggle between King and Parliament. That we know anything at all about John Locke, Sr. of Pensford, is because he was the father of one of England's greatest philosophers.

John Locke, the future philosopher, was born at his grandparents' home in Wrington, a quiet village lying between Bristol and the Mendip Hills in the serenely beautiful county of Somersetshire. He was baptized in the Parish Church at Publow on August 29, 1632. His mother was Agnes Keene of Wrington, the daughter of a tanner. She died when Locke was twenty-two. He afterwards described her as "a very pious woman and an affectionate mother." [2] His attorney father, the senior John Locke, took his bride to live in the nearby village of Beluton located on the river Chew amid the lovely orchards and rolling hills of the West Country. The family home was an agreeable Tudor farmhouse set on a hill overlooking the Mendip Hills. Locke always spoke of his father "with great respect and affection," according to Locke's close friend, Lady Masham. Locke told her that his father "used a conduct towards him when young that he often spoke of afterwards with approbation." [3] The elder Locke kept his son in awe of him when he was a boy, but relaxed his severe behavior by degrees as John grew up, until finally "he lived perfectly with him as a friend." [4]

A PURITAN FAMILY

Both parents were from Puritan families. John and his younger brother, Thomas (born in 1637), were brought up on the doctrines of John Calvin (1509-1564), the great Geneva reformer. Dr. Samuel Crook, the rector of their parish who married John and Agnes Locke, was of a strong Puritan stamp and fearlessly upheld Calvinist views on: the importance of the Scriptures; the centrality of the sermon in the church service; the requirement of personal conversion to Jesus Christ for membership in the Church; and the importance of representative church government. [5] The Lockes must surely have been well taught by Dr. Crook in these fundamental tenets of Calvinism. From Dr. Crook as well as from his pious mother and father, young John must have gained his lifelong love and reverence for the Holy Scriptures as the Word of God. Basil Willey indicates that Locke shared John Milton's reverence for the Bible and that this was typical of the Puritan outlook on life. [6]

Little is known about Locke's education as a child. James L. Axtell theorizes that he may have been sent to live with his uncle in Bristol and attend school there for a time or he may have been educated at home by his parents or by a tutor. Axtell notes that education by a tutor is the one educational method Locke later recommended as best for the child. "If indeed Locke did receive the major part or all of his elementary education

---

2 Maurice Cranston, *John Locke*, New York: The Macmillan Co., 1957, 13.

3 Cited in Thomas Fowler, *Locke*, (London, 1888, reprint ed., New York: AMS press, Inc., 1968), 1.

4 Fowler, 1-2.

5 See Cranston, 1-4, for a discussion of this strong-minded Puritan.

6 See Basil Willey, *The Seventeenth Century*, Garden City, New York: Doubleday & Company, Inc., 1953 (1st edition, 1934), 271.

from his parents, and if he enjoyed his family life as a boy as much as he later said he did, then perhaps this may have contributed to his preference for education in the home."[7] On the other hand, as Axtell suggests, he may have received part of his education from a teacher in the village, or perhaps Dr. Crook gave him his early lessons, for pastors often conducted classes for children. His ideas on education would certainly have been influential with Locke's parents since they shared his Puritan approach to life.

Dr. Crook persisted in his Puritan preaching and teaching despite the disapproval of his bishop, William Piers, who held to the apostolic succession of bishops as the correct form of church government and who adhered to the old traditions of the Anglican liturgy and ritual. The contest within the Church of England between Anglicans like Bishop Piers and the new Puritans, typified by Dr. Crook, played an important role in precipitating the English Civil Wars. These wars broke out as a protest against Charles I's attempt to rule as an absolute monarch without the check of Parliament upon his actions. To the Puritan there could be no absolute ruler except God. Historian John Richard Green's comments on the Puritan character are also suggestive of the kind of views that young John must have learned from his family:

> The temper of the Puritan was eminently a temper of law. The diligence with which he searched the Scriptures sprang from his earnestness to discover a Divine Will which in all things, great or small, he might implicitly obey. But this implicit obedience was reserved for the Divine Will alone; for human ordinances derived their strength only from their correspondence with the revealed law of God. The Puritan was bound by his very religion to examine every claim made on his civil and spiritual obedience by the powers that be; and to own or reject the claim, as it accorded with the higher duty which he owed to God.[8]

A NEW AND HIGHER SENSE OF POLITICAL ORDER

Green also remarks that the religious beliefs of the Calvinist were necessarily accompanied by a "new and higher sense of political order."[9] Human laws were accounted valid only as they accorded with the higher law of

---

7 James L. Axtell, *The Educational Writings of John Locke, A Critical Edition*, Yale University: Cambridge University Press, 1968), 71.

8 John Richard Green, *A Short History of The English People*, New York and London: Harper & Brothers Publishers, 1898, 479.

9 John Richard Green, *The History of the English People*, Chicago and New York: Belford, Clarke & Co., 1886, 3:17-18.

God revealed in the Scriptures. The new movement to purify the Church and the nation of ungodly laws and reliance on a monarch as an absolute ruler had made its way slowly but steadily. Puritanism was opposed vigorously by Elizabeth I (1533-1603) and even more so by her successor, James I (1566-1625) who insisted in his *True Law of Free Monarchy* that Kings had a divine right to absolute rule. In his view the king was responsible only to himself—not to Parliament, nor to the people. "It is atheism and blasphemy and a high contempt in a subject," he declared, "to dispute what a king can do, or to say that a King cannot do this or that."[10] He was stoutly resisted by Puritan churchmen and by Parliament, as was his son, Charles I (1600-1649) when he continued his father's absolutism by declaring in 1626: "Remember, Parliaments are altogether in my power for their calling, sitting, and dissolution; therefore, as I find the fruits of them good or evil, they are to continue or not to be."[11]

THE MISRULE OF CHARLES I

After Charles I dissolved Parliament in that same year, he tried to rule without it for eleven turbulent years. It was not without reason that John Locke later remarked that no sooner was he born than he found himself in a storm, for the nation was plunged into a constitutional struggle between King and Parliament, between monarchical absolutism and parliamentary Puritanism. According to English law, no taxes could be raised without the consent of Parliament. To get around this, the King asked for a free "gift" from the people to make up for the subsidy that Parliament had refused to grant him. In many counties, however, the people vehemently resisted declaring they would not give unless "by way of Parliament!" The northern counties defied the King. One Lincolnshire community drove the Crown's commissioners from the town. The king's illegal demands did not end there; he went on to demand a forced "loan." When this stratagem failed to raise the amount of money Charles believed necessary to meet his needs, he called the historic Parliament of 1628 which drew up that landmark document, the Petition of Right, in which were stated four basic principles: 1) No taxation without the consent of Parliament; 2) no troops to be boarded in citizens' homes without their consent; 3) no martial law in time of peace; 4) no subject to be denied trial by jury; and 5) no arbitrary imprisonment. Charles signed the document but it soon became clear that he had no intention of complying with its demands.

10 Green, 70.
11 Green, 123.

In 1634, when Locke was ten years old, Charles I again attempted to raise a revenue without the consent of Parliament, this time by a demand for "Ship Money," a tax levied ostensibly to protect English ports from foreign attack. The King's arbitrary taxation must have been particularly worrisome to Locke's father, because—as clerk to the Justices of the Peace for Somersetshire—he had the unpleasant task of assessing and collecting the King's revenue in that county. The experience of having to go against his own principles must have been deeply galling to the elder Locke. As a Puritan, he heartily disapproved of collecting this revenue and as heartily supported the protests of Parliament against the King's arbitrary use of power.

THE WAR AGAINST THE SCOTS

If these illegal attempts to raise revenue irritated the people and exasperated the House of Commons, the King's war against the Scots filled both Parliament and people with the deepest misgivings. Nothing could have been more unpopular in a nation yearning for more religious toleration than the King's efforts, begun in 1636, to force the Scots to accept the Church of England's Book of Common Prayer. At home, Charles had further angered the Puritans by his appointment in 1636 of William Laud, the unrelenting foe of Puritanism, as Archbishop of Canterbury.

THE LONG PARLIAMENT

After his war with the Scots took a bad turn, Charles found himself in desperate need of money to fund his army and, in November 1640, was driven to call another Parliament. This historic "Long Parliament" was made up of many members who had never served there before. They were overwhelmingly Puritan in sentiment. The Puritan preachers played a large part in forming the opinions of those who made up this historic body whose work led to the war that broke out between King and Parliament. Maurice Ashley notes that "it was Puritanism that aroused, by its spiritual and ideological appeal, the ardour of Oliver Cromwell, and men like him who in the last resort were prepared to do battle with the monarchy; and it may be doubted if without that inspiration the parliamentary armies would have had the moral strength to overcome the disappointments and setbacks of the first year of the war." [12]

---

12 Maurice Ashley in *Oliver Cromwell and The Puritan Revolution*, New York: Collier Books Edition, 1966, 39. Ashley also cites Professor Haller as saying that the Puritan preachers "were the men who did most in the long run to prepare the temper of the Long Parliament."

The Long Parliament upheld unwaveringly to the importance of the "fundamental laws" of the land, notably that the King had no right to rule without the advice and consent of Parliament. In the civil realm, the questions of taxation and reformation of the Church loomed largest. Had Charles made any genuine attempt to come to terms with the issues, many members of Parliament would have been eager to work out a compromise. Most did not want to abolish the monarchy, but only to keep it within its constitutional bounds. Every time the King appeared to be yielding, however, it was soon discovered that this was only a ruse. Finally, Parliament voted to send a Grand Remonstrance which, among other things, demanded that cabinet ministers be appointed only with the advice and consent of Parliament.

Upon receiving the Remonstrance, Charles acted with fatal rashness. Believing Parliament more divided than it really was, he planned to arrest four of its leaders. When word of his intentions reached them prematurely, they fled to the City of London which refused to give them up. By this act, the King finally made it clear to Parliament that all hope of compromise was useless. As the American colonists were to discover later in relation to another king, revolution was the reluctant, but inevitable, answer to tyranny.

Throughout the summer of 1642 there were ominous rumblings as the gathering clouds of war hung over the nation. There were isolated skirmishes—preludes to the battles to come. At last the storm clouds broke and the Civil War began, with Englishmen riding to the side of either King or Parliament. Throughout this stormy period, young John Locke must have heard many a discussion in his home of the issues at stake and of what the future might demand of his father.

When the war began in 1642, Locke's father promptly declared his support of the parliamentary cause in a meeting held in the parish church at Publow. A few weeks later, he joined the army that was mustering to the defense of Parliament. His son's life-long devotion to the natural and constitutional rights of Englishmen may well have begun when he saw his father ride off to defend Parliament as captain of a troop of cavalry. Thomas Fowler says of this formative period in the future philosopher's life: "Though the fortunes of the family undoubtedly suffered from this step on the part of the young attorney, the political and religious interests which it created and kept alive in his household must have contributed in no small degree to shape the character and determine the sympathies of his elder son."[13]

---

13 Fowler, 2.

EDUCATION AT
WESTMINSTER SCHOOL

In 1647, despite his reduced circumstances, the elder Locke was able to send John, then fifteen, to the prestigious Westminster School in London. That he was able to find a place there for his son was probably owing to his friendship with Colonel Popham, a prominent landowner in his district and an important client. The parliamentary armies had virtually won the war by 1647, but the Master of Westminster at this time, Dr. Richard Busby—dreaded by the boys for his harsh discipline—was a staunch royalist.[14] Despite his uncompromising royalist ideas, however, Dr. Busby harbored a deep suspicion of powerful men and taught his charges never to accept their views without careful examination. The young schoolboy from the West Country hardly could have been given a better grounding in learning to think for himself than this counsel from the irascible Dr. Busby. While a severe disciplinarian (his pupils called him Dr. "Richard Birch-hard"), he also knew how to introduce humor into is teaching and had an underlying kindness which won over many of his students. For those who worked hard and showed self-discipline, he was not backward in showing his approval. After three years at Westminster, Locke was one of twenty boys elected to a King's Scholarship which gave them free lodgings at the school and a chance to win a scholarship to Oxford or Cambridge within the next two-year period. Dr. Busby tutored him so that he might have a better chance of winning a challenge competition in grammar and classical literature. Locke was successful and was among six who were given a scholarship to Christ Church, Oxford, one of the finest colleges in the university.

OXFORD STUDIES
UNDER DR. JOHN OWEN

Locke was twenty when he entered Christ Church, Oxford, in 1652. A victorious Oliver Cromwell (1596-1658) was Chancellor of the College and Dr. John Owen, his former Chaplain, was Dean of Christ Church and Vice Chancellor. The Dean was a rarity for his age: a man of tolerant religious views. Locke's future devotion to the cause of religious liberty may find its roots here at Oxford in the teaching of Dr. Owen who, like the Lord Protector himself, was an Independent in religious matters. Locke's tutor,

---

14 See Maurice Cranston, *John Locke*, 18-20. Locke was attending Westminster School when Charles I, having been tried by the House of Commons, was executed (on January 30, 1649) nearby in White-hall Palace Yard.

Thomas Cole, also was an Independent.[15] The term Independent had various shades of meaning, but in general applied to those who believed in extending religious toleration in varying degrees to dissenters from the established Church. Oliver Cromwell and Dr. Owen were among those Independents who still believed in a national church but they supported the idea that individual congregations within the Church of England should be accorded a large measure of self-government.

They stopped short of the view increasingly held by other Independents—who were first known as Brownists (for their leader, Reverend John Browne) and then Separatists—that the Biblical standard of the early Christian Church should prevail: that each congregation should be completely autonomous, answerable only to God for its actions. The Separatists, from whom sprang the Pilgrim Fathers and American Congregationalism, held that there was, Scripturally speaking, no such thing as a national church, but only local independent congregations which might advise and aid one another, but none of which had the right to dictate policy to the others. By Locke's time, many of these people had been "harried out of the land" by James I, seeking safe haven first in Holland and later, in the case of the Pilgrims, in the New World. Other champions of Congregationalism remained in England, however, and there were many other dissenters from the Established Church, such as the Baptists, who had supported Cromwell and for whom he felt a genuine sympathy and concern.[16]

Whether they believed in an established church made up of semi-independent, self-governing congregations, or whether they espoused the more radical idea of completely independent congregations without a national church, the Independents all sought to protect the individual's liberty of conscience. Dr. Owen was among the first of these advocates of religious toleration for dissenters. Basing his views on the Bible, Owen maintained that there was no justification for the idea—held by Catholics and Anglicans alike—that heresy should be rooted out by the power of government. In Maurice Cranston's words: "Owen maintained that all men should be free to think and worship as they pleased as long as their faith did not lead them to disturb peace and order. The duty of Government,

---

15 Thomas Cole was only five or six years older than Locke and had only recently received his M.A. degree. When Locke graduated in 1656, Cole became principal of St. Mary's Hall, but later when the monarchy was restored he was dismissed for nonconformity. He then started a nonconformist academy at Nettlebed, Oxfordshire.

16 For more on the gradations of belief among the Independents, see Maurice Ashley, *Oliver Cromwell and the Puritan Revolution*, New York: Collier Books, 1966), 116. See also H. H. Brailaford, *The Levellers and the English Revolution* (Stanford, California: Stanford University Press, 1961), 30.

he said, was to maintain order and not to impose religion."[17] In later years Owen suffered for his non-conformity but became an increasingly courageous defender of religious toleration. Even after the Restoration, he was a courageous supporter of Congregationalism.[18] Young Locke soon became conversant with the Dean's views which, in the future, he would expand beyond mere "toleration" to an espousal of full religious liberty for one of His Majesty's colonies in the New World. Lord King, the author of the first full-scale biography of Locke, believed that Englishmen of his day owed "any true notion of religious liberty, or any general freedom of conscience to the Independents at the time of the Commonwealth" and to Locke who was "their most illustrious and enlightened disciple."[19]

LOCKE GRAPPLES WITH THE CHURCH/STATE RELATIONSHIP

Locke's first appearance in print was in a volume of academic poems, edited by Dr. Owen, in honor of Oliver Cromwell, now Lord Protector of England, on the occasion of his victory over the Dutch in 1653. This showed that he had attracted the favorable attention of Dr. Owen. The ferment of thought at Oxford, where discussion of civil and political liberty was in the very air, caused Locke to explore these subjects. All of his early correspondence and his notes on his developing ideas reveal his preoccupation with the question of the bounds of governmental authority and show him grappling with the church/state relationship. He also began to grapple with the idea of the Law of Nature, that law which God made evident to all rational human beings.[20]

DISSATISFACTION WITH OXFORD'S TEACHING METHODS

In addition to his lively interest in religion and politics, Locke found himself increasingly attracted to scientific investigation and the study of

---

17 Cranston, 14.

18 Owen, a graduate of Queen's College, Oxford, with a doctorate in divinity (1653), left the college because of Archbishop Laud's intolerant statutes and became a private chaplain to a nobleman; as vicar of Coggeshall, Essex, wrote a treatise in favor of congregational autonomy in church government in 1648. Preached before Parliament several times. Supported Cromwell in his opposition to the Crown. In 1660, Charles II removed him from his post as Dean of Christ Church. He was indicted in 1665 for holding non-conformist assemblies in Oxford; he then moved to London and published anonymous tracts defending religious liberty. When Charles II decided to woo dissenters, Owen had an interview with the King who gave him money for nonconformists and allowed him to preach to an independent congregation in Leadenhall St., London, 1673. He contended for the historical position of Congregationalism, 1680-81.

19 Lord King, *The Life of John Locke, with Extracts from His Correspondence, Journals, and Common-Place Books*, London: Henry Colburn, 1829, 176.

20 See Chapter 6 for a discussion of Locke's views on the Law of Nature.

medicine. But he found the teaching methods at Oxford dry and dusty and he had a strong aversion to learning by scholastic disputations. In later years he urged his friend Edward Clarke to,

> be sure not to let your son be bred up in the art and formality of disputing, either practising it himself, or admiring it in others; unless, instead of an able man, you desire to have him an insignificant wrangler, opinionator in discourse, and priding himself in contradicting others.... There cannot be anything so disingenuous, so unbecoming a gentleman, or any one who pretends to be a rational creature, as not to yield to plain reason and the conviction of clear arguments. Is there any thing more inconsistent with civil conversation, and the end of all debate, than not to take an answer, though ever so full and satisfactory.... For this, in short, is the way and perfection of logical disputes, that the opponent never takes any answer, nor the respondent ever yields to any argument.[21]

Thomas Fowler may well have been right in his view that Locke gained more from the friendships he formed at Oxford and from discussion with his fellow students in the college rooms or during afternoon walks than he did from many of the prescribed courses.[22] According to those who knew him well, he had a great capacity for friendship. His good friend, Lady Masham, wrote that he "sought the company of pleasant and witty men, with whom he likewise took great delight in corresponding by letters; and in conversation and in these correspondences he spent for some years much of his time."[23] Indeed, Locke had a talent for forming life-long friendships. Even the Locke shown in the melancholy portrait of his old age was still a warm-hearted, kindly man to whom the society of his friends meant much. He also greatly enjoyed the society of children and young people. As Richard Aaron has perceptively noted: "Essentially, his nature was warm, and generous."[24] Locke's character, which we can see gradually forming at Oxford, was far from being that of the dispassionate philosopher we are tempted to imagine when we read the calm, cool cadences of his arguments in the *Essay* or *The Two Treatises of Government*.

---

21 John Locke, *Some Thoughts Concerning Education*, 1690, in Works, 10 vols., London, 1823, reprint ed. Germany: Scientia Verlag Aalen, 1963, 9:178.

22 Fowler, 7-8.

23 Fowler, 8.

24 Richard I. Aaron, *John Locke*, 1937, Oxford: The Clarendon Press, 1965, 47.

A LIFE-LONG LOVE OF TRUTH

He was as ardent and constant in his life-long love of truth as in his love of his friends. Moreover, throughout his life he retained what Richard Aaron referred to as "his deep religious piety." [25] Beginning during his Oxford years, he sought to find the truth of things in God himself. Later, he wrote in his essay, *Of Study* (1677):

> It is a duty we owe to God as the fountain and author of all truth, who is truth itself, and 'tis a duty also we owe our own selves if we will deal candidly and sincerely with our own souls, to have our minds constantly disposed to entertain and receive truth wheresoever we meet with it, or under whatsoever appearance of plain or ordinary, strange, new, or perhaps displeasing, it may come in our way. Truth is the proper object, the proper riches and furniture of the mind, and according as his stock of this is, so is the difference and value of one man above another. [26]

LOCKE AS TEACHER

Locke received his M.A. degree in 1658, the year Oliver Cromwell died leaving the reins of power in the slack hands of his son, Richard. In 1660, the fateful year when members of Parliament summoned Charles I's son home from his continental exile to reestablish the monarchy, Locke was appointed Greek Lecturer at Christ Church, thus shifting from student to teacher. The following year he became a teacher of Rhetoric and in 1662 he took up the office of Censor of Moral Philosophy, the college's senior disciplinary office under that of the Dean. It was not a position he had sought and he apparently assumed it reluctantly. But in December of 1664, when he was finishing his term of office, he warmly commended his students in a gracious speech he gave in Christ Church Hall. The talk showed his approach to discipline and to education which he saw as resting on two pillars—theology and philosophy.

> Certainly he finds himself in a tight corner and rules under an unfair law who is not allowed to use his free judgement in matters of reward or punishment, who is distracted by discordant cries on either side, of pardon on one hand and the rod on the other. Though perhaps ancient tradition might call for the latter, it certainly does not befit my right hand nor your behaviour. For

---

25 Aaron, 49.
26 John Locke, *Of Study* (1677), reprinted in Axtell, 415.

you have devoted yourself so well to the study of the things that to most of you I have been not so much a Censor and taskmaster as a witness and applauder of your hard work. Faults, if faults there were, you have so atoned for that they only offered an opportunity to us both—for you to earn and for me to give praise.... But let no one, should he have a guilty feeling, imagine that I have said this as a formality and that, as those who bid farewell are wont to do, I praise those things which have not really met with my approval: but let him rather learn to love and cherish that virtue whose merit is so great that it overflows upon those around and profits even him who has it not. But if anyone should wish to make this virtue his own, there are two chief places that must be frequented early and often: the hall where they may learn to debate and the temple where they may learn to pray; for thus they become philosophers and thus theologians.[27]

At this period, Locke also served as a tutor to several students and it appears that they were devoted to him. With one of them, John Alford, he carried on a correspondence into the 1680s. The role of tutor in the English university was (and is) an important one, for it was the tutor who not only assisted students in their studies but directed them to books which could be of help, discussed the authors with them and how well they understood what they were reading. One grateful father, the Earl of Berkeley, wrote to Locke: "I return you my hearty thanks for your great care of my son." He spoke of his "extraordinary opinion" of Locke's abilities and piety and of his "excellent qualifications for the well-governing of youth."[28]

LOCKE GRAPPLES WITH CHURCH/STATE RELATIONS

The year 1660 was not only the year Locke first was appointed a teacher at Christ Church, but it was also the year he wrote his first important work, an unpublished essay on "Whether the Civil Magistrate May Lawfully Impose and Determine the Use of Indifferent Things in Reference to Religious Worship." In this essay, he came down firmly on the side of the magistrate's authority. At this time, Locke believed that men should submit to the rule of the civil magistrate in all "indifferent things" in the Church, i.e., regarding various methods of worship and religious ceremonies. These had nothing to do, he thought, with believing or not believing

---

27 Cited by Axtell, 43.
28 See Axtell, 41.

certain fundamental doctrines. He could not see why men quarreled over these externals.

In his preface to the work (written a year later, as he was preparing it for possible publication), he asserted that "there is no one can have a greater respect and veneration for authority than I. I no sooner perceived myself in the world but I found myself in a storm which has lasted almost hitherto," he explained, referring to the bloody Civil Wars that had rent England asunder, only to be followed by bitter dissension in Parliament as to the form of government to be adopted after Charles I's execution. Therefore, he said, he could not but "entertain the approaches of a calm with the greatest joy and satisfaction...." He felt obliged "to endeavour the continuance" of the blessing of such a calm "by disposing men's minds to obedience to that government which has brought with it the quiet and settlement which our own giddy folly had put beyond the reach not only of our contrivance but hopes." [29]

ENGLAND THREATENED BY NEAR ANARCHY

Locke's reason for championing governmental authority over the churches—which he never did again—was probably because of the near-anarchy that threatened England. The period of the Lord Protector's rule had been beset by factionalism, each religious and political group loudly demanding that it be allowed to impose its ideas on the rest. Some members of Parliament wanted to see a completely reformed civil government which, in their view, ought to conform to the pattern of the primitive Christian Church, that is, it ought to be republican. Most members, however, could only conceive of a monarchical government with its concomitant, a State Church.

When Oliver Cromwell refused to be made King, Parliament was forced into the position of greater responsibility than its members were ready to assume. Suddenly faced with the power for which it had struggled, it bogged down into endless floundering debates on the character and role of civil government and was torn asunder by the views of widely differing factions.

QUARRELING FACTIONS IN PARLIAMENT

Among these factions were: The Army—generally republican in governmental theory and independent in religion—but which, like Cromwell, believed in an extremely strong executive; the oligarchic republicans,

---

29 Cranston, 61.

intent on keeping power in the hands of a select few by birth and position (the old feudal view); the religious republicans of Puritan stamp who
also wanted to keep power in the hands of a select few—the "saved"; the
democratic republicans, a small and sometimes quite radical group, led by
John Lillburne, called by his enemies a "leveller," which wanted a single-
chamber legislative body representing all the people with no limitations
or qualifications for the elective franchise; and the monarchists who were
just waiting for an opportunity to topple the Commonwealth and restore
the monarchy.[30]

OPTIMISTIC ACCLAIM FOR CHARLES II

Between such disparate elements unity of plan and purpose became impossible, thus making the rise of a "strong man" inevitable. Although called
Lord Protector, Cromwell exercised many of the powers of a king, usually
wisely. After his death, Englishmen were once again faced with the old,
unresolved question: How should England be governed? Clearly, the ir-
resolute Richard Cromwell would never be the wise and firm ruler that
his father was. Very quickly the ranks of the monarchical group in Parliament swelled. In 1660, the year that the 27-year-old Locke was wrestling
with the extent of the civil magistrate's powers over religion, the Royalists
in Parliament won out. Charles II landed at Dover on May 25 to much
optimistic acclaim. Thus ended the English Commonwealth.

LOCKE'S VIEWS ON THE RESTORATION

Locke was among those who rejoiced to see the Restoration. Like many
other thoughtful men, he had become disgusted with the intoxication
for power which had driven the contending factions within the Commonwealth to oppose each other so bitterly—to the detriment of the
nation. He believed that a return to the rule of a monarch, if balanced
and checked by Parliament, was the remedy for England's civil ills. In his
unpublished essay on the powers of the civil magistrate, he wrote of his
conviction—that were the freedom his opponents contended for "generally
indulged in England, it would prove only a liberty for contention, censure,

---

30 H.L. Brailaford says that Lillburne proclaimed that God gave man "a rational soul or understanding"
   creating him after His own image, and that all men and women were equal before God, no one
   having the right to rule over others without their consent. Unlike strict Calvinists who thought of
   the world as divided between the elect and the damned, Lillburne based his concept of society on
   the equality of men and women as God's image, since, despite the Fall, they possessed this rational
   soul and were, to that extent, still godlike. See Brailaford's *The Levellers and the English Revolution*,
   Stanford: Stanford University Press, 1961.

and persecution."[31] He had not, he said, "the same apprehension of liberty as some have, or can think the benefits of it to consist in a liberty for men, at pleasure, to adopt themselves children of God, and from thence assume a title to inheritance here, and proclaim themselves heirs of the whole world, nor a liberty for ambitious men to pull down well-framed constitutions that out of the ruins they may build themselves fortunes, nor a liberty to be Christians so as not to be subjects."[32]

Although Locke's thoughts in 1660 crystallized into a defense of authority, it was constitutional, not arbitrary authority he had in mind. Thus, he wrote in the essay of "a body of laws so well composed" that to preserve them "was the only security of this nation's settlement." Peter Laslett's observations on this unpublished essay are perceptive: "Even in this, to us his earliest, his most authoritarian mood, Locke is revealed as a constitutionalist, and a man convinced of the fundamental distinction between secular and spiritual power, political and religious authority."[33]

The reign of England's new monarch was to put a period to Locke's "sanguine expectations of the future," as Fowler notes. All too soon the tendencies of the new government toward persecution of dissenters came to the fore. It was not long before Locke would see the wisdom of John Owen's position on religious toleration and to advance similar views on the subject, finally arriving at full religious liberty. His mature views were soon to be adopted by Englishmen living in the New World.

LOCKE'S INTEREST IN SCIENCE AND MEDICINE

Early in 1661, he received a severe blow: his father died at age 54. His death was followed soon after by that of Locke's younger brother, Thomas, who succumbed to tuberculosis. Suddenly, the gregarious young Oxford scholar, age twenty-seven, was alone in the world. Locke's own health was never robust. Indeed, he suffered increasingly severe bouts of asthma throughout his life. He was convinced it was likely that he, too, would come down with consumption and, like his brother, would die an early death. This conviction may have been one reason for wanting to change the career his father had chosen for him in the Church. Locke had entered Oxford on a clerical studentship and was expected to take holy orders upon receiving his master's degree. There was also another reason he wanted

---

31 From Locke's paper on powers of the Civil Magistrate, as cited by Lord King, 1:14.
32 Lord King, 1:14.
33 See Peter Laslett's Introduction to Locke's *Two Treatises of Government*, Mentor Book edition, New York and Toronto: The New American Library, 1965, 32-33.

to change his studentship. He had developed a keen interest not only in politics and religion, but also in scientific and medical research. This was the third important strand in his Oxford experience. Although expected to go into the Church, these interests led him to believe he was better fitted to become a doctor than a clergyman. By 1666, he received permission to continue his medical studies and to keep his studentship at Christ Church, even though he was not in Holy Orders. In addition to his medical studies he also studied botany and herbal medicine and assisted Robert Boyle (1627-1691) in his laboratory from time to time.[34] Although he never took an M.D. degree, Locke practiced medicine informally throughout his life with considerable success.

DIPLOMATIC TRAVELS

Late in 1665, Locke took time out from his duties at Oxford to serve as secretary to Sir Walter Vane who was sent on an embassy to the Elector of Brandenburg. (Locke probably owed this good fortune to William Godolphin, an old school friend, then active in Court circles.) It was Locke's first visit to the Continent, and he greatly enjoyed his two months in France. Most of the diplomatic papers sent home are in Locke's handwriting but, as Thomas Fowler notes, Locke's letters to Boyle and his life-long friend, John Strachey, are much more interesting.

Strachey lived at Sutton Court, not far from Locke's family home at Pensford. He was only two years younger than Locke and attended Lincoln College, Oxford, while Locke was a student at Christ Church College. Locke early made a fast friend of John Strachey. To Strachey he wrote a letter revealing his respect for the Catholic priests he had met and he said that he had received many courtesies from them for which he would always be grateful.[35] He attended the church services of Catholics, Lutherans, and Calvinists and was impressed by the mutual harmony in which they lived at Cleves. In a letter to Boyle, he wrote:

> The distance in their churches gets not into their houses. They quietly permit one another to choose their way to heaven; for I cannot observe any quarrels or animosities amongst them upon the account of religion. This good correspondence is owing partly to the power of the magistrate, and partly to the prudence and good

---

34 Robert Boyle, born in Ireland in 1627, settled in Oxford in 1654. He experimented in Pneumatics, improving the air-pump. A devout Christian, he worked for the propagation of the Gospel in the East while he was a director of the East India Company. He died in 1691.

35 Fowler, 15.

nature of the people, who, as I find by inquiring, entertain different opinions without any secret hatred or rancour." [36]

PROSPECTS FOR A DIPLOMATIC CAREER

So well did Locke perform his duties in this diplomatic assignment that on his return to England he was offered another post as secretary to the newly-appointed ambassador to Spain. The offer tempted him with its prospect of a diplomatic career. After much hesitation, he turned it down. He did so partly because of his bouts with asthma which made necessary frequent periods of rest and recuperation. An equally important consideration may well have been his desire to pursue the contemplative life of an Oxford scholar. He was to try repeatedly to flee from a strenuous life of action to the quiet life of the scholar, only to be drawn back into public affairs. On this occasion, he wrote to a friend: "Whether I have let slip the minute which they say everyone has once in his life to make himself, I cannot tell." [37] He had not done so, of course. A far greater moment was to appear in July of 1666—one which afforded him an extraordinary opportunity for public service and for his own development as a political and philosophical thinker.

---

36 Ibid.
37 Ibid.

CHAPTER TWO

Entry into the World of Whig Politics

He was wont to say, that wisdom lay in the heart, and
not the head; and that it was not the want of knowledge,
but the perverseness of the will, that filled men's
actions with folly, and their lives with disorder.

JOHN LOCKE
(on the Earl of Shaftesbury[38])

IT was an entirely unexpected event that brought Locke, at the age of
thirty-five, into the heart of English Whig politics. This was his meeting with Anthony Ashley Cooper, then Lord Ashley, who was to become
a celebrated statesman at the court of Charles II. It was Charles who later
made him the Earl of Shaftesbury. Paradoxically, Locke's entry into the
heady world of high-level politics came about because of his expertise as a
medical man. Lord Ashley came to Oxford to consult Dr. David Thomas,
a friend of Locke's who, being called away unexpectedly, entrusted Ashley
to Locke's care. In addition to his medical knowledge, Locke was a polished
and pleasant conversationalist with no little wit. Ashley, a shrewd appraiser
of men's characters, evidently was struck by Locke's diverse interests and
abilities, particularly his medical knowledge. It was as medical advisor,
therefore, that the young Oxford professor and tutor was invited to join
Ashley's household. Soon, he was to play other roles, one of which was
tutor to Ashley's son and grandson. Of more importance to his intellectual development was his work as Ashley's political researcher and "ghost
writer." Locke's good friend, Lady Masham, wrote that from 1667, "he was
with my Lord Ashley as a man at home and lived in that family much
esteemed, not only by my lord, but by all the friends of the family."[39]

---

38 John Locke, "Memoirs Relating to the Life of Anthony, First Earl of Shaftesbury," in *Works*, 9:272.
39 Cited by Fowler, 18.

Saving Lord Ashley's Life

As family physician, Locke is credited with saving Ashley's life by directing a tricky operation to remove an abscess from his liver. For the times, the operation was something of a miracle, and Ashley extolled Locke's medical wisdom to all his friends.[40] But he soon recognized that his medical advisor might be even more useful to him as a private secretary. He saw that Locke's greatest talents lay in philosophical and political writing and research. Lord Ashley's grandson, the third Earl of Shaftesbury, for whose education Locke had been made responsible, wrote that "Mr. Locke grew so much in esteem with my Grandfather that, as great a man as he had experienced him in physic, he looked upon this as but his least part. He encouraged him to turn his thoughts another way.... He put him upon the study of the religious and civil affairs of the nation with whatsoever related to the business of a minister of state, in which he was so successful that my Grandfather began soon to use him as a friend and consult with him on all occasions of that kind."[41]

Ashley not only put his library at Locke's disposal but he also shared with him his own extensive knowledge of both practical and theoretical politics. Ashley was an ardent champion of parliamentary government and a foe of religious persecution. With his patron's approval, Locke wrote *An Essay on Toleration* (1667) which, though never published, probably was circulated among his lordship's friends and may well have been produced as a policy document for Ashley's use. It contains the germs of Locke's future philosophy of politics and religion, which were fully developed in his *Letter Concerning Toleration* (1689), his *Two Treatises Of Civil Government*, (1690) and *The Reasonableness of Christianity* (1695).

Ashley was a complex man of considerable intellectual acumen but he was not an orthodox Christian. His motivation for wanting greater religious toleration was probably because he wanted to see greater freedom for his own unorthodox, deistic views. Locke may well have begun to see the dangers of deism through association with this brilliant but worldly patron. In his old age, when his ship finally sailed out of the turbulent sea of politics into the calm waters of philosophical meditation, Locke wrote *The Reasonableness of Christianity* in order to persuade the deists of the truth of Biblical revelation.

---

40 Peter Laslett remarks that "All that political influence could do was directed toward Locke's promotion in his profession of academic medicine, and he was provided for financially, though his obstinate independence evidently made it difficult for Ashley to go as far as he wanted." See Laslette, 38.

41 Cited by Fowler, 39.

CONTINUED MEDICAL AND SCIENTIFIC RESEARCH

Locke's interest in medicine and scientific research also continued apace. In 1668, he became a Fellow of the Royal Society, sponsored by Sir Paul Neile, a founder of the Society and a close friend of Lord Ashley's. While at Exeter House he also met Thomas Sydenham, the greatest English physician of the time. The two men hit it off, and soon Locke was helping him in his medical practice and his research on the cause of smallpox. On April 2, 1668, Sydenham wrote to Boyle of "my friend Mr. Locke" and several years later, in 1676, he wrote to another physician friend that Locke was "a man whom, in the acuteness of his intellect, in the steadiness of his judgment, and in the simplicity, that is, in the excellence of his manners, I confidently declare to have amongst the men of our own time few equals and no superior."[42] Sydenham and Locke worked closely together to determine the cause of smallpox. They each made careful case histories during several epidemics which swept through England in both the 1660s and 1670s. They did not succeed in tracing it to its source, but came to important conclusions as to what medical methods did not cure smallpox, and the most sensible form of treatment of a disease for which doctors had not as yet found a cure: a good diet to build up strength so that nature could aid in repelling the disease.

LOCKE'S CONTRIBUTION TO
THE CAROLINA CONSTITUTIONS

One of Locke's most interesting secretarial assignments for Lord Ashley, one which aroused in him a keen interest in America, was the drafting of *The Fundamental Constitutions of Carolina* of 1669. In 1663, Ashley had become one of eight noblemen whom Charles II made "lords proprietors" of Carolina (then one colony). The foremost among these gentlemen was George Monk, Duke of Albemarle, who had engineered Charles II's restoration to the throne, and Edward Hyde, Earl of Clarendon, another staunch supporter of the restored monarchy. The remaining six were: Locke's patron, Lord Ashley; Lord Craven, Lord Berkeley, and his brother, Sir William Berkeley, governor of Virginia; Sir George Carteret, and Sir John Colleton. The feudalistic document the proprietors drew up hardly reflected Locke's own views on government. He simply seems to have been the scribe who took down what was dictated to him. The articles relating to religion, however, Locke claimed as his own. There was to be freedom for religion, but

---

42 Fowler, 21-22.

not freedom from religion. The first article pertaining to religion read:

> XCV. No man shall be permitted to be a freeman of Carolina, or to have any estate or habitation within it, that doth not acknowledge a God; and that God is publicly and solemnly to be worshipped."[43]

Another article explained that

> "since the natives...are utterly strangers to Christianity, whose idolatry, ignorance, or mistake, gives us no right to expel, or use them ill; and [since] those who remove from other parts to plant there, will unavoidably be of different opinions concerning matters of religion...and it will not be reasonable for us on this account to keep them out; that civil peace may be maintained amidst the diversity of opinions, and our agreement and compact with all men may be duly and faithfully observed;...and also that Jews, heathens, and other dissenters from the purity of the Christian religion, may not be scared and kept at a distance from it, but by having an opportunity of acquainting themselves with the truth and reasonableness of its doctrines, and the peaceableness and inoffensiveness of its professors, may by good usage and persuasion...be won over to embrace and unfeignedly receive the truth; therefore any seven or more persons, agreeing in any religion, shall constitute a church or profession...."[44]

These different churches were forbidden either to molest each other or to "use any reproachful, reviling or abusive language against the religion of any church or profession, that being the certain way of disturbing the peace, and of hindering the conversion of any to the truth."[45]

Because of these liberal provisions, which also were outlined in *Advertisements* Locke drew up to recruit colonists, many persecuted French Protestants began to migrate to Carolina. But another religious article was inserted at the insistence of some of the proprietors, much against Locke's wishes, as he explained to one of his friends to whom he sent a copy of the Constitutions.[46] That article stipulated that the Church of England should be planted in the colony as soon as practicable as "the only true and orthodox [church]" and that "it alone should be allowed to receive public maintenance, by grant of parliament."[47]

---

43 *The Fundamental Constitutions of Carolina* in John Locke, *Works*, 10:193.
44 John Locke, *Works*, 10:194-95.
45 *Works*, 10:195.
46 Ibid. See note on 194.
47 Ibid., 194.

The complicated form of government the lords proprietor devised proved unworkable and, as historian John Fiske noted, "it was never anything but a dead letter, and civil government sprouted up as spontaneously in Carolina as if neither statesman nor philosopher had ever given thought to the subject."[48] The only real achievement was that the publication of the *Fundamental Constitutions* in 1670, 1682 and 1698 drew persecuted Protestants, not only from France but from England and Scotland. To this day Charleston, South Carolina is noted for its many historical churches including those described in Locke's times as dissenting churches, such as the Congregational, Presbyterian, and French Huguenot. The aspiration after religious liberty, which motivated so many of the original settlers, could not be rooted out and, after the War of Independence, it finally prevailed.

THE ENGLISH LATITUDINARIANS

At the time Locke was working on *The Fundamental Constitutions of Carolina*, he was also very interested in the Latitudinarian movement in the Church of England, from which came his preferred solution to the problems of religious diversity. The Latitudinarians believed that the Anglican articles of faith should be reduced to a very small number so that Christians with diverse doctrinal views could remain within the fold of the Church of England.

It was in 1668 that Locke became a member of the Reverend Benjamin Whichcote's congregation of St. Lawrence Jewry in the City of London. Benjamin Whichcote (1609-1683) had been Provost of King's College, Cambridge between 1644 and 1660 and was a leading Latitudinarian in the Church of England. He was not only a Latitudinarian; he was also the "guiding spirit" of the "Cambridge Platonists," a group of philosophers at Cambridge who sought to reconcile Divine Revelation with reason, which they saw "as the candle of the Lord." While Locke probably liked Whichcote's definition of reason as: "the candle of the Lord," he would have been more inclined to suggest reconciling reason with Divine Revelation, with which he was soon to deal as he wrestled with just how much reason can be expected to understand and what must be left to the Divine Revelation given to men in the Holy Bible.

Basil Willey has pointed out that most of the Cambridge Platonists were Puritans as seen in their connection with Emmanuel College which was

---

48 John Fiske, *Old Virginia and Her Neighbours*, Two Volumes, Boston and New York: Houghton, Mifflin and Company, 1900, 2:274.

considered by many at the time as a "seminary of Puritanism."[49] Although raised among Puritans, their views differed from the prevailing Puritan espousal of predestination. They thought of love as God's supreme gift to man.[50] With the followers of the Dutch theologian, Jacobus Arminius (1560-1609), they did not believe that God arbitrarily chooses some to be saved and others to be damned, but that all who believe in Christ are predestined to salvation. As Carl Bangs explains, "Arminius stands firmly in the tradition of Reformed theology in insisting that salvation is by grace alone and that human ability or merit must be excluded as a cause of salvation. It is faith in Christ alone that places a sinner in the company of the elect."[51] Arminian in doctrine, the Cambridge Platonists rejected Calvinism because of what they saw as its arbitrary portrayal of Divine sovereignty. With the Arminians, they believed that God had given man free will to choose or reject Jesus Christ as Saviour. With the Arminians, they also rejected the Calvinist view that Christ died only for the elect. Rather, they held that Christ died for all men, that salvation is by faith alone, that anyone who believes in Christ is saved, that those who reject God's grace are lost, and that God does not elect particular individuals for either heaven or hell.

If Locke was not already familiar with the doctrines of Arminius, he was soon to be influenced by some of his ideas through Reverend Whichcote's sermons and also by his friendship with other Cambridge Platonists.

MORAL LAWS AS THE EXPRESSION OF GOD'S WILL

Locke was impressed by Whichcote's latitudinarian ideas but disagreed with his view that the goodness of an action resulted simply from its conformity with the nature of things as discerned by reason. Such a view was opposed to the Calvinist idea that moral laws are simply the expression of God's will. Locke discerned that without God there could be no true moral law. That God's moral law was good was for Locke a given. God himself was good, therefore His will was good. Things were not good in themselves, however. They were morally right because God decreed them to be so by his sovereign will. In this, he remained Calvinist. Although at this time, Locke did not believe that moral rules had been "imprinted in our

---

49 See Basil Willey, *The Seventeenth Century Background*, 141.

50 See Kenneth Scott Latourette, *A History of Christianity*, New York: Harper & Brothers, 1953, 825.

51 Carl Bangs, Arminius, *A Study in the Dutch Reformation*, 2d ed., Grand Rapids, Michigan: Francis Asbury Press of Zondervan Publishing House, 1985, 198.

minds immediately by the hand of God," he believed they were readily recognizable. He was soon to write in his book, *The Essay on Human Understanding*:

> I grant the existence of God is so many ways manifest, and the obedience we owe him so congruous to the light of reason, that a great part of mankind give testimony to the law of nature; but yet I think it must be allowed, that several moral rules may receive from mankind a very general approbation, without either knowing or admitting the true ground of morality; which can only be the will and law of a God, who sees men in the dark, has in his hand rewards and punishments, and power enough to call to account the proudest offender...."[52]

Later he wrote (in Book III of his *Essay on Human Understanding*) of reason as natural revelation coming from God and of Divine Revelation as "a new set of discoveries communicated by God immediately, which reason vouches the truth of, by the testimony and proofs it gives that they come from God...." He was to return repeatedly to the necessity of reason and Revelation as always tied together because man's unassisted reason never could provide him with a true moral code through reason alone.[53]

FRIENDSHIP WITH DAMARIS CUDWORTH

Locke was also linked with another of the Cambridge Platonists' leading lights, the Reverend Ralph Cudworth (1617-1688) through his friendship with Cudworth's daughter, Damaris (later Lady Masham) whom he met in 1682 and who was to become one of his closest friends. Exceptionally well educated by her father, Damaris was both charming and intelligent. She also may have been not only an intellectual friend with whom Locke could discuss his ideas, but the woman he came to love and hoped one day to marry. Their correspondence under the names of "Philander" and "Philoclea" indicates something more than mere friendship, as do the poems they sent to each other within a year of their first meeting. Their mutual friends twitted Locke about his attachment to Damaris, but dramatic events intervened to separate them for more than five years. When next they met, Damaris had married Sir Francis Masham, a country gentleman who had been a widower.

---

52 John Locke, *Essay on Human Understanding* in *Works*, 1:38.
53 *Essay, Works*, 3:149.

REVEREND CUDWORTH'S
COURAGEOUS PLEA FOR TOLERATION

It appears that Locke met Damaris and her mother when they were visiting in London, but may never have met her father. He knew Reverend Cudworth's writings, however, and was impressed with his large, inclusive view that stressed the love of God. Cudworth had also displayed considerable courage in a sermon he had preached before the House of Commons in 1647 in which he had taken on the powerful Presbyterian faction in the House which was bent on passing severe punishments on those whom it declared were religious heretics. In his sermon, Cudworth fearlessly proposed toleration for those who dissented from the prevailing orthodoxy. Despite the eloquence of his sermon, which was published and republished many times, the proposed "Ordinance for the Suppression of Blasphemies and Heresies" passed the House anyway. This Ordinance stipulated that anyone who denied the doctrine of the Trinity, or the divinity of Christ, or that the Bible was the Word of God, or the resurrection of the body, or a future day of judgment, and who refused to recant when put on trial, would be put to death. For those who declared that man by nature had been given free will to turn to God, or who declared that there was a Purgatory, or that images used in Churches were lawful, or that infant baptism was unlawful, the penalty was imprisonment.[54]

Interested though Locke was in the latitudinarian movement in England as expressed in the views of Whichcote and Cudworth, his own religious articles in *The Fundamental Constitutions of Carolina* show that he viewed full religious liberty as the ideal solution to the problem of religious diversity. He may have concluded, though, that was not to be hoped for in England.

THE ESSAY ON
HUMAN UNDERSTANDING

While in Lord Ashley's employ, Locke also began his great philosophical work, *The Essay on Human Understanding*, finishing the first draft in July 1671. In his "Epistle to the Reader" Locke explained that the Essay was begun after "five or six friends meeting at my chamber, and discoursing on a subject very remote from this, found themselves quickly at a stand,

---

54 Later, under the Commonwealth, these extreme measures were abandoned and, as noted previously, a large measure of toleration for religious dissent prevailed under Oliver Cromwell during the Interregnum. See J. R. Green, 569, and J. H. Adamson and H. F. Folland, Sir Harry Vane: *His Life and Times*, Boston: Gambit Incorporated, 1973, 243-44.

by the difficulties that rose on every side." [55]

Locke then explained that,

> After we had a while puzzled ourselves, without coming any nearer a resolution of those doubts which perplexed us, it came into my thoughts, that we took a wrong course; and that before we set ourselves upon inquiries of that nature, it was necessary to examine our own abilities, and see what objects our understandings were, or were not, fitted to deal with." [56]

It is not my purpose to analyze the *Essay* exhaustively in these pages, but only to highlight those concepts which sometimes have been portrayed as contrary to Christianity. Such a one is Locke's denial that men are born with certain innate ideas. Yet while he asserted that man's mind starts out like a blank page on which experience traces its outlines, he also maintained that what he termed experience is made up of "two fountains" or sources of knowledge—sensation and reflection.

> Our observations employed either about external sensible objects, or about the internal operations of our minds, perceived and re-flected on by ourselves, is that which supplies our understandings with all the materials of thinking. These two are the fountains of knowledge, from whence all the ideas we have, or can naturally have, do spring. [57]

It is important to recognize that this is a very different view from the one later advanced by the Sensationalist philosophers of the French Enlightenment, who held that sensation was the sole source of man's knowledge and studiously ignored Locke's "other fountain" (reflection) even as they blandly attributed their sensationalist philosophy to him. [58] It differs, too, from the view advanced by the materialist philosopher Thomas Hobbes (1588-1679) who wrote in his *Leviathan* that "The original of all the thoughts of men is that which we call Sense, for there is no conception in a man's mind which hath not at first, totally or by parts, been begotten upon the organs of sense." [59]

---

55 John Locke, *Works*, 1:xlvi. Two of the "five or six friends" were his Oxford friends, Dr. Thomas, and James Tyrell, one of Locke's closest friends from his Oxford days. Tyrell was the author of an ambitious *General History of England, Both Ecclesiastical and Civil*, the first three volumes of which were published between 1696-1704. See Axtell's note in *The Educational Writings of John Locke*, 400.

56 *Works*, 1:xlvi-xlvii.

57 Locke, *Essay on Human Understanding*, in *Works*, 1:82-83.

58 See Chapter 11 for a full discussion of the French misuse of Locke's philosophy of the mind.

59 See Fowler, 134.

MAN ENDOWED WITH INNATE FACULTIES

Locke's view was that although man was not born with innate ideas, he was born with innate *faculties* which God had given him to evaluate experience—faculties such as thinking, willing, judging, memorizing. While one "fountain," or source of knowledge, was from without (sensation), the other was from within (reflection). As Fowler observed, "His theory of knowledge may fairly be called an experiential, but it cannot with any truth be called a sensationalist theory." [60] Lockean scholar Richard I. Aaron made the same point when he wrote: "It is frequently assumed that Locke's denial of innate knowledge is equivalent to the assertion that the one kind of knowledge which exists is sensory.... The outcome of the polemic against innate ideas according to this view is a pure sensationalism. Now there is nothing in the text to justify the very big assumption that is being made here...." [61] In fact, despite Locke's denial that God had gifted men with an innate, ready-made set of ideas, he affirmed that they were endowed with the faculty of reason with which to understand God and the universe, at least to the degree that God had given man the wisdom to understand His will. Locke was always convinced that there was much that lay beyond man's reason. Indeed, what prompted Locke to write the *Essay* was his desire to discover what God had put within the range of his comprehension and what, on the other hand, must lie forever beyond the power of human understanding—unless enlightened by Divine Revelation. In the following passage from his Introduction to the *Essay*, Locke set forth his view on the degree of understanding God has bestowed upon man:

> For, though the comprehension of our understanding comes exceeding short of the vast extent of things; yet we shall have cause enough to magnify the bountiful Author of our being, for that proportion and degree of knowledge he has bestowed upon us, so far above all the rest of the inhabitants of this our mansion. Men have reason to be well satisfied with what God hath thought fit for them, since He has given them (as St. Peter says)...whatsoever is necessary for the conveniences of life and information of virtue; and has put within their discovery the comfortable provision for this life, and the way that leads to a better. [62]

---

60 Fowler, 134. See also Richard I. Aaron, *John Locke*, 84, discussion Locke's "innate capabilities."
61 John Locke, Introduction, *Essay on Human Understanding*, in *Works*, 1:3-4.
62 Ibid., 1:4.

Therefore, he thought, it was wise for men to content themselves with the variety and beauty God had put within the range of their understanding and not to "quarrel with their own constitution, and throw away the blessing their hands are filled with, because they are not big enough to grasp every thing."[63] Locke did not stop with the reasoning powers God has given man. He discerned that God communicates to man in two different ways—through reason and Revelation.

> Reason is natural revelation, whereby the eternal Father of light, and fountain of all knowledge, communicates to mankind that portion of truth which he has laid within the reach of their natural faculties: revelation is natural reason enlarged by a new set of discoveries communicated by God immediately, which reason vouches the truth of, by the testimony and proofs it gives that they come from God.[64]

Locke was to expand upon this theme later in *The Reasonableness of Christianity* in which he maintained that man's reason, if unassisted by Divine Revelation, never could provide him with a true moral code. This view, iterated and reiterated by Locke, is certainly not consonant with deism which rejects Biblical revelation. Still less is it the conviction of a godless rationalist bent on undermining Christianity, as Locke has sometimes been portrayed.[65] On the contrary, as he wrote to the Bishop of Worcester:

> The Holy Scripture is to me, and always will be, the constant guide of my assent; and I will always hearken to it, as containing the infallible truth relating to things of highest concernment. And I wish I could say there are no mysteries in it; I acknowledge there are to me, and I fear always will be. But where I want the evidence of things, there yet is ground enough for me to believe, because God has said it; and I will presently condemn and quit any opinion of mine, as soon as I am shown that it is contrary to any revelation in the Holy Scripture.[66]

---

63 Ibid., 1:4.

64 *Essay*, in *Works*, 3:149.

65 See Leo Strauss's treatment of Locke in *Natural Right and History* (Chicago: University of Chicago Press, 1953), 165-66 and 202-51 and Thomas L. Pangle's assertions in *The Spirit of Modern Republicanism: The Moral Vision of the American Founders and the Philosophy of Locke* (Chicago: University of Chicago Press, 1988), that Locke was attempting to "undermine the Bible's supreme suprarational authority" (147) and that Locke—and Spinoza—"carried out, for the sake...of the god of reason, a subversion of the received Scriptures" (153).

66 *Works*, 4:96.

LOCKE'S MANY ROLES
IN THE ASHLEY HOUSEHOLD

The years in Lord Ashley's household did not give Locke much time for introspection, however, as his duties involved the wearing of at least three hats: As a medical man, his time was often taken up with attending to the Ashley family's health; as Lord Ashley's private secretary, he was often called upon to write position papers for him and to research matters pertaining to the Earl's official duties; as tutor, he taught Ashley's son and grandson. He was even called upon to find a wife for the son, Anthony Ashley, when he had reached age seventeen. According to the grandson, writing when he had become the third Earl of Shaftesbury, "My father was too young and inexperienced to choose a wife for himself, and my grandfather too much in business to choose one for him." Therefore, as he explained, "all was thrown upon Mr. Locke, who being already so good a judge of men, my grandfather doubted not of his equal judgment in women. He departed from him, entrusted and sworn, as Abraham's head servant 'that ruled over all that he had,' and went into a far country 'to seek for his son a wife,' whom he as successfully found."[67] Locke made many discreet inquiries and chose Lady Dorothy Manners, the daughter of the Earl of Rutland. He then accompanied the boy to the Earl's home, Belvoir Castle. Here he negotiated the marriage between the two young people. Locke must have chosen wisely, for the match turned out to be a very happy one. Later, he attended assiduously to Lady Dorothy's health and assisted at the birth of a son on February 6, 1671.

EVILS OF ARRANGED MARRIAGES

Here, we pause to consider the custom of arranged marriages among the aristocracy and also the gentry at this period. Usually, these marriages involved some material advantage to the families involved and the bride often had no choice in the matter. These were seldom love matches, although some turned out well which was apparently the case for young Anthony Ashley and his Lady Dorothy. As time went on, though, Locke may have had cause to reconsider as he observed other arranged marriages among the aristocracy.

He writes in the *Second Treatise of Government*, Chapter VII, "Of Political or Civil Society," some startling comments on marriage as mainly for procreation and that the wife "has in many Cases a Liberty to separate

---

67 See Fowler, 20-21.

from [her husband] where natural Right or their Contract allows it" and that "the Children under such Separation fall to the Father or Mother's Lot, as such Contract does determine."[68] These comments on marriage seem to show Locke as a man bound by the customs of his time, rather than as a far-sighted philosopher. But he does seem to be looking for a way out for unhappy wives who often were forced into marriages that brought then much unhappiness and took place just because of material advantages to the families involved.

LOCKE LEAVES FOR FRANCE

Not surprisingly, perhaps, Locke began to suffer from overwork. By 1672, he had a severe cough which warned him that he might go into tuberculosis as had his brother. The smoky, polluted air of London was always difficult for him to endure. He was forced periodically to retreat from its toxic fumes. So, with his patron's blessing, he jumped at the opportunity to accompany the Countess of Northumberland on a short visit to France. While in Paris, he discovered a new book by the philosopher Pierre Nicole (1625-1693) titled *Essais de Morale*. Impressed with Nicole's Christian approach to ethics, he translated three of the essays and sent them to Lady Ashley as a gift. Thomas Fowler sees this as "evidence of the depth and sincerity of Locke's religious convictions."[69]

Although the precarious state of his health was undoubtedly troubling to Locke, he had a resilient, good-natured temperament. Ever the keen observer, his letters from France to his Somerset friend John Strachey are full of merriment and satire at the expense of the French court. In October 1672, he informed his friend with mock pomposity that it was now time he were "beatified by the refined conversation of a man that knows the difference between a black and white feather, and who can tell you which side of his two-handed hat ought to be turned up, and which only supported by an audace. I fear you have the unpardonable ignorance not to know what an audace is; to oblige you then, know that what an untravelled Englishman would take to be a piece of ordinary loop lace made use of to support the overgrown brim of a flapping hat has by the virtuosos and accomplished gallants of Paris, when I was there, been decreed to be an audace. And thus you may reap the benefit of what cost me many a step. O the advantage of travel! You see what a blessing it is to visit foreign

---

68 *Second Treatise*, par. 82, 1714 edition in Hall, *Christian History*, 1:79.
69 Fowler, 25.

countries and improve the knowledge of men and manners." [70]

Locke tells his friend of seeing the usual tourist sights—the Louvre, the Seine, and the Pont Neuf, and then comments ironically on "the perfection and glory of all, the King of France himself," and the "vast and magnificent buildings as big almost as others dominions" that were prepared only for his use. He comments shrewdly that "there be a great many other two legged creatures, but 'tis not the way of that country much to consider them...." [71]

POLITICAL FORTUNES AND MISFORTUNES

Shortly after Locke's return to England in the late autumn of 1672, his patron, who had been made the Earl of Shaftesbury in April, also was made Lord High Chancellor of England and saw to it that Locke was appointed Secretary of Presentations with a salary of three hundred pounds a year. Shaftesbury's good fortune did not last long, however. A year later, in November 1673, he seriously displeased the King by his vehement defense of a bill in Parliament (the Test Act) designed to exclude Catholics from civil or military employment. If passed, the bill threatened to remove the King's brother, James, the Duke of York, from his post as Lord High Admiral, because he was suspected of being a Catholic. Indeed, when the bill was introduced, James declared that he was a Roman Catholic and resigned his post. Other prominent Catholics followed suit. The series of admissions and resignations had a profound effect on public opinion convincing many that the Catholic Party at court did indeed pose a threat to Protestant England.

TOLERATION FOR DISSENTERS—BUT AT A PRICE

Up to this time, Shaftesbury, in spite of his strong support of Parliamentary power, had usually supported the King in his foreign policies, even when Charles joined Louis XIV of France in his war against the Netherlands. For his support, Shaftesbury gained from the King a Declaration of Indulgence which resulted in toleration for the numerous dissenters who had long been persecuted by the Church of England. "Ministers returned," says historian John Richard Green, "after years of banishment, to their homes and flocks. Chapels reopened. The gaols were emptied. [John] Bunyan left his prison at Bedford; and hundreds of Quakers, who had been the special objects of persecution, were set free to worship God after their own fashion." [72]

---

70 Letter of John Locke to John Strachey, October 1672, in Benjamin Rand, *The correspondence of John Locke and Edward Clarke*, 77.

71 Ibid., 78.

72 Green, *Short History of the English People*, 640.

THE KING'S DUPLICITY REVEALED

It was with astonishment and bitterness, therefore, that Shaftesbury learned through the Duke of Arlington, one of the King's ministers, of a secret treaty Charles had made with the King of France. Worked out at Dover in May 1670 between Charles and his sister, Henriette, the Duchess of Orleans, it was of extraordinary duplicity. In this secret treaty, it was agreed that Charles would soon declare that he was a Roman Catholic. If this should cause unrest in his country, the French army would come to his aid. He would also receive an annual subsidy from King Louis in the amount of three hundred thousand pounds a year if he could bring England into the war against the Netherlands.[73]

DISMISSAL AND DANGER

Now in possession of this shocking story by one of the King's trusted councilors, Shaftesbury did an about-face and strongly opposed the war against the Netherlands. The result was that the King prorogued Parliament in November 1673 and dismissed Shaftesbury from his post as Chancellor. As an associate of Shaftesbury's, Locke now lost his lucrative post as Secretary of Presentations. He did not, however, distance himself from Shaftesbury. On the contrary, as the third Earl of Shaftesbury wrote,

> When my grandfather quitted the Court and began to be in danger from it, Mr. Locke now shared with him in dangers, as before in honours and advantages. He entrusted him with his secretest negotiations, and made use of his assistant pen in matters that nearly concerned the State and were fit to be made public.[74]

Oddly, Locke who had been made Secretary to the Council of Trade and Foreign Plantations just before Shaftesbury's fall, retained the position until the end of the council in 1675, although there is no record that his salary was ever paid. Shaftesbury more than made up for the loss of the post by giving Locke an annuity of one hundred pounds a year. This sum, along with money from Locke's property in Somersetshire, and interest from one or two loans and mortgages, left him in fairly good financial circumstances. He was not a gentleman of leisure, however, if it is true that Shaftesbury was still using his "assistant pen" in behind-the-scenes political maneuverings.

---

73 Ibid., 638–39.
74 Cited by Fowler, 26.

THE ANTI-WAR PARTY

Shaftesbury mobilized the anti-war party in Parliament to push for peace. Finally, in 1674, the King yielded reluctantly to their demands, and peace was concluded with the Dutch. Charles still had not announced his conversion to the Catholic faith. At the moment, his policy was to allay the fears of his Protestant subjects by agreeing to the marriage of Mary, the Protestant daughter of his brother James, to the Dutch Protestant ruler, Prince William of Orange. He thought this a clever way to neutralize any designs William might have on England. Like his father, Charles II ruled by an intricate system of duplicity using one person or group to counter another, sometimes favoring non-conformists, sometimes the Anglican Church, sometimes Protestant members of Parliament (like Shaftesbury) and sometimes the Catholic Party at his Court.

SHAFTESBURY IMPRISONED IN THE TOWER OF LONDON

In November 1675, Locke once again found that his lungs demanded he get away from the polluted air of London. He determined to try a health resort in Montpelier which had a distinguished medical school attached. Here he remained until the spring of 1677 when, at Shaftesbury's request, he left for Paris to act as tutor and traveling companion to Sir John Banks' son. He remained abroad for two more years traveling throughout France with his pupil. It was just as well that he was out of the country as his patron had run into rough political waters. Lord Danby, now Chancellor, seeing Shaftesbury as an obstacle to his efforts to reconcile the King and Parliament engineered a coup in February 1677 whereby the Earl and several supporters were imprisoned in the Tower of London on trumped-up charges of contempt of the House of Commons. Here Shaftesbury remained until November when he was released.

Early in 1679, he sent an urgent note to Locke summoning him home. Locke hastened back, arriving in London on April 30 where he took up residence again in Shaftesbury's home. He found that his patron's fortunes had turned once again; he had been made President of a reorganized Privy Council made up of thirty prominent members of Parliament, rather than mere Crown nominees. The situation looked hopeful. Shaftesbury continued to hammer away at the need for a bill excluding James from inheriting the throne. He knew, however, that Charles would try to use his influence with the House of Lords to see that such a bill did not become law. So he decided to put his weight in the House of Commons behind preparing a Remonstrance designed to put public opinion firmly behind his efforts. Officials of the City of London were ready to speak before the Commons in favor of Shaftesbury's bill. Seeing where matters were heading, Charles abruptly dissolved Parliament in May 1679.

A DIVIDED OPPOSITION

It is an irony of history that Charles II's delaying tactics would have been of no avail had Parliament been of one mind. Unhappily, a serious divergence of opinion had developed between 1) those who favored exclusion in favor of a Protestant successor to Charles already in line for the throne, (that is, the Princess Mary and her husband William of Orange), and 2) those who favored placing on the throne the Duke of Monmouth, Charles II's illegitimate son. Shaftesbury was one of those who wanted to see Monmouth on the throne. He apparently feared that William of Orange might turn out to be just as autocratic as Charles, whereas the Duke of Monmouth, a young man inexperienced in politics, would be less of a threat to the rights of Parliament and the people. Charles detected the split between Shaftesbury and many of his former allies in Parliament and, in October 1679, he summarily dismissed Shaftesbury from his post as President of the new council.

Charles was unable, however, to obtain more funds from Louis XIV and was being flooded with petitions from all over the country to call another Parliament. Many of these petitions were being prepared by Shaftesbury and sent to every town for signatures. Others wrote to abhor the acts of the petitioners. "The country was divided," wrote Green, "into two great factions known as 'petitioners' and 'abhorrers,' the germs of the two great parties of 'Whigs and Tories' which have played so prominent a part in our political history from the time of the Exclusion Bill."[75]

CHARLES FORCED
TO CALL ANOTHER PARLIAMENT

Charles was forced to call another Parliament for November 1680 at which Shaftesbury at last pushed through the Exclusion Bill in the House of Commons, only to be vetoed by the House of Lords. He then made a final "despairing effort to do the work of exclusion by a Bill of Divorce, which would have enabled the King to put away his Queen on the ground

---

75 Green, 657.

of barrenness, and by a fresh marriage to give a Protestant heir to the throne." [76] This effort, too, failed. Meanwhile, Monmouth toured the country trying to gain public support, and riots broke out in London. The King abruptly prorogued Parliament at the end of the year. In March 1681, when he next called for it to assemble, it was in Oxford, rather than in turbulent London. What happened at the historic Oxford Parliament led to another turning point in the life of John Locke.

---

76 Green, 657.

CHAPTER THREE

Danger and Exile

I have found here in another country [Holland]...for all that is
dearest...good-will, love, kindness—bonds that are stronger than
blood—I have experienced amongst you. It is owing to this
fellow-feeling which has always been shown to me by your
countrymen, that, though absent from my own people and exposed
to every kind of trouble, I have never yet felt sick at heart.

JOHN LOCKE
(1689[77])

IT has long been believed that Locke played hardly any role in Shaftesbury's political maneuverings, but Maurice Cranston's biography and
Peter Laslett's detective work in the Introduction to his edition of Locke's
Two Treatises of Government reveal that Locke was probably much more
active in aiding Shaftesbury in his political goals than has been assumed,
and this at a time when Shaftesbury was contemplating armed resistance
to the crown after the Exclusion Bill failed.[78] To be sure, some of Locke's
aid was of a merely practical nature, such as his arranging for lodgings for
Shaftesbury and his entourage in Oxford. But particular attention should
be given to the third Earl of Shaftesbury's comments that his grandfather
"entrusted him [Locke] with his secretest negotiations and made use of
his assistant pen in matters that nearly concerned the state," since it now
appears that Locke was not a detached observer of Shaftesbury's political
action. It has been discovered, for instance, that Locke probably drafted
Shaftesbury's "Instructions to the Knights of the County of...for Their
Conduct in Parliament," which, according to Laslett, has claims to being
the first modern document of party politics. A copy of the document written in Locke's hand was found in the Shaftesbury papers. That Locke may

---

77 John Locke, "Memoirs Relating to the Life of Anthony, First Earl of Shaftesbury," in *Works*, 9:272.
78 See chapters 14 and 16 of Cranston's biography; see also page 44 of Laslett's Introduction to Locke's
   Two Treatises of Government.

have become wholeheartedly involved in plans to topple Charles could well have arisen from the events that took place during the Oxford Parliament.

FOREIGN MONEY FREES
THE KING FROM PARLIAMENT

Believing that Charles's financial needs were such that he must agree to Parliament's demands in exchange for a subsidy, Shaftesbury again introduced an Exclusion Bill. Unknown to him, however, the King had entered into another secret agreement with Louis XIV in which Charles pledged—in exchange for another substantial subsidy from France—to withdraw from the Grand Alliance William of Orange was creating to oppose Louis. Therefore, Charles could snap his fingers at Parliament. He no longer had to go there, hat in hand, begging for money. But if he made himself independent of Parliament by his acceptance of funding from a foreign government, he also made himself dependent on the will of a foreign king, and surely this was treason to England.

As soon as Shaftesbury proposed an Exclusion Bill, the King immediately adjourned Parliament after it had sat for only eight days. He then issued a royal declaration appealing to the nation for justice. His choice of Oxford for the meeting with Parliament called up visions of the days of the Civil War in his father's reign and aroused fears throughout the land that another civil war could break out. The King portrayed himself as a patient monarch who had been imposed upon by a recalcitrant Parliament. As a result, the King's lofty appeal to the nation for justice was greeted with an outflow of loyalty all over the country. Somehow war must be prevented. It was clear to Shaftesbury, however, that Charles II, like his father, intended to rule as an absolute monarch without consulting Parliament.[79] At this point, Locke may well have been ready to support the idea of "an appeal to Heaven."[80]

On July 2, 1681, Shaftesbury was arrested and charged with plotting to overthrow Charles. The Middlesex Grand Jury ignored the indictment and when Shaftesbury was released from the Tower, Londoners celebrated with bonfires and pealing of church bells. Now free again, Shaftesbury continued to conspire against the King. Far from staying aloof, Locke accompanied his patron to Cassiobury, the home of the Duke of Essex, on September 15 where, says Laslett, "a meeting of the Whig leaders was scheduled at the

---

79 In fact, Charles called no further Parliaments for the rest of his reign.

80 In paragraphs 240-242 of Locke's *Second Treatise Of Civil Government*, he discusses when a people have a right to dissolve a government and make "an appeal to heaven" for justice.

height of what is sometimes called the Insurrection Plot."[81] As rumors of the meetings at Cassiobury leaked out, Shaftesbury realized that he must flee the country or else risk being tried and executed as a traitor.[82] He left clandestinely for Holland early in December 1682 and upon arriving in Amsterdam petitioned the government there for citizenship. His petition was granted. This prevented his being sent back to England for trial. Unhappily, Shaftesbury died in January 1683, of "gout of the stomach." Therefore, as Laslett points out, when Locke visited Cassiobury again in April 1683, after Shaftesbury's death, it must have been his own deliberate decision. What was discussed at this meeting? We do not know. We do know that the visit took place just when the Rye House Plot against Charles was underway.[83] At Sir Algernon Sydney's subsequent trial for treason, the Crown used Sydney's *Discourses Concerning Government*, which they had found in manuscript form in his home, to show that his sentiments were republican and hostile to monarchy. This manuscript formed an integral part of the Crown prosecution which led to Sidney's execution.

LOCKE'S PRECARIOUS POSITION

What must Locke have been thinking at this time? Locke's position as an associate of Shaftesbury's and suspected of having written against the government suddenly left him in an exceedingly precarious condition, much more precarious than has previously been supposed, for more than Locke's visits to Cassiobury was involved. Laslett maintains that Locke began what we now know as his *Two Treatises Of Civil Government*, not after returning from exile in Holland in 1688, or even while in exile there, but much earlier—indeed while living at Shaftesbury's London home as his principal aide and advisor. In other words, *Of Civil Government* was not a defense of a revolution, but a demand for one. It appears that Locke may have begun work on the book in 1679 and that his writing it was a direct result of discussions with Shaftesbury and others.

---

81 Peter Laslett, John Locke, *Two Treatises of Government*, 45.

82 This happened later to Sir Algernon Sydney, one of the frequent guests at Cassiobury, who was beheaded for his part in the Assassination, or Rye House Plot. Essex died while imprisoned in the Tower. Locke preserved a manuscript that suggested Essex had not died a natural death but had been murdered, which indicates that this was his own view.

83 The Rye House Plot was hatched by some hotheads who planned to assassinate both Charles and his brother as they went by the Rye-house on their way to Newmarket. A very different plot and actors took place at the same time between the leaders of the Country Party, among them Lord Essex, Lord Russell and Sir Algernon Sydney. This was a conspiracy to foment agitation calling for a new Parliament but the Crown insisted the two events were connected.

HOLLAND BECKONS

Having written such a revolutionary document, a work which completely demolished the Divine Right of Kings doctrine, it is no wonder that Locke realized his life was in danger. If he wished to go on being of use, he would have to flee the country. Like Shaftesbury and so many other persecuted people before him, Locke chose Holland in the United States of the Netherlands. Here, earlier in the century, the Pilgrim Fathers had fled because Holland was known for religious toleration. The present William of Orange (1650-1702), Stadtholder of Holland, was descended from another William of Orange, the celebrated William the Silent (1533-1584), who formed a league among seven provinces (Holland, Zealand, Utrecht, Friesland, Gelderland, Gronigen, and Overyssel) in 1579. This was the foundation of the Dutch republic. Two years later, these united provinces, or states, declared themselves independent of their Spanish overlords. There were to be years of war with Spain before their independence was finally acknowledged in 1648. Originally a Roman Catholic, William the Silent became an ardent Calvinist but would not set himself up as judge over other Christians and determined that all professed Christians of whatever denomination would be free to worship without molestation from the state. Holland became a haven for both English Puritans and Separatists and also became an asylum for political refugees whose views had displeased the rulers of their lands.

When Locke arrived in Holland, it was the home of countless distinguished scholars and theologians, both native and foreign. His sojourn there was to prove a very stimulating one. He arrived in Amsterdam in the autumn of 1683, a fifty-one year old refugee in not very good health. So secret was his departure from England that he did not even tell Damaris Cudworth until after his arrival in Holland. Although there was some talk of her coming over for a visit, nothing came of this idea. Locke's letters to her were fewer than might have been expected, so he ought not to have been surprised that Damaris did not wait for his return and, in 1685, married the widower Sir Francis Masham. She may have realized that Locke, older than she, was set in his bachelor ways and was moving irrevocably out of her orbit, perhaps never to return to England. He, too, may have realized that with the age difference, his poor health, and an uncertain life as an exile in a foreign country, it was best to forget the idea of marriage. On his last visit to France, his sentiments in regard to love and marriage were expressed in a letter he wrote to a friend, in which he admitted: "My health is the only mistress I have a long time courted, and is so coy a one that I think it will take up the remainder of my days to obtain her good graces and keep her in good humour."[84] Although there was a coolness in Locke's correspondence with Damaris after he learned of her marriage, this was only momentary. Their friendship and mutual esteem continued throughout the remainder of his life.

DUTCH FRIENDSHIPS

Soon after his arrival in Holland, Locke renewed his friendship with Dr. Peter Guenellon, a prominent physician in Amsterdam whom he had met formerly in Paris. Guenellon introduced him to the leading intellectual, scientific, and theological figures in Amsterdam. Among them was Philip van Limborch (1674-1712) who was an Arminian, or Remonstrant, professor of theology in the city and one of the most important theologians in Holland. A big, burly, genial man, Guemellon was to become one of Locke's closest friends. Locke came to respect and in some measure share Arminian theological views. Certainly, he admired their toleration of those who differed from them and their reliance on Scripture rather than creeds.[85]

DISPUTES OVER ARMINIAN DOCTRINES

Locke was undoubtedly interested to learn that Limborch was not only an important Remonstrant theologian in his own right but was also the grand nephew of Simon Episcopius (1583-1643), another celebrated Remonstrant theologian who, in 1634, became head of their first seminary in Amsterdam.[86] Arminians came to be called "Remonstrants" from a paper titled "A Remonstrance" which they presented to the States-General in 1610 laying out their theological positions and protesting the persecution they were receiving from Calvinists. Their leader, Jacobus Arminius (1559-1609), was born in Oudeswater as Jacob Harmenszoon, shortened to Harmensz, but when he became a scholar he took a Latin name, as was customary. The name he chose was Arminius for the leader of the Germanic tribes who rebelled against the tyranny of Rome; Arminius (18 B.C.-A.D. 19) made it his life's work to bring about the independence of the Germanic tribes from

---

84 Fowler, 30.

85 Episcopius wrote a creed but was quick to say that this Confession of Faith should be used as a guide but not to force someone else into his formulation of faith. See Robert M. Bartlett, *The Pilgrim Way*, (Philadelphia: Pilgrim Press. 1971), 169.

86 The Pilgrims Fathers' minister, Reverend John Robinson, when they were living in exile in Holland, took the Calvinist position in his debate with Episcopius at the University of Leyden in 1610. He was shocked and grieved later when the Arminians were severely persecuted because he did not believe in persecution, but in courteous dialogue with those of differing theological views.

Roman rule. This must have resonated with Jacob because his countrymen were battling Spain for their independence from Spanish rule. His father had died in 1558 and Jacob's education was then conducted by Theodore Aemelius, a priest in the then still Catholic town. In 1575, a professor at Marburg befriended him and took him to Marburg to be enrolled in the university. Scarcely had they arrived, however, when they heard the terrible news that Oudewater had been attacked by the Spaniards and that almost all its inhabitants, including women and children, had been slain. He returned at once to Oudewater to find that his mother, his brothers and sisters and, indeed, all his family were dead. Not knowing what else to do, he went back to Marburg. Later, hearing that a university had started in Leiden, he returned to Holland where he studied at the University of Leiden (1576-1582) and then at Geneva (1582-86).

He was ordained in the Dutch Reformed Church in Amsterdam in 1588 and called to be a professor of theology at Leiden University in 1603. Considered a fine scholar, he only ran into trouble with the church when he expressed some views doubting the Calvinist interpretation of predestination. The last six years of his life were filled with theological controversy which the gentle, reticent Arminius entered into reluctantly. Nevertheless, he stood steadfastly by his convictions. His final view of predestination was that God elects to eternal life those who respond to His offer of salvation. He believed this was in accord with God's infinite mercy.[87] This was a view Locke expressed in his *Reasonableness of Christianity*, written late in life, although he never lost track of the sovereignty of God. For him, freedom of the will to accept or reject God's offer of salvation in Jesus Christ was not dependant on man's rational nature per se, but on God's gift of grace.[88]

Locke was probably familiar with the disputes between the Calvinists and the Arminians in the Dutch Reformed Church. It became a controversy so bitter that the States-General finally summoned Church leaders to a Synod of Dort (or Dordrecht, to give the town's full name) on November 13, 1618, to settle the theological matters under dispute, among which were predestination and freedom of the will. The document under scrutiny was the famous Arminian Remonstrance of 1610. Its five points declared that: 1) Election or condemnation was conditioned by the rational faith or non-faith of man; 2) the Atonement, while for all, was efficacious only for the person of faith; 3) unless aided by the Holy Spirit, no one is able to respond to the will of God; 4) Grace is not irresistible; and

---

87 Carl Bangs. *Arminius*, an excellent biography and detailed study of the reformer's theological views.
88 See, for example, par. 166 in *The Reasonableness of Christianity* (any complete edition).

5) although believers are able to resist sin, they may fall from grace.[89]

The delegates to the Synod were all staunch Calvinists, but after the opening of the meeting, Episcopius, leader of the Arminians since the death of Jacob Arminius, and a dozen other Remonstrants were allowed to attend some of the assemblies. They attended as the accused, however, not as participants. The Synod of Dort, because of its composition (all Calvinists) declared in favor of Calvinism and against the Arminians who were everywhere ousted from their posts as ministers and teachers. At least a dozen were exiled, including Episcopius. He lived in Antwerp, Paris, and Rouen during this period. As one writer has observed: "The aftermath of the Synod of Dort, which started out to be just another assembly of divines and academicians, forms a blot on the escutcheon of Dutch tolerance.... Its implications in the field of divinity were sad enough, since they reflected an abandonment of the benevolent outlook of William the Silent...of the traditional sanctuary granted to Jews, Roman Catholics, and all brands of Protestant rebels."[90] The fever of persecution passed, however, and Episcopius came home in 1626. In 1629, the works of Arminius finally were published in Leiden. In 1630, the Arminians were accorded legal toleration.

ATTEMPTS TO FORCE LOCKE TO RETURN TO ENGLAND

By the time of Locke's arrival in Holland, religious toleration was once again well established in the Dutch Republic and Locke was free to move around the country. In the autumn of 1684, he visited many cities. His health seemed to benefit from the climate better than it had in the much-vaunted Montpellier. Perhaps, though, as Fowler remarks, his improved health may not have been so much the result of the change in climate as pleasant companionship and "the variety of interests—political, commercial, literary, and theological—which the Dutch nation at that time so pre-eminently afforded."[91] But this pleasant existence was to be abruptly curtailed. In November, when Locke was back in Amsterdam, he received word from the dean of Christ Church summoning him to Oxford. While considering whether or not to obey this summons, he learned that he had been expelled from Christ Church and thus deprived of all the benefits of

---

89 In the eighteenth century, the Wesleys espoused Arminian doctrines and John Wesley wrote in *The Arminian Magazine*, which he edited, that "God willeth all men to be saved, by speaking the truth in love." The Arminian emphasis on the grace of God influenced the growth of the Methodist movements in England and the United States.

90 Robert Merrill Bartlett, *The Pilgrim Way*, 171.

91 Fowler, 45.

his studentship. This showed him the sinister nature of the summons, and he did not comply. This was not to be the last attempt to get him to return to England. For the moment, though, all was quiet and Locke spent that winter in Utrecht in writing and study. Being away from England and out of the turmoil of politics was actually an advantage for Locke the writer, as Lady Masham noted. "In Holland, he had full leisure to prosecute his thoughts on the subject of the *Essay on Human Understanding*—a work which, in probability, he never would have finished had he continued in England."[92]

ENGLAND SEEKS HIS EXTRADITION

On February 6, 1685, Charles II died. Brother James prepared to ascend the throne, but he was not unchallenged. Charles's illegitimate son, the Duke of Monmouth, decided to mount an insurrection. He failed, was imprisoned and executed. Because of Locke's association with the Earl of Shaftesbury, his name was on a list the Crown sent to the Dutch government on May 7, 1686, of eighty-four "dangerous" persons, supposedly plotters against the King's life. When William of Orange received it, he sent copies to the magistrates of Amsterdam and other towns where traitors might be hiding. There seems to have been a tacit understanding, however, that if Locke stayed out of sight he would not be picked up and returned to England. (Indeed, there is no record that the Dutch ever surrendered to England any of the people on the King's list.)

Locke could not be sure that he would not be arrested, however, and he returned from Utrecht to Amsterdam to take up residence in the home of Dr. Veen, his friend Dr. Guenellon's father-in-law. He intended to lay low for some time, but his isolation was broken by visits from Limborch and others. Locke took the name of Dr. Van der Linden, and on a short visit to Cleves, he used the name Lamy.

Meanwhile, friends at home were at work on his behalf. William Penn, a school fellow from his Oxford days, went to King James and asked for a pardon for Locke. The Earl of Pembroke also petitioned the King for a pardon and wrote to Locke jubilantly on August 20 that the King had agreed to pardon him. All he had to do was to come home. "I told him," Pembroke wrote, "I would then bring you to kiss his hand, and he was fully satisfied I should."[93] Locke declined to come home or to accept the

---

92 Cited by Fowler, 46.
93 See Fowler, 48.

pardon, replying that he had "no occasion for a pardon, having been guilty of no crime."[94] He continued his concealment and his identity as Dr. Van der Linden.

FRIENDSHIP WITH JEAN LE CLERC

In 1685 or 1686, Limborch introduced Locke to a young man who was to play an immensely important role in Locke's work as an author. This was Jean Le Clerc, a professor of theology and Hebrew at the Remonstrant college in Amsterdam. Although young, Le Clerc already had an established reputation as a philosopher and theologian. Born in Geneva in 1657, he had traveled widely before settling in Amsterdam. More liberal in his religious views than Locke, he nevertheless became a good friend, mainly because of his efforts to get Locke's works translated into French and published. He first approached Locke about writing something for publication in his *Bibliotheque Universelle*, one of the first literary journals on the continent. Locke obliged him with a short piece on how to arrange materials in a common-place book.[95] It appeared, translated into French, in the July issue of Le Clerc's publication under the title "Methode Nouvelle de Dresser Les Recueils." (Later, in 1688, an abstract of his *Essay on Human Understanding* appeared in an issue of the *Bibliotheque Universelle*.)

THE EPISTOLA DE TOLERANTIA

Probably inspired by discussions on Dutch toleration with his friend Limborch and his own passionate desire to advance the cause of religious toleration in England, Locke wrote a treatise on the subject while he was in Holland. It expanded upon the themes in his earlier unpublished *Essay on Toleration* and introduced ideas developed further in his *Essay on Human Understanding* and the *Two Treatises of Government*.[96] For example, one of the reasons Locke gives for toleration of those who hold differing religious convictions is because of the limitations of the human mind which attempts to judge matters beyond its powers. This was the central concern of the *Essay*. The proper role of civil government also is introduced in

---

94 Ibid.

95 Such notebooks were very popular in Great Britain during the seventeenth and eighteenth centuries and in her North American colonies. In Noah Webster's first edition of *An American Dictionary of the English Language* in 1828, he defines a common-place book as "a book in which are registered such facts, opinions, or observations as are deemed worthy of notice or remembrance, so disposed that any one may be easily found."

96 Patrick Romanell, in his Introduction to a modern edition of the *Letter on Toleration*, declares that "it contains the master key to his entire philosophy." See John Locke, *A Letter Concerning Toleration* (New York: The Liberal Arts Press, 2d. ed., 1955), 7.

relation to religious toleration. In the *Second Treatise of Government*, Locke developed fully his ideas on the role of civil government in relation to the rights of the individual to his life, liberty, and property.

Locke's treatise on toleration is a passionate and eloquent plea for Christians to follow the example of Christ who "sent out his soldiers to the subduing of nations, and gathering them into His church, not armed with the sword or other instruments of force, but prepared with the Gospel of peace and with the exemplary holiness of their conversation."[97] It was written in Latin, the language of scholars, and was entitled *Epistola de Tolerania;* Locke gave it to his friend Limborch, who promptly got it published (anonymously) in Gouda, Holland, in 1689. Dutch and French translations followed and, in the same year, it was translated into English by William Popple, an English merchant and scholar living in London, and published as *A Letter Concerning Toleration.*

EQUAL AND IMPARTIAL LIBERTY NEEDED

It was Popple who penned the eloquent words in his preface to the book entitled "To the Reader": "Absolute liberty, just and true liberty, equal and impartial liberty, is the thing we stand in need of."[98] They were printed in italics and Locke could not have missed them when he read Popple's translation. It is significant that he never took issue with Popple about these words, nor does the record show that he did with anyone else. Some scholars, such as Patrick Romanell, have thought that Popple's words were at variance with the tenor of the book which they say pleads for toleration, rather than religious liberty. Views pointing toward religious liberty are in the letter, however, which is not surprising when we remember Locke's articles on religious liberty in the *Carolina Constitutions.*[99] That he did not address the difference between religious toleration and religious liberty head-on in *A Letter Concerning Toleration* is probably because he well knew that it would be many long years before England would be ready to accept such a radical idea. If, on the other hand, Englishmen could be persuaded to see the different roles of Church and State and the proper role of the civil magistrate in relation to the Church, this would go a long way to prepare the ground for toleration and, eventually, religious liberty.

---

97 Locke, *A Letter Concerning Toleration, Works*, 6:8-9.

98 *Works*, 6:4.

99 See, for example, his comments on the church being a voluntary society in which individuals bind themselves voluntarily, (surely a reference to the dissenting churches), rather than an institution into which one is born (an oblique reference to the Church of England), in *Works*, 6:13.

THE BANNER OF CHRIST

This first *Letter Concerning Toleration* (there were to be three more, written as rebuttals to a garrulous critic) is notable for its presentation of the idea of a separation between Church and State. Locke makes it clear that such a separation is in order to protect the Church (and dissenting churches) from the power of the state, and also the state from churchmen intent on levying civil penalties (such as confiscation of property, imprisonment, and loss of life) for alleged religious heresies. He reminds the reader that "If the Gospel and the apostles may be credited, no man can be a Christian without charity, and without that faith which works, not by force, but by love." He goes on to say: "Now I appeal to the consciences of those that persecute, torment, destroy, and kill other men upon pretence of religion, whether they do it out of friendship and kindness towards them, or no?"[100] He admonishes the reader:

> Whosoever will list himself under the banner of Christ, must, in the first place, above all things, make war upon his own lusts and vices. It is in vain for any man to usurp the name of Christian without holiness of life, purity of manners, and benignity and meekness of spirit. 'Let every one that nameth the name of Christ depart from iniquity,' 2 Tim. ii. 19. 'Thou, when thou art converted, strengthen thy brethren,' said our Lord to Peter, Luke xxii. 32. The toleration of those that differ from others in matters of religion, is so agreeable to the Gospel of Jesus Christ, and to the genuine reason of mankind, that it seems monstrous for men to be so blind, as not to perceive the necessity and advantage of it in so clear a light.[101]

THE JUST BOUNDS BETWEEN
CIVIL GOVERNMENT AND RELIGION

He then sets forth a way to prevent persecution. In order that "some may not colour their spirit of persecution and unchristian cruelty with a pretense of care of the public weal and observation of the laws, and that others, under pretense of religion, may not seek impunity for their libertinism and licentiousness; in a word, that none may impose either upon himself or others, by the pretenses of loyalty and obedience to the prince, or of tenderness and sincerity in the worship of God; I esteem it above all things necessary to distinguish exactly the business of civil government

---

100 *Works*, 6:6.
101 *Works*, 6:6.

from that of religion, and to settle the just bounds that lie between the one and the other. If this be not done, there can be no end put to the controversies that will be always arising between those that have, or at least pretend to have, on the one side, a concernment for the interest of men's souls, and, on the other side, a care of the commonwealth." [102]

WHAT IS THE COMMONWEALTH?

He defines the commonwealth as "a society of men constituted only for the procuring, preserving, and advancing their own civil interests." [103] What are these civil interests? Locke defines them as "life, liberty, health, and indolency of body; and the possession of outward things, such as money, lands, houses, furniture, and the like." [104] Here we see his extended definition of property as including not only physical possessions, but also the individual's very life and liberty.

He declared that the duty of the civil magistrate is to secure to everyone "the just possession of the things belonging to this life" and to punish those who violate any other man's rights. But the "care of souls" does not belong to the civil magistrate. He gave three reasons for this:

> First, Because...it appears not that God has ever given any such authority to one man over another, as to compel anyone to his religion. Nor can any such power be vested in the magistrate by the consent of the people; because no man can so far abandon the care of his own salvation as blindly to leave it to the choice of any other, whether prince or subject, to prescribe to him what faith or worship he shall embrace.... All the life and power of true religion consists in the inward and full persuasion of the mind; and faith is not faith without believing....
>
> In the second place, The care of souls cannot belong to the civil magistrate, because his power consists only in outward force: but true and saving religion consists in the inward persuasion of the mind, without which nothing can be acceptable to God.... Confiscation of estate, imprisonment, torments, nothing of that nature can have any such efficacy as to make men change the inward judgment that they have framed of things.
>
> In the third place, The care of men's souls cannot belong to the magistrate; because, though the rigour of laws and the force of penalties were capable to convince and change men's minds, yet

---

102 *Works*, 6:9.
103 *Works*, 6:9–10.
104 *Works*, 6:10.

would not that help at all to the salvation of their souls. For, there being but one truth, one way to heaven; what hope is there that more men would be led into it, if they had no other rule to follow but the religion of the court, and were put under a necessity to quit the light of their own reason, to oppose the dictates of their own consciences, and blindly to resign up themselves to the will of their governors.... In the variety and contradiction of opinions in religion, wherein the princes of this world are as divided as in their secular interests, the narrow way would be much straightened....[105]

Locke was aware of the religious upheavals England had been put through by the sudden changes in religion imposed on Englishmen by changes in monarchs, so that England was one day Catholic and the next Protestant, later Catholic once more, then Protestant. Further on in the *Letter* he wrote that English history affords examples,

[I]n the reigns of Henry VIII, Edward VI, Mary, and Elizabeth, how easily and smoothly the clergy changed their decrees, their articles of faith, their form of worship, every thing, according to the inclinations of those kings and queens. Yet were those kings and queens of such different minds in points of religion, and enjoined thereupon such different things, that no man in his wits, I had almost said none but an atheist, will presume to say that any sincere and upright worshipper of God could, with a safe conscience, obey their several decrees.[106]

WHAT IS A CHURCH?

Locke then considers what a church is. He does not use "the Church" because he is not concerned with defining what the Church of England is, but what a Christian church is, of whatever denomination. "A Church then I take to be a voluntary society of men, joining themselves of their own accord, in order to the public worshipping of God, in such a manner as they judge acceptable to him, and effectual to the salvation of their souls."[107] This definition and the following sentence make it clear that he was certainly not describing the Church of England or any other state church. He boldly states his case:

I say, it is a free and voluntary society. Nobody is born a member of any church; otherwise the religion of parents would descend unto children by the same right of inheritance as their temporal

---

105 *Works*, 6:10–12.
106 *Works*, 6:27.
107 *Works*, 6:13.

estates, and every one would hold his faith by the same tenure he does his lands, than which nothing can be more absurd.... No man by nature is bound unto any particular church or sect, but every one joins himself voluntarily to that society in which he believes he has found that profession and worship which is truly acceptable to God. The hope of salvation, as it was the only cause of his entrance into that communion, so it can be the only reason of his stay there.[108]

This is a direct denial of the position of the Church of England into which men and women were indeed "born" and from which it was dangerous to withdraw. Earlier, the Pilgrims had learned that those who desired to do so were often thrown into prison, there to rot, or else were tried and executed on trumped-up charges of treason. According as Kings blew hot or cold on the subject, persecution would be stronger or milder. As noted earlier, Charles II sometimes persecuted dissenters or, if he thought it politically advantageous, permitted them to worship unmolested. But when dissenters believed that a church had become corrupt and no longer godly, they felt that they should be free to leave and worship in a manner they believed was, as Locke wrote, "truly acceptable to God." Locke's conclusion of the matter is that "No member of a religious society can be tied with any other bonds but what proceed from the certain expectation of eternal life. A church then is a society of members voluntarily uniting to this end." [109]

How Much Power
Does a Church Have?

A church must be governed by some laws and rules agreed upon by its members, Locke goes on to explain, but these are laws involving its forms and times of worship, admitting or dismissing members, kinds of officers, etc. If a member of a church disputes its teachings or form of worship, or is living a life not in harmony with the teachings of Christ, the only proper compulsive power of a church should be exhortation, admonition, and advice. "If by these means the offenders will not be reclaimed, and the erroneous convinced, there remains nothing farther to be done, but that such stubborn and obstinate persons, who give no ground to hope for their reformation, should be cast out and separated from the society. This is the last and utmost force of ecclesiastical authority." [110]

---

108 *Works*, 6:13.
109 *Works*, 6:13.
110 *Works*, 6:16.

THE EXTENT OF THE CIVIL MAGISTRATE'S POWER OVER RELIGION

Since the offence is spiritual and not material, the civil magistrate cannot be called upon to impose civil penalties upon the excommunicated person. Nor does any private person have the right "to prejudice another person in his civil enjoyments, because he is of another church or religion. All the rights and franchises that belong to him as a man, or as a denison, are inviolably to be preserved to him. These are not the business of religion." [111] Locke goes on to stress that "No violence nor injury is to be offered him, whether he be Christian or pagan." He follows up these words with an eloquent, evangelical statement:

> Nay, we must not content our selves with the narrow measures of bare justice: charity, bounty, and liberality must be added to it. This the Gospel enjoins, this reason directs, and this that natural fellowship we are born into requires of us.[112]

He insists that the authority of the clergy is confined to the church, "nor can it in any manner be extended to civil affairs; because the church itself is a thing absolutely separate and distinct from the commonwealth. The boundaries on both sides are fixed and immoveable. He jumbles heaven and earth together, the things most remote and opposite, who mixes these societies, which are, in their original, end, business, and in everything, perfectly distinct, and infinitely different from each other." [113]

THE DUTIES OF THE MAGISTRATE TOWARD THE CHURCHES

Locke sees the duties of the magistrate in regard to the churches as largely to refrain from interfering in their affairs. Regarding their outward worship, for example, Locke says that "the magistrate has no power to enforce by law, either in his own church, or much less in another, the use of any rites or ceremonies whatsoever in the worship of God. And this, not only because these churches are free societies, but because whatsoever is practiced in the worship of God is only so far justifiable as it is believed by those that practice it to be acceptable unto him. —Whatsoever is not done with that assurance of faith is neither well in itself, nor can it be acceptable to God." [114] Here he anticipates his reader's probable question by asking

---

111 *Works*, 6:17.
112 *Works*, 6:17.
113 *Works*, 6:21.
114 *Works*, 6:29.

"if some congregations should have a mind to sacrifice infants, or, as the primitive Christians were falsely accused, lustfully pollute themselves in promiscuous uncleanness, or practise any other such heinous enormities, is the magistrate obliged to tolerate them, because they are committed in a religious assembly?"[115] He answers no, because "these things are not lawful in the ordinary course of life, nor in any private house; and, therefore, neither are they so in the worship of God, or in any religious meeting." Therefore, the magistrate can only legitimately interfere in the worship services of a church if the members or leaders of that church are injuring or destroying the life, liberty, or property of another human being. These come within the purview of the magistrate, but not the religious teaching of the church or its forms of worship.

LIMITS ON TOLERATION

Locke's conclusion is that there are only four kinds of churches that ought not to be tolerated. First, those churches whose opinions would destroy "those moral rules which are necessary to the preservation of civil society" ought not to be tolerated by the magistrate. But he believes these would be rare occurrences because "no sect can easily arrive to such a degree of madness, as that it should think fit to teach, for doctrines of religion, such things as manifestly undermine the foundations of society, and are therefore condemned by the judgment of all mankind: because their own interest, peace, reputation, everything would be thereby endangered."[116]

A second group is those people or churches who are intolerant of other churches and would interfere with their affairs or who teach that kings not of their faith may be forcibly dethroned. Such persons or churches have no right to be tolerated by the magistrate, "for what do all these and the like doctrines signify, but that they may, and are ready upon occasion to seize the government and possess themselves of the estates and fortunes of their fellow-subjects; and that they only ask leave to be tolerated by the magistrates so long, until they find themselves strong enough to effect it."[117]

A third group that has no right to be tolerated by the magistrate is a church "which is constituted upon such a bottom, that all those who enter it, do thereby, *ipso facto*, deliver themselves up to the protection and service of another prince. For by this means the magistrate would give way to the settling of a foreign jurisdiction in his own country, and suffer his own

---

115 *Works*, 6:33.
116 *Works*, 6:45.
117 *Works*, 6:46.

people to be listed, as it were, for soldiers against his own government." [118]

This is an obvious allusion to the conspiracies of English Roman Catholics against Queen Elizabeth's life, their plot to dethrone and kill her, and substitute in her place the Catholic Mary, Queen of Scots, all in accord with the desires of the Catholic Church. He may also have been thinking of the Pope who promised a bounty to the man who would assassinate William the Silent. Locke is still so cautious, though, that the example he gives is of a Mahometan who declares that while he is faithful to his religion, in everything else he is a faithful subject of England. Locke points out the inconsistency here, because he still owes obedience to the decrees of the mufti of Constantinople. [119] From this passage, it is clear that Locke's objection to the real religion in question is that the adherents of the Roman Catholics of his day was not just to their religious beliefs, but to the political decrees of their Pope whenever he urged interference in the internal affairs of England, a Protestant nation.

EVIL RESULTS OF DENYING THE EXISTENCE OF GOD

"Lastly," he says, "Those are not at all to be tolerated who deny the being of God. Promises, covenants, and oaths, which are the bonds of human society, can have no hold upon an atheist. The taking away of God, though but even in thought, dissolves all. Besides also, those that by their atheism undermine and destroy all religion, can have no pretence of religion whereupon to challenge the privilege of a toleration." [120] This passage makes it clear that Locke believed it impossible for a nation to have a genuine and workable moral system which denies the existence of God. For without God, who is to say what is moral or immoral, lawful or unlawful? Thus, when he writes of Church and State as separate, the state caring for the civil affairs of its citizens and the Church (or churches) of their spiritual well-being, he does not mean that the state is not governed by the moral principles of Christianity. All of his writings show that he expects civil government to rest on a Christian moral basis.

THE GLORIOUS REVOLUTION

This quiet period of reflection and writing, so fruitful for his work as a thinker and an author, soon changed. He moved to Rotterdam where he

---

118 *Works*, 6:46.

119 An example today would be that of Islamic writer Solomon Rushdie, whose books so incurred the ire of the Moslem leaders in his country, that they ordered any of the faithful who knew his whereabouts to kill him.

120 *Works*, 6:47.

remained during the rest of his stay in Holland. The move seems to have been connected with political events taking place there. James II failed to heed the advice of his brother Charles II who, on his deathbed, warned him not to try to impose the Catholic faith on England. Instead, James moved quickly to put Catholics in all the important posts in the army and forcibly installed his own Catholic nominees as heads of Christ Church, Oxford, and of Magdalen College. He filled his Privy Council with Catholics including his Jesuit adviser, Father Petre. A Catholic was made head of the fleet. The notorious Judge Jeffreys was appointed Lord Chancellor.

By 1687, secret negotiations were well under way between William of Orange, who was a staunch Calvinist, and members of Parliament who wished to rid England of James II's rule and install William and his wife, Mary, James's Protestant daughter, on the throne of England. William's court was at Rotterdam and there, too, was Lord Mordaunt, later the Earl of Peterborough, who shortly before had left England to live in Holland. It is believed that Locke, as a friend of Lord Mordaunt, was introduced to Prince William and the Princess Mary, and that he played some role in advising Mordaunt and others, perhaps on the proper role of the royal pair as elected sovereigns and the need for a Declaration of Rights. A letter Locke wrote to his friend Limborch in February 1687, hints at what was going on. He wrote: "To politics I gave but little thought at Amsterdam; here I cannot pay much attention to literature." [121]

Despite his undoubted preoccupation with politics during the latter period of his life in Holland, he produced an abstract of his *Essay on Human Understanding* which Le Clerc published in the January 1688 *Bibliotheque Universelle*, with the French translation by Le Clerc. Several copies of Locke's condensation of his great work were produced with a short dedication to Locke's friend, the Earl of Pembroke.

While in Rotterdam, he lived in the home of Benjamin Furley, an English Quaker and bibliophile, where he enjoyed much domestic comfort with the family and especially delighted in Furley's children, among them a little boy of four or five named Arent whom he called "my little friend." Locke loved children and greatly enjoyed their company. He advised Furley on the boy's education, as he did for so many of his other friends like Edward Clarke, a Somerset friend who had married a cousin of Locke's and with whom he corresponded regularly while in Holland. The series of letters he wrote to Clarke and his wife on the education of their son

---

121 Fowler, 52.

later were the basis of his book, *Some Thoughts on Education* (1690).[122]

By autumn of 1688 William of Orange, having been given the go-ahead by the States-General to his plan to invade England, was gathering a fleet together with the aid of numerous English Lords, such as the Earl of Shrewsbury who donated 2,000 pounds toward the expedition. Sons of Tory nobles, such as the sons of the Marquis of Winchester, Lord Danby and Lord Peterborough, also flocked to William's side.

William set out for England on November 1, 1688 with a force made up mainly of Hollanders and English and Scottish exiles prepared to fight James II.[123] By some accounts he left with a fleet of 600 transports (another account mentions only 200 to 300 transports), and 50 men-of-war. His own vessel flew a banner that read: *"Pro religione et libertate—je maintiendrai"* (For religion and liberty—I will maintain). There were 4,000 English and Scottish troops in this fleet, plus two regiments of English emigres and four regiments of Dutch troops which reached Torbay on November 5.

As it turned out, it was to be virtually a bloodless revolution. On entering Exeter, William's army was greeted with cheers. Town after town threw open their gates to William and his army, looking upon them as liberators from the tyranny of James and as defenders of the Protestant faith. By the time William reached Salisbury, where James II's forces were stationed, he found them leaderless, their officers having abandoned the fight, and ready to disperse peaceably. In despair, James fled to France.[124] Once arrived in London, William was met by a delegation from both Houses of Parliament requesting him to take provisional government of the kingdom and to send out letters inviting the electors of every town and county to send representatives to a Convention to be held in January 1689.

THE CONVENTION PARLIAMENT

At the Convention, learning that Mary had resolved not to reign independently of her husband, it was decided that William and Mary would be acknowledged as joint sovereigns of England, but that William alone would rule. A parliamentary committee, led by John Somers, a young lawyer who was to become one of England's leading statesmen, drew up a Declaration of Rights which was presented to William and Mary on February 13 in the

---

122 The letters are scattered throughout Benjamin Rand's excellent *Correspondence of John Locke and Edward Clarke*, Plainview, New York, 1927, reprinted 1975.

123 Bryan Bevan discusses the origins of William's family in his excellent biography, *King William III, Prince of Orange: The First European*, London: The Rubicon Press, 1997. He explains that Orange was a French principality that was long fought over between Holland and France, 4.

124 For more details on the landing of William, see Bevan, 20, and Green's *Short History of England*, 681.

banqueting-room at Whitehall Palace. Here they signed the document that made them England's elected sovereigns sworn to uphold the provisions of the Declaration.

Somers was a good friend of Locke's. He had been a strong supporter of Shaftesbury's policies. Locke was still in Holland when the Convention Parliament drafted the Declaration of Rights, but it reflects Locke's views. His ideas on what should be included may well have been transmitted to Somers. In any case, Locke was to have a profound effect on the policies of the government when Somers came to lead it, and was to exert an influence on King William who came to have great respect for Locke's wisdom and integrity. Discussion of the English Declaration of Rights and Locke's role in English politics during the reign of William III is discussed in Chapter 5.

Meanwhile, we follow Locke and the royal party as they wait for the go-ahead from the King for their departure for England. Locke is believed to have had many interviews with the new Queen of England and had been charged by Lord Mordaunt who was in London with the King, to escort Lady Mordaunt back to England. It was not until February 11, 1689, however, that Locke and Lady Mordaunt left the Hague with the royal party. They set foot on Greenwich the following day. What emotions Locke must have felt to be at last in his own beloved England once again, free to see the many friends from whom he had been separated for more than five years, and free to visit his home and relations in Somersetshire. He probably had no idea of the demands that would soon be made upon him to support the new Whig administration with his political talents. He was probably looking forward to the joy of getting his books published in England where they could not have been published before 1688 and what Englishmen were soon to call "the Glorious Revolution."

CHAPTER FOUR

Safe Harbor

You ask me "what is the shortest and surest way, for a young
gentleman, to attain a true knowledge of the Christian religion, in the
full and just extent of it?"...And to this I have a short and plain answer:
"Let him study the Holy Scripture, especially the New Testament."
Therein are contained the words of eternal life. It has God for
its author; salvation for its end; and truth, without any
mixture of error for its matter.

JOHN LOCKE
(*A Letter to the Reverend Mr. Richard King,* 25 August 1703[125])

WHEN John Locke set foot on English soil once again, he must
have had a feeling of elation, gratitude, and relief; he was, after
all, returning to an England with tremendous possibilities for an improved
constitutional system under William and Mary. The relief he felt at being
home once again must have been tempered by caution, however, because
it was not yet apparent that "the Glorious Revolution" would be a lasting
one. Locke has been accused of being too timorous and cautious, too
loath to acknowledge that he was the author of *The Two Treatises Of Civil
Government,* even after the revolution had taken place. This is easy to say
from our standpoint today. We know that when the English Bill of Rights
became law and William and Mary took the throne as elected sovereigns,
this marked the beginning of constitutional monarchy in England, a system
that in its broad outlines has continued to our own day. Locke, however,
could not see ahead and could not be certain that the pendulum might not
swing again in the direction of tyranny, as it had done before. He could not
be sure that William's throne was truly secure. In fact, it was not. There
were still many Tories in England who wished for the return of James II to
the throne. To them, Locke's political ideas were much too radical.

---

125 In *Works,* 10:306.

Take the idea of compact, on which Locke's system is based. The Tories would agree on the idea of compact, but their idea of compact was different. They saw the English form of government as based on a compact or covenant between the king and the nobility, whereas Locke's compact was among the people who would then decide on the kind of government they wanted and the extent of its powers, as they found them beneficial or hurtful to their natural God-given rights to "life, liberty, and property." Locke's great work on government championed the cause of limited government and rejected absolute power wherever lodged. Locke knew from previous experience that such views were anathema to James and those who had supported him, however quiet they might be now. He may have feared that it would be only a matter of time before there would be some plot against the achievements of the Revolution.

Indeed, the Earl of Marlborough, who had betrayed his master, King James, and joined William's side, soon secretly conspired to oust William and put Queen Mary's sister, the Princess Anne, on the throne. Marlborough's wife had insinuated herself into Anne's friendship; the princess was completely governed by her new friend's wishes. What could be better for the ambitious Marlborough?[126] There was also the ever-present danger of Louis XIV's forces invading England and restoring James to the throne by force and, at the same time, returning England to the Roman Catholic fold.

As will be seen in the following chapter, Locke became an advisor to King William and to the leading Whig politicians who crafted the Bill of Rights and the Toleration Bill. He was in a position to know the various dangers threatening the fledgling constitutional monarchy. It should hardly be surprising, therefore, to find that he was extremely cautious about acknowledging his authorship of the *Two Treatises* when they were published in England in 1690. He had good reason to be. To imply that he was simply of a very timorous nature or had an exaggerated sense of personal danger is to ignore the historical events going on at the time, not to mention the earlier power changes in England that Locke had already experienced firsthand.

PUBLICATION OF THE ESSAY
AND THE TWO TREATISES

While Locke never acknowledged—except in his will—that he was the author of the *Two Treatises*, he did acknowledge his *Essay Concerning*

---

126 See Green's account of the Marlboroughs and their manipulation of Anne, in his *Short History of the English People*, 705–707.

Human Understanding when it was published. In 1689, Locke wrote the dedication to the Earl of Pembroke, who had taken a great interest in the work. Printing then started on the work; along the way, Locke sent proof-sheets to Jean Le Clerc in Holland for him to review. Locke was meticulous about what he wanted typographically, and apparently found the printers not always cooperative. Finally, in early 1690, the book was available to the public. Locke sent copies to his friends and must have felt considerable pleasure at finally getting the book into print. He received, says Fowler, £30 for the copyright, which certainly seems a small sum until one considers that Milton only received £10 for *Paradise Lost*. Sales of the *Essay* soon became brisk and several more editions were necessary in Locke's lifetime.

Publication of the *Essay* embroiled him in a lengthy controversy with the Bishop of Worcester who wrote two letters to Locke (to which Locke responded), the burden of which was that Locke's "new way of ideas," of arriving at knowledge and certainty by reason, would undermine the mysteries of the faith, particularly the doctrine of the Trinity. Locke painstakingly laid out his reasons for believing that what he had written was not hurtful to any of the mysteries of the Christian faith. "If your lordship had showed me any thing in my book, that contained or implied any opposition in it to any thing revealed in holy writ concerning the Trinity, or any other doctrine contained in the Bible, I should have been thereby obliged to your lordship for freeing me from that mistake, and for affording me an opportunity to own to the world that obligation, by publicly retracting my error."[127] He continued with an eloquent statement of his Christian faith:

> The holy scripture is to me, and always will be, the constant guide of my assent; and I shall always hearken to it, as containing infallible truth, relating to things of the highest concernment. And I wish I could say, there were no mysteries in it: I acknowledge there are to me, and I fear always will be. But where I want the evidence of things, there yet is ground enough for me to believe, because God has said it: and I shall presently condemn and quit any opinion of mine, as soon as I am shown that it is contrary to any revelation in the holy scripture.[128]

Locke received another letter from the Bishop, however, with new objections. The Bishop wrote that "in an age, wherein the mysteries of faith

---

127 John Locke, A Letter to The Right Reverend Edward, Lord Bishop of Worcester, 1697, in *Works*, 4:96.
128 Letter to the Bishop of Worcester, 4:96.

are so much exposed, by the promoters of scepticism and infidelity, it is a thing of dangerous consequence to start such new methods of certainty, as are apt to leave men's minds more doubtful than before...." Locke replied that "I humbly conceive the certainty of faith...has nothing to do with the certainty of knowledge." He went on to declare:

> Faith stands by itself, and upon grounds of its own; nor can be removed from them, and placed on those of knowledge. Their grounds are so far from being the same, or having anything common, that when it is brought to certainty, faith is destroyed; it is knowledge then, and faith no longer.... I believe, that Jesus Christ was crucified, dead and buried, rose again the third day from the dead, and ascended into heaven;...let the grounds of knowledge be resolved into what any one pleases, it touches not my faith; the foundation of that stands as sure as before, and cannot be at all shaken by it....[129]

This was not to be the end of the controversy, however, as the Bishop wrote another lengthy reply bringing up new issues. In particular, he was disturbed by Locke's views on the resurrection of the body. The Bishop maintained that the body resurrected was the same body that one had at the time of death. He says "the reason of believing the resurrection of the same body, upon my grounds, is from the idea of identity." Locke replied in the most courteous manner:

> Give me leave, my lord, to say that the reason of believing any article of the Christian faith (such as your lordship is here speaking of) to me and upon my grounds, is its being a part of Divine Revelation.... The resurrection of the dead I acknowledge to be an article of the Christian faith: but that the resurrection of the same body, in your lordship's sense of the same body, is an article of the Christian faith, is what, I confess, I do not yet know.[130]

In the following paragraph he pointed out: "In the New Testament (wherein, I think, are contained all the articles of the Christian faith) I find our Saviour and the apostles to preach the resurrection of the dead, and the resurrection from the dead, in many places: but I do not remember any place in the New Testament (where the general resurrection at the last day is spoken of) any such expression as the resurrection of the

---

129 Mr. Locke's Reply to the Right Reverend the Lord Bishop of Worcester's Answer to His Letter, *Works*, 4:121, 146–47.
130 Mr. Locke's Reply to the Bishop of Worcester's Answer to his Second Letter, *Works*, 4:303.

body, much less the same body." [131] He then remarked that when he speaks of the resurrection, St. Paul does not refer to "your bodies" but to "you" (1 Corinthians 6:14). The point Locke endeavored to make in his long passage on this question is that personal identity is more than our material bodies. Locke reminded the bishop that even such bodies as we have here on earth are not the same throughout our earthly lifetime, but are constantly changing, hence:

> ...your lordship will easily see, that the body he had, when an embryo in the womb, when a child playing in coats, when a man marrying a wife, and when bed-rid, dying of a consumption, and at last, which he shall have after his resurrection; are each of them his body, though neither of them be the same body, the one with the other. [132]

1 John 3:2 reminds the Christian that "Beloved, now we are children of God; and it has not been revealed what we shall be, but we know that when He is revealed, we shall be like Him, for we shall see Him as He is." Locke would surely agree with this.

John Yolton's summary of Locke's thoughts on this subject is apt: "The point Locke is making is simply that 'whatever matter is vitally united to his soul, is his body, as much as is that which was united to it when he was born, or in any other part of his life.' [133] What is important for the resurrection is that the dead shall rise, that the person will be judged." [134]

RETIREMENT AT OATES

This lengthy correspondence with the Bishop of Worcester did not begin until 1697, after Locke had moved from London to semi-retirement in the country. When he first returned to England in 1689, Locke took rooms in London in the lodging house of a Mrs. Smithsby in Dorset Court, Channel Row, Westminster. Here he stayed for two years until he found the heavy fogs and coal smoke of London insupportable. He was grateful to be asked by Lord Mordaunt, now made the Earl of Monmouth, to come and stay with him for a time at his residence at Parson's Green, a suburb of London. He also visited Damaris Masham and her husband, Sir Francis, in their home, a charming moated manor-house in High Laver, Essex.

---

131 Ibid., 304.
132 Ibid., 308.
133 Quoting from Locke, *Works*, 4:314.
134 John W. Yolton, *Locke, An Introduction*, Oxford: Basil Blackwell Ltd., 1985, 97.

Approximately twenty miles from London, it was in a lovely countryside where the air was even better than in suburban Parson's Green. It is described as being "in quiet surroundings a mile distant from the little church of High Laver. A country lane bordered with fine trees led up to the mansion. The lawn in front of it was approached by a causeway built across a pond. There were splendid shady trees and walks with rustic seats. The grounds of the manor were surrounded by a moat, and hence it is spoken of in Locke's letters as 'the moated castle.'"[135] It was indeed an idyllic location.

After a bad attack of asthma in the autumn of 1690, the Mashams urged him to come to them, and Locke spent several months at Oates. Both Sir Francis and Lady Masham urged him to escape permanently from the bad air of London and make his home with them. He was undoubtedly touched by their offer but would not consider it unless he were to pay his proportion of the household's expenses. In the Spring of 1691, the Mashams agreed to accept his terms and, as Lady Masham wrote, "Mr. Locke then believed himself at home with us, and resolved, if it pleased God, here to end his days, as he did."[136] The following pages deal mainly with his personal life at Oates. His political life is outlined in the next chapter.

SAFE HARBOR AT LAST

Upon his removal to Oates and the tranquil countryside of High Laver, Locke must have felt that he had arrived in safe harbor at last. To be sure, he was often pulled back into the turbulent waters of politics, often had to run up to London for weeks at a time to discuss political strategy with the leaders of the new government and with King William. This necessitated his keeping rooms in Westminster and later in Lincoln's Inn Fields. The greater part of his time, however, was spent at Oates where he had the quiet and leisure he needed to continue his writing and to receive his friends.

He found the household at Oates most congenial. Damaris' mother, now a widow, lived with Sir Francis and Lady Masham. The Mashams young son, Francis, then age six, as well as Sir Francis's fourteen-year-old daughter, Esther, by his first wife, completed the family circle. Locke and the Mashams shared some of the same friends. It was probably through Locke's cousin, Mary Clarke, and her husband, Edward, that Locke first

---

135 See Biographical Study by Benjamin Rand, in *The Correspondence of John Locke and Edward Clarke*, 34.

136 Cited by Rand, 34, from an account of Locke's life written by Lady Masham after his death and sent to Le Clerc, January 12, 1705.

met Damaris Cudworth and her mother when they were all staying in London. Mary and Damaris were fast friends, and the Clarkes and their children frequently visited Locke and the Mashams at Oates. Damaris was particularly fond of the Clarke's son (the boy for whom Edward Clarke had solicited Locke's suggestions for his proper education), and the lad often stayed at Oates for visits of several months. While there, he studied under Locke's supervision. Mary Clarke also sought suggestions from Locke on how her daughter Betty, a little girl of ten, should be educated. Locke grew very fond of this bright little girl with whom he would playfully banter, suiting his talk to her understanding as was his way in talking with "the little ones."

LOCKE'S TALENT FOR FRIENDSHIP

Locke had a talent for friendship. His many friends were the source of his unceasing care and sometimes his anxiety. He advised them on their health; he advised them on the education of their children; he advised them on their business or political activities. He also helped them in any way he could with the problems they encountered. His letters show a warm, caring, and generous spirit. In the case of Edward Clarke, Locke owed much to him, for Clarke took care of his property and business affairs in Somerset during his absence in Holland. He and his wife, Locke's cousin Mary, visited Locke late in his stay in Holland. Clarke was elected to the second parliament in King William's reign and therefore spent a lot of time in London where he frequently turned to Locke for advice and help. Locke often expressed in his letters to Clarke his gratitude for his friend's care on his behalf. Always concerned about his friend's health and that of his children, he wrote to Clarke in an anxious tone when Mary was expecting a baby:

> Dear Sir,
>
> I begin now to be in pain by your silence. The latest date I have from you being the 3rd October, which I may now call a long month since. For as there is nobody to whom I have greater obligations than to you, so I can truly say that whether I consider gratitude, friendship, or inclination, there is nobody in the world can upon any of these scores be more concerned for you and yours than I am upon every one of them. And if I may with freedom tell it you, I can with great sincerity assure you that that which most sensibly touches in my own private affairs is my absence from a man I so perfectly love and esteem and my being out of the way

of giving him those marks I would of it…must tell you again I am in pain till I hear from you. I know that the painful hour must by this time have overtaken your lady, and I long to hear that 'tis safely over: when you assure me of that, and that she and you and the little ones are well, I shall be at rest and be at much more ease than I am at present.…

I am, Dear Sir, your most affectionate and most obliged servant,

J. Locke[137]

When in London Locke saw a good deal of young Lord Ashley, grandson of Locke's patron, the first Earl of Shaftesbury, for whose early education Locke had been responsible. After being sent to Winchester and traveling on the Continent, as young gentlemen were expected to do, Ashley was living again in London at his father's house. He always called Locke his "foster-father," and they had many lively philosophic discussions at Locke's lodgings. He also visited Locke at Oates. He was soon to become the third Earl of Shaftesbury, and an influential politician to whom Locke also gave his counsel and advice.

Locke was always delighted to act as a foster-father to his friends' children. Arent Furley, son of his old Rotterdam friend, was a visitor at Oates to whom he acted *in loco parentis* while Arent was in England. Locke helped him learn English and later, in 1702, assisted him in finding a secretarial position with Lord Peterborough on a naval expedition against the Spanish in the West Indies. Limborch's son also received his hospitality at Oates. He helped other friends find tutors for their sons.

Locke seems to have had a real affection for young people. They certainly responded to his kindly and witty conversation, for Locke knew how to suit his conversation to those around him. To young people, he showed his concern for their interests and ambitions and exhibited his sense of humor. He was gallant with the ladies and full of charming compliments and gentle raillery. Lady Masham remarked that while he often spoke against raillery of the unkind sort, "he knew how to give a pleasant and agreeable Turn to everything he said. If he rally'd his Friends, it was either for some inconsiderable Faults, or, something which 'twas for their Benefit to make known.… He never jested with the natural Infirmities, or Misfortunes of any Persons." [138]

---

137 Benjamin Rand, ed., *The Correspondence of John Locke and Edward Clarke*, 99–100.

138 Quoted from Lady Masham by Jean Le Clerc in his *Life and Character of Mr. John Locke*, reprinted in Locke's *Essay Concerning Human Understanding*, Chicago: The Open Door Publishing Co., 1905, i.

Lady Masham also remarked on his ability to suit "his Discourse to the meanest Capacities" and noted that "he conversed very freely, and willingly with all sorts of Persons, endeavouring to Learn something from them: And this proceeded not only from his genteel Education, but from his professed Opinion, that some good thing or other might be learn'd from any Person whatsoever." [139] It appears that Locke was also a stickler for courtesy and gracious manners. Lady Masham's remarks on why he so much disliked bad manners, further illumine Locke's character:

> If there was anything that he cou'd not bear, 'twas ill Manners… when he perceived they did not arise from want of Conversation, and Knowledge of the World, but from Pride, Ill-nature, Brutality, and other Vices of that Nature. Otherwise he was very far from despising any Persons, though their Persons were never so mean. He look'd on Civility to be not only something very agreeable and proper…but also a Duty of Christianity, and which ought to be more pressed, *and urged upon Men* than it commonly is." [140]

A FRIEND FROM IRELAND

Another good friend was the Irishman, William Molyneux, who represented the University of Dublin in the Irish Parliament for some years and had a strong sense of the importance of Irish home rule. Except for one brief visit to England in 1698, the friendship was through a six-year correspondence. It became a close friendship nonetheless. Locke wrote to Molyneux at the beginning of their correspondence that "meeting with few men in the world, whose acquaintance I find much reason to covet, I make more than ordinary haste into the familiarity of a rational inquirer after, and lover of truth, whenever I can light on any such." [141] Locke first became aware of Molyneux in 1692 when he sent him a copy of a book he had written in which he paid tribute to Locke and his *Essay*. Locke replied to his letter, and so began their correspondence. Locke asked Molyneux to help him with his revisions on the *Essay* and to tell him of "its mistakes and defects" and anything superfluous which ought to be left out of the second edition. Molyneux took him at his word and frankly gave his opinion on points he thought could be better expressed, or where he thought Locke was perhaps at fault. Far from being ruffled by his friend's critiques,

---

139 Lady Masham, xlviii.
140 Lady Masham, xlix.
141 John Locke to William Molyneux, September 20, 1692, in *Works*, 9:293.

Locke showed his openness to constructive criticism and expressed much appreciation for the suggestions that Molyneux offered.

THE GOSPEL'S PERFECT BODY OF ETHICS

When Molyneux suggested that Locke write a "treatise of morals," Locke considered the matter and gathered some materials together for such a work, but finally decided that this was an unnecessary project. He wrote to Molyneux: "Did the world want a rule, I confess there could be no work so necessary, nor so commendable. But the Gospel contains so perfect a body of ethics, that reason may be excused from that inquiry, since she may find man's duty clearer and easier in revelation than in herself." [142]

Both men suffered from frequent illness, and when Molyneux wrote, after a long period of silence, of a severe illness that had felled him for several months, Locke replied that he could not, "without great trouble, hear of any indisposition of yours: your friendship, which Heaven has bestowed on me, as one of the greatest blessing I can enjoy, for the remainder of my life, is what I value at so high a rate, that I cannot consider myself within danger of losing a person, every way so dear to me, without very great uneasiness of mind." [143] After Molyneux's brief visit to London and to Oates in 1698 both men looked forward to meeting again the following year, when Molyneux hoped to return to England. But this was not to be. Locke learned in October from the letter of a mutual friend that Molyneux had died. Sadly, Locke replied that "his worth, and his friendship to me, made him an inestimable treasure, which I must regret the loss of, the little remainder of my life, without any hopes of repairing it in any way." He then wrote with characteristic concern: "I should be glad, if what I owed the father could enable me to do any service to his son." [144]

SOME THOUGHTS CONCERNING EDUCATION

It was Molyneux who had urged Locke to turn into a book his letters to Clarke on the education of his son, Edward. He believed such a volume would be of great help to many fathers like himself. Locke's *Some Thoughts Concerning Education* was published in July 1693 with a dedication to Edward Clarke. It was to become a tremendously influential book and was printed in English at least twenty-one times during the eighteenth century. It was also published in French, Dutch, German, Italian, and Swedish; Czech

---

142 John Locke to William Molyneux, March 30, 1696, in *Works*, 9:377.
143 John Locke to William Molyneux, July 2, 1696, in *Works*, 9:383.
144 John Locke to Mr. Burrridge, October 27, 1698, in *Works*, 9:458.

and Spanish translations were added in the nineteenth century. It had considerable influence on American families and educators at that period.

PIERRE COSTE TRANSLATES LOCKE'S WORKS

In a letter to Molyneux of May 3, 1697, Locke had alluded to a young friend of Jean Le Clerc's, Pierre Coste (1668-1747), who had translated Locke's book on education into French. He commented that Le Clerc had often "spoken of him to me with commendation and esteem."[145] Coste's Dutch translation was published in 1695 in Amsterdam. In August of 1696 Coste began to translate the *Essay* into French. According to James Axtell, "This young French Huguenot was to do more for the spread of Locke's name and works throughout Europe than any other person."[146]

Pierre Coste was born in the old Mediterranean town of Uzes in Languedoc. His father, a wool merchant, sent him to a school at Anduze and, when Pierre was fifteen, to Geneva to attend the University there. It was only a year later that the Edict of Nantes, which had afforded religious toleration to French Protestants, was revoked by Louis XII, and the young teen-ager found himself unable to return to his homeland. He studied for the ministry and continued his classical studies in Hebrew, Greek, Latin, Italian, and *belles lettres* while he lived in Switzerland. At the completion of his studies he moved to Leyden in Holland. After a short time as pastor of a Walloon Church there, he apparently decided in 1690 that his calling was to be a scholar rather than a clergyman. He became a proofreader for a publishing company, but before long he put his language skills to work on "the task that was to consume the rest of his life, that of bringing many of the best English works, specially those of Locke, to French-speaking Europe."[147]

Locke decided that this young man who had done such an excellent job translating the *Education* should come to England so that they could work together on the translation of the *Essay*. He invited him to Oates, where Sir Francis desired him to tutor his son, Francis (known to the family as Frank). Coste was in residence at Oates by August of 1697. Locke worked with him, often rewriting his thoughts to make them easier for Coste to translate. As a translator the young Frenchman had long been convinced that the best way to translate an author's work into the French language was not to try to do so word for word, but to thoroughly understand his meaning and then simply express it anew in French. His

---

145 John Locke to William Molyneux, May 3, 1697, in *Works*, 9:416.
146 James L. Axtell, *The Educational Writings of John Locke*, 16.
147 Axtell, 88.

excellent translation finally was published in 1700 as *Essay Philosophique sur l'Entendement Humain*. He was to remain at Oates as Locke's secretary and aide until the philosopher's death, after which he wrote an important eulogy of the great philosopher in a letter which was published in the *Nouvelles de la Republique des Lettres*.

THE REASONABLENESS OF CHRISTIANITY

In 1695, when Coste was beginning his translation of Locke's book on education, Locke was deeply involved in writing *An Essay on the Reasonableness of Christianity as Delivered in the Scriptures* which came out the following year. Locke intended it specifically as a way to convert deists who did not believe in—and thus saw no need for—Biblical revelation. He was surprised by the criticism his work stirred up and wrote later to one who defended the book and became a new friend, of his motives in writing the work and his reflections on what his Biblical studies revealed to him as he wrote it:

> The wonderful harmony, that the farther I went disclosed itself, tending to the same points, in all the parts of the sacred history of the Gospel, was of no small weight with me.... But when I had gone through the whole, and saw what a plain, simple, reasonable thing Christianity was, suited to all conditions and capacities; and in the morality of it now, with divine authority, established into a legible law, so far surpassing all that philosophy and human reason had attained to...I was flattered to think it might be of some use in the world; especially to those, who thought either that there was no need of revelation at all, or that the revelation of our Saviour required the belief of such articles for salvation, which the settled notions, and their way of reasoning in some, and want of understanding in others, made impossible to them. Upon these two topics the objections seemed to turn, which were with most assurance made by Deists against Christianity; but against Christianity misunderstood. It seemed to me, that there needed no more to show them the weakness of their exceptions, but to lay plainly before them the doctrine of our Saviour and his apostles, as delivered in the Scriptures, and not as taught by the several sects of Christians.[148]

Nevertheless, *The Reasonableness of Christianity* was attacked in a highly vituperative spirit by the Reverend John Edwards (1637-1716), a Cambridge

---

148 John Locke, *A Second Vindication of The Reasonableness of Christianity, Works*, 7:188.

clergyman, in his book *Thoughts concerning the Causes and Occasions of Atheism*. He proclaimed that Locke's book was "all over Socinianized," in the mistaken belief that followers of the religious reformer Faustus Socinus favored the cause of atheism.[149] While some of Locke's religious views were similar to those of Socinus, such as a stress on ethics and the importance of living a moral life in obedience to the Scriptures, he did not share the Socinian view that Christians should accept nothing in the Bible that was above reason. Some of his closest thinking on the subject of the extent of authority to be granted to reason is in *The Essay on Human Understanding*, Book IV, Chapter 17, par. 23, where he draws clear distinctions between what is "according to, above, and contrary to reason." Here he explained his thoughts on these three aspects of reason:

1) According to reason are such propositions, whose truth we can discover by examining and tracing those ideas we have from sensation and reflection, and by natural deduction find to be true or probable.

2) Above reason are such propositions, whose truth or probability we cannot by reason derive from those principles.

3) Contrary to reason are such propositions, as are inconsistent with, or irreconcilable to, our clear and distinct ideas.

He concludes, "Thus the existence of one God is according to reason; the existence of more than one God contrary to reason; the resurrection of the dead above reason."[150] Nor did he repudiate the doctrine of the Trinity, although it may well have been a doctrine that mystified him. Therefore, unlike Socinus, he was simply silent on the subject, apparently willing to accept it on the grounds of Divine Revelation. As he explained to the Bishop of Worcester, there were many things in the Bible which were mysteries to him but which he took on faith because "God had said it." To accuse Locke of atheism was, of course, an absurd accusation. Locke's book is itself a refutation of that charge. Nevertheless, Locke took up his pen again—wearily, one imagines—to refute Edwards' charges.

In response to Edwards' claim that he failed "to mention the advantages

---

149 Fausus Socinus (1539-1604) was an Italian theologian, born in Siena, Italy. He spread the doctrines of his uncle, Laelius Socinus, who maintained that the Trinity was a pagan doctrine that denied the unity of the Godhead and that Christ was a created being and not God incarnate. The Socinians became a powerful body in Poland and Hungary. Their statement of beliefs is known as the Racovian Catechism for Racow in Poland where it was first published. Their church was known as the Unitarian Brethren. They believed that the Son and the Holy Spirit were persons begotten by the one God and Father, but inferior to Him. Later some Socinians believed that Jesus was just the greatest prophet appointed by God; others still believed him a mere man, born as other men were and therefore not deserving of worship.

150 John Locke, *Works*, 3:136.

and benefits of Christ's coming into the world, and appearing in the flesh, he hath not one syllable of his satisfying for us, or by his death, purchasing life or salvation, or any thing that sounds like it," Locke cited the places where he had written of Jesus Christ restoring men to life in the resurrection and that he specifically had written, "He that hath incurred death for his own transgression, cannot *lay down his life for another,* as our Saviour professes he did."[151] In writing of Jesus as the Messiah, far from making him a mere man, he used the same term the Jews used for the divine Son of God.

Indeed, in *The Reasonableness of Christianity* Locke stressed as the fundamental article of belief for the Christian: that Jesus Christ is the Messiah. He cited many places in the New Testament where it is brought out, as in the Gospel of St. John, Chapter 20:30-31, in which John says that many other signs did Jesus before his disciples and in many other places the apostles preached the same doctrine, which are not written in these books, "But these are written that you may believe that Jesus is the Messiah, the Son of God; and that believing you may have life in his name." Locke commented that: "what St. John thought necessary and sufficient to be believed, for the attaining eternal life, he here tells us."[152] To the possible objection that this could not be a saving faith, for even the devils believed that Jesus was the Messiah, Locke replied that "they could not be saved by any faith, to whom it was not proposed as a means of salvation, nor ever promised to be counted for righteousness. This was an act of grace shown only to man-kind.... [T]hough the devils believed, yet they could not be saved by the covenant of grace," because they lacked repentance, which Locke goes on to say "is as absolute a condition of the covenant of grace as faith and as necessary to be performed as that."[153]

Despite the fact that Locke explicitly pointed out the divinity of Jesus and cited his birth by a virgin, His miracles, and His Resurrection from the dead as facts that demonstrate His divinity,[154] Edwards returned to the

---

151 John Locke, *A Vindication of the Reasonableness of Christianity,* etc., from Mr. Edwards's Reflections, *Works,* 7:162-63.

152 John Locke, *The Reasonableness of Christianity, Works,* 7:101.

153 Ibid., 7:102-3.

154 On the Virgin Birth, see *The Reasonableness of Christianity, Works,* 7:106: "God, nevertheless, out of his infinite mercy, willing to bestow eternal life on mortal men, sends Jesus Christ into the world; who being conceived in the womb of a virgin (that had not known man) by the immediate power of God, was properly the Son of God.... So that being the Son of God, he was, like the Father, immortal; as he tells us, John v. 26, "As the Father hath life in Himself, so hath He given to the Son to have life in Himself." Of his miracles, see especially, page 32. See also Locke's *A Discourse of Miracles.*

fray in another attack on the book, and Locke wrote a *Second Vindication* in which appears one of his most eloquent passages:

> As men, we have God for our King, and are under the law of reason: as Christians, we have Jesus the Messiah for our King, and are under the law revealed by him in the Gospel. And though every Christian…be obliged to study both the law of nature and the revealed law, that in them he may know the will of God, and of Jesus Christ, whom he hath sent…he that believes one eternal, invisible God, his Lord and King, ceases thereby to be an atheist; and he that believes Jesus to be the Messiah, his King, ordained by God, thereby becomes Christian, is delivered from the power of darkness, and is translated into the kingdom of the Son of God; is actually within the covenant of grace, and has that faith, which shall be imputed to him for righteousness; and, if he continues in his allegiance to this his King, shall receive the reward, eternal life.[155]

This passage, by its passion, seems to be a fundamental statement of Locke's faith in Jesus Christ as Saviour and Lord. It also refers to his convictions on the different roles reason and Revelation play in the life of the Christian. It should be remembered that Locke emphasized throughout *The Reasonableness of Christianity* that man's unassisted reason could not give him all he needed to know to live aright here on earth, much less to find salvation in the world to come. (There is much more on Locke's views on the Law of Nature, Reason, and Revelation in Chapter Six.)

FRIENDSHIP WITH THE REVEREND SAMUEL BOLD

The whole wearisome exercise of refuting his opponent, a task Locke heartily disliked but believed to be necessary, had one positive by-product. It brought into his life a new friend and one who published a refutation of Edwards' attacks on *The Reasonableness of Christianity*. This was the Reverend Samuel Bold (1649-1737), a clergyman from Dorset who for fifty-five years was the rector of Steeple in the Isle of Purbeck. During James II's reign he was imprisoned for a sermon he delivered against persecution, and for a pamphlet he had published entitled, *A Plea For Moderation*. He was known as a man of genuine piety who held sound Christian doctrine, and led an exemplary life. In 1697, Bold began to write several tracts against opponents of *The Essay Concerning Human Understanding* and *The Reasonableness of*

---

155 John Locke, *A Second Vindication of The Reasonableness of Christianity, Works,* 7:229.

Christianity. Locke acknowledged his support in his *Second Vindication*. In 1703, Reverend Bold visited him at Oates. Locke tried to dissuade him from making any further responses to Reverend Edwards' attacks. After Locke's death, however, Bold's sense of the injustice that had been done to his friend was so great that he published several more papers defending him.

As an interesting aside, in 1702, Locke's *Essay* received support from a most unexpected source. A Mrs. Cockburn, a young woman of twenty-three, published her *Defence of the Essay*. It was published anonymously, but Locke got her name from her bookseller and wrote to her a gracious letter expressing his appreciation. Years later, in 1726, she published a letter to a Dr. Holdsworth, taking him to task for his criticisms concerning Locke's ideas on the Resurrection and, later still, an elaborate *Vindication of Mr. Locke's Christian Principles*.[156]

LOCKE'S FRIENDSHIP WITH ISAAC NEWTON

Another cherished friendship of Locke's was with Sir Isaac Newton (1643-1727), the great English physicist and mathematician, who was a trail blazer in the study of optics and formulated the basic principles of modern physics which led to his ground-breaking theory of universal gravitation. Regarded as the greatest scientist of his time, his *Principia* (1687) has been deemed one of the most important scientific works ever written. The two men were both members of the Royal Society. Their mutual friend Robert Boyle (1627-1691),[157] a well-known Irish physicist, probably brought them together. In 1689, Locke closely studied Newton's paper, "A Demonstration that the Planets," by their gravity towards the Sun, may move in Ellipses. Deeply impressed by Newton's powers, Locke praised "the incomparable Mr. Newton" in his epistle to the reader which preceded his *Essay Concerning Human Understanding* and likened himself to a mere under-labourer clearing the ground for others:

> The commonwealth of learning is not at this time without master-builders, whose mighty designs in advancing the sciences will leave lasting monuments to the admiration of posterity: but every one must not hope to be a Boyle, or a Sydenham: and in an age that produces such masters as the great Huygenius and the incomparable Mr. Newton, with some others of that strain; it is ambition

---

156 See *Works*, Preface by the Editor, vii.

157 Born in Lismore Castle, Ireland, Robert Boyle settled at Oxford in 1654. He experimented in pneumatics and improved the air pump. When he was a director of the East India Company, he worked for the propagation of Christianity throughout the East.

enough to be employed as an under-labourer in clearing the ground a little, and removing some of the rubbish that lies in the way to knowledge....[158]

Locke and Newton also saw a good deal of each other during the recoinage crisis (to be discussed in the next chapter) and without Newton's help as Warden of the Mint, the currency reform that Locke was promoting might never have taken place. Knowing of Newton's need for a position that would provide him with financial support, Locke had helped him obtain this position through his political friends at Court. Newton visited him at Oates in January 1691 where they probably had many scientific and political discussions (Newton had been a member of the Convention Parliament in 1689). They also probably talked about theological matters which increasingly engrossed both of them. Newton took a great interest in Biblical prophecy and Divine Providence.

Earlier, in 1690, Newton had corresponded with Locke concerning two commonly used proof texts for the Trinity (1 John 5:7 and 1 Timothy 3:16) which he had investigated and believed to have been spuriously inserted by Bishop Jerome into the Latin Vulgate.[159] Newton sent a draft of his paper to Locke who offered to send it to Holland to be translated and published by his friend Jean Le Clerc. At first, Newton agreed to this, but later decided it ought not to be published, as the paper's rejection of these two proof passages could be taken as a rejection of the doctrine of the Trinity. Locke therefore cancelled the project. Le Clerc regretted it but retained the passage from 1 John 5:7 in his own translation of the New Testament, even though it might not be authentic, because, as he explained to Locke: "Nevertheless, this passage, having been accepted into our Bibles, it has not seemed advisable to omit it, as Luther did in his version."[160]

When Newton visited Oates again in 1701, he was eager to see the *Paraphrases on St. Paul's Epistle to the Corinthians* on which Locke was then at work and took parts of the work back with him to London for further perusal. There was some trouble in getting him to return the manuscript in timely fashion, so Locke asked his cousin Peter King to call on Newton and try to get the material returned, but to do so in a most tactful way,

---

158 John Locke, Epistle to the Reader, *Essay Concerning Human Understanding, Works,* 1:1.

159 Later scholarship traces the origin of 1 John 5:7 to either Africa or Spain and dates it toward the end of the fourth century. Therefore, it appears that Jerome simply continued to include it in the Latin Vulgate. See H. McLachlan's *The Religious Opinions of Milton, Locke, and Newton* (Manchester: Manchester University Press, 1941; reprint ed., New York: Russell and Russell, 1972, 133.

160 My translation. Cited in French by McLachlan, 132-33.

as Newton was quick to take offence. He wrote to King: "Mr. Newton is really a very valuable man, not only for his wonderful skill in mathematics, but in divinity, too, and his great knowledge in the scriptures, wherein I know few his equals."[161] Locke's cousin evidently was sufficiently tactful and was able to retrieve Locke's manuscript for which Newton expressed his approval. Despite Locke's admiration for Newton who seemed to be tending toward Unitarian views, there is no evidence that Locke was a Unitarian. He seems to have been willing to leave whatever doubts he may have had about the mystery of the Trinity in the hands of God. It was something that was above reason, and so a matter of faith. It will be recalled that in a letter to the Bishop of Worcester Locke wrote:

> The Holy Scripture is to me, and always will be, the constant guide of my assent; and I shall always hearken to it, as containing infallible truth, relating to things of the highest concernment. And I wish I could say, there were no mysteries in it: I acknowledge there are to me, and I fear always will be. But where I want the evidence of things, there yet is ground enough for me to believe, because God has said it: and I shall presently condemn and quit any opinion of mine, as soon as I am shown that it is contrary to any revelation in the Holy Scripture.[162]

Later in the year that Newton first visited him, their mutual friend Robert Boyle died. He and Locke had been friends since their Oxford days. Locke went up to London to visit Boyle shortly before his death and became his literary executor. Boyle left to him the editing of his work on *The General History of the Air* on which Locke worked conscientiously during the remainder of the year.

Locke not only had a talent for making friends, but for keeping them. Most of his friends were long-standing ones, such as Dr. Thomas, the Oxford physician who recommended him to Lord Ashley, and Sir James Tyrrell, another friend from Oxford days, who corresponded with Locke until the latter's death. Tyrrell was also one of the "five or six friends" with whom he met to discuss philosophical matters, as Locke related in the beginning of his *Essay Concerning Human Understanding*. Locke viewed his friends as blessings sent from God (see his letter to Molyneux cited earlier) and greatly appreciated their individual characters.

---

161 John Locke to Peter King, April 30, 1703 in H. McLachlan, 101.
162 Letter to the Bishop of Worcester, 1697, in *Works*, 4:96.

PETER KING —
COUSIN AND ADOPTED SON

As he grew older, however, he must have become keenly aware that he would have no children of his own. He did have, however, a young cousin named Peter King. (Locke's uncle, Peter Locke, had a daughter who had married Jeremy King, a merchant in business in Exeter. Their son, Peter, was born in 1669.) He worked for a time in his father's business in Exeter. On one of his visits to the family, Locke discovered that the boy devoured books and had a great desire for learning. He persuaded Peter's parents to let him study for one of the learned professions. What schools he may have attended in England is not known, but he did study the classics, law, and theology for a time at the University of Leyden when Locke was living in Holland. While there, King wrote a treatise entitled, *An Enquiry into the Constitution and Discipline of the Primitive Church* in which he stated that the Presbyterian form of government was the original form of government of the Christian Church. Such views as these would make it impossible for him to become a minister in the Church of England, although he evidently had a great interest in theology. By 1694, he became a student of the law at the Middle Temple in London and in 1698 he became a member of the Bar. During this period he was a frequent visitor at Oates. Locke also visited him in his chambers in London.

Soon King became a very successful barrister. In 1700, he ran for election to the House of Commons in which he sat during several Parliaments. Though never an outstanding speaker, he soon became known as a sound thinker and an honest politician, which must have made Locke very proud of him. He was to rise to the positions of Lord Chief Justice of the Common Pleas and Lord High Chancellor of England and would be given the title of Lord King of Ockham, a title borne by his four sons in succession. It was his great-grandson, also named Peter, who collected documents and letters connected with Locke and wrote the first full-scale biography of him.[163]

Peter King was a frequent visitor at Oates and at least once came down from London with Lord Ashley with whom he had formed a close friendship. Early in June, Locke urged his cousin to come and see him, because he was sure the end was coming soon and he wanted to have time to converse with "one who not only is the nearest but the dearest to me

---

163 The family is presently represented by the Earl of Lovelace.

of any man in the world." [164] When King was married in September 1704, Locke wanted to give the bridal pair a fine party at Oates, even though his own physical condition was worsening, and, as he expressed it, "the deterioration of the cottage was not far off." King was to choose what he and his bride wanted for their wedding feast and it was to be cooked by a chef who had formerly been employed by Lord Shaftesbury. It was with great joy that Locke welcomed the young couple to the festivities in their honor and doubtless with great pride in his young cousin for whom he foresaw a fine future as lawyer and statesman. [165]

THE PARAPHRASES OF SAINT PAUL

The Paraphrases of Saint Paul was Locke's last work which he finished but did not live to see published. Indeed, he may not have intended it for publication, but rather for his own spiritual edification. Conversations with Lady Masham may well have inspired him to undertake the task. It is known that Lady Masham wrote a *Discourse on the Love of God*, which was published in 1696. Undoubtedly, the two friends discussed their writing together and benefited from each others' insights. Down the years, Locke always found inspiration for his writing from meetings with his friends where they exchanged ideas with each other.

As age gained on him, he seemed more and more desirous of understanding the Scriptures better. His friend Le Clerc wrote:

> Some Years before his Death, he apply'd himself intirely to the Study of the Holy Scriptures, and found so much Pleasure therein, that he was very much troubled he had apply'd his Mind to that Study no sooner.... This study of the Holy Scriptures wrought in him a lively and sincere, though unaffected Piety.... He had a deep Sense of the Divine Wisdom, that discovers it self in those methods God has taken in saving Men; and when he discoursed about it, he cou'd not forbear joyning with the Apostle in the Exclamation: *O the depth of the Riches and Wisdom of God.* And he was perswaded that all Persons woul'd [sic] be of the same mind, who shoul'd [sic] read the Scriptures without prejudice and this Study

---

164 Cited by Fowler, 124.

165 In April of 1704, sensing the end was coming soon, Locke made his will. To his friends and relations and dependents he left tokens of his regard, but of his personal property, half went to Frank Masham and half to Peter King, the latter of whom was to be his sole executor. Locke left all his manuscripts to King and half of his landed property, the other half going to another cousin, Peter Stratton. He directed that his funeral be conducted simply and the money saved by avoiding ostentation was to go to four labourers on the farm at Oates.

he very frequently recommended to those, with whom he conversed towards the latter end of his Life. This Application of these
Holy Writings, had given him a more noble and compleat Idea of
the Christian Religion than he had before....[166]

One of those to whom he wrote concerning reading the Bible was
his kinsman the Reverend Richard King who had asked him in a letter,
"what is the shortest and surest way, for a young gentleman, to attain a
true knowledge of the Christian religion, in the full and just extent of it?"
Locke answered: "Let him study the Holy Scripture, especially the New
Testament. Therein are contained the words of eternal life. It has God for
its author; salvation for its end; and truth, without any mixture of error,
for its matter."[167] He went on to answer Reverend King's question regarding morality and recommended again that the Bible is the most important
book to study. For further study he suggested the sermons of three great
divines of the church of England, Dr. Barrow, Archbishop Tillotson, and
Dr. Whichcote. To the Reverend King's second letter inquiring "what is
the best way of interpreting the sacred Scripture?" Locke answered with
some helpful suggestions for how to read the Bible:

> Taking "interpreting" to mean "understanding," I think the best
> way for understanding the Scripture, or the New Testament, (for
> of that the question will here be in the first place) is to read it
> assiduously and diligently; and, if it can be, in the original. I
> do not mean, to read every day some certain number of chap-
> ters, as is usual; but to read it so, as to study and consider, and
> not to leave till you are satisfied that you have got the true
> meaning.[168]

To help in finding the true meaning, he suggests the use of commentaries such as Matthew Poole's *Synopsis Criticorum*; Dr. Hammond's book
on the New Testament, and Dr. Whitby's *Commentaries*, with the caution
that no Bible commentator is infallible, only the Holy Scriptures "which
were dictated by the infallible Spirit of God."[169] He suggested that the
first study should be that of the four Evangelists. "They all treating of the
same subject do give great light to one another; and, I think, may with

---

166 Jean Le Clerc, *The Life and Character of Mr. John Locke*, in Locke's *Essay Concerning Human Understanding*, Books II and IV, (Chicago: The Open Court Publishing Company, 1906), xliv.
167 John Locke, *A Letter to the Reverend Mr. Richard King*, dated 25 August 1703, in *Works*, 10:306.
168 John Locke, *A Letter to the Reverend Mr. Richard King*, undated, in *Works*, 10:310.
169 Ibid.

the greatest advantage, be read in harmony. To this purpose Monsieur Le Clerc's, or Mr. Whiston's *Harmony of the Four Evangelists*, will be of use, and save a great deal of time and trouble.... They are now both in English, and Le Clerc's has a paraphrase. But if you would read the Evangelists in the original, Mr. Le Clerc's editions of the *Harmoney* in Greek and Latin will be best." [170]

Here he also described his own method of studying the Scriptures which he used in his study of the life and teachings of Jesus in *The Reasonableness of Christianity* and upon which he expanded in his "Essay for the Understanding of St. Paul's Epistles, by consulting St. Paul himself," which introduces *The Paraphrases of St. Paul*. Locke undertook this work to get a clearer understanding of St. Paul's letters which would show him the context in which they were written and what particular problems they were addressing. He found that it was necessary to ignore chapter headings and simply to read the whole letter through repeatedly, just as one would read a letter from a friend—not a few paragraphs at a time, and then putting the rest off until another day. One would read all of one's friend's letter, and if unclear as to its meaning, one would read it again—and again—if need be. Locke recommends reading a letter of St. Paul's "to see what was the main subject and tendency of it; or if it had several views and purposes in it...to discover what those different matters were, and where the author concluded one, and began another...." [171]

ST. PAUL INSTRUCTED BY GOD

Locke studied each letter repeatedly in order to grasp as much of Paul's intentions as he possibly could, because, as he wrote: "I remembered that St. Paul was miraculously called to the ministry of the Gospel, and declared to be a chosen vessel; that he had the whole doctrine of the Gospel from God, by immediate revelation; and was appointed to be the apostle of the Gentiles, for the propagating of it in the heathen world." He saw that Paul had "a large stock of Jewish learning he had taken in, at the feet of Gamaliel" and that "God himself had condescended to be his instructor and teacher. The light of the Gospel he had received from the Fountain and Father of light himself...." [172]

---

170 Ibid., *Works*, 10:310-11.

171 John Locke, "An Essay for the understanding of St. Paul's Epistles, by consulting St. Paul himself," in *A Paraphrase and Notes on the Epistles of St. Paul to the Galatians, Corinthians, Romans, Ephesians*, 1705-1707, in *Works*, 8:14.

172 Ibid., 8:15.

Philosophies Mislead Men from True Sense of the Scripture

He was very chary of the role various philosophies had played in "misleading men from the true sense of the sacred Scripture."[173] He pointed out:

> In the ages wherein Platonism prevailed, the converts to Christianity of that school, on all occasions, interpreted holy writ according to the notions they had imbibed from that philosophy. Aristotle's doctrine had the same effect in its turn; and when it degenerated in to the peripateticism of the schools, that, too, brought its notions and distinctions into divinity, and affixed them to the terms of the sacred Scripture. And we may see still how, at this day, every one's philosophy regulates every one's interpretation of the word of God.[174]

Locke did not make the mistake of the medieval philosophers who placed so much reliance on Aristotle's teaching, for example, that his ideas almost assume a normative status, with the teachings of Jesus confirming them, rather than the other way around.[175] In the true spirit of the Reformation, which gives the individual the right to interpret the Scriptures for himself, Locke remarks:

> For if I blindly, and with an implicit faith, take the pope's interpretation of the sacred Scripture, without examining whether it be Christ's meaning, it is the pope I believe in, and not in Christ; it is his authority I rest upon.... It is the same thing, when I set up any other man in Christ's place and make him the authentic interpreter of sacred Scripture to myself. He may possibly understand the sacred Scripture as right as any man: but I shall do well to examine myself, whether that, which I do not know, nay, which (in the way I take) I can never know, can justify me in making myself his disciple, instead of Jesus Christ's, who of right is alone, and ought to be, my only Lord and Master: and it will be no less sacrilege in me, to substitute to myself any other in his room, to be a prophet to me, than to be my king or priest.[176]

He concluded by saying that he did not want to impose his interpretation on others. "The same reasons that led me into the meaning, which

---

173 Ibid., 8:20.
174 Ibid.
175 The effect of Aristotelian thought is discussed further in Chapter 6.
176 Ibid., 8:22.

prevailed on my mind, are set down with it: as far as they carry light and conviction to any other man's understanding, so far, I hope, my labour may be of some use to him; beyond the evidence it carries with it, I advise him not to follow mine, nor any man's interpretation." This is simply because "We are all men, liable to errors, and infected with them. . . ." He concluded by observing that we "have this sure way to preserve ourselves, everyone, from danger by them, if, laying aside sloth, carelessness, prejudice, party, and a reverence of men, we betake ourselves, in earnest, to the study of the way to salvation, in those holy writings, wherein God has revealed it from heaven, and proposed it to the world, seeking our religion, where we are sure it is in truth to be found, comparing spiritual things with spiritual." [177]

It is significant that Locke's most eloquent words are when he is discussing the Holy Scriptures. Yet his present-day detractors either ignore, misquote, or disparage his words on the Christian faith and on his own deep faith as mere lip-service to religion, as words which he did not really mean. To assert that a writer did not mean what he wrote is a leap of faith in the wrong direction! It is unfair, because Locke is not here to defend himself. These assertions can be disproved, however, by considering his own words, the facts of his life, and the testimony of Christians who knew him well.

Some critics have mistakenly believed that Locke accused St. Paul of corrupting the Gospel in his *Paraphrases*. If they had read what we have quoted above from Locke's essay at the beginning of the *Paraphrases* and the book that followed, it would have been impossible to come to this conclusion. Other critics who have read the *Paraphrases* appear only to have done so from a hostile, prejudiced point of view and seem to be following the lead of University of Chicago professor Dr. Leo Strauss.

Such a critic is Thomas L. Pangle who objects to Locke's paraphrase on 1 Corinthians 16:1-2 on the Christian's duty to give to needy brethren because, according to Pangle, Locke believes that if there is no gain, the Christian need not give money to the poor.[178] But let us put side by side what St. Paul says and Locke's paraphrase in order to see if Pangle's remarks are justifiable deductions:

The Scriptures say, "as God hath prospered him." Locke says, "as he thrives in his calling." According to the dictionary, "to thrive" means "to prosper." Nowhere in any of Locke's works—or in his personal life is there a suggestion that if he has not gained, he has no duty to give to others more

---

177 Ibid., 8:23.
178 See Thomas L. Pangle, *The Spirit of Modern Republicanism*, 306.

St. Paul	Locke's Paraphrase
Now concerning the collection for the saints, as I have given order to the churches of Galatia, even so do ye. Upon the first day of the week, let every one of you lay by him in store, as God hath prospered him, that there be no gatherings when I come.	As to the collection for the converts to Christianity, who are at Jerusalem I would have you do as I have directed the churches of Galatia. Let every one of you, according as he thrives in his calling, lay aside some part of his gain by itself, which the first day of the week, let him put into the treasury, that there be no need of any gathering when I come.

needy than himself. But Pangle repeatedly accuses Locke of lacking charity by similarly stretched claims. He says that rather than seeing charity as a duty enjoined by God, he sees it only as a right of the poor to the surplus of the wealthy, an interesting Marxist twist to Locke's words, but here is what Locke actually wrote in that connection (from the *First Treatise*):

> But we know God hath not left one man so to the mercy of another, that he may starve him if he please: God the Lord and Father of all, has given no one of his children such a property in his peculiar portion of the things of this world, but that he has given his needy brother a right to the surplusage of his goods; so that it cannot justly be denied him, when his pressing wants call for it: and therefore no man could ever have a just power over the life of another by right of property in land or possessions; *since it would always be a sin, in any man of estate, to let his brother perish for want of affording him relief out of his plenty.* As justice gives every man a title to the product of his honest industry, and the fair acquisitions of his ancestors descended to him; so charity gives everyman a title to so much out of another's plenty, as will keep him from extreme want, where he has no means to subsist otherwise: and a man can no more justly make use of another's necessity, to force him to become his vassal, by withholding that relief *God requires him to afford to the wants of his brother,* than he that has more strength can seize upon a weaker, master him to his obedience, and with a dagger at his throat offer him death or slavery.[179]

Locke's Charitable Character

Clearly, those who are poor do have a moral claim on us, and Locke also points out above that God requires us to relieve the wants of the poor. This

---

179 Locke, *The First Treatise,* par. 42, in *Two Treatises of Government, Works:* 5:242-43. Italics added for emphasis.

then is a duty laid upon those with the means to help. Locke is perfectly aware of this. Locke's life was an illustration of his own concerns for the needy, and his practical efforts to help them in the place where he lived witness to his character. In her biographical sketch of Locke, Lady Masham remarked that "he was very charitable to the Poor, except such Persons as were Idle or Prophane, and spent the Sunday in the Alehouses, and went not to Church." Her remarks on his attitude toward the poor is telling:

> But above all, he did compassionate those, who after they had labour'd as long as their Strength wou'd hold, were reduced to Poverty. He said it was not enough to keep them from starving, but that such a Provision ought to be made for them, that they might live comfortably. Accordingly he sought occasions of doing Good to those who deserved it; and often when he walked out, he wou'd visit the Poor of the Neighbourhood, and give them somewhat to supply their Necessities, or buy the Remedies which he prescribed them, if they were sick, and had no other Physician.[180]

LOCKE'S FAREWELL LETTER TO PETER KING

A few days after the party Locke gave for his cousin Peter King and the younger Peter's bride, Locke believed that his end was not far off and so wrote to Peter with an "earnest request to you to take care of the youngest son of Sir Francis and Lady Masham in all his concerns, as if he were your brother."[181] (This King did. As soon as he became Lord Chancellor, he helped Frank Masham find employment in His Majesty's government as Accountant-General in the Court of Chancery.) In his farewell letter to Peter, Locke spoke from his heart: "I wish you all manner of prosperity in this world, and the everlasting happiness of the world to come. That I loved you, I think you are convinced."[182]

Jean Le Clerc, writing of the last period of Locke's earthly life, says that "a few weeks before his Death, he perceiv'd he shou'd not long live, but yet he continued as chearful and pleasant as before."[183] Lady Masham and her daughter Esther took care of him—to the extent that he would let them—and found him to be an uncomplaining and cheerful patient. Lady Masham wrote that "The weakness of his Health was a Disturbance

---

180 Lady Masham, cited by Jean Le Clerc in *The Life and Character of Mr. John Locke*, in Locke's *Essay Concerning Human Understanding*, Books II and IV, Chicago: The Open Court Publishing Company, 1905, 1.

181 See Fowler, 125.

182 Fowler, 125.

183 Le Clerc, *Life and Character of Locke*, in Locke's *Essay on Human Understanding*, xliii.

to none but himself and that "he bore up under his Afflictions very patiently."[184] At length, a few days before his death, he called for the parish minister to give him the sacrament which he took, professing that he was in perfect charity with all men and in "sincere communion with the whole Church of Christ, by whatever name Christ's followers call themselves."[185]

LOCKE EXALTS GOD'S LOVE IN JUSTIFYING MAN THROUGH FAITH IN JESUS CHRIST

Pierre Coste, the French translator of his works and his secretary for the last seven years, wrote an account of his life which relates the manner of Locke's death and his confession of faith in Jesus Christ as his Lord and Saviour. Coste wrote that two days before his death Locke's breathing was so bad that he had to stay in bed. Since he was unable to attend evening prayers, he asked that he should be remembered by the family at that time, whereupon

> Lady Masham told him, that, if he would, the whole family should come and pray by him in his chamber. He answered, he should be very glad to have it so, if it would not give too much trouble; there he was prayed for particularly. After this, he gave some orders with great serenity of mind; and, an occasion offering of speaking of the goodness of God, he especially exalted the love which God showed to man, in justifying him by faith in Jesus Christ. He returned thanks, in particular, for having called him to the knowledge of that Divine Saviour. He exhorted all about him to read the Holy Scripture attentively, and to apply themselves sincerely to the practice of all their duties; adding, expressly, that "by this means they would be more happy in this world, and secure to themselves the possession of eternal felicity in the other."[186]

The next day he was carried into his study to sit in an armchair. Here Lady Masham read to him from the Psalms as his earthly life ebbed away. The end came at about three in the afternoon of October 28, 1704. Lady Masham relates that "His death was like his life, truly pious, yet natural, easy, and unaffected; nor can time, I think, ever produce a more eminent example of reason and religion than he was living and dying."[187]

---

184 Lady Masham, cited by Le Clerc, lii-liii.

185 See Fowler, 124-26.

186 See *Works*, 10:73, for "The Character of Mr. Locke," by Pierre Coste, printed originally in the *Nouvelles de la Republiques des Lettres*, for February 1705, art. II, 154.

187 Cited in Fowler, 126.

Locke was buried in the churchyard of the old Parish Church of High Laver. The epitaph he wrote for himself is on the wall above the tomb and tells the reader of it that "he had lived content with his own insignificance: that, brought up among letters, he had advanced just so far as to make an acceptable offering to truth alone: if the traveller wanted an example of a good life, he would find one in the Gospel; if of vice, would that he could find one nowhere; if of mortality, there and everywhere."[188]

Although we here take leave of John Locke, the private person and sincere Christian, we will meet him again in the next chapter as a public servant and advisor to William III and to the statesmen who were most influential in the years immediately following the English Revolution of 1688. We will discover Locke's considerable impact on "The Glorious Revolution" and see how it prepared the way for the American Revolution.

OATES, THE LAST HOME OF JOHN LOCKE
1632–1704

Illustration from *English Literature: An Illustrated Record* by Richard Garnett.
Published by William Heinemann, London, 1903.
©LookandLearn.com. Used by permission.

"[H]e quit this life in a spirit of calm thankfulness for the blessings which he had enjoyed and in the firm hope of a happy immortality. He died in his study, where Lady Masham had been reading the Psalms to him.... He had lived to see the triumph of most of the causes for which he had fought; he had combined with singular success the active and the contemplative life, winning the respect of the learned world and the gratitude of a great king whose favours were never lightly granted; his latter years had been spent in peace, prosperity, and domestic happiness; and his influence was destined to spread in ever-widening circles throughout the century which was just beginning."

("John Locke," by Charlie Dunbar Broad, 1887-1971, in *A Locke Miscellany*, ed. by Jean S. Yolton.)

---

188 Fowler, 126.

PART TWO

The Glorious Revolution: Locke Adapted

Thou hast here the beginning and
end of a discourse concerning government;
what fate has otherwise disposed of the papers that
should have filled up the middle, ... it is not worthwhile to tell thee.
These which remain I hope are sufficient to establish the throne
of our great restorer, our present king William;
to make good his title in the consent of the people;
... and to justify to the world, the people of England, whose
love of their just and natural rights, with their resolution to preserve them,
saved the nation when it was on the very brink of slavery and ruin.

JOHN LOCKE
(from The Preface to *Two Treatises of Government*[189])

---

189 John Locke, Preface to the *Two Treatises of Government* in Works, 5:209.

CHAPTER FIVE

Locke's Influence on English Politics During the Reign of William and Mary

IT has been said that through the "Glorious Revolution" the government of England became "Locke institutionalized." But some historians have said that Locke played a very little role, if any, in the actual revolution that placed William and Mary on the throne or on the subsequent drafting of the Declaration of Rights. The truth regarding Locke's influence on these events lies somewhere between these two positions.

As is evident from the quotation that begins Part Two, Locke termed King William "our great restorer" of the people's rights. He seemed content to let his *Two Treatises* serve as the rationale for the new monarch's legitimacy even though he had begun writing his work years earlier to aid the Earl of Shaftesbury in the revolution the latter hoped, but failed, to achieve. There were, however, many implications in Locke's *Second Treatise* which went far beyond the old English system.

GOVERNMENT AS A NEW KIND OF COMPACT

There was, for instance, Locke's idea of civil government as a compact—not just between King and Parliament—but between the members of the community which have set up the government and then entrusted the office holders to govern in accord with the specifications of the original compact or constitution. To Locke, government was emphatically a trust, in which those who held power (*both* king and parliament) were trustees of the people, who could be replaced if not faithful to their trust. Locke wrote in par. 221 of the *Second Treatise* that governments may be dissolved "when the Legislative, or the Prince, either of them act contrary to their Trust." [190]

It is also significant that when speaking governmentally, Locke used the term "compact" rather than "contract." There is a very good reason for this. In a contract there are two equal parties, each of whom gets something out of the contract. Locke did not see civil government as a contract between two equal parties, nor did he see the government as a "partner" of the people. It was a trust, as noted above. Those who govern do so on behalf of the people and may be removed if they disobey the terms of the trust. While most English Whigs approved of such a view, the Tories did not. Many of them longed to see the old Stuart hereditary dynasty restored, despite its history of claiming absolute power over the people and its evident contempt for Parliament.

THE ROLE OF THE LEGISLATIVE BRANCH

Even more distinctive than Locke's particular view of compact as the basis of civil government was his conception of the role of the legislative branch of government. He did not see the legislative as co-equal with the monarch. He saw it as *the most important branch* of government. This must have made an impression on the Whig politicians who, although they supported William as King, were determined to curb the royal powers effectively and to maintain, if not expand, the powers of Parliament. To be sure, a long time was to elapse before the power of Parliament would become truly supreme and the role of the English monarch would become one of titular head of state, shorn of all direct political power.[191] These great changes, however, which had been desired by forward-looking members of Parliament for years, were finally begun in the Glorious Revolution and the English Bill of Rights. As historian John Richard Green shrewdly observed:

> In outer seeming, the Revolution of 1688 had only transferred the sovereignty over England from James to William and Mary. In actual fact it had given a powerful and decisive impulse to the great

---

190 John Locke, *Second Treatise Of Civil Government*, facsimile, 1714, in Hall, *Christian History*, 1:117.

191 Americans came up with a different solution in the Constitution of the United States, with its separation of powers between the executive, legislative, and judicial branches, each with its own area of power and each balancing the others. But the executive power was spelled out clearly in the Constitution wherein the chief executive was elected for only four years at a time. The Founding Fathers saw the legislative branch as the most important one, since the law-making power was in its hands, but it feared that even this branch could become despotic without checks upon it; hence the checks and balances in the Federal system. Hence, too, the primacy—but not the supremacy—of the legislative power in the American system.

constitutional progress which was transferring the sovereignty from the King to the House of Commons. From the moment when its sole right to tax the nation was established by the Bill of Rights, and when its own resolve settled the practice of granting none but annual supplies to the Crown, the House of Commons became the supreme power in the State.[192]

THE DRAFTING OF THE DECLARATION OF RIGHTS

There is, therefore, a sense in which the English Constitution did become "Locke institutionalized." The idea that Locke had no impact on the drafting of the Declaration of Rights of 1688 because he was still in Holland during the drafting process leaves out several important facts: *First*, we know that Locke had been brought into contact with William and Mary in Holland by Lord Mordaunt (the future Earl of Monmouth and then the Earl of Peterborough). Mordaunt was in Holland to negotiate terms with William and Mary. Locke had met Lord Mordaunt earlier through his patron, the Earl of Shaftesbury, and they had become good friends. It was, therefore, no accident that Locke moved to Rotterdam near the Hague. According to Thomas Fowler, "there can be no doubt that Locke was taking an active share in the schemes that were in preparation."[193] *Second*, Locke was also a friend of Sir John Somers who played a leading role in the Convention Parliament which drew up the Declaration of Rights.[194] Locke had also known Somers during his days with Shaftesbury in the early 1680s. Somers became an intimate friend after Locke's return

---

192 Green, *Short History of the English People*, 696. The English system differs from the American system in another important way: Parliament may rescind or change any part of the English Constitution. The English Constitution, furthermore, is not one single document, but a collection of documents: The Assize of Clarendon (1166) establishing the English jury system; The Magna Carta (1215) listing the rights of both Barons and freemen; The Writ of Summons to Parliament (1295) summoning not just the barons, but two knights from each county and two citizens from each town, thus heralding the beginning of the House of Commons; the Habeas Corpus Act (1679) which legally put an end to arbitrary imprisonment; The Bill of Rights (1689). These and later documents and legal precedents form the English Constitution.

193 Fowler, 52.

194 Born in Worcestershire of a family of the country gentry, Somers matriculated at Trinity College, Oxford, in 1667, and in 1676 became a member of the Bar at the Middle Temple, London. He became well known as the defender of seven bishops who, in June 1688, were arrested for sedition by James II. The jury found the bishops not guilty, and it was widely held that Somers' eloquence in defending the bishops won the case. As head of a committee to draft a Bill of Rights at the Parliamentary Convention which elected William and Mary to the throne, it is believed that his was the pen that drafted most of the document. William III appointed him Attorney General in 1692 and Lord Keeper of the Seal in 1693. By 1696, he was the King's leading advisor. In 1697, the King made Somers Lord High Chancellor and a peer of the realm. In 1700, he was forced to resign this post because of Tory attacks. Despite these Tory attacks, he was a man of unimpeachable virtue. "Lord Somers," said Horace Walpole, "was one of those divine men who, like a chapel in a palace, remain unprofaned, while all the rest is tyranny, corruption, and folly."

to Holland and often turned to him for advice in his rapidly advancing political career which culminated in his being made the chief minister to King William from 1696-1700 and leader of the Whigs from 1696-1716.

It will be recalled, too, that when Lord Mordaunt left for England with Prince William, he arranged for Locke to accompany Lady Mordaunt and the future Queen Mary home when it was safe for them to do so. He and Locke very probably had discussed the politics of the accession of William and Mary and what kind of statement the new monarchs would have to sign before receiving the crown. Professor Laslett doubted that Locke could have had any influence on the writing of the Declaration because he did not arrive in London until February 11, and the Declaration had already been drafted on the 12th and was presented to William and Mary on the 13th in the great Banqueting Room at Whitehall Palace.

LOCKE'S INDIRECT ROLE AT THE CONVENTION

Nevertheless, Laslett noted that some of the arguments presented at the Convention sounded very much like what Locke wrote in the *Second Treatise*. When one considers that Sir John Somers was on the committee that drafted the document and was probably the primary drafter, the Lockean connection is clear. The paragraphs Laslett mentions are pars. 217 and 219. The first of them, on the dissolution of government, reads:

> *Fourthly*, the Delivery also of the People into the Subjection of a foreign Power, either by the Prince, or by the Legislative, is certainly a *Change of the Legislative*, and so a *Dissolution of the Government*. For the end why People entered into Society being to be preserved one intire, free, independent Society, to be governed by its own Laws; this is lost, whenever they are given up into the Power of another.[195]

Examples of this in recent English history were fresh in the minds of the delegates. There were, for example, Charles II's delivering the political policies of England into the hands of Louis XIV of France, and then James II's designing to put England once again under the authority of the Church of Rome. The Declaration of Rights drawn up by the Parliamentary committee headed by Sir John Somers, included securities for Protestants for the free exercise of their religion and bound the new sovereigns to maintain the Protestant religion and the laws and liberties of England.

Paragraph 219 of Locke's *Second Treatise*, to which Laslett referred

---

195 See *Second Treatise*, in Hall, *Christian History of the Constitution*, 1:116.

as also similar to arguments made at the Convention, seems to refer to James II's fleeing from the country and so appearing to have abdicated his obligations to the nation. This paragraph is believed to have been inserted by Locke into the *Second Treatise* at the time of the Revolution.

> There is one Way more whereby such a Government may be dissolved, and that is, when he who has the supream executive Power, neglects and abandons that Charge, so that the Laws already made can no longer be put in Execution. This is demonstratively to reduce all to Anarchy, and so effectually *to dissolve the Government*.[196]

The Convention adopted the idea that James had, in effect, abdicated his kingship when he fled to France. James would have disagreed, of course, and would have pointed out (not without reason) that the hostility of Parliament and his own people and the arrival in England of William of Orange with an army had caused his flight. Using the Lockean idea of abdication as a cause for the dissolution of a government, however, seemed to the Convention to be the easiest way of handling the shift in power from James to his daughter and her husband. For one thing, it was a somewhat more palatable idea to the Tories than a bald acknowledgment that they were dethroning James in favor of Princess Mary and her Dutch prince.

Although, as Laslett pointed out, there is no evidence in Locke's letters that he communicated these or other ideas to members of the Convention, he was definitely part of the English group surrounding William and Mary who were busy figuring out the rationale for getting them on the throne. That Locke's views were considered important may be seen in a letter Lady Mordaunt wrote from the Hague to Locke in Rotterdam on the eve of their return to England. In it she spoke of King James as a king "who went out like a farthing candle, and has given us by this Convention an occasion not only of mending the Government but of melting it down and making all new, which makes me wish you were there to give them a right scheme of government...."[197]

PROVISIONS OF THE BILL OF RIGHTS

Of course, the government was not melted down and made all new. The Declaration of Rights, which was soon turned into a Bill of Rights and passed by Parliament into law, contained much that stemmed from the earlier documents such as the Petition of Right presented to Charles I in

---

196 Ibid., par. 219, 1:117.
197 See Laslett, 58.

1628. The Petition in turn reiterated rights claimed in the great Magna Carta. The difference was that the Declaration of Rights was not a *petition*, but a series of *conditions* given to the proposed new sovereigns to which they had to agree in order to be elected monarchs of England. In a way similar to the beginning of the American Declaration of Independence, the document began by recapitulating the misgovernment of the king. It also emphasized his attempt "to subvert and extirpate the Protestant religion and the laws and liberties of this kingdom." [198]

It continued by condemning:

➤ His suspending of laws and their execution without parliament's consent;

➤ His prosecuting "divers worthy prelates for humbly petitioning to be excused from concurring to the said assumed power";

➤ His erecting an ecclesiastical commission;

➤ His levying money for use of the crown without Parliament's permission;

➤ His raising a standing army in time of peace, without Parliament's permission, and quartering soldiers contrary to law;

➤ His disarming his Protestant subjects, "at a time when papists were both armed and employed, contrary to law";

➤ His violations of the freedom of election of members to Parliament;

➤ His prosecution in the court of King's bench "for matters and causes cognizable only in parliament" and for other arbitrary and illegal acts;

➤ His requiring excessive fines and inflicting illegal and cruel punishments;

➤ His granting fines and forfeitures before judgment had been made against the persons concerned.

The Declaration then stated that the Lords and Commons, in vindicating and asserting their ancient rights and liberties, declared illegal:

➤ The suspending of laws or their execution without the consent of parliament.

➤ The court of commissioners for ecclesiastical causes, and any similar court.

➤ Levying money for the crown without consent of parliament.

---

198 For the text of the Bill of Rights, presented above in brief summary, see Hall, *Christian History*, 1:44-47.

➤ The raising of a standing army in time of peace, unless with the consent of parliament.

After having declared what was illegal, the Declaration then listed the following rights of his majesty's subjects:

➤ The right of subjects to petition the King without being committed or prosecuted.

➤ The right of Protestants to bear defensive arms "suitable to their defence and as allowed by law."

➤ The right of free election of members of parliament.

➤ The right to freedom of speech and debates in parliament which ought not to be impeached or questioned in any court or place outside of parliament.

➤ That neither excessive bail nor excessive fines ought to be imposed nor cruel and unusual punishments inflicted.

➤ That jurors ought to be duly impaneled and returned and jurors in trials for high treason should be freeholders.

➤ That all grants and promises of fines and forfeitures before an individual's conviction of a crime are illegal and void.

➤ That Parliaments should be held frequently to consider redress of all grievances and for amending, strengthening, and preserving of the laws.

Clearly, an important theme runs through the English Bill of Rights: That Parliament or the courts must decide what is just and right. Henceforth, neither the rights of Parliament nor the legal processes of English law were to be obstructed or contravened by the monarch.

SUPREMACY OF THE LAW
AND THE LEGISLATIVE BRANCH

The supremacy of law, along with the supremacy of the legislative branch of government, are emphasized in Locke's *Two Treatises of Government*. He repeatedly refers to parliament as the supreme branch of government but also deals with limitations on its powers:

> Though the *Legislative* ... be the *supream* Power in every Commonwealth; yet, *First*, It is *not*, nor can possibly be absolutely *Arbitrary* over the Lives and Fortunes of the People ... For no Body can

transfer to another more Power, than he has in himself; and no Body has an absolute Arbitrary Power over himself, or over any other, to destroy his own Life, or take away the Life or Property of another.[199]

As for law, Locke traced it back to God, the supreme lawmaker, who had made it discernible by men through His "Law of Nature," planted in their hearts.[200] Thus, he declared that "the Law of Nature stands as an Eternal Rule to all Men, *Legislators*, as well as others."[201] Thus, too, the laws of the legislative branch cannot be arbitrary, nor can it rule by extemporary decrees, but "*is bound to dispense Justice, and decide the Rights of the Subject by promulgated standing Laws, and known Authoris'd Judges.*"[202] Locke also insisted that the Law must be designed for no other end than the good of the people, that the legislative branch must not raise taxes without the consent of the people and, finally, that the legislative power could not transfer the power of making laws any where else than where the people have placed it.[203]

These views, which ultimately prevailed in the English constitutional system, were quite different from what earlier governmental reformers had championed, which was a balance between the powers of the monarch and the powers of parliament. Monarchs frequently resisted Parliament and even tried to rule without it. Then, as we have seen from the days of James I, the Stuart monarchy sought to rule by "Divine Right." This divine-right-to-rule theory was strongly resisted by parliament whose leaders insisted that it was no part of the English system which had developed from the days of Magna Carta (1215). That great covenant made between King John and his barons limited the powers of the monarch and outlined the rights to be enjoyed by his subjects.

---

199 See John Locke, *Second Treatise of Government*, par. 135, in Hall, *Christian History*, 1:93–94. See also par. 132 in which he refers to "the supream Power, which is the Legislative" and par. 149, which states, in part, "that there can be but one supream Power, which is the Legislative, to which all the rest must be subordinate, yet the Legislative being only a Fiduciary Power to act for certain end, there remains still in the People a supream Power to remove or alter the Legislative, when they find the Legislative act contrary to the trust reposed in them."

200 See Chapter 6 for a detailed discussion of the Law of Nature as understood by the ancient Greeks and Romans, by St. Paul in the New Testament, by the medieval Christian Church, and by John Locke.

201 See par. 135 of *Second Treatise*, in Hall, *Christian History*, 1:94.

202 Ibid., par. 136.

203 Ibid., pars. 142, 96. Although there is nothing in the English constitutional system to stop Parliament from transferring its powers to others or another, or, indeed from abolishing itself, it is unlikely to ever do any of these things as long as veneration for the Constitution of England exists in Parliament and among the people.

The Great Charter is the foundation of the English Constitution because it was the first time that just government had been claimed as a right that existed despite the will of the king. The demands outlined in the Magna Carta insisted upon justice and property rights not only for the barons but for the "free man." The King also must rule by law and not merely by his own will. King John signed the Great Charter unwillingly, and many kings thereafter sought to rule arbitrarily and to seize the property of their subjects arbitrarily. The Stuart monarchs (James I, Charles I, and Charles II) were particularly astute, as we have seen, at manipulating parliament by false promises—or else ruling without it. (Recollect, too, that Charles II was able to do so because of secret foreign subsidies from Louis XIV.) Members of Parliament often reminded kings that they did not rule alone, but with Parliament, or "in Parliament" as the expression went.[204]

LOCKE'S VIGOROUS OPPOSITION TO ABSOLUTE MONARCHY

Locke contested absolute monarchy vigorously in his *First Treatise of Government* (written to refute Sir Robert Filmer's book, *Patriarcha: or the Natural Power of Kings*, 1680). Locke summarized what he describes as Filmer's "short system of politics," using a direct quote from Filmer:

> "Men are not born free, and therefore could never have the liberty to choose either governors, or forms of government." Princes have their power absolute, and by divine right; for slaves could never have a right to compact or consent. Adam was an absolute monarch, and so are all princes ever since.[205]

Locke denied all of Filmer's claims for absolute monarchy as descending from Adam, pointing out that far from being made a universal monarch, Adam was cast out of paradise.

> This was not a time, when Adam could expect any favours, any grant of privileges, from his offended Maker...God sets him to work for his living, and seems rather to give him a spade into his

---

204 In his speeches to Parliament, James I frequently referred to a king's absolute power to rule. In a speech from the Star Chamber, he declared that "As it is atheism and blasphemy to dispute what God can do, so it is presumption and a high contempt in a subject to dispute what a King can do, or to say that a King cannot do this or that." (Green, *Short History*, 478) But, as Green wrote, "The claim of absolutism was met in words which sound like a prelude to the Petition of Right." (Green, 478) An address to the King from Parliament declared that "Your Majesty would be misinformed if any man should deliver that the Kings of England have any absolute power in themselves either to alter religion, or to make any laws concerning the same, otherwise than as in temporal causes, by consent of Parliament." (Green, 478).

205 John Locke, *First Treatise of Government*, Book I, Chapter I, par. 5, in *Works*, 5:214.

hand to subdue the earth, than a scepter to rule over its inhabitants. "In the sweat of thy face thou shalt eat thy bread," says God
to him, v. 19.[206]

As to Filmer's claim that Adam's title descended to monarchs by his
right of fatherhood, Locke makes a truly eloquent statement about the
nature of life and the bounds of fatherly rights which anticipates his major
theme developed in the *Second Treatise* that none can claim absolute power
over other men, for all are God's workmanship.

> They who say the father gives life to his children are so dazzled
> with the thoughts of monarchy, that they do not, as they ought,
> remember God, who is "the author and giver of life:...it is in
> Him alone that we live, move, and have our being."...To give
> life to that which has yet no being, is to frame and make a living
> creature, fashion the parts, and mould and suit them to their uses;
> and having proportioned and fitted them together, to put into
> them a living soul. He that could do this, might indeed have some
> pretence to destroy his own workmanship. But is there any one so
> bold that dares thus far arrogate to himself the incomprehensible
> works of the Almighty? Who alone did at first, and continues still
> to make a living soul, He alone can breathe in the breath of life.[207]

Although Locke never said that hereditary monarchy in and of itself was
wrong, his bias on the subject of the executive power in the *Two Treatises*
supports the idea that when a ruler fails to uphold the trust given him to
rule for the good of the people, he may be removed and the Crown given
to another. In other words, Locke supported elective monarchy. It worked
on the occasion of electing William and Mary, but it did not become a
part of the British system.

The hereditary monarchy resumed with a proviso in the 1701 Act
of Settlement that every sovereign must be a member of the Anglican
Church. It was decreed that if William died without issue (and, in fact,
Mary died in 1694 without bearing him children, and the King did not
remarry), the crown would pass to Mary's sister, Anne, and if she died
without issue the crown would go to Sophia of Hanover, a granddaughter
of King James I, and her heirs.

Although Locke admired William, viewing him as the courageous deliverer of England from the scourge of Louis XIV, and appeared to be content

---

206 *First Treatise*, Book I, Chapter V, par. 45, in *Works*, 5:245. (See also *Second Treatise*, par. 6.)
207 *First Treatise*, Book I, Chapter VI, pars. 52–53, in *Works*, 5:251–52.

with the English monarchical system as it then existed under William and Mary, he named in his *Second Treatise of Government* the traditional options that a people might choose as their form of government: *Democracy*, where the community "may imploy all that Power in making Laws for the Community from time to time, and executing those Laws by Officers of their own appointing," or an Oligarchy where the community puts "the Power of making Laws into the hands of a select few Men, and their Heirs or Successors," or a *Monarchy* where they put the power of making laws into the hands of one man. "If to him and his Heirs, it is an *Hereditary Monarchy*: If to him only for Life, but upon his Death the Power only of nominating a Successor to return to them; an *Elective Monarchy*." Here Locke also discusses the right of the community to make "compounded and mixed Forms of Government, as they think good." [208] Next, in a paragraph which emphasizes the critical importance of the Legislative Power, he explains that,

> [I]f the Legislative Power be at first given by the Majority to one or more Persons only for their Lives, or any limited time, and then the supream Power to revert to them again; when it is so reverted, the Community may dispose of it again anew into what hands they please, and so constitute a new Form of Government. For the *Form of Government depending upon the placing the* supream Power, which is *the Legislative*, it being impossible to conceive that an inferior Power, should prescribe to a superior, or any but the supream [power] make Laws, according as the Power of making Laws is placed, such is the *Form of the Common-wealth*.[209]

Locke's conviction that the "State all Men are naturally in, and that is, a *State of perfect Freedom* to order their Actions, and dispose of their Possessions, and Persons as they think fit, within the bounds of the Law of Nature, without asking leave, or depending upon the Will of any other Man," [210] struck a responsive chord in the minds of colonial Americans who chafed against the arbitrary and unfair government of Great Britain over her colonies by the middle of the 1700s. The question for them was: Did men have a natural right to their lives, liberties, and properties and

---

208 Locke, *Second Treatise*, Ch. X: Of the Forms of a Commonwealth, par. 132, in Hall, *Christian History*, 1:92.

209 Ibid., par. 132, 1:92-93. Locke cautions that by the word Commonwealth, "I must be understood all along to mean, not a Democracy, or any Form of Government, but *any Independent Community* which the *Latines* signified by the word *Civitas*, to which the word which best answers in our language is *Commonwealth*...." par. 133, 1:93.

210 Ibid., Of the State of Nature, par. 4, 1:58.

did they have a right to erect a government that would protect them? Their brothers in England reasoned from historical precedent rather than from Locke's natural rights theory and believed that the rising power of Parliament and its checks upon the powers of the monarch were sufficient to ensure their liberties.

Thus, England was content to incorporate a number of Lockean ideas into their existing monarchical/parliamentary system. Locke's emphasis on the legislative power as the most important power found, as we have seen, a ready audience among English Whigs. So did the idea that kings must rule for the good of the people, or be called to account for it. (English Parliaments had done just that in successfully calling both Charles I and now James II to account for their misrule.) In the Act of Succession of 1701, they placed many restrictions upon the monarch: 1) that judges were not to be removed from office except with the consent of both Houses of Parliament; 2) that no monarch born outside Great Britain could engage in war to defend his territories on the continent unless with the consent of Parliament; 3) that the monarch could not go abroad without its consent; 4) that no foreigner should be allowed to sit in parliament—or be on the Privy Council. (The last three of these were criticisms of William III's activities in defense of Holland, his going abroad when he chose, and allowing foreigners to be members of his Privy Council.) Though Tories may have grumbled about Lockean denials of the monarch's power, Whigs appreciated the wisdom of these restrictions. In fact, from this time on, the powers of the monarchy were gradually curtailed.

THE TOLERATION ACT

Locke's interest in political theory and in its application to the present situation was great, but his interest in religious toleration was perhaps even greater. It is said that Somers turned to him to help frame the Toleration Bill (1689) which followed hard on the heels of the Bill of Rights. Locke had high hopes that full religious toleration would at last be accorded to the many persecuted dissenters from the Church of England. This, however, did not happen. The bill which was passed into law ended up being full of provisos and exceptions which Locke deplored.[211] In a letter to his Dutch friend, Philip Van Limborch, Locke admitted that:

---

211 No toleration was to be accorded to anyone who believed in transubstantiation or failed to believe in the Trinity. Moreover, no dissenting minister could exercise his ministry if he failed to subscribe to at least thirty-four of the thirty-nine articles of the Anglican Church. Quakers were forced to make a special declaration of belief in the Trinity and in the Scriptures as divinely inspired.

Toleration has indeed been granted, but not with that latitude which you and men like you, true Christians without ambition or envy, would desire. But it is something to have got thus far. On these beginnings I hope are laid the foundations of liberty and peace on which the Church of Christ will hereafter be established.[212]

As a Latitudinarian, Locke was also disappointed that the Comprehension Bill, which was designed to make it easier for dissenters to remain in the Church of England, was violently opposed by the Anglican clergy and failed to pass. Although disappointed, Locke must have been encouraged that the King was completely opposed to religious persecution (even as was that earlier Prince of Orange, William the Silent) and that he had strongly supported the Comprehension Bill. When the Scots recognized William III as their king, through a Claim of Right (similar to England's Declaration), they refused to accept the Toleration Act, and expressed their determination to recognize only the Presbyterian Church. The King remained firm in his purpose that there be no religious persecution, declaring that "We never could be of that mind that violence was suited to the advancing of true religion, nor do we intend that our authority shall ever be a tool to the irregular passions of any party."[213] His stand must have endeared him to Locke. Certainly the new monarch had a high view of Locke's worth.

THE KING OFFERS LOCKE IMPORTANT DIPLOMATIC POSTS

Immediately upon his accession, William offered Locke an ambassadorship to Frederick I, Elector of Brandenburg. Locke was aware that this was an important appointment—indeed one of the most important—as Frederick was an ally upon whom William relied in his opposition to Louis XIV's machinations to subjugate Europe to France. In a letter to Lord Mordaunt, Locke explained why he was declining the King's offer. "It is the most touching displeasure," he wrote, "I have ever received from that weak and broken constitution of my health, which has so long threatened my life, that it now affords me not a body suitable to my mind, in so desirable an occasion of serving his Majesty." He also feared that his temperate habits (he drank no alcohol) would make it difficult for him to play the convivial role needed for his position. As he explained, "I know no such rack in the

212 Fowler, 57.
213 Green, *Short History*, 686.

world to draw out men's thoughts as a well managed bottle. If therefore, it were fit for me to advise in this case, I should think it more for the king's interest to send a man of equal parts, that could drink his share, than the soberest man in the kingdom."[214]

But the King persisted in offering Locke another ambassadorship, this time to Vienna. If this would not suit, Locke was invited to name any diplomatic post he wanted. Locke earnestly explained that his health prevented him from doing justice to any of these positions, but that he was very willing to accept such work in England that he believed he could accomplish to the King's credit. "If there be anything, "he wrote, "wherein I may flatter myself I have attained any degree of capacity to serve his Majesty, it is in some little knowledge I perhaps may have in the constitutions of my country, the temper of my countrymen, and the divisions amongst them, whereby I persuade myself I may be more useful to him at home...."[215]

The King then offered him a post as a Commissioner of Appeals, an office with small remuneration and little work. Later, in 1695, Locke was appointed to a revived Council on Trade and Plantations. Although Locke worked conscientiously as one of its commissioners from 1695 until deteriorating health caused his resignation in 1700, he did not make any innovative political or economic contributions through this medium. Rather, he conscientiously followed English custom in supporting protection of English manufactures in foreign trade, making suggestions on how to discourage Irish woolen manufacture, which was viewed as one of England's most important exports. Locke's report on this subject of manufactures proposed encouraging the linen manufacture in Ireland and English importation of linen from Ireland in order to compensate Ireland for the loss of the woolen trade which England viewed as its peculiar monopoly. That Locke was appointed to this committee was because the Whigs, under Sir John Somers, were finally in the political ascendancy, for they did not come to power immediately after the Revolution, as might have been expected.

WILLIAM III'S COALITION GOVERNMENT

In fact, immediately after the Revolution, William was anxious to conciliate all political elements in the country. Therefore, he formed a coalition

---

214 Fowler, 55.
215 Fowler, 55.

government which included many Tories. This offended the Whigs who wanted to punish Tories who had supported Charles II's and James II's illegal acts. The King, however, wanted to end the squabbling between the two factions in order to be able to concentrate on the great danger facing him on the continent: the increasing power of Louis XIV. William knew that the Whigs were full of consternation and wondered that he could be so ungrateful to his supporters. He believed, however, that it was essential for him to conciliate the Tories, not only because of Louis XIV's attempts to dominate Europe, but for another pressing reason—the dangerous political situation in Ireland.

FRANCE BACKS JAMES II'S EFFORTS TO REGAIN HIS THRONE

As early as April, 1689, with substantial aid from France, James had gone to Ireland to rouse his fellow Catholics to restore him to the throne. This resulted in the House of Commons quickly voting supplies to William so that he could fight this uprising in Ireland. In May war was declared against France. It had long been William's objective to bring England into an alliance against France. He had tried earlier to get Charles II to join him (not knowing that Charles was being funded by Louis XIV through the secret Treaty of Dover) and after Charles's death had tried to persuade James II to join the alliance against France (not knowing that James had renewed the Treaty of Dover with the French). Now, at last, there was hope that England could be drawn into the fight against France on the continent as well as in Ireland.

The war in Ireland did not go well. When William learned that France had sent 7,000 soldiers there to support James, he left for Ireland. Here he led the decisive Battle of the Boyne on July 1, 1690.* William then returned home to make plans to defend Holland, leaving the task of the final subduing of Ireland to John Churchill, the Duke of Marlborough. Marlborough largely accomplished this task in only twenty-three days, capturing both Cork and Kinsale. As for the King, he had returned to England none too soon, for Louis XIV's forces were making alarming inroads on the continent. France was winning battles in Flanders and in Italy. In England, even before William left for Ireland, Tory traitors were hoping to see the French fleet off the coast. This would be a signal for an uprising to put James II back on his throne.

---

* For an interesting narrative of the prior related events of 1688-89, see *The Brave Boys of Derry, or No Surrender*, written by W. Stanley Martin in 1900, republished by Nordskog Publishing Inc., 2010.

The French Fleet Enters the Channel

Indeed, even while William was on his way to Ireland, the French admiral, Tourville, entered the Channel. He was engaged by English and Dutch vessels, but repulsed them. When night fell they were forced to shelter in the Thames. The French fleet was now master of the Channel. The invitation to the Tories in England to revolt and recall their former king had arrived. But then the French made a fatal mistake. They proceeded to land on English soil and burned the coastal town of Teighmouth. Patriotic Englishmen were up in arms. Even many Tories who wanted James II back on the throne had no stomach to support foreign incursions into England. When word reached England of William's resounding victory in Ireland at the Battle of the Boyne, Tory efforts to restore James to the throne were dampened.

The situation on the Continent was so serious, though, that William left England immediately for Flanders accompanied by an English army. But William's hopes of joining with his allies against France in a victorious battle were disappointed. France was too fast for them. While he looked on in helpless fury, a French army of a hundred thousand captured Mons, the strongest fortress in the Netherlands. When word of this disaster reached England, Tory hopes of unseating him revived. Lord Clarendon and Lord Dartmouth sent letters to James. Even some Whigs, such as the Earl of Shrewsbury, feeling they had been thrust aside in favor of Tories, also corresponded with James. Historian Green tells us that the devious Marlborough, who had just fought valiantly in Ireland for William's cause, now decided to put all his efforts into ousting William and getting James's daughter, Anne, declared Queen. But for one man, this might, indeed, have happened.

England Delivered from Invasion

Edward Russell had just become admiral of the navy and was suspected of having strong sympathies for James. So great was the conviction in the minds of the French that Russell was with them and would surrender to them, that Louis XIV ordered Admiral Tourville to engage the far greater fleet headed by Admiral Russell. Russell, however, was not made of base metal. He warned the supporters of James with whom he had been in contact: "Do not think I will let the French triumph over us in our own seas. If I meet them I will fight them, even though King James were on board."[216]

---

216 Green, *Short History*, 696.

His strong attack on the French immediately disabused them of their illusion, but too late. Tourville's fifty vessels were too few before the onslaught of the ninety ships under Russell's command. At last, the French fleet was forced to sail away along the rocky coastline of Cotentin. Only twenty-two of their ships reached St. Malo. Thirteen tried to take refuge in the bays of Cherbourg and La Hogue, but the English fleet pursued them and burnt ship after ship. This ended all threat of invasion. William's throne was saved. Although the war dragged on, this was an important turning-point. From this time, France lost her superior naval power and, more important, her soldiers and sailors began to lose their confidence. Had Russell been the traitor they supposed, England's political history might have been very different. William, fighting heroically in the Netherlands, might have been unseated by James, and with a resurgence of faith in the seemingly omnipotent power of France, the whole of the map of Europe might have been changed for many years. To patriotic Protestant Englishmen, it was clear that Divine Providence had turned away Louis XIV's wrath and protected England from coming under the heel of Catholic France.

RISE OF THE WHIG "JUNTO"

Russell went on to become one of a group of prominent and influential Whig politicians known as the "Junto."[217] From 1694 to 1698, five Whigs ruled the domestic policies of England: Russell (later Lord Orford) as first lord of the Admiralty; Lord Wharton (an experienced party manager); Lord Shrewsbury, as Secretary of State; and Locke's friends, Sir John Somers as Lord Keeper (later Lord Chancellor), and Charles Montague as Chancellor of the Exchequer. They came to power because, as the war dragged on and cost England more and more money, the Tories waxed cold and became anxious for peace negotiations. Only the Whigs remained resolute supporters of the war. Thus, William abandoned his idea of a coalition government and gave the Whigs the controlling cabinet posts. It was not a moment too soon. The Tories were trying to restrict the size of the army, and England was in dire financial straits.

---

217 Junto is from a Spanish word meaning "council." According to Noah Webster's 1828 *An American Dictionary of the English Language*, it means "a select council or assembly, which deliberates in secret on any affair of government." It was a pejorative term to describe a meeting of men for secret deliberations and perhaps intrigue for party purposes. Tories during William and Mary's reign used the term contemptuously to describe this group of influential Whigs.

Establishment of
the Bank of England

Montague had already come up with a plan which was to establish a Bank of England. In twelve days, it raised 1,200,000 pounds from the people and lent it to the government at 8 per cent.[218] While in London in June of 1694, Locke subscribed 500 pounds to the new bank. Thus he became one of the original proprietors of the Bank of England. The founding of the Bank was a significant event in the reign of William and Mary. In Maurice Ashley's opinion, the subsequent Peace of Ryswick, concluded in September 1697, was the product of England's financial strength, as well as "the persistence of King William III (who like George Washington, never knew that he was beaten), and the influence of sea power...."[219]

The day after Locke invested in the Bank of England he wrote to his friend Edward Clarke, who was serving in Parliament at the time, "Last night the subscriptions amounted to 1,100,000 pounds, and to-night I suppose they are all full."[220] In this same letter he spoke of meeting the Lord Keeper (John Somers, now Lord Somers) who expressed an interest in talking with him before he left town.

The Influence of "The College"
on English Politics

Somers, who was twenty years Locke's junior, frequently asked for his counsel on political matters. As early as 1689, he asked Locke whether he should attend parliament or go on circuit. In 1690, they had exchanged views on the currency problems plaguing England. But it was after 1694, when the Whigs began to exercise real power, that Locke began to be of greatest use to the government through his practical advice on reforming the coinage and abolishing the Licensing Act that restricted freedom of

---

218 "In return it was incorporated as the first English joint-stock bank and allowed to issue notes [which did not, however, rank as legal tender] and discount bills. This loan from the Bank to the Government did not have ever to be fully repaid so long as the interest was forthcoming, and thus is the origin of [the English] present funded national debt." (Maurice Ashley, in *England in the Seventeenth Century*, 185.) Ashley also noted that the Bank of England, and later the East India company which also lent money to the government at 8 per cent, "owed their powers to parliament and might not lend to the Crown without parliament's consent...."

219 Maurice Ashley, *England in the Seventeenth Century*, 1952. Baltimore, Maryland: Penguin Books, 1967, 187.

220 Letter of John Locke to Edward Clarke, June 30, 1694, in Benjamin Rand, *The Correspondence of John Locke and Edward Clarke*, 395. Maurice Ashley points out (in *England in the Seventeenth Century*, 185), that when people invested in the Bank of England or the new East India Company, "they not only helped King William III to make war, but also ensured the permanence of the revolution of 1688."

the press. Locke's influence on practical legislation demonstrates another side of his mental makeup. He proved that he was not just a brilliant abstract thinker but an eminently practical one as well. Certainly, this is an unusual combination. He was a tireless researcher and produced long, detailed pamphlets on the coinage problem, a subject that would seem outside his fields of expertise—diverse as they already were including medicine, science, philosophy, education, and political theory. Yet, his thorough knowledge of the coinage problem and the issues involved in the Licensing Act, together with his well-reasoned, common-sense solutions, won the admiration and respect of Whig political leaders.

Most of Locke's influence was filtered through what Laslett has called "a knot of Lockean members of parliament." Their work was facilitated by meetings and correspondence as members of a group Locke founded and called "the College."[221] This was similar to other groups Locke had started over the years to discuss philosophical or political matters—such as the group that met in Shaftesbury's home in London (that discussion group sparked his writing of the *Essay on Human Understanding*) and in Rotterdam where the members met at "the Lantern" to exchange opinions on a variety of subjects.

This new group met whenever possible at Locke's lodgings in London or at the chambers of one of the other members, but most of its work was carried on through correspondence. According to Laslett, Somers was its patron. The correspondence, however, is mainly that of Locke and two of his friends, Edward Clarke—whom he humorously styled "Sir Grave," "the Grave Squire," or "Squire Edward," and John Freke, to whom he referred in the correspondence as "the Bachelor," "Bachelor John," or "Squire John."

EDWARD CLARKE: LOCKE'S VOICE IN PARLIAMENT

Edward Clarke's 20-year span of service in parliament began in 1690, when he was elected as a member from Taunton, in his own county of Somersetshire. He was in the first session of the second parliament of William III. All told, Clarke served the constituency of Taunton in eight parliaments, the last one being the second session of the second parliament of the reign of Queen Anne in 1709-10. Although the "College" enjoyed convivial evenings together, "...the promotion of important legislation in Parliament" as Benjamin Rand observed, "appears to have been a more important

---

221 Laslett, 52.

object...the advancement of various measures by the group being carried out largely through the agency of Clarke as a member of Parliament." [222]

THE COLLEGE ADVOCATES
FREEDOM OF THE ENGLISH PRESS

One great opportunity to influence the government came through efforts to repeal the Licensing Act restricting what could or could not be printed. The English press had never known freedom. Under Elizabeth I, dissenters from the Church of England who published books advancing their theological ideas, could be arbitrarily imprisoned and sometimes executed on trumped up charges of treason. [223] Charles II's Licensing Act was still in force in the spring of 1695. [224] In Parliament's 1695-96 session, the House of Commons decided to renew a number of statutes, but to strike out the Licensing Act. The House of Lords disagreed, however, and put it back on the list of those acts to be renewed. The House of Commons refused to accept this change and, after a conference between both houses of Parliament, with Edward Clarke as the leading representative of the House of Commons, the Lords decided to drop their objections.

During this Conference, a paper detailing the reasons of the House for abolishing the Licensing Act was circulated. It is believed to have been written by Locke. Certainly the reasons given corresponded with those Locke had detailed earlier in a paper opposing the Licensing Act. The crux of Locke's argument lay in his question: "Why a man should not have liberty to print whatever he would speak, and be answerable for the one, just as he is for the other, if he transgresses the law in either." [225] Instead of licensing publications, he suggested, "Let the printer or bookseller be answerable for whatever is against law in the book, as if he were the author, unless he can produce the person he had it from, which is all the restraint ought to be upon printing." [226]

---

222 Rand, 41.

223 Two famous cases involved John Greenwood, a dissenting minister, and Henry Barrowe, a young law student, who tried to help Greenwood when he was cast into prison and was himself arrested and imprisoned. After languishing in prison for several years with intermittent questioning by the churchmen who had ordered their arrest, they were finally transferred to a civil court where they were tried and convicted of writing seditious books, although their writings were theological and not political and both men affirmed their loyalty to the Queen. They were both executed at Tyburn on April 6, 1593. These men justly became known as martyrs for their faith.

224 We have seen how Sir Algernon Sydney was executed for his political writings during the reign of Charles II.

225 Fowler, 83.

226 Fowler, 83.

LOCKE'S EFFORTS TO REFORM THE CURRENCY

The other great matter engrossing the attention of Locke and the "College" was the prickly question of how to reform the coinage which had become clipped and debased to an extent that threatened the entire commerce of the nation. The debased state of the coinage was not only a danger to the domestic economy, but also a deterrent to funding the King's efforts on the continent to stop Louis XIV's expansionism. An underlying problem was that two kinds of silver money were in circulation: hammered money (whose rims were unmarked) and milled money—so called from being produced in a coining-mill. Milled coins bore a legend on the rim of the larger ones and graining on the rim of the smaller coins so that they could not be clipped. Another difference between the two kinds of coins was that milled coins were almost completely circular, while hammered coins were irregular in shape. Obviously, the hammered coins could be easily clipped, while the milled coins were completely protected against this stealthy depreciation of value. Milled coins were introduced by the mint in 1663, but the old hammered coins were left in circulation. Because the milled money was always worth its weight in silver, but the hammered money was valued at something above its intrinsic worth, the milled money was often melted down or sent abroad, which meant that the hammered money was the coinage most often used in England.

> The milled money disappeared almost as fast as it was coined, and the hammered money was clipped and pared more and more, till it was often not worth half or even a third of the sum for which it passed. At Oxford, indeed, a hundred pounds worth of the current silver money, which ought to have weighed four hundred ounces, was found to weigh only a hundred and sixteen.[227]

This meant that the cost of goods was constantly rising, and when payments were made, there was usually a great deal of argument between buyer and seller as to the correct amount of money due. In some parts of the country, a guinea, for example, was worth twenty-two shillings; elsewhere, it might be worth as much as thirty shillings. Its value might have increased more than that, except that the government pegged it at 30 shillings when used to pay taxes.

Locke had been concerned about this issue as early as 1672, when he wrote that "It is only the quantity of the silver that is in [the coin], that

---

227 Fowler, 84.

is, and eternally will be, the measure of its value."[228] When he returned to England in 1689, Locke began to urge currency reform and to talk to all his friends about the dangers facing the country if it were not reformed. Lady Masham recalled that when visiting her lodgings in London, "the company there, finding him often afflicted about a matter which nobody else took any notice of, have rallied him upon this uneasiness as being a visionary trouble, he has more than once replied, 'We might laugh at it, but it would not be long before we should want money to send our servants to market with for bread and meat,' which was so true, five or six years after, that there was not a family in England who did not find this a difficulty."[229]

When Edward Clarke became a member of Parliament, Locke shared his views with him on the dangers facing the country if the currency was not reformed. Clarke agreed with him. Locke quickly produced a tract titled, "Some Considerations on the Lowering of Interest and Raising the Value of Money in a letter sent to a member of Parliament, 1691." The member in question was Sir John Somers, who had urged him to undertake the task. In this tract he opposed vigorously current efforts to solve the currency problem by "raising the value of money," which meant nothing more than to depreciate its intrinsic value by putting less silver into a shilling or a crown.

Clarke wrote to Locke on December 15, 1691, that he had circulated several copies of his paper among the members of parliament and that "all that have read the Considerations are clearly of opinion that the arguments therein are abundantly sufficient to destroy that bill, and all future attempts of the like kind. I hear the whole treatise generally much approved of and commended, for the many useful notions therein touching *money, trade,* and *taxing.*"[230] Clarke was premature, however, in his declaration of victory. No actions were taken by the Tory-controlled parliament at that time to rectify the situation. Rather, the authorities relied on apprehending (and hanging) those caught clipping coins. This was hardly an effective remedy.

THE WHIGS BECOME THE PREDOMINANT POWER

It was not until 1694 that the Whigs began to predominate on the political scene. Just after the establishment of the Bank of England, Locke's friend, Charles Montague was made Chancellor of the Exchequer. Then, when the

---

228 Rand, *Correspondence of John Locke and Edward Clarke,* 42.

229 Fowler, 86-87.

230 Letter of Edward Clarke to John Locke, 15th December, 1691 in Rand, *Correspondence of John Locke and Edward Clarke,* 324.

King left for the Continent in May, 1695, Locke's good friends, Lord Keeper of the Seal Somers and the Earl of Pembroke became two of the seven Lords Justices, appointed to govern England during the King's absence. The time for action had come at last. William Lowndes who recently had been made Secretary of the Treasury reported that the silver coins brought into the exchequer during a three-month period of 1695 should have weighed 221,418 ounces. The actual weight, however, was 113,771 ounces.

Locke was asked to come up to London from his residence in Oates and discuss the matter with the Lords Justices. They were interested in what he had to say, but Lowndes, although he agreed on the necessity of immediate remedial action, had a different solution: Depreciate the currency by one-fifth. To Locke, this was to make the government the major clipper of coin! It was also to deprive every creditor of one-fifth of his debts. Therefore, he advised the council of the Lords Justices to recoin at full value.

On September 21, knowing Locke was in London at the time, Somers asked him to meet him the next morning because he wanted to get Locke's opinion of a rebuttal that Lowndes had written to Locke's plan to reform the coinage. Shortly after, Lowndes published his paper in book form, titling it *A Report Containing an Essay for the Amendment of the Silver Coins.* Somers urged Locke to reply, which he did, quickly writing a 100-page pamphlet, *Further Considerations Concerning the Raising the Value of Money.* It was submitted to the Lords Justices, printed, and published by the end of December.

Locke began his pamphlet by reminding his readers of several important monetary definitions. First he asserted that "Silver is the instrument and measure of commerce in all the civilized and trading parts of the world." Second, he declared that "It is the instrument of commerce by its intrinsic value." What is this intrinsic value? He affirms that "the intrinsic value of silver, considered as money, is that estimate which common consent has placed on it...."[231]

What else defines the value of silver? Locke answers:

> Silver is the measure of commerce by its quantity, which is the measure also of its intrinsic value. If one grain of silver has an intrinsic value in it, two grains of silver have double that intrinsic value, and three grains treble, and so on proportionably. This we have daily experience of in common buying and selling; for if one ounce of silver will buy, i.e., is of equal value to, one bushel of

---

231 John Locke, *Works,* 5:138.

wheat, two ounces of silver will buy two bushels of the same wheat, i.e., have double the value.[232]

In discussing the coining of silver, he reminds the reader that "The coining of silver, or making money of it, is the ascertaining of its quantity by a public mark, the better to fit it for commerce."[233] He then outlines the three things necessary for coined money: "1. Pieces of exactly the same weight and fineness. 2. A stamp set on those pieces by the public authority of that country. 3. A known denomination given to these pieces by the same authority."[234] He pointed out that the stamp on a coin is a kind of public voucher "that a piece of such denomination is of such a weight, and of such a fineness, i.e., has so much silver in it. That precise weight and fineness, by law appropriated to the pieces of each denomination, is called the standard."[235]

In two telling paragraphs, Locke made it clear that clipping money is raising it without public authority. The piece bears the same denomination but now has less silver in it. What Lowndes has proposed, therefore, is to do exactly the same thing by public authority! The difference is that when done illegally, no one is forced to accept clipped money, but when the standard is arbitrarily altered by the government, everyone is obliged to receive the clipped money. What will be the result? According to Locke,

> Altering the standard, by raising the money, will not get to the public, or bring to the mint to be coined, one ounce of silver: but will defraud the king, the church, the universities and hospitals, &c. of so much of their settled revenue as the money is raised, *v.g.* twenty per cent. [sic] if the money (as is proposed) be raised one-fifth. It will weaken, if not totally destroy, the public faith, when all that have trusted the public, and assisted our present necessities, upon acts of parliament, in the million lottery, bank act, and other loans, shall be defrauded of twenty per cent. of what those acts of parliament were security for. And to conclude, this raising our money will defraud all private men of twenty per cent. in all their debts and settled revenues.[236]

Montague introduced a series of resolutions in the House of Commons which followed Locke's suggestions for reform of the coinage. The

232 John Locke, *Works*, 5:140.
233 John Locke, *Works*, 5:141.
234 John Locke, *Works*, 5:141-42.
235 John Locke, *Works*, 5:142.
236 John Locke, *Works*, 5:146.

resolutions prompted prolonged debate in the House, but on December 10, 1695 they finally passed. The terms of the new act involved calling for and recoining the clipped silver as milled money according to the old standard of weight and fineness, "the point for which [Locke] had fought so persistently."[237] The loss was to be covered by the Exchequer; so as not to be disrupting to trade the transition was to be gradual. After a certain day, clipped coins would be accepted only to pay taxes or loans. At a later date, clipped coins would no longer be legal tender for any transactions.[238]

Money was scarce during the transition from the old system to the new, but at length the coinage of the realm was properly reformed, largely owing to the clarity and persuasiveness of Locke's arguments and the efforts of the statesmen whom he influenced through the efforts of the "college," particularly Edward Clarke. Thomas Fowler expresses the general view regarding not only the coinage reform but also the Licensing Act and breaking the monopoly of the Stationer's Company, that "had it not been for [Locke's] clearness of vision, and the persistence of his philanthropic efforts, these measures might have been indefinitely retarded or clogged with provisos and compromises which might have robbed them of more than half their effects."[239]

RENEWED THREATS TO ENGLAND

Clearly, Locke's influence on the development of English politics and economics was of great importance during the reign of William III. Intensely patriotic, Locke watched the political scene anxiously even after his complete retirement to Oates. The winter of 1701-2 saw some critical events, as England was poised to enter the war of the Spanish Succession. In September of 1700, England had entered a Grand Alliance against France with Holland, the Austrian empire, and the United Provinces, which were soon joined by Denmark, Sweden, the Palatinate, and most of the German States. No sooner had this treaty been signed than the news came that James II had died in France, and Louis XIV had ordered his son, born of Mary of Modena, shortly before his flight to France, to be proclaimed King of England and received at his court with full honors.

The new parliament that met on December 30, was thoroughly alarmed

---

237 Fowler, 90.

238 A further bill was necessary to resolve a challenge from Lowndes and his supporters. It carried easily but because of difficulties with the Lords, this bill had to be abandoned and a new one introduced on January 13, including the same provisions as the former bill. It was passed rapidly and assented to by the King on January 21, 1696.

239 Fowler, 91.

and determined to support the Protestant succession in England. When King William opened Parliament with a stirring speech, there was a burst of excitement and patriotic devotion that radiated out through the country. His speech urged his subjects to unity and the burying of everything that divided them so that they might make an effective opposition to French attempts to saddle England once again with "a popish prince." The speech, printed in English, Dutch—and French—was framed and hung on the wall of many a protestant home in England and abroad.

Four days later, Locke urgently requested his nephew, Peter King, who was in parliament, to send him a copy of the King's speech. He also suggested that in addition to the support shown by both houses of Parliament, the city of London and all the counties of England should "with joined hearts and hands return his Majesty addresses of thanks for his taking such care of them." He urged Peter King to "Think of this with yourself and think of it with others who can and ought to think how to save us out of the hands of France, into which we must fall, unless the whole nation exert its utmost vigour, and that speedily." He continued by observing that he could not conceive "how any one of the house can sleep till he sees England in a better state of defence, and how he can talk of anything else till that is done." He need not have worried. A majority of the House voted substantial supplies and measures be taken to ensure the Protestant succession to the crown of England. A few days after this, however, King William died from a tubercular lung and after many years of suffering as an asthmatic. The long war with France (which had seemed ended by the Treaty of Ryswick) went on under William's successor, James II's daughter, Queen Anne and her commander-in-chief, Marlborough until a year before her death in 1713.

There is something touching in the devotion Locke felt for King William and his desire to see him supported in his heroic battle against the spreading power of Louis XIV. Although there were rumors that Shaftesbury had been a secret republican, there is no evidence that Locke was anything but loyal to the monarchical/parliamentary system of government of his day. He may not have imagined that anything better than this system of government actually would be realizable in England. If so, he could scarcely have imagined that Englishmen inhabiting Great Britain's colonies in North America would take his ideas far beyond their partial adoption by the English political system. Indeed, while England adapted Locke's ideas to its own system, it was left to these Englishmen over the seas to adopt them wholeheartedly.

PART THREE

The American Revolution: Locke Adopted

'[T]is plain in Fact, that human Reason unassisted,
failed men in its great and proper business of Morality.
It never from unquestionable Principles, by clear Deductions,
made out an entire Body of the Law of Nature.
And he that shall collect all the moral Rules of the Philosophers,
and compare them with those in the New Testament,
will find them to come short of the Morality delivered by
our Saviour, and taught by his Apostles....

JOHN LOCKE
(*The Reasonableness of Christianity as Deliver'd in the Scriptures*[240])

---

240 John Locke, *The Reasonableness of Christianity*, in Hall, *Christian History* (Vol. 2: *Christian Self-Government with Union*), 2:87.

CHAPTER SIX

The Law of Nature in John Locke's Writings: A Break with Classic Natural Law?

THOMAS JEFFERSON (1743-1826) called him one of "the three greatest men that ever lived."[241] The American colonial clergy extolled his defense of man's God-given rights to "life, liberty, and property" and taught his political principles to their congregations. In his Plymouth Anniversary Sermon of 1774, the Reverend Gad Hitchcock (1718-1803) expressed the thoughts of many a minister when he referred to him as "that prince of philosophers...."[242] James Madison (1751-1836) declared that his political writings were "admirably calculated to impress on young minds the right of Nations to establish their own Governments, and to inspire a love of free ones."[243] Madison also paraphrased his extended view of property in his own writing on the subject.[244]

The object of all this admiration was, of course, John Locke who was known to the Founding Father generation as "the great Mr. Locke" because of his *Two Treatises Of Civil Government* (1690) justifying England's "Glorious Revolution" of 1688 which placed William and Mary on the

---

241 See Noble E. Cunningham, Jr., *In Pursuit of Reason: The Life of Thomas Jefferson* (Baton Rouge and London: Louisiana State University Press, 1987), 129. The other two great men he cited were Bacon and Newton.

242 See Gad Hitchcock, *A Sermon Preached at Plymouth December 22, 1774*, in Hall, *Christian History of the American Revolution*, 1975, 41c.

243 Letter of Madison in, *James Madison, A Biography in His Own Words*, 2 vols. Ed., Merrill D. Peterson. Introduction by Robert A. Rutland, New York: Newsweek Books, 1974, 2:383.

244 See James Madison's essay "Property," 1792, in *Letters and Other Writings of James Madison*, in 4 vols., Philadelphia: J.B. Lippincott & Co., 1867, 4:478-480; or excerpt in Hall, *Christian History*, 1:248A.

throne as sovereigns elected by Parliament and sworn to uphold the Bill of Rights produced by that body in 1689. Among other statements of rights of the English people, it will be recalled that this bill declared that no taxes were to be levied on the people except by the consent of Parliament.

To the American colonists, the English Bill of Rights came to be revered as embodying the rights of *all* Englishmen, whether living in Great Britain or in her colonies across the seas. That the political ideas of "the celebrated Locke" had played a role in "the great settlement" of 1689 was discussed in the colonial press. In 1773, that redoubtable Puritan patriot, Samuel Adams (1722-1803), extolled Locke's *Two Treatises Of Civil Government* in a front-page article published in the *Boston Gazette* of March 1, declaring that they were "universally read and admired by all Lovers of Liberty."[245] He also asserted that "It is well known among the learned, that Mr. Locke's two Treatises on Government, of which this [the *Second Treatise*] is by far the most Valuable, contributed more essentially to the establishing of the Throne of our Great Deliverer King William, and consequently to securing of the Protestant Succession, than the Battle of the Boyne, or indeed all the Victories since obtained." Adams went on to claim that:

> This *Essay* alone, well studied and attended to, will give to every intelligent Reader a better View of the Rights of Men and of Englishmen, and a clearer Insight into the Principles of the British Constitution, than all the Discourses on Government.... It should be early and carefully explained by every Father to his Son, by every Preceptor in our public and private Schools to his Pupils, and by every Mother to her Daughter.

The *Two Treatises* were among the most widely cited political writings in colonial America. Many members of the influential New England clergy taught Lockean principles of government to their congregations in their Election Sermons using Locke's treatises. They were also familiar with his writings on religious toleration and on the extent of the human understanding. He was quoted by the New England clergy as early as 1738, and after 1763 references to him became more and more numerous. He was cited not only by prominent ministers in towns like Boston, but also by country parsons.[246]

There was scarcely a Founding Father who did not quote from Locke in

---

245 This quote and the two that follow are from the front page of the *Boston Gazette* for March 1, 1773, reproduced in Hall, *Christian History*, Vol. 2, 2:69.

246 See Alice Baldwin's landmark study, *The New England Clergy and The American Revolution*, 1928, New York: Frederick Ungar Publishing Co., 1958, 7-8.

his writings. Locke's assertion that just civil government was originated by compact; that men were the workmanship of God from whom they received their rights to life, liberty, and property; and that the only legitimate end of government was the defense of these rights struck a responsive chord in the minds of colonial Americans. As the day grew closer when independence from Great Britain must either be claimed or rejected, Locke's views on the right of revolution were increasingly consulted and quoted. When independence finally came, Jefferson paraphrased Locke as he wrote the Declaration of Independence.[247] Later, Lockean ideas found their way into the United States Constitution, particularly the Bill of Rights.

WIDESPREAD MISUNDERSTANDING OF LOCKE'S VIEWS

John Locke drew heavily on the Bible in his writing of both the *First* and *Second Treatises Of Civil Government*, but he also drew heavily on the Law of Nature. Since the American Founding Fathers closely followed Locke's ideas on the Law of Nature as undergirding all just legal statutes, it is important to understand what this term meant to him and to them. It is particularly important because a widespread misunderstanding of the term "the Law of Nature" and of Locke's views on this subject has gained currency in recent years. First, let us be clear what the Law of Nature is and what it is not. Many people today confuse the term with the laws of nature that govern plants and animal life.

Rather, the term Law of Nature refers to the law that God implanted in man at the Creation, as a famous English jurist, Edward Coke (1552-1634), observed when he wrote that "the law of nature is that which God at the time of creation of the nature of man infused into his heart, for his preservation and direction; and this is *lex aeterna*, the moral law, called also the law of nature."[248]

William Blackstone (1723-1780), the famous English jurist, codified English common law which itself had its root in Christianity. Blackstone provided colonial Americans with a detailed study of both the Law of

---

247 Locke wrote in his *Second Treatise Of Civil Government*, Chapter XIX, of "a long train of abuses, prevarications, and artifices, all tending the same way," which Jefferson changed to "a long train of abuses and usurpations pursuing invariably the same object...." Locke wrote of "the People, who are more disposed to suffer from right themselves by Resistance...." In Jefferson's wording, this became, "mankind are more disposed to suffer while evils are sufferable than to right themselves...." For the Locke quotes see facsimile edition of the *Second Treatise* in Hall, *Christian History*, 1:119-20.

248 See Gary T. Amos, *Defending the Declaration: How the Bible and Christianity Influenced the Writing of the Declaration of Independence.* Wolgemuth and Hyatt, Publishers, Inc., Brentwood, Tennessee, 1989, 43.

Nature and the Revealed Law in the Scriptures. He wrote in his *Commentaries on the Laws of England*:

> This law of nature, being coeval with mankind and dictated by God Himself, is of course superior in obligation to any other. It is binding over all the globe in all countries, and at all times: no human laws are of any validity, if contrary to this; and such of them as are valid derive all their force, and all their authority, mediately or immediately, from this original. But in order to apply this to the particular exigencies of each individual, it is still necessary to have recourse to human reason.... And if our reason were always, as in our first ancestor before his transgression, clear and perfect, unruffled by passions, unclouded by prejudice, unimpaired by disease or intemperance, the task would be pleasant and easy; we should need no other guide but this. But every man now finds the contrary in his own experience....[249]

Clearly, the Revealed Law in the Scriptures was necessary, as Blackstone notes:

> This has given manifold occasion for the benign interposition of divine providence; which, in compassion to the frailty, the imperfection, and the blindness of human reason, hath been pleased, at sundry times and in divers [sic] manners, to discover and enforce its laws by an immediate and direct revelation. The doctrines thus delivered we call the revealed or divine law, and they are to be found only in the Holy Scriptures. These precepts, when revealed, are found upon comparison, to be really a part of the original law of nature..."[250]

He concludes that "Upon these two foundations, the law of nature and the law of revelation, depend all human laws; that is to say, no human laws should be suffered to contradict these."[251]

Practicing attorney and former professor of law and government at Regent University (then CBN University) Gary Amos argues:

> The Christian practice of speaking of the "law of nature" and the "law of God" as a single law grew out of the church's reading of the New Testament in Romans 1 and 2. There the Apostle Paul denounced a mistake of certain legalists who claimed that the only

---

249 William Blackstone, *Commentaries on the Laws of England* (1765), in Hall, *Christian History*, 1:142.
250 Ibid., 142-143.
251 Ibid., 143.

valid "law of God" was the Mosaic legislation in the Pentateuch.... They tried to honor God's law by making Biblical law the only law of God. The Apostle pointed out that to say this was not to protect God's law, but to deny God's law because God Himself gives general revelation in nature and in men's hearts. In the name of honoring the law, the legalists were in fact repudiating the law of God and consequently attacking God's sovereignty and omnipotence."[252]

Amos adds,

> By dividing the law of the Bible into moral, ceremonial, and judicial (political) law, Locke was in agreement with the *Westminster Confession of Faith*, the *Westminster Larger Catechism*, John Calvin, and even Thomas Aquinas.[253]

> To say that the term "law of nature" is contrary to Calvinism and Reformed thinking is strange indeed, since it was always part of Calvinist legal theory. The idea is prominent in the most favored of all Reformed Creeds, the Westminster Confession (1646): 'As it is of the law of nature...so, in his Word, by a positive, moral and perpetual commandment, binding all men in all ages.'"[254]

Consider, however, John Calvin's view of the Law of Nature in Chapter 2 of his *Institutes*:

> For conscience, instead of allowing us to stifle our perceptions, and sleep on without interruption, acts as an inward witness and monitor, reminds us of what we owe to God, points out the distinction between good and evil, and thereby convicts us of departure from duty. But man, being immured in the darkness of error, is scarcely able, by means of that natural law, to form any tolerable idea of the worship (godly manner of living) which is acceptable to God. At all events, he is very far from forming any correct knowledge of it. In addition to this, he is so swollen with arrogance and ambition, and so blinded with self-love, that he is unable to survey, and, as it were, descend into himself, that he may so learn to humble and abase himself, and confess his misery. Therefore, as a necessary remedy, both for our dullness and our contumacy, the Lord has given us his written Law, which, by its sure attestations, removes the obscurity of the law of nature, and also, by shaking

---

252 Gary T. Amos, *Defending the Declaration*, 44.
253 Amos, 59.
254 Amos, 61 (regarding the Sabbath, Chapter XXI, VII).

off our lethargy, makes a more lively and permanent impression on our minds.[255]

(However, as will be seen in the final chapter of this book, Calvin presents a more sympathetic interpretation of the Law of Nature.)

Other complaints about the Law of Nature also come from two groups of scholars citing different reasons for their objections.

First, some Christian scholars view the Law of Nature as just a concept derived from pagan classical scholars and have concluded that it has no place in Christianity. So, their reasoning goes, if our Founding Fathers were following political ideas based on the Law of Nature, they were following non-Christian, or even anti-Christian ideas, whether they were aware of this or not.[256] In this view, the Declaration of Independence and the Constitution start from a flawed basis.

Second, other scholars applaud the adoption by the medieval Christian Church of Aristotle's philosophy of natural law. To them, this classical version of the Law of Nature is the true one. These scholars believe that a serious break with the medieval tradition occurred in the seventeenth century when, according to them, philosophers such as John Locke diluted, secularized, or perverted the medieval view. The result was what they refer to as "modern natural law" in contradistinction to "classic natural law" doctrines. Among scholars holding these views is the respected historian Forrest McDonald who asserts that Locke's theory of natural rights is "a perversion of the Western World's natural law tradition...."[257] In regard to Locke and his ideas on the Law of Nature, University of Chicago professor Leo Strauss and his students and followers maintain the same stance. To Strauss, Locke was one of the primary exponents of modern natural right and natural law theories. Strauss maintained that with the arrival of these "modern" natural law theories, the old (and true) theory as advanced by Thomas Aquinas (1227-1274), Aristotle (384-322 B.C.), and Plato (425-327 B.C.) was replaced by a modern rationalist viewpoint, typified by Locke, that secularized natural law and cut it off from its medieval Christian moorings.

---

255 John Calvin, *Calvin's Institutes, Book Two*, Chapter 8 (on the Ten Commandments), Section 1 (Grand Rapids: Associated Publishers and Authors, no date), 186.

256 See C. Gregg Singer, *A Theological Interpretation of American History*, (Phillipsberg, N.J.: Presbyterian and Reformed Publishing Co., 1981). He declared that the Declaration of Independence reflected ideas about God and man that were deistic rather than Christian, that the Declaration presented a view of God and man that was anti-Christian, 40. See also Rousas J. Rushdoony's statements that natural law is a pagan Greek concept and is in opposition to Biblical law in *The Politics of Guilt and Pity* (Vallecito, California: Ross House Books, 1970), 99.

257 See *Imprimis* (July 1983). Reprinted by permission from *Imprimis*, the national speech digest of Hillsdale College, www.hillsdale.edu.

Much has been said about the Law of Nature in this book. John Locke acknowledged and used it in many of his discussions on man's right to "life, liberty, and property." He found it useful to invoke at a time when there was bitter controversy among Christians as to the right interpretation of the Bible. But Locke has some particularly relevant words for us today in his book, *The Reasonableness of Christianity* which he wrote to convince deists of the divinity of Jesus. Here, he wrote:

> 'Tis true there is a Law of Nature; but who is there that ever did, or undertook to give it us all entire, as a Law?... Where was there ever any such Code, that mankind might have recourse to, as their unerring Rule, before our Saviour's time?... Such a Law of Morality Jesus Christ hath given us in the New Testament.... Here Morality has a sure Standard, that Revelation vouches, and Reason cannot gainsay, nor question.[258]

Today, when Christians are experiencing unprecedented attacks on their constitutional rights to religious liberty, these words are particularly relevant. Happily, most Christian denominations today are not at bitter theological odds with each other as many were in Locke's time. Now is the time for them to stand together against rulings by judges who oppose the right of Christian parents to uphold the sanctity of human life and the nature of marriage as defined in the Bible. Parents also know that they must claim their constitutional rights to religious liberty and their right to home teach their children if they wish to do so. Pastors know they must oppose efforts by the government to tell them what Biblical teachings they can or cannot preach. Today, it is vital that Christians defend their heritage by turning to the Bible's "sure standard," and "unerring rule" as their sole guide.

NATURAL LAW TRANSFORMED
BY THE PROTESTANT REFORMATION

Those philosophers and historians who believe that there was a break between Thomistic natural law doctrines and later views of the Law of Nature are, I believe, correct. But the idea that the break was owing to a secularization of the older natural law tradition is, I believe, an extraordinary mistake. A break in the natural law tradition did indeed occur, but it was as a result of the Protestant Reformation, which emphasized the importance of the individual and of his liberty of conscience as well as his rights in

---

258 John Locke, "The Reasonableness of Christianity" (1714) in Hall, *Christian History*, 2:89-90.

regard to religious worship and political liberty. This was something quite different from classic and medieval natural law theories, which emphasized duties rather than rights, and viewed the individual as subordinate to the whole. Politically, that view meant that the individual was subordinate to the state. The Reformation asserted the right of the individual to read the Bible for himself and prayerfully to interpret it with the help of the Holy Spirit and by the use of his God-given reasoning powers. The desire to fashion churches after the New Testament model also played a great role in the Reformation; and the idea of godly and just church government in accord with that model naturally spread to the idea of justice and right in the sphere of civil government. In both Church and State, the dignity of the individual emerged more and more in men's hearts as the result of their study of the Bible.

THE LAW OF NATURE IN THE ANCIENT WORLD

The best minds of the ancient world had no Bible to guide them; they only had recourse to their reason. The philosophers of ancient Greece tried to discover what was the good life according to nature and what was the best form of government for mankind, the one most in accord with his nature. To see how the shift occurred between the older natural law tradition that appeared in Greece and Rome and the one that came to the fore during the Protestant Reformation, it is necessary to go back to the ancients and discover what the Law of Nature was as seen through the eyes of these philosophers of the pre-Christian world. It is evident that they—Plato and Aristotle, in particular—had some notion of a divine power behind and supporting natural law. Sometimes it was spoken of as "of the gods," but sometimes as coming from one God.

The Greek philosophers of antiquity, although surrounded by the worshippers of many gods with many different ideas of right and wrong, sought for answers as to what was naturally good and right for man. To do this, they realized they needed to know the nature of man, his natural constitution, and a life in accordance with that nature. They recognized that what distinguishes man from beasts is his ability to reason and to understand. Therefore, they saw the good life as the life in accordance with man's nature. They also believed that the good life was one of virtue and excellence. But their view of virtue and excellence fell short of the one we understand from Scripture.

PLATO: THE STATE GOVERNED
BY AN INTELLECTUAL ELITE

Among the ancient philosophers there were differences regarding what they viewed as the best form of government for man, the one most in accord with his nature. Plato and his teacher, the celebrated Socrates, reasoned that the "best" government was of an intellectual elite who would know better than the ignorant man what was "right" for him; only the "superior" man could know how to render to a man "his due." An ideal government by the elite, however, was impossible to bring to realization. Therefore, in practical terms, it would be necessary to modify this ideal system by allowing the "unwise" to have the power of consent over the decrees of the "wise." Thus, a balance would be kept, although the results would be far inferior to the ideal. In this Socratic/Platonic ideal government, the guardians of the state would select the strongest and most intelligent men and women who, without possessions of their own, would be brought together in communal housing. Marriage would be only for procreation; the children would be raised communally without knowing who their actual parents were.[259] The Socratic/Platonic view was that happiness resides in the State as a whole rather than in individual lives.[260]

ARISTOTLE: THE STATE
AS EVOLUTIONARY DEVELOPMENT

Aristotle saw man as a "political animal," as naturally social, and the state as the outcome of his need for sociality. He reasoned that the state was an evolutionary development with man moving from primitive society toward political society, wherein he believed the individual would find his fullest development as a member of the state. So, for Aristotle, too, the state was of primary importance and man, the individual, was secondary and necessarily subordinate to the state. He wrote:

> ...and therefore, if the earlier forms of society are natural, so is the state, for it is the end of them and the nature is the end. For what each thing is when fully developed we call its nature, whether we are speaking of a man, a horse, or a family.... Hence it is evident that the state is a creation of nature, and that man is by nature a political animal.... Thus the state is by nature clearly prior to

---

259 Plato's *Republic*, Book V, trans. B. Jowett, in *Plato: Five Great Dialogues* (New York: Walter J. Black, Inc., 1942), 343-53.
260 Plato's *Republic*, Book IV, 308.

the family and to the individual, since the whole is of necessity
prior to the part....[261]

Again, in the *Nichomachean Ethics*, he wrote: "For even if the good of
an individual is identical with the good of a state, yet the good of the state
is evidently greater and more perfect to attain or to preserve. For though
the good of an individual by himself is something worth working for, to
ensure the good of a nation or a state is nobler and more divine."[262]

GOOD LAWS DETERMINED
BY THE FORM OF GOVERNMENT

Aristotle's famous forms of government—monarchy, aristocracy, constitutional government—and their perversions—tyranny, oligarchy, and
democracy—have been widely studied and his views on their virtues and
vices are still valid. He reasoned that forms of government, whether by
one, the few, or the many, are "true forms" if they govern with a view to
the common interest; whereas those that govern only with a view to their
own private interests are perversions: "For tyranny is a kind of monarchy
which has in view the interest of the monarch only, oligarchy has in view
the interest of the wealthy; democracy, of the needy; none, of the common good of all."[263] But how to arrive at the common good? How to give
each man what is his due? Aristotle was perplexed as to how to discover
what laws are good or evil. It appeared to him that what was good under
a monarchical form of government was bad under a constitutional form.
Or, what was good under a democracy would be bad under an oligarchy.
He ended by being uneasy about the nature of law.

> But what are good laws has not yet been clearly explained; the old
> difficulty remains. The goodness or badness, justice or injustice of
> laws depends of necessity on the constitution of states. If so, true
> forms of government will of necessity have just laws, and perverted
> forms of government will have unjust laws.[264]

But just in what sense? Aristotle admits that "it will be clearly seen
that all the partisans of different forms of government speak of a part

---

261 Aristotle's *Politics*, Book I, Chapter 2, in *Aristotle on Man and the Universe*, New York: Walter J.
Black, Inc., 1943, 251-52.

262 Aristotle's *Nichomachean Ethics*, Book I, Chapter 1, in *Aristotle on Man and the Universe*, ed. Louise
Ropes Loomis, New York: Walter J. Black, 1943, 88.

263 Aristotle's *Politics*, Book III, Chapter 7, in *Aristotle on Man and the Universe*, 299.

264 Ibid., Book III, Chapter 11, 306.

of justice only."[265] Aristotle reasoned brilliantly, but could get only so far in his quest for what is natural to man and what is the best form of government because, lacking Divine Revelation, he had no way of arriving at an absolute standard that went beyond merely human reason.

Cicero's View
of Natural Law

Later, in Rome, Marcus Tullio Cicero (106-43 B.C.) came closer to an awareness of the divine origin of natural right and natural law. He believed in one God who was the Lawmaker. (Possibly he also believed that there were other gods, or at least paid lip service to them.) He wrote in *The Law*, Book I: "Of all the questions which are ever the subject of discussion among learned men there is none more important thoroughly to understand than this, that man is born for justice, and that law and equity have not been established by opinion, but by nature."[266] He saw reason as giving man "many advantages over beasts" and that "there is but one essential justice which cements society, and one law which establishes this justice. This law is right reason, which is the true rule of all commandments and prohibitions. Whoever neglects this law, whether written or unwritten, is necessarily unjust and wicked."[267] He went on to assert that "we have no other rule by which we may be capable of distinguishing between a good or a bad law than that of nature" and that "the power of the law of nature is not only far more ancient than any existence of states and peoples, *but is coequal with God himself,* who beholds and governs both heaven and earth. For it is impossible that the divine mind can exist in a state devoid of reason; and divine reason must necessarily be possessed of a power to determine what is virtuous and what is vicious."[268]

What to say then about bad laws? "If then in the majority of nations, many pernicious and mischievous enactments are made, which have no more right to the name of law than the mutual engagements of robbers, are we bound to call them laws? For…we cannot call that the true law of a people, of whatever kind it may be, if it enjoins what is injurious, let the people receive it as they will." He concludes this paragraph with this declaration of the nature of law: "For law is the just distinction between

---

265 Ibid., *Book III*, Chapter 9, 302.
266 Marcus Tullio Cicero, *The Treatises of Cicero*, tr., C.D. Yonge, London, 1853, "On the Laws, Book I, in *The Western Tradition*, Boston: D.C. Heath and Company, 1959, 117.
267 Ibid., 117, 119.
268 Ibid., 120. Emphasis added.

right and wrong, made conformable to that most ancient nature of all, the original and principal regulator of all things, by which the laws of men should be measured...."[269]

Cicero spoke in the dying days of the Roman Republic, and his words fell on deaf ears. He seemed to be speaking from the republic's glorious past but, in fact, his words were pointed toward the future when men would hold much clearer ideas about the Law of Nature, which finally came from the Revelation of God's Word in the Bible.

MEDIEVAL NATURAL LAW

By the time medieval Church theologians were adopting Aristotle, the Church rather than the Scriptures, claimed to be the source of Christian revelation, the door of salvation through which the believer entered the Kingdom. Thomas Aquinas (1225-1274), in his learned *Summa Theologica*, followed Aristotle's view of man as a "political animal" and believed with Aristotle that the state is "by nature." But for Aquinas, as a Christian, nature and natural law were not self-existing but were the product of Providence. For him natural law became a secondary cause, an instrument of Divine Providence. Still thinking in feudal terms, however, Thomas held that the Pope was the supreme earthly ruler, not only in the spiritual, but also in the secular realm, that this was true through the eternal law of God and the order of nature in which inferiors obey superiors.

Aquinas saw the secular power as joined to the spiritual through the Pope who was the head of both powers.[270] He also asserted that the secular power was ruled by the Spiritual power so that it is proper for prelate to intervene in matters temporal that are subject him, or which the secular powers have given to him.[271] To Aquinas, the *ecclesia* embraced the *res publica*, the latter having no separate existence. Order was a prime concern of Aquinas. For this reason, he was much more concerned with a well-ordered state than with individual rights. Otto A. Bird has observed that while Aquinas had a lot to say about natural law, he said little about individual rights.[272]

---

269 Ibid., 121.

270 See Thomas Aquinas' *Commentary on the Sentences of Peter Lombard*, II, 44, *expositio textus*, cited by Dino Bigongiari in *The Political Ideas of St. Thomas Aquinas*, New York: Hafner Publishing Co., Inc., 1953, see xxxiv.

271 See Aquinas, *The Summa Theologica*, II-II, Q. 60, A. 6, in *Political Ideas of Thomas Aquinas*, see xxxiv.

272 See Otto A. Bird, *The Idea of Justice*, New York: Frederick A. Praeger, 1967, 122.

THE BEST FORM OF GOVERNMENT
ACCORDING TO THOMAS AQUINAS

As a part of his feudal view of life, with the Pope as supreme sovereign, Aquinas naturally viewed monarchy (when good) as the best form of government. Aquinas admitted, however, that when bad, it can constitute the most naked form of tyranny. He also admitted that in an "unjust government" the ruling power will become more harmful the more unitary it becomes.[273] But Aquinas was confronted by a basic difficulty in trying to reconcile monarchy, as he saw it, with his Christian convictions regarding justice and the moral law. If the monarch is absolutely sovereign—and this is how Aquinas saw him—then there is no other earthly power to make him institute or obey laws of justice. The favorite maxims of Roman law were that whatever the prince willed had the force of law and that the sovereign is above the law and may not be bound by it. This was a pagan idea, but it had received sanction by the Church when the Church allowed itself to be adopted and protected by the Roman emperors. Aquinas fully accepted this view, although he realized it presented a severe problem in relation to the idea of justice. It was his conclusion, however, that kings *ought* to rule in accord with good laws, but that they could not properly be forced to do so. The obligation to respect justice rested on the conscience of the sovereign which bade him obey the Law of Nature implanted in him as in other men. But what if he did not obey the Law of Nature? In order to explain why God permitted tyrants to rule, Aquinas had to fall back on the idea that they must have been sent to punish a wicked people.

AQUINAS MISLED
BY HIS RELIANCE ON ARISTOTLE

I do not wish to appear dismissive of the Christian contributions of Thomas Aquinas to an understanding of natural law. His system of thought stressed the Eternal Law of God as supreme and the Law of Nature, or the Law of God "written in our hearts" (see Romans 2:13-15) as secondary. Nevertheless, he was sometimes misled by his reliance on Aristotelian philosophy. Dr. J. Budziszewski has addressed this problem in his excellent book *Written on the Heart: The Case for Natural Law*. An admirer of Thomas Aquinas, he is nevertheless aware of the problem posed by his reliance on Aristotle. He writes:

---

273 See Aquinas, *On Kingship (De Regimine Principium)*, Book I, Chapter III, in *The Political Ideas of St. Thomas Aquinas*, 182.

There is much for a Christian to complain of in Thomas Aquinas, and I speak as one who loves him. Though he knows that every-thing other than God is utterly dependent on God, he sometimes gives the impression that what goes on in nature is somehow less dependent on him than are the effects of his grace. Though he knows that there can be no sin without the complicity of the mind, he sometimes gives the impression that the mind has not fallen as far as the rest of us.[274]

What is the reason for this? Dr. Budziszewski believes that one reason may be because Aquinas began his reasoning with the pagan philosophers, rather than beginning with the Scriptures.[275] Therefore, there are certain things in the writings of Thomas Aquinas that ought not to be there simply because of his reliance on pagan sources which led him into misinterpreting the Scripture.[276]

For example, Dr. Budziszewski discusses the way Aquinas speaks about the common good. He finds that there is a defect in it that does not come from natural law but from Aristotle, particularly Aristotle's way of dealing with the parts and the whole. As we have seen, to Aristotle, the whole is prior to its parts. This raises a problem when thinking about the relation-ship between a state and its citizens. Are we to believe that the citizen is a part of the state?

Dr. Budziszewski believes that this is not a view Christians should ac-cept. Christians are part of the body of Christ, but this means that our meaning and identity come from our relationship with Him, rather than the state.[277] Much as he admires Thomas Aquinas, Dr. Budziszewski be-lieves that Aquinas and those who follow him have too easily accepted Aristotle's opinions regarding "parts and wholes." This is no mere intellec-tual quibble; it can have serious consequences. In Dr. Budziszewski's words:

> To hold that citizens and subjects belong to the City is not an
> ennobling imitation of the idea that believers belong to Christ
> but a debasing perversion of it. It is, in the most literal sense,
> an idolatry. The one idea says that for the sake of my neighbor I
> should sacrifice myself; the other implies that for the sake of the
> state I may have to sacrifice my neighbor.[278]

---

274 Budziszewski, *Written on the Heart: The Case for Natural Law*, Downers Grove, Illinois: InterVarsity Press, 1997, 190. This is an excellent exploration of the subject.

275 See *Written on the Heart*, Ibid.

276 Ibid.

277 Ibid.

278 *Written on the Heart*, 95.

NATURAL LAW SEPARATE
FROM GOD'S ETERNAL LAW?

There is another problem with the natural law philosophy of Aquinas which also is attributable to his adoption of Aristotelian ideas; he some-times gives the impression that he thought of natural law as separate from, although related to, God's eternal law. It would not be fair to say that he intended such a division, since he wrote that "the light of natural reason, whereby we discern what is good and what is evil, which is the function of the natural law is nothing else than an imprint on us of the divine light."[279] As such, natural law is the rational creature's limited "participa-tion of the eternal law." (It is limited because "The human reason cannot have a full participation of the divine reason but according to its own mode and imperfectly.")[280]

Nevertheless, elsewhere the reasoning of Aquinas suggests that natural law is sufficient for man in this world; it is only because man is destined for eternal life that he needs the Eternal Law as well as the Law of Nature. Aquinas maintained that if man had no other end than what related to his natural faculties, he would need no further direction than natural law and the human laws coming from it. But because man was destined for eternal life and happiness, he also should be governed by laws directly from God.[281] He follows this up later, in his Reply to Objection I (which said that there was no need for a divine law in addition to the natural law and human laws derived from them): He points out that in addition to natural law pertaining to his human nature, man has a supernatural end that needs to be directed in a higher way. Hence the additional law given by God, whereby man more perfectly understands the eternal law.[282]

A GROWING DIVISION
BETWEEN NATURE AND GRACE

It is easy to see how the unbeliever could take the natural law teachings of Aquinas and, not believing in God or eternal life, could simply cut them off from any connection with eternal law. He could then proceed to live on this earth quite adequately (such would be the theory) by the

---

279 See *The Summa Theologica*, (First Part of the Second Part), Question 91, Second Article: "Whether there is in us a Natural Law?" in *The Political Ideas of St. Thomas Aquinas*, 13-14.

280 Ibid., 15.

281 See *The Summa Theologica*, Question 91, Fourth Article: "Whether there was any need for a Divine Law?" in *The Political Ideas of St. Thomas Aquinas*, 17.

282 Ibid., 15.

sole use of human reason with natural law viewed from a purely human basis.[283] Although Thomas Aquinas could not foresee the growing division which occurred between reason and Revelation, nature and Grace, a basic dualism was deduced by succeeding generations and, by the time of the Renaissance, humanism held full sway with the divine element very much in the background. It would seem that the reason for this Thomistic dualism was because of the great theologian's admiration for Aristotle, whose philosophy he attempted to blend with Christianity and use as his authority in much of his writing. As a Christian, Aquinas wrote many fine and correct theological statements about natural law based on his understanding of the Scriptures. When he spoke as an Aristotelian, however, he adopted the emphases of Aristotle's pre-Christian teachings. Thus, man needed eternal law because of his spiritual life to come, while his unassisted reason would be quite adequate for life on earth.

LOCKE SAW THE NEED
FOR DIVINE REVELATION

It was precisely the limitations of the "unassisted reason" to guide man correctly here on earth which John Locke clearly discerned. He knew that Divine Revelation was absolutely essential to guide man here and now, as well as in the life to come. He did not rely on the works of pagan philosophers, believing that their moral systems left much to be desired. Indeed, he was convinced that men's adherence to various philosophies played a role in "misleading men from the true sense of the sacred Scripture."[284]

> He that will attentively read the Christian writers, after the age of the apostles, will easily find how much the philosophy they were tinctured with influenced them in their understanding of the books of the Old and New Testament. In the ages wherein Platonism prevailed, the converts to Christianity of that school, on all occasions, interpreted holy writ according to the notions they had imbibed from that philosophy. Aristotle's doctrine had the same effect in its turn; and when it degenerated into the peripateticism of the schools, that, too, brought its notions and distinctions into divinity, and affixed them to the terms of the sacred Scripture. And

---

283 See Dr. Francis A. Schaeffer's *Escape From Reason*, Chicago: Henry Regnery Company, 1965, for a provocative discussion of Thomas Aquinas and the autonomous realm of reason.

284 John Locke, "An Essay for the understanding of St. Paul's Epistles, by consulting St. Paul himself," in *A Paraphrase and Notes on the Epistles of St. Paul to the Galatians, Corinthians, Romans, Ephesians,* in *Works,* 8:20.

we may see still how, at this day, everyone's philosophy regulates every one's interpretation of the word of God.[285]

He thought that "we shall, therefore, in vain go about to interpret [the apostles' words] by the notions of our philosophy, and the doctrines of men delivered in our schools. This is to explain the apostles' meaning by what they never thought of whilst they were writing; which is not the way to find their sense, in what they delivered, but our own, and to take up, from their writings, not what they left there for us, but what we bring along with us in ourselves."[286] As to how to interpret the Scripture without the use of philosophy, Locke wrote in a letter to the Reverend Richard King:

> The Christian religion is a revelation from God almighty, which is contained in the Bible, and so all the knowledge you can have of it must be derived from thence. "What is the best way of inter-preting Scripture?" Taking "interpreting" to mean "understanding," I think the best way for understanding the Scripture...is to read it assiduously and diligently; and, if it can be, in the original. I do not mean, to read every day some certain number of chapters, as is usual; but to read it so, as to study and consider, and not to leave till you are satisfied that you have got the true meaning.[287]

He recommended the use of several Commentaries, (Matthew Poole's *Synopsis Criticorum*, Dr. Hammond's commentary on the New Testament and Dr. Whitby's) with a caution that no Bible commentator is infallible, only the Holy Scriptures "which were dictated by the infallible Spirit of God."[288] Locke's approach to the Bible reflected his upbringing. Through-out his entire life he maintained the Puritan's deep reverence for the Bible as the Word of God. Although often depicted today as one who believed only in "natural religion" and that there was no need for Revelation, such was far from the truth. In fact, he wrote *The Reasonableness of Christian-ity as Deliver'd in the Scriptures*, to convince the deists of the necessity of Biblical Revelation. He wrote:

> But "natural Religion" in its full extent, was no where, that I know of, taken care of by the force of natural Reason.... It would seem by the little that has hitherto been done in it, that 'tis too hard a Task for unassisted Reason, to establish Morality in all its Parts

---

285 Ibid.
286 Ibid., 8:21.
287 John Locke, *A Letter to the Reverend Mr. Richard King*, in *Works*, 10:310.
288 John Locke, *A Letter to the Reverend Mr. Richard King*, undated, in *Works*, 10:311.

upon its true Foundations, with a clear and convincing Light.... We see how unsuccessful in this, the Attempts of Philosophers were before our Saviour's time. How short their several Systems came of the perfection of a true and compleat Morality is very visible.[289]

LOCKE'S BIBLICAL APPROACH TO GOD'S LAW OF NATURE

Locke contends that, far from being sufficient for man, human reason actually had failed him, because "it never from unquestionable Principles, by clear Deductions, made out an entire Body of the Law of Nature. And he that shall collect all the moral Rules of the Philosophers, and compare them with those contained in the New Testament, will find them to come short of the Morality delivered by our Saviour and taught by his Apostles...."[290] In contrast to this approach, Locke adhered to the Biblical view of the Law of Nature as explained by St. Paul in his Epistle to the Romans, Chapter 2, Verses 14-15. Here Paul compared the Word of God, revealed in the Scriptures, with the Work of God, revealed in His Law of Nature planted in men's hearts from the beginning of creation.

> For when the Gentiles, which have not the law, do by nature the things contained in the law, these, having not the law, are a law unto themselves: Which shew the work of the law written in their hearts, their conscience also bearing witness, and their thoughts the meanwhile accusing or else excusing one another.[291]

In Locke's *Paraphrases and Notes on the Epistles of St. Paul*, he renders this passage as follows:

> For when the Gentiles who have no positive law given them by God, do, by the direction of the light of nature, observe or keep to the moral rectitude, contained in the positive law, given by God to the Israelites, they, being without any positive law given them, have nevertheless a law within themselves; And show the rule of law written in their hearts, their conscience also bearing witness to that law, they amongst themselves, in the reasoning of their own minds, accusing or excusing one another.[292]

---

289 John Locke, *The Reasonableness of Christianity, as Delivered in the Scriptures*, 1714, in Hall, *Christian History*, 2:86–87.

290 Ibid., 2:87.

291 As rendered by The King James Version of the Bible.

292 *Paraphrases of St. Paul*, in *Works*, 8:265–66.

Locke comments that "though, from Adam to Christ, there was no revealed, positive law, but that given to the Israelites; yet it is certain that, by Jesus Christ, a positive law from heaven is given to all mankind, and that those to whom this has been promulgated, by the preaching of the Gospel, are all under it, and shall be judged by it."[293]

REASON AND REVELATION

Locke saw clearly that God had revealed Himself in two ways: through the Law of Nature and through the positive law revealed in the Scriptures, in other words through Reason and Revelation. In Locke's *Essay Concerning Human Understanding*, he gives these illuminating definitions of Reason and Revelation:

> Reason is natural revelation, whereby the eternal Father of light, and fountain of all knowledge, communicates to mankind that portion of truth which he had laid within the reach of their natural faculties: revelation is natural reason enlarged by a new set of discoveries communicated by God immediately, which reason vouches the truth of, by the testimony and proofs it gives that they come from God.[294]

Here he uses Reason in a very different sense from man's "unassisted reason." Note what he says about this kind of reason. It is "natural revelation." Who is doing the revealing to man? It is God, the eternal Father of light. Obviously, this is a much higher view of reason than that espoused by the deist who saw reason as a purely human faculty detached from the Creator. The following statement also brings out how God guides our reasoning processes: "When we find out an idea by whose intervention, we discover the connection of two others, this is a revelation from God to us by the use of reason. For then we come to know a truth that we did not know before. When God declares any truth to us, this is a revelation to us by the voice of his spirit, and we are advanced in our knowledge."[295]

GOD'S GIFT OF INTUITION

One might say that this is a revelation God gives to the human mind through a flash of intuition. Locke says in the *Essay Concerning Human*

---

293 Ibid., 265.
294 John Locke, *Essay Concerning Human Understanding*, Book IV, Chapter XIX, par. 4, in *Works*, 3:149.
295 *Essay*, Book IV, Chapter VII, in *Works*, 3:31.

Understanding that there are three kinds of knowledge: *intuitive* (the immediate perception of self-evident truths), *demonstrative* (requiring a logical reasoning process), and sensitive (arrived at through the five senses.) [296] Under *Intuitive Knowledge*, Locke observes:

> This part of knowledge is irresistible, and like bright sunshine forces itself immediately to be perceived, as soon as ever the mind turns its view that way; and leaves no room for hesitation, doubt, or examination, but the mind is presently filled with the clear light of it.[297]

He follows this passage with a highly significant comment that "it is on this intuition that depends all the certainty and evidence of all our knowledge...." How does man come to have this intuitive knowledge? Through "a revelation of God to us from the voice of reason." When Locke uses "Reason" in this way, it is, as noted above, much more akin to intuition. It is an immediate perception in the mind rather than a laborious thinking process. Moreover, it is necessary in every step of demonstrative reason. "Now, in every step reason makes in demonstrative knowledge, there is an intuitive knowledge of that agreement or disagreement it seeks with the next intermediate idea, which it uses as a proof.... By which it is plain, that every step in reasoning that produces knowledge has intuitive certainty."[298]

THE LAW OF NATURE AS THE WILL OF GOD

In his *Second Treatise Of Civil Government*, Locke also refers to the Law of Nature as "the eternal rule of all men" and as "the will of God." Paragraph 135 reads:

---

296 *Essay*, Book IV, Chapter II, "Of the Degrees of our Knowledge," for Locke's discussion of the three kinds of knowledge.

297 *Essay*, Book IV, Chapter II, par. 1, in *Works*, 2:320.

298 *Essay*, Book IV, Chapter II, par. 7, in *Works*, 2:323. See Basil Willey's discussion on Locke's three kinds of knowledge in *The Seventeenth Century Background*, 271–76. See also Gary T. Amos, in his excellent study, *Defending the Declaration: How the Bible and Christianity Influenced the Writing of the Declaration of Independence*, Brentwood, Tennessee: Wolgemuth & Hyatt Publisher, Inc., 1989, 93–94. From Webster's 1828 *American Dictionary* definition of **intuition**: "A looking on; a sight or view; but restricted to mental view or perception. Particularly and appropriately, the act by which the mind perceives the agreement or disagreement of two ideas, or the truth of things, immediately, or the moment they are presented, without the intervention of other ideas, or without reasoning and deduction." Some Christians, however, may prefer a stronger identification of *intuition* with Biblical wisdom, aided by the Holy Spirit. They believe that such a basis for *intuition* is properly in Biblical knowledge proved through its fruits. In this light, Locke's view of the certainty of **intuition** rings true to them.

Thus the law of Nature stands as an Eternal Rule to all Men, Legislators as well as others. The Rules that they make for other Men's actions, must, as well as their own, & other Men's Actions, be conformable to the Law of Nature, i.e., the Will of God, of which that is a declaration, and the fundamental Law of Nature being the preservation of Mankind, no Human Sanction can be good, or valid against it.[299]

Here he links the Law of Nature to an Eternal Rule for all men, and as the Will of God, which is the preservation of all mankind. Elsewhere in the *Second Treatise* he speaks of "common Reason and Equity" as "that measure God has set to the actions of Men for their mutual Security" (par. 8). Reason is also defined as "the common Rule and Measure, God hath given to Mankind...." (par. 11) Finally, Locke declares that "the Municipal Laws of Countries...are only so far right, as they are founded on the Law of Nature, by which they are to be regulated and interpreted." (par. 12)

THE DIFFERENCE BETWEEN THE LAW OF NATURE AND NATURAL LAW

The discerning reader of the *Two Treatises* will notice that Locke most often uses the term "the Law of Nature" rather than the term "natural law." Why is this? It may well be because the term natural law meant to him moral law understood or developed by the human mind, as seen in the works of the pagan philosophers of antiquity, while the Law of Nature, as he understood it, was the Law of God revealed to man *through* reason.[300]

Most important of all, he explained (in *The Reasonableness of Christianity*) the superiority of the Divine Moral law in the Scriptures as presenting the entire Law of Nature beyond what human reason could discern:

'Tis true, there is a Law of Nature; but who is there that ever did, or undertook to give it to us all entire, as a Law?...Where was there any such code that mankind might have recourse to, as their unerring Rule, before our Saviour's time?... Such a Law of Morality Jesus

---

299 Facsimile edition of *Second Treatise*, in Hall, *Christian History*, 1:94.

300 According to Gary Amos, this distinction between the Law of Nature and Natural Law was in use in the 1770s. In *Defending the Declaration*, 186 (note 22 of Chapter 2), he explained that: "'Law of nature' meant the objectively revealed moral law of God, first in nature (called 'general revelation' by Christian theologians), then in the positive moral law of Scripture. 'Natural law' denoted the fallen understanding or mental perception in man's mind of the law of nature. Some deists used the term 'natural law' to speak of man's ability to reason his way to a perfect understanding of natural justice."

Christ hath given us in the New Testament...by Revelation. We have from him a full and sufficient Rule for our direction, and conformable to that of Reason.... Here Morality has a sure Standard, that Revelation vouches and Reason cannot gainsay, nor question; but both together witness to come from God, the great Law maker. And such an one as this out of the New Testament, I think the World never had, nor can any one say is any where else to be found....[301]

To recapitulate: In Locke's philosophy of life and of political relationships, he saw Reason and Revelation as twin aspects of the Godhead, hence, as also twin aspects of man's living—never as two antagonistic forces pulling against each other. Locke saw the Law of Nature as the Will of God revealed to man subjectively through reason. Revelation he saw as the Will of God revealed to man objectively through the Holy Scriptures which confirmed and completed the Law of Nature and gave it authority as the Law of God.

As one becomes acquainted with Locke's deeply Christian understanding of the Law of Nature, we can see more clearly why the Founding Fathers and the Founding Clergy, if I may so name them, were so impressed by his writings on natural rights and the proper role of civil government in protecting them. As the years wore on in their debate with the Mother Country over infringements of their Charter and constitutional rights, both clergy and laymen read with increasing interest Locke's writing on the Law of Nature and on the nature of just civil government which, according to Locke, exists to protect men's God-given natural rights to their "Lives, Liberties, and Estates, which I call by the general Name, *Property.*"[302]

Doubtless, they also appreciated his eloquent words in Paragraph 6 of the *Second Treatise* defining mankind as "being all the Workmanship of one Omnipotent, and infinitely wise Maker: All the Servants of one Sovereign Master, sent into the World by his Order, and about his Business, they are his Property, whose Workmanship they are, made to last during his, not one anothers Pleasure: And being furnished with like Faculties, sharing all in one Community of Nature, there cannot be supposed any such *Subordination* among us, that may authorize us to destroy one another as if we were made for one another's Uses,..." and Locke reminds the reader that mankind, "may not unless it be to do

---

301 John Locke, *The Reasonableness of Christianity,* in Hall, *Christian History,* 2:89-90.
302 Locke, *Second Treatise Of Civil Government,* par. 123, in Hall, *Christian History,* 1:91.

Justice on an Offender, take away, or impair the Life, or what tends to the Preservation of the Life, the Liberty, Health, Limb, or Goods of another." [303]

In the next chapter, we will see just how closely the New England clergy followed Locke in their reasoning when Great Britain began to threaten the lives, liberties, and property of their people.

---

303 Ibid., par. 6, 1:58.

CHAPTER SEVEN

The New England Clergy and "The Great Mr. Locke"

The original of Government is Divine.
It is from God,
by His Sovereign Constitution and Appointment.

REVEREND EBENEZER PEMBERTON
(*Massachusetts Election Sermon*, 1710)

A STUDY of the Colonies from their earliest days to the War of Independence shows that the ideas in the Declaration of Independence and later in the Constitution of the United States were far from being the work of a few brilliant political leaders. In fact, they began at the grass roots level. The progress of these ideas and their embedding, as it were, in the American consciousness was in great measure the work of the colonial clergy. This was particularly true of the Congregationalist clergy, in New England, although it is only fair to say that distinguished ministers in other colonies and of other denominations also wielded considerable political influence.[304] But the New England clergy played a particularly

---

[304] There was, for example, Dr. John Witherspoon, the Scottish minister who became president of the Presbyterian College of New Jersey in 1768 and soon was a strong defender of colonial rights. He gave James Madison a thorough education in the fundamental principles of government and evidently instilled in him Locke's expanded idea of property as more than human possessions. Dr. Witherspoon wrote in a magazine article in April 1776 that "if therefore we yield up our temporal property, we at the same time deliver the conscience into bondage." Years later, in 1791, Madison wrote in an essay that "Government is instituted to protect property of every sort.... Conscience is the most sacred of all property...." See James Madison, *Letters and Other Writings of James Madison*, 4 vols., Philadelphia: J. B. Lippincott & Co., 1867, 4:478-480. Dr. Witherspoon inspired his students with a spirit of patriotism, and at least eighty-six graduates of Princeton became active in government. He himself served in Congress for seven years, beginning in 1776. He was a signer of the Declaration of Independence (to which he is thought to have contributed the phrase, "with a firm reliance on the protection of Divine Providence"). For more on John Witherspoon as educator and politician see Mary-Elaine Swanson, *The Education of James Madison: A Model For Today*, Montgomery, Alabama: The Hoffman Center, 1994, and Mary-Elaine Swanson, "James Madison and the Presbyterian Idea of Man and Government," in *Religion and Political Culture in Jefferson's Virginia*, eds. Garrett Ward Sheldon and Daniel L. Dreisbach, Lanham, Maryland: Rowman & Littlefield Publishers, Inc., 2000, 119-132.

conspicuous and decisive part in forming the groundwork of a large body of public opinion in the New England colonies—and elsewhere in the colonies through the circulation of their printed sermons. These courageous ministers educated their congregations year in and year out in what they saw as the fundamental Christian principles of government. What they taught soon produced leaders who gave their pastors' teachings a voice in the civil realm.[305]

DISTINCTIVE FORMS OF CHURCH GOVERNMENT

What was it about their theology that caused these New England ministers to take such a lively interest in government? To answer this question, one must first understand that the Congregationalists (and also the Presbyterians), although dissenters from the Church of England, were true sons of the Reformation. As I have written elsewhere:

> That great religious movement, we should remember, was not only about questions of individual conscience. It was quite as much about how the church should be governed. Anglicans, both in Great Britain and her North American colonies, were content with Henry VIII's Reformation which abolished allegiance to the Pope, made the English monarch head of the Church, and retained the old authority of Archbishop and bishops. But Congregational and Presbyterian dissenters from the Church of England, particularly those who had come to America in search of liberty to worship in accord with their religious convictions, believed that Christ's church should not be governed by any earthly monarch or bishopric. Rather, the dissenters' view was that it should be governed directly by the whole Congregation (as in the Congregational Church) or by their representatives, the elders, or Presbyters (as in the Presbyterian Church).[306]

The names of these churches reflect their distinctive forms of government. This is also true of the American descendant of the Church of England, which came to be known as the Episcopal Church, often called a monarchical form of government because power flows from the top down. The Presbyterian form of government may be termed aristocratic with elders chosen to represent the members and make decisions for them, with

---

305 See Chapter 8 for a discussion of the work of two prominent examples of lay leaders raised up by the New England Clergy—James Otis and Samuel Adams.

306 Swanson, "James Madison and the Presbyterian Idea of Man and Government," in *Religion and Political Culture in Jefferson's Virginia*, 120.

extended representative judicial presbyteries over numbers of congregations. The third form of government—often called democratic, but perhaps better termed republican—was historically that of the Congregational Church with power flowing reciprocally—i.e., where "church government [was] by consent and election, maintaining that each congregation is independent of others, and has the right to choose its own pastor and govern itself...."[307]

In New England we are dealing primarily with the Congregational church beginning with the church of the Pilgrim Fathers in Plymouth colony. A study of the New England colonies shows that they were begun by plantation covenants or compacts which were modeled after their church covenants. Through the faith and courage of "the first comers" these colonies gradually put down deep roots and prospered despite the desperate difficulties of their early days.

THE IDENTITY OF PURITAN THEOLOGY AND AMERICAN POLITICAL THOUGHT

The story of the profound influence of the clergy on New England's political life has not been given as much attention as it deserves. A debt is owed to Alice Baldwin who first revealed in her landmark work, *The New England Clergy and The American Revolution*, "the intimate relation of the New England minister to the thought and life of eighteenth-century New England...."[308] The purpose of her excellent study was, as she explained, "to make clear the similarity, the identity of Puritan theology, and fundamental political thought" and to show how the New England clergy made their doctrine of political philosophy thoroughly familiar to New England churchgoers. Their work began long before 1763. (But intense political debates began when Great Britain imposed a Stamp Tax on all kinds of paper including all legal documents, newspapers, pamphlets, etc.)

The ministers taught their congregations about the Law of Nature, man's natural rights, and the social compact that created civil government. Often they used John Locke to support their arguments. Alice Baldwin wrote that they taught "the fundamental principle of constitutional law, that government, like its citizens, is bounded by law and when it transcends its authority it acts illegally."[309]

---

307 Noah Webster, 1828, *American Dictionary of the English Language.*

308 Alice M. Baldwin, *The New England Clergy and The American Revolution*, 1928, New York: Frederick Ungar Publishing Co., 1958, xii.

309 Baldwin, xii.

A LEARNED CLERGY DRAWS ON LOCKE
IN THEIR SERMONS

It is important to recognize that New England ministers of the eighteenth century were largely a "learned clergy." Many of them were graduates of Harvard or of Yale. It should also be added that they were well-read, not only in theology but in a wide range of subjects and authors, including the writings of John Locke. They read not only his *Two Treatises of Government*, but also his *Essay Concerning Human Understanding* and his *Reasonableness of Christianity*. They found Locke's ideas congenial to their own understanding of these subjects.

The ministers preached not only on Sunday but also on any special days dictated by the colonial assemblies, such as thanksgiving days and days of fasting and prayer. In large towns, like Boston, they also gave a weekly lecture on some topic of current interest. So they had many opportunities to educate their congregations in matters theological and political.

GOVERNMENT BY COVENANT AND COMPACT

The most striking thing about New England theology is the role of covenanting that played such an important role in the establishment of the Congregational Churches throughout New England. Not only were the churches but also their civil governments created by covenant. Thus, their societies had two covenants—their church covenants and their "plantation covenants."

By the eighteenth century, the New England clergy believed, along with Locke, in the Law of Nature as a divine law. Clearly, they also believed that civil as well as church government ought to be based on a covenant or compact. Indeed, they could point to New England's first civil covenant in the Pilgrims' Mayflower Compact of 1620 which stands as the first concrete example of this theory in the New World. Of course, it can be traced back much further than Locke and seventeenth century England. Indeed, it has its roots in the Biblical idea of the covenant.

It is no wonder then, as Dr. Andrew C. McLaughlin wrote, that the covenant was "the central and pivotal idea in the organization of a church."[310] He traced this idea to the Separatist clergy (from whom came the Pilgrim Fathers). It was, he says, their conviction "that people can establish their own church by coming together and entering into a covenant or contract

---

310 Andrew C. McLaughlin, *The Foundations of American Constitutionalism*, Greenwich, Conn., Fawcett Publications, Inc., 1961, 20.

of mutual support."[311] This idea, in turn, was predicated upon the idea that the individual was important to God and that individuals had the right to come together in a self-governing body under His guidance. This was as opposite as it could be from the Church of England's idea that men were born into an earthly monarch's Church to which they owed unquestioning loyalty and in which the individual certainly did not have the right of private judgment.

AFTER THE MAYFLOWER COMPACT

After the Mayflower Compact of 1620, compacts were entered into at the beginning of the Massachusetts Bay Colony (1630); Rhode Island's colonists, under Roger Williams, drew up a written covenant in 1637 establishing their colony; and The Fundamental Articles of New Haven (1639) were that colony's "plantation covenant."

McLaughlin was struck by the remarkable continuity of these doctrines which were widely known and accepted in New England by the time of the American Revolution.

> If we trace this line even incompletely and see the continuity of these doctrines, we do not need to suppose that the men of the American Revolution only rummaged about during an anxious emergency to find in Milton, Sidney, or Locke support for the position they were prepared to take against George III.[312]

Locke, Sidney, and Milton were already well known by New Englanders, and, indeed throughout the colonies. As did Alice Baldwin, Dr. McLaughlin also noted the "conspicuous role" of the New England clergy during the American Revolution. "The philosophy of the seventeenth century was repeated over and over again by New England divines, who preached about a law of reason and a law of God, the sacredness of covenant and the divine character of government."[313]

THE TWO BASIC GOVERNMENTAL IDEAS
OF THE NEW ENGLAND CLERGY

McLaughlin defined the two basic governmental ideas of the New England clergy as: (1) the individual's right of self-determination and (2) his right to join with others to form a body—either church or colony—"which could

---

311 McLaughlin, 20-21.
312 McLaughlin, 70-71.
313 McLaughlin, 71.

have real existence and, within its scope, real power." McLaughlin then cited John Locke as the philosopher "who in the field of politics put forth these doctrines with special cogency and clearness."[314]

CHRISTIAN MORALITY SEEN AS THE ONLY FOUNDATION OF JUST LAWS

The political education of the New England clergy was naturally uppermost in their election sermons. Here was an excellent opportunity to discuss governmental matters. In Massachusetts, Connecticut, and Plymouth (before it was absorbed by Massachusetts), and in Vermont after 1778, the governor's council selected a minister to preach a sermon on the day the people's representatives were chosen to sit in the Assembly for the coming year. Election day was always in the Spring. Historian John Wingate Thornton describes the importance of these sermons in his own colony of Massachusetts:

> The clergy were generally consulted by the civil authorities; and not infrequently the suggestions from the pulpit, on election days and other special occasions, were enacted into laws. The statute-book, the reflex of the age, shows this influence. *The State was developed out of the Church.*
>
> The annual "Election Sermon"—a perpetual memorial, continued down through the generations from century to century—still bears witness that our fathers ever began their civil year and its responsibilities with an appeal to Heaven, and recognized *Christian morality as the only basis of good laws.*[315]

ELECTION DAY AND ARTILLERY SERMONS

In Massachusetts, a few days after the election day sermon, another sermon was preached on the artillery election day, the day when the officers were reelected, or new officers chosen. The general election minister was chosen alternately by the council and Assembly. The sermon was printed with a copy going to each representative and one or more for the minister.

---

314 McLaughlin, 72.

315 John Wingate Thornton, *The Pulpit of the American Revolution*, Boston, 1860. Cited in Hall, *Christian History of the American Revolution*, 191. Emphasis in the original. The Massachusetts Bay colony's charter stipulated that there should be elected a governor, deputy-governor, and eighteen assistants who were to be chosen in their "general court, or assemblie," on "the last Wednesday in Easter Terme, yearely, for the year ensuing." Commencing about 1633, the governor and his assistants appointed a minister to preach a sermon on the day of election. In 1691, the charter issued by William and Mary established the last Wednesday in May as election-day and thus it remained.

The Reverend William Gordon of Roxbury, Massachusetts, who actively supported the War of Independence, left some illuminating remarks on these election sermons which explain why the ministers giving them were so at ease on the subject of government, be it civil or religious. He wrote of the ministers of New England, as being "mostly Congregationalists,"

> who are from that very circumstance, more attached and habituated to the principles of liberty than if they had spiritual superiors to lord it over them.... They oppose arbitrary rule in civil concerns from the love of freedom, as well as from a desire of guarding against its introduction into religious matters.... As the patriots have prevailed, the preachers of each [election] sermon have been the zealous friends of liberty; and the passages most adapted to promote the spread and love of it have been selected and circulated far and wide by means of newspapers.... Thus, by their labors in the pulpit, and by furnishing the prints with occasional essays, the ministers have forwarded and strengthened, and that not a little, the opposition to the exercise of that parliamentary claim of right to bind the colonies in all cases whatever.[316]

Miss Baldwin noted that "for a hundred years before the Revolution and year by year throughout the long conflict, these sermons dealt with matters of government."[317] They were read not only in their own communities but were often sent to friends in England and in other colonies, and "were distributed regularly to the country towns where they became, as [Justin] Winsor styles them, 'text-books of politics.'"[318] But these election sermons were not the New England clergy's only opportunity to educate their communities in the principles of government; there were political sermons given to their own congregations; letters or articles addressed to the local newspaper; pamphlets; and correspondence with ministers and friends both in their own colony and elsewhere.

SOURCES OF THE
NEW ENGLAND PASTORS' POLITICAL THEORIES

The New England pastors' political theories were derived first of all from the Scriptures, then from Greek and Roman authors, and finally from the works of John Locke.

---

316 Cited by Thornton, in Hall, *Christian History of the American Revolution,* 191–92.
317 Baldwin, 6.
318 Justin Winsor, *Memorial History of Boston,* 4 vols. Boston, 1881, 3:120, cited by Baldwin, 6.

The Bible

But the Bible was the New England minister's primary source in developing his political theories. Here were to be found in the Old Testament many examples of God covenanting with His people, of the limits God's laws placed on all people (kings included), of the Law of Nature, and of what was referred to as "the divine constitution." This the ministers viewed as three-fold: it included Old Testament law; the Law of Christ in the New Testament; and God's Law of Nature. Along with their study of the Bible, they also studied various Bible commentaries such as those by Matthew Henry, Matthew Pool, and Daniel Whitby (the latter's commentaries it will be recalled, Locke used and recommended as a reliable source.)

Greek and Roman Authors

Another source of political ideas were such authors of Greek and Roman antiquity as Aristotle, Plato, Cicero, and others. It is important to recognize, however, that although both pastors and laymen of the Revolutionary period found these authors' writings interesting, they also realized that they were inadequate to their own situation. Scholar Bernard Bailyn points out that the views of these authors merely provided the clergy with helpful illustrations of their use in the ancient world but did not play a role in determining what kind of government was appropriate for their own time.[319]

The Works of John Locke

"The next great source," says Miss Baldwin, "was the works of John Locke, his essays on religious toleration and human understanding as well as those on government."[320] Miss Baldwin's research revealed that Locke was quoted by name as early as 1738 and especially after 1763. Even when he does not appear in a text by name, his political ideas and even phrases from his works are used. The clergy referred to him as "the great Mr. Locke," "the celebrated Locke," or simply as "Mr. Locke."[321] The clergy

---

319 See Bernard Bailyn, *The Ideological Origins of the American Revolution* (Cambridge, Massachusetts: The Belknap Press of Harvard University Press, 1967), 26. Bailyn also contends that Enlightenment ideas were more influential with the colonists. He includes Locke in this camp. This, as I have noted in Chapter 6, is a common error of many authors who have not sufficiently studied Locke to discover his strong Biblical moorings.

320 Baldwin, 7.

321 Other writers on government and their works that the clergy were also fond of quoting included: Sir Algernon Sydney's *Discourses Concerning Government* (a new edition came out in 1772); Samuel Puffendorf's *The Law of Nature and Nations* (1703); the Baron de Montesquieu's *Spirit of the Laws* (1748); Sir Edward Coke's *Institutes of the Laws of England* (1628); James Harrington's *Oceana*, (1656) and his *Political Discourses* (1660); Locke's friend Lord Somers in *A Collection of Scarce and Valuable Tracts* (1748-52); Emmerich de Vattel's *The Law of Nations, or Principles of the Law of Nature Applied to the Conduct and Affairs of Nations and Sovereigns* (1760); J. J. Burlemaqui, *Principles of Natural and Politic Law*, 2 vols., (1748).

found his ideas congenial, particularly his handling of the Law of Nature as the Law of God and his insistence on government founded upon compact with consent of the governed.

REASON AND NATURE
AS THE VOICE OF GOD

To the common assertion that the clergy of eighteenth century New England were following Reason and Nature rather than sound Biblical theology, Miss Baldwin replies that the clergy of the eighteenth century, even as those of the seventeenth, "believed Reason and Nature but the voice of God and the laws of Nature as truly those of God as the laws found in the Scripture. This they said repeatedly and thus gave a sacred significance to the laws of Nature and the arguments from Reason." [322] Along with Locke who, it will be remembered, came from a Puritan family, these New England ministers saw the Law of Nature as the Law of God and that Reason is that law written in men's hearts "as with a pen of iron and the point of a diamond," as wrote one pastor. [323]

JARED ELIOT:
THE FIRST PASTOR TO QUOTE LOCKE

We have already seen that Locke's great contribution to the study of the Law of Nature was in his discerning that it did not constitute an autonomous realm for man's intellect, nor was it a substitute for Revelation. Rather, it was a branch of divine law. So it was that the New England clergy saw it. In 1738, Jared Eliot (1685-1763), a pastor of Killingworth, Connecticut, brought out a thorough study of government, its nature and origins, containing the first known reference to John Locke by a New England pastor who cited him by name. [324]

Using Lockean terms, Eliot began by discussing man in the State of Nature declaring that just such an account of man is given in the Bible in the story of Ishmael. In speaking of sovereignty, Eliot declared that it

---

322 Baldwin, 29, note 22.

323 Boston clergyman, Jonathan Mayhew, cited by Baldwin, 15. As an Arminian, one who believed in free will, he was harshly criticized by Calvinists; nevertheless, it appears that he also believed firmly in the sovereignty of God. See Baldwin, 18.

324 Jared Eliot was a minister, physician, and scholar who pastored the Congregational Church at Killingworth, Connecticut, from 1709 until his death. His grandfather was John Eliot, the Apostle to the Indians. In addition to his work as a pastor, he was also a physician well-known for his treatment of insanity and chronic complaints. He was consulted more than any other New England physician. He was also a close student of the natural sciences and was the first to introduce the white mulberry tree into Connecticut and with it the silkworm. In 1735, he published "Religion Supported by Reason and Revelation." His "Sermon on the Taking of Louisburg," published in 1745, was widely read.

is a "fundamental principle of government," that sovereignty "must lodge somewhere." [325] He concluded that where the community rightly places it is in the legislative branch of government which must be supreme (thus agreeing with Locke). He lauded the British system of government as having as its corner-stone that "no man's Life, Limb, Name, or Estate, shall be taken away but by his Peers, and by the known Law of the Land." He presented the government of the British colonies as "little Models" of the home government, in which the people enjoyed the same liberties and, in addition, the liberty of electing their own legislators from among themselves. He acknowledged that the liberty known in the state of nature became limited under government, but this was only in order to protect the common good. Law, he declared, is the basis of civil liberty. If the legislature makes laws that are inconsistent with God's laws, or if it undermines the commonwealth's foundations, then men must imitate the example of the Apostles and obey God rather than men. These words seemed to be a definite warning to the legislators of the colony!

At this time the people of Connecticut were complaining of heavy taxation and many believed they were being unjustly deprived of their "liberty and property." Eliot expressed concern about so many people being heavily in debt. "He wondered that honest men and Christians should glory in cheating the people through customs dues." [326] Here we can see the first rumbling of discontent regarding taxes believed to be unjust and a pastor using the ideas of John Locke in laying out what a government should look like and how it should function.

RELIGIOUS DISAGREEMENTS PREPARE MINISTERS TO GRAPPLE WITH POLITICAL CONTROVERSIES

In the years before the Stamp Act, the ministers developed their political ideas even when called upon to deal with religious, rather than political, disagreements. They had to grapple with such ecclesiastical problems as contention over changes in the government of the Congregational Church, the persecution of evangelists during the Great Awakening, and widespread fears of an American Episcopacy.

---

325 Of course, no state of nature, independent of God's providence exists, and as He commands civil government (at least in germ form) in Genesis 9:6 over all men, no man is absolutely without government. However, he may be in a given situation relatively independent of civil government, such as cited. Thus, Locke's *State of Nature* is often considered as a useful philosophical abstraction, relative to and in contrast with the state of a man in civil association. The term sovereignty also should be qualified as between man and man, because Scripture makes clear that God Himself possesses all sovereignty. So man's relative sovereignty is limited and derivative.

326 Baldwin's wording, 48.

The first religious disagreement was an internal one among Congregational churches and dealt with a serious change in their church government. Most Congregationalists believed in democratic independent churches with power in the hands of all the members of each congregation, although the power of the elders was also acknowledged. Many believed strongly in achieving a balance between the democratic and representative elements of government in the Congregational polity. Many also still cherished the independence of each church, and the councils they held jointly were deemed to be purely advisory, not compulsory. But with the increase of Presbyterian Churches, particularly in Connecticut, moves were made to establish an order where the elders held more power and where the decisions of Synods or councils would be binding upon all of the churches.

CONNECTICUT ADOPTS THE SAYBROOK PLATFORM

The Saybrook Platform was drafted by a Synod of only twelve ministers and four laymen. Although it was not really representative of the general feelings of the people, the Connecticut Assembly made it law in 1700 (and so it remained until 1784). The Saybrook Platform made mandatory regional Consociations which would decisively exercise church discipline through a delegated council of the Consociation of churches. If a church or an individual refused to accept their decision, they would stand in contempt of the Consociation. This change in Congregational church government was bitterly resented by those who wished to retain the original Congregational polity of independent churches. Feelings ran high against Governor Saltonstall, who had urged passage of the platform into Connecticut law.[327]

Feelings ran even higher when a law was passed by the Assembly in 1717 permitting the voters of a town to choose the minister of a church, whether or not they were actually members of that church. During discussions on a similar attempt to establish a Synod in Massachusetts with

---

327 For a detailed account of the Saybrook Platform, see H. Shelton Smith, Robert T. Handy, and Lefferts A. Loetscher's *American Christianity*, 3 vols. (New York: Charles Scribner's Sons, 1960), I:225. Passage of the Saybrook Platform provoked a spirited response from Rev. John Wise, an Ipswich pastor, in his *The Churches Quarrel Espoused . . .*, 1710. This was followed by an influential work, not only in its own day, but in 1772 when it was reissued and read avidly by the public which applied to the civil realm the political ideas Wise had laid down in support of religious liberty. That work was *A Vindication of Government of the New England Churches*. Wise wrote in strikingly Lockean terms of man's fundamental rights in the state of nature which ought not to be abrogated by civil government. He never cited Locke, however, but rather used Puffendorf as his authority. The latter was a contemporary of Locke's, living from 1631 to 1704, and wrote his best-known work, *The Law of Nature and Nations* in 1703. In a letter written in August of that year to a relation, the Rev. Richard King, Locke recommended "Puffendorf's little Treatise…." See John Locke, *Works*, 10:308.

superior power over the churches, Reverend John Barnard pleaded for the power of individual churches to be defended and for freedom of the individual conscience when he addressed a ministerial convention in 1738. He declared (in terms that would have pleased Locke):

> The civil Magistrate has nothing to do, to enter with his Directions and Restraints, of Temporal Laws...into these matters. A people have still an unalienable Right to make the best of their Bibles. And when the civil Powers shall take upon them, to form churches, to ascertain who shall, and who shall not, belong to this or that particular church...and when Church-Men...shall pretend to exert an Authority over other Churches, and anathematize those that will not tamely submit themselves to their Determinations; I say, if ever such Principles and Practices should obtain among us, I must have leave to lament over our Churches...."[328]

CONTROVERSIES OVER THE GREAT AWAKENING

The next prominent religious controversy was at the time of "the Great Awakening," a widespread evangelical revival that began in earnest in 1740 with the arrival in New England of the great English evangelist, George Whitefield (1714-70). He taught that all could experience "the new birth" irrespective of rank or position, because all were equal in God's eyes. Ordinary people could easily follow his dynamic teaching, and some began to say that anyone, if filled with the Spirit, could become a minister without going to a seminary or college to be trained in the Bible. Many ministers who had at first welcomed Whitefield warmly, began to view his ministry with less favor fearing the loss of a learned clergy. They also resented allegations by some intemperate itinerant preachers that those who disapproved of their evangelistic fervor were "unconverted." Soon churches and ministers were deeply divided, some supporting and some condemning the Awakening. People began to be divided into "Old Lights" and "New Lights." Soon the "Old Lights" began to persecute the "New Lights." This was particularly the case in Connecticut where the authorities tried to extinguish the influence of those who supported Whitefield. In May 1742, the Assembly forbade any itinerant minister to preach in a town without the consent of the minister there. If he did so, he would have to pay a penalty. If he were a minister from another colony he was subject

---

328 John Barnard, *Convention Sermon of 1738*, cited by Baldwin, 54. Miss Baldwin believed that this was the first use by the clergy of the word "unalienable" in connection with rights.

to expulsion from Connecticut as a vagrant. More laws opposed to the Awakening were passed.

LOCKE'S "UNANSWERABLE LETTER OF TOLERATION"

In 1743 the Assembly repealed their own toleration act of 1708 and passed another act preventing the formation of new Congregational churches without the permission of the legislature. Alice Baldwin relates how ministers in the east part of the colony petitioned the Assembly against this law, while their brothers in Hartford and New Haven supported it.

> Those who opposed it argued that their rights under the constitution and the Act of Toleration of William and Mary were ignored, their rights under their covenants with their churches not maintained and that they were denied the right of trial.... They protested against the interference of the state in religious affairs and referred to Locke and his "unanswerable Letter of Toleration, which we are glad to hear is like [sic] to have a new Edition in this Country.'"[329]

Baldwin goes on to relate how their protests were ignored and the laws against "New Lights" continued. Boys were expelled from Yale for attending New Light meetings and the seniors punished for having Locke's *Letter on Toleration* printed; ministers were deposed for itineracy or for ordaining New Light ministers; men and sometimes women, too, were imprisoned for their conscience's sake. The authorities even removed Justices of the Peace and other governmental officers if they were known to be "New Lights," and the Assembly refused to seat "New Light" representatives.[330]

ELISHA WILLIAMS' DETAILED EXPOSITION OF LOCKE

It was against this gloomy canvas that a flash of light appeared in a 66-page pamphlet written by the Reverend Elisha Williams (1694-1755) entitled *The Essential Rights and Liberties of Protestants: a Seasonable Plea for Liberty of Conscience and the Right of Private Judgment in matters of Religion, without any control from Human Authority*. Reverend Williams was a follower of George Whitefield, and his pamphlet was written to defend the liberties of

---

329 Baldwin, 60.

330 David Brainerd was expelled from Yale and seniors there were disciplined for printing Locke's *Letter on Toleration*. (See Alice Baldwin, 61.)

the "New Lights" against the ministers who opposed them.[331] His pamphlet is notable for its detailed exposition of Locke's *Second Treatise*. Not content with merely citing a few passages, he examined the treatise closely and began his discussion of the origin and end of civil government with a detailed summary titled "a Short Sketch of what the celebrated Mr. Lock [sic] in his *Treatise of Government* has largely demonstrated; and in which it is justly to be presumed all are agreed who understand the natural Rights of Mankind."[332]

Three things lacking in the State of Nature

Discussing the rights of men in the State of Nature he agreed with Locke that "because in such a State of Nature, every man must be Judge of the Breach of the Law of Nature and Executioner too, (even in his own Case) and the greater Part being no strict Observers of Equity and Justice; the Enjoyment of Property in this State is not very safe. Three things are wanting in this State (as the celebrated Lock observes) to render them safe...."[333] Here he lists the three things Locke mentioned (in his chapter, "Of the Ends of Political Society and Government") as: 1) an established known law as the standard of right and wrong; 2) known and impartial judges; 3) the power to enforce their sentences, when right, and to execute them.

The remedy: "to unite together into a Commonwealth"

Reverend Williams, like Locke before him, concluded that the remedy for the lack of these three things is "to unite together into a Commonwealth." As to what natural rights were given up after uniting into a commonwealth, he said that one could easily tell what natural rights the people had entrusted to government "by considering the end for which they had been yielded"; then, in a paraphrase of Locke, he asserted that

---

331 Elisha Williams, a clergyman's son, was born in Hatfield, Massachusetts, and filled several roles in his lifetime: as minister, teacher, lawmaker, and judge. After graduating from Harvard and completing law studies, he became Clerk of the Connecticut Assembly. In 1716 he began four years as tutor to delinquent youths in the town of Wethersfield. At this time he also began to study for the ministry and was ordained pastor of Newington Church, near Hartford in 1721. Between 1725 and 1739 he was rector of Yale University. He then served in the Connecticut Assembly and as a judge of the Superior Court. During the expedition on Louisburg in 1745, he served as an army chaplain and the following year he was made colonel of a regiment. He went to England in 1749 to plead the cause of his men who were owed back pay. He returned to America and died in Wethersfield. For more on this remarkable minister, see my biography in Hall, *Christian History of the American Revolution*, 185.

332 Elisha Williams, *The Essential Rights and Liberties of Protestants...*, in Hall, *Christian History of the American Revolution*, 185a.

333 Williams, 185a.

"The great End of civil Government, is the Preservation of their Persons, their Liberties and Estates, or their Property."[334] This is the extent of the power of civil government over the members of the commonwealth. "This I rest on as certain," he declares, "that no more natural Liberty or Power is given up than is necessary for the Preservation of Person and Property."[335]

Religious Liberty Retained

Having explained what he deemed to be the limited powers of civil government, Williams went on to discuss religious liberty. He affirmed the rights of all men to read the Scriptures for themselves and judge whether those who instruct them in the Scriptures are doing so rightly. He declared that "The members of a Civil State do retain their natural Liberty or Right of judging for themselves in Matters of Religion. Every Man has an equal right to follow the Dictates of his own Conscience in the Affairs of Religion." He went on to say that "Every one is under an indispensible Obligation to search the Scriptures for himself...and to make the best Use of it he can for his own Information in the Will of God, the Nature and Duties of Christianity." Williams also boldly asserted that the individual has "an unalienable Right to judge of the Sense and Meaning of it, and to follow his Judgment wherever it leads him; even an equal Right with any Rulers be they Civil or Ecclesiastical." He affirmed strongly that "No Action is a religious Action without Understanding and Choice in the Agent. Whence it follows, the Rights of Conscience are sacred and equal in all and strictly speaking unalienable."[336] He pointed out further that woven into man's very nature is his power of thinking and reasoning. Therefore, he declared:

> A Man may alienate some Branches of Property and give up his Right in them to others; but he cannot transfer the *Rights of Conscience*, unless he would destroy his rational and moral Powers, or substitute some other to be judged for him at the Tribunal of God.[337]

---

334 Williams, 185a, 185b. The paraphrased passage is from pars. 123 and 124 of the *Second Treatise* where Locke wrote: "And 'tis not without Reason, that he seeks out, and is willing to joyn in Society with others, who are already united, or have a Mind to unite, for the mutual Preservation of their Lives, Liberties, and Estates, which I call by the general Name, Property. The great and Chief End therefore, of Men's uniting into Commonwealths, and putting themselves under Government, is the Preservation of their Property. To which in the state of Nature there are many things wanting."

335 Williams, 186b.

336 Williams, 186d–187b.

337 Williams, 187b.

Where religious authority resides

He pursued the idea of where religious authority resides and concludes that it does not reside anywhere but in the Holy Scriptures. In words that remind one of Locke's *Letter on Toleration*, he wrote:

> What is taught by any established Church, and not contained in Scripture, is indeed the Doctrine of that Church, but not of CHRIST: For none can make Laws to oblige the Church of CHRIST but CHRIST himself.... Again if CHRIST be the *Lord* of the *Conscience*, the sole King in his own Kingdom; then it will follow, that *all such* as in any Manner or Degree *assume* the Power of directing and governing the Consciences of Men, are justly chargeable with *invading* his rightful Dominion; He alone having the Right they claim.[338]

With biting irony he suggested that for anyone to assume power over the consciences of men is like declaring the Scriptures to be defective and insufficient, "and therefore that our Lord who has left us the *Scriptures* for that Purpose, did not know what was necessary and sufficient for us, and has given us a Law, the Defects of which were to be supplied by the wisdom of some of his own wiser Disciples, such would do well to consider, who impose their own Doctrines, Interpretations or Decisions upon any Men by Punishments, legal Incapacities, or any other Methods besides those used and directed to in the sacred Scriptures."[339]

But he did not just inveigh against powers outside of us trying to bind the conscience, but also exhorted each individual to take care what he accepts as truth and upon what authority.

> To submit our Consciences to the Guidance of any Man or Order of Men, is not to reason and act according to our own Understanding; but to take every thing for true, that our spiritual Guide affirms to be so, and that meerly [sic] upon his Authority, without examining into, or seeing the Truth and Reasonableness of it: And in every Instance wherein we thus submit our selves to the Direction of any humane [human] Authority, so far we set aside and renounce all other Authority, our own Light and Reason, and even the Word of God and CHRIST: And the Authority of the Guide we subject our selves unto is substituted in the Stead of all these.... And therefore if our Consciences are under the direction of any humane Authority as to religious Matters; they cease to be under the Direction of CHRIST.[340]

---

338 Williams, 188d–189a.
339 Williams, 189b.
340 Williams, 189b–d.

"CLEAR EVIDENCE OF THE TRANSMISSION THROUGH THE CLERGY OF THE THEORIES OF LOCKE"

In this pamphlet there is, as Alice Baldwin has noted, "clear evidence of the transmission through the clergy of the theories of Locke."[341] Here, too, is an example of "a minister using the very arguments of 1775, declaring that subjects and rulers are bound by the constitution and that a law violating natural and constitutional rights is no law and requires no obedience." This shows, that long before this time, the clergy were confronting and grappling with the issues of individual liberty as challenged by the authorities opposed to the Great Awakening. The very same points they made in connection with religious liberty were as applicable to civil liberty, as may be seen in the sermons and pamphlets of 1775 and 1776.

FEARS OF AN AMERICAN EPISCOPACY

Another matter of grave concern for the dissenting clergy in New England was the possible design of Parliament to saddle New England with an American bishop. They feared that this would mean the gradual or abrupt extinction of the religious liberty which they had fled to the New World to enjoy. In a letter to the Reverend Jedidiah Morse in 1815, John Adams recalled how "the apprehension of episcopacy contributed, fifty years ago, as much as any other cause, to arouse the attention, not only of the inquiring mind, but of the common people, and urge them to close thinking on the constitutional authority of Parliament over the colonies...."[342] In fact, objections to the office of a bishop in America, were based on the power of Parliament to create one. The Church of England had no power to do so outside of Great Britain. "There is no power, or pretended power," wrote Adams, "less than Parliament, that can create Bishops in America."

As New Englanders pondered this question, Adams suggested that their reasoning proceeded along this line:

> ...if Parliament can erect dioceses [sic] and appoint Bishops, they may introduce the whole hierarchy, establish [sic] tythes, forbid marriages [by other than Church of England clergy], establish religion [i.e., the Church of England as the only lawful church], forbid dissenters, make schism heresy, impose penalties extending to life and limbs, as well as to liberty and property.[343]

341 Baldwin, 68.
342 John Adams, Letter to the Reverend Dr. Jedidiah Morse, dated December 2, 1815, in Hall, *Christian History*, 2:41.
343 Ibid, 2:42.

Why the powers of the Church of England were greater in Virginia than in New England

Adams also recalled that members of the Church of England in Massachusetts at that time (as well as subsequently) were greatly outnumbered by Congregationalists, Presbyterians, Anabaptists, Methodists, Quakers, and Moravians. The case in Virginia was very different. Here, he related, "the Church of England was established by law, in exclusion and without toleration of any other denomination. The British Statute, called the Act of Uniformity, was acknowledged as law, and carried into execution by the magistrates." [344]

Strong influence of the Church of England in New York

In New York, the Church of England had such a great influence with the royal governors, counselors, and judges, Adams wrote, "that they dared to grant large tracts of lands to the churches of England, and laid the foundation of the ample riches they still hold; while no other denomination could obtain any [land]." [345]

JONATHAN MAYHEW: CHAMPION OF RELIGIOUS AND CIVIL LIBERTY

In addition to the alarm over the possible action of Parliament in regard to setting up an episcopacy in New England, there was concern as to the actions of the Church of England's "Society for the Propagation of the Gospel." Adams maintained sturdily in his letter to Dr. Morse that the members of the Society "had long perverted their resources from their original design, to the support of Church of England ministers." He then mentioned that "Dr. Mayhew appeared with his comparison between the charter and conduct of the society, shewing their non-conformity with each other." [346]

Jonathan Mayhew (1720-66) was the pastor of the West Church in

---

344 Ibid. Adams does not mention that Virginia did not acknowledge the Toleration Act of 1689, the act on which Locke labored, as applicable to Great Britain's colonies. They told dissenters that it applied only in England. For this reason, the Reverend Samuel Davies, that eloquent Presbyterian pastor, whom Patrick Henry so admired, went to England to find out for himself whether the act applied to the colonies or not. Being told by the authorities there that it did, indeed, apply to the colonies, he brought this information back with him to Virginia. Although the situation improved in Virginia, dissenters were forced to support the Church of England financially as well as their own, and there was still considerable persecution. Young James Madison was indignant at the persecution and jailing of a Baptist pastor in a county adjacent to his own. The charge was that he had been preaching without a license. It is said that the pastor was undeterred and continued to preach through the bars of his cell.

345 Ibid., 42-43.

346 Ibid., 44.

Boston, and became famous for his sermon delivered, in 1750, on *Unlimited Submission and Non-Resistance to the Higher Powers*. His election sermon of 1754 reiterated many of the same ideas used in the 1750 sermon. He was then a young preacher whose vigorous language and bold courage in confronting first, the question of an American Episcopate and then civil as well as religious liberty, stirred men's hearts and started his congregation to think seriously on these issues. Indeed, Baldwin tells us that from 1748 until his untimely death in 1766, "he preached and wrote for the cause so dear to his heart."[347] He was a friend of the patriot leaders in Boston, including James Otis and Samuel Adams (about which there is more in the next chapter).[348] In Mayhew's sermon on the repeal of the Stamp Tax in 1766, he gives these autobiographical details:

> Having been initiated in youth in the doctrines of civil liberty as they were taught by such men as Plato, Demosthenes, Cicero, and other renowned persons, among the ancients; and such as Sydney and Milton, Locke and Hoadley, among the moderns, I liked them; they seemed rational. And having learnt from the holy Scriptures that wise, brave, and virtuous men were always friends to liberty,—that God gave the Israelites a king in his anger, because they had not sense and virtue enough to like a free commonwealth,—and that where 'the Spirit of the Lord is, there is liberty,'—this made me conclude that freedom was a great blessing...."[349]

MAYHEW'S "DISCOURSE CONCERNING UNLIMITED SUBMISSION AND NON-RESISTANCE TO THE HIGHER POWERS"

The ostensible occasion of Mayhew's sermon, preached in January, 1750, was to honor the memory of King Charles I on the anniversary of his death, to honor him indeed, as a saintly man, whose character the Episcopal clergymen in England likened to that of Jesus, and to bemoan his fate at the hand of a rebellious people. Since the time of the Restoration of the Stuart monarchy under Charles's son, Charles II, it had been mandatory to

---

347 Baldwin, 44.

348 Jonathan Mayhew was the son of Experience Mayhew, a distinguished missionary to the Indians. He graduated with honors from Harvard in 1744 and was called to be the pastor of the West Church in Boston in 1747, and here he remained until his death. He preached a practical Christianity based on the Scriptures. In theology, he was an Arminian, that is, one who believed in free will. He strongly supported individual responsibility and private judgment and was a fearless supporter of civil liberty.

349 Cited by J. Wingate Thornton, *The Pulpit of the American Revolution* (1860), in Hall, *Christian History*, 1:374.

celebrate the anniversary of Charles I's death as a fast day and to preach from the pulpit sermons on the subject of unlimited submission and non-resistance to the higher powers. In New England, too, the Episcopal governors saw to it that this day was proclaimed a fast day and that all ministers were to preach on Charles I and submission to the higher powers.

Mayhew was already deeply concerned about the Anglican Society for the Propagation of the Gospel and what he believed to be the Society's misuse of their funds. Thus he decided to take on not only the impious characterizations of Charles I by the Anglican ecclesiastics, but their misuse of Biblical teaching on government, particularly Romans 13:1-8.

Mayhew answers objections to "preaching politics"

In Mayhew's preface to his discourse, he comments that "It is hoped that but few will think the subject of it an improper one to be discoursed on in the pulpit, under a notion that this is preaching politics instead of Christ. However, to remove all prejudices of this sort, I beg it may be remembered that 'all Scripture is profitable for doctrine, for reproof, for correction, for instruction in righteousness.' Why, then, should not those parts of Scripture which relate to civil government be examined and explained from the desk, as well as others?"[350] He also uttered a warning that is as pertinent today as when he gave it:

> Civil Tyranny is usually small in its beginning like "the drop of a bucket," till at length, like a mighty torrent, or the raging waves of the sea, it bears down all before it, and deluges whole countries and empires....[351]

What Scripture says about civil government

Reverend Mayhew begins the body of his sermon by explaining why it is important for a Christian to have a correct understanding of civil government:

> It is evident that the affairs of civil government may properly fall under a moral and religious consideration.... For, although there be a sense, and a very plain and important sense, in which Christ's kingdom is not of this world, his inspired apostles have, nevertheless, laid down some general principles concerning the office of civil rulers, and the duty of subjects, together with the reason and

---

350 Jonathan Mayhew, *Sermon on Unlimited Submission and Non-Resistance to the Higher Powers* (1750), in John Wingate Thornton, *The Pulpit of the American Revolution*, Boston: Gould and Lincoln, 1860, 47.

351 Ibid., 50.

obligation of that duty. And from hence it follows, that it is proper for all who acknowledge the authority of Jesus Christ, and the inspiration of his apostles, to endeavor to understand what is in fact the doctrine which they have delivered concerning this matter. It is the duty of Christian magistrates to inform themselves what it is which their religion teaches concerning the nature and design of their office. And it is equally the duty of all Christian people to inform themselves what it is which their religion teaches concerning that subjection which they owe to the higher powers.[352]

Analysis of Romans 13:1-8 on the authority of the civil magistrate

He refers to the passage from Romans as "the most full and express of any in the New Testament relating to rulers and subjects; and therefore I thought it proper to ground upon it what I had to propose to you with reference to the authority of the civil magistrate, and the subjection which is due to him."[353]

Of great concern to Mayhew was the assumed power of the Church of England to act through the civil authorities to the detriment of dissenters. He made a pointed reference to the proper role of civil rulers (as he believed St. Paul intended) in Romans 13:4. The terms of his argument coincide with what Locke had written in his *Letter on Toleration* on the proper duties of the magistrate which he, too, had obviously derived from Scripture.[354] Reverend Mayhew wrote:

> It is manifest that when the apostle speaks of it as the office of civil rulers to encourage what is good and to punish what is evil, he speaks only of civil good and evil. They are to consult the good of society, as such; not to dictate in religious concerns; not to make laws for the government of men's consciences, and to inflict civil penalties for religious crimes...to give them authority in religious matters, would have been, in effect, to give them authority to extirpate the Christian religion, and to establish the idolatries and superstitions of paganism. And can any one reasonably suppose

---

352 Ibid., 53.

353 Ibid., 54.

354 See Locke's *Letter Concerning Toleration* on the duties of the civil magistrate as not extending to the care of men's souls but only to their civil concerns, *Works*, 6:10-11. See also Locke's introduction to Romans 13 and the duty of Christians to the civil magistrate. Here he says "That St. Paul, in this direction to the Romans, does not so much describe the magistrates that then were in Rome, as tells whence they, and all magistrates, every where, have their authority; and for what end they have it, and should use it." See Locke's "Paraphrase and Notes on St. Paul's Epistle to the Romans" in *A Paraphrase and Notes on the Epistles of St. Paul*, in *Works*, 8:366.

that the apostle had any intention to extend the authority of rulers beyond concerns merely civil and political, to the overthrowing of that religion which he himself was so zealous in propagating?[355]

After a lengthy and close analysis of Romans 13:1-8, Reverend Mayhew sums up his conclusions on the apostle's doctrine concerning the office of civil rulers and the duty of subjects: That civil rulers are, indeed, the ministers of God; that disobedience to them "in the due exercise of their authority" is indeed a sin against God; but that the reason to be subject to the higher powers is when the magistrate's office is properly used for the general welfare."[356]

In words that again are reminiscent of Locke, he declares that not even a parent can demand the absolute and unlimited submission of his children since his authority is only for their good and terminates when they reach their majority.[357] Nor is the Biblical injunction to servants to obey their masters or wives to obey their husbands an absolute one. "But," he asks, "who supposes that the apostle ever intended to teach that children, servants, and wives, should, in all cases whatever, obey their parents, masters, and husbands respectively, never making any opposition to their will, even although they should require them to break the commandments of God, or should causelessly make an attempt upon their lives? No one puts such a sense upon these expressions, however absolute and unlimited."[358]

When magistrates are no longer the ministers of God

He goes on to assert boldly and unequivocally: "When once magistrates act contrary to their office, and the end of their institution, — when they rob and ruin the public, instead of being guardians of its peace and welfare, — they immediately cease to be the ordinance of ministers of God,

---

355 Mayhew's Sermon in Thornton, 58, note a.

356 Mayhew's Sermon in Thornton, 60-61.

357 In the *Second Treatise of Government*, Locke wrote (in Chapter VI, "Of Paternal Power") that "the Father's Power of commanding extends no farther than the Minority of his Children, and to a degree only fit for the Discipline and Government of that Age [of his children]." See also his remarks in the following chapter on the relations between husbands and wives and masters and servants where he points out that the husband has no absolute rights over his wife, children or servants. (See par. 86.)

358 Mayhew's Sermon in Thornton, 66. Here Mayhew also advances the idea that the apostle's views were directed to Christians who (falsely) believed that they no longer owed obedience to any civil magistracy. "Now it is with persons of this licentious opinion and character that the apostle is concerned; and all that was directly to his point was to show that they were bound to submit to magistracy in general." Regarding the duties of parents to their children, Locke asserts (par. 66) that they have not been given "an Authority to make Laws and dispose as they please, of their Lives or Liberties." He repeatedly brings out that the authority of parents extends only to the well-being of their children. *Second Treatise*, par. 66.

and no more deserve that glorious character than common pirates and highwaymen." Here he echoes Locke's comments in the *The Two Treatises of Government*, where he characterizes such men as robbers and pirates.[359]

Government as a trust

His remarks on government as a trust whose only true authority lies in the people's consent, without which it is lawless force and usurpation, contain more echoes of Locke who insisted repeatedly that civil government was a trust. Mayhew wrote:

> Whoever considers the nature of civil government, must indeed be sensible that a great degree of implicit confidence must unavoidably be placed in those that bear rule: this is implied in the very notion of authority's being originally a trust committed by the people to those who are vested with it,—as all just and righteous authority is. All besides is mere lawless force and usurpation; neither God nor nature having given any man a right of dominion over any society independently of that society's approbation and consent to be governed by him.[360]

When neither the law of reason nor of religion requires submission to those in authority

Like Locke, Mayhew notes that "it cannot be supposed that the public affairs of any state should be always administered in the best manner possible," and may even be poorly managed, but that this is not sufficient to legitimate disobedience to the higher powers.[361] Following such a principle would throw all into anarchy. "But it is equally evident, upon the other hand, that those in authority may abuse their trust and power to such a degree, that neither the law of reason nor of religion requires that any obedience or submission should be paid to them...." On the contrary, their authority should be put into other hands which will exercise it "to those good purposes for which it was given."[362]

---

359 See passages in Locke's *Two Treatises of Government* where he speaks of pirates (Book I:IX, par. 81) and of robbers and pirates (Book II:XVI, par. 176) in connection with unjust power over men.

360 Mayhew's *Sermon on Unlimited Submission*, in Thornton, 86, note a. On Locke's view of civil government as a trust, see *Second Treatise*, pars. 22, 134, 136, 156, 171, 231, and particularly, par. 142 on the bounds of the power entrusted to legislators and pars. 221, 222, 239, 240, 242 on the dissolving of a government that acts contrary to its trust.

361 Locke denies the supposition that the people will want to set up a new legislature over small issues. Locke says: "...such Revolutions happen not upon every little mismanagement in public affairs." It is only if there are "a long train of abuses...all tending the same way," that the people "rouze themselves" and are willing to put the rule into the hands of those "who may secure to them the ends for which Government was at first erected." (*Second Treatise*, par. 25.)

362 Mayhew's Sermon in Thornton, 87, note a.

Both rulers and people are bound by the law and the constitution

Regarding the doctrine of unlimited submission to civil government, so assiduously advanced by the Church of England, Mayhew declared bluntly: "We may very safely assert these two things in general, without undermining government: One is, that no civil rulers are to be obeyed when they enjoin things that are inconsistent with the commands of God."[363] And, like Locke, Mayhew believed firmly that both rulers and people are equally bound by the law and the constitution.

Charles I's crimes against his people exposed

As to the supposedly saintly character of Charles I, Mayhew hesitated not a moment to expose the truth about that "unhappy king" who victimized his people and—as was typical of the Stuarts—believed no one had a right to challenge his actions. He reminded his congregation, lest they had forgotten, that Charles had sent many members of both houses of Parliament to the Tower for opposing his arbitrary attempts to raise money without their consent; that he had imprisoned countless numbers of merchants and gentry for refusing to pay his illegal taxes; and that he had refused to call Parliament for twelve years, "during all which time he governed in an absolute, lawless, and despotic manner." He reminded them, too, that during this time Charles constantly promoted Roman Catholics to the highest offices of trust in the government and aided France to massacre thousands of French Protestants at Rochelle. Worst of all, in 1627, he sent a large sum of money to Germany to pay for foreign troops to aid him in putting down any insurrection of his own people resulting from his illegal taxation. Finally, he entered the House of Commons surrounded by an armed force to demand five of its most important members to be given into his hands. "This," Mayhew concluded, "was a prelude to that unnatural war which he soon after levied against his own dutiful subjects...."[364]

Reasons for the Anglican clergy's saintly portrayal of Charles I

Nevertheless, even though a Hanoverian monarch now occupied the throne, and the last Stuart king had gone into exile because of his arrogance at the time of the Glorious Revolution, the Anglican clergy still

---

363 Mayhew's Sermon in Thornton, 86.
364 Mayhew's Sermon in Thornton, 90-92, 101-02.

insisted on portraying Charles as a saint, and those who had established a true constitutional monarchy, as villains of the worst kind. Mayhew saw this as evidence that Charles was beloved by the Anglican clergy because he always gave them the right to persecute dissenters as much as they liked—as long as they were his willing tools.

Toward the end of this remarkably courageous sermon, Mayhew expressed his hope that the anniversary of the death of Charles I, though often used for bad purposes by the established clergy, might serve a good end by becoming "a standing memento that Britons will not be slaves, and a warning to all corrupt counsellors and ministers not to go too far in advising to arbitrary, despotic measures." [365]

MAYHEW CONTINUES
TO RESIST BRITISH TYRANNY

By the time of the Stamp Act, Mayhew was a strong supporter of the Boston patriotic resistance to British tyranny. He was known in both the colonies and the Mother Country for his vigorous defense of the rights of the colonists and, in particular, their right to resist unjust laws imposed by Great Britain—laws which had not been passed by the colonists' own legislators and hence had not received the sanction of the people. His sermon on the repeal of the Stamp Tax, titled *The Snare Broken*, was published six days after he gave it, and a second edition appeared the following year. This was followed by its publication in England.

A "communion of colonies" likened to a "communion of churches"

After the repeal of the Stamp Tax Mayhew suggested to James Otis that the Massachusetts Assembly send congratulatory letters to the other assemblies because of their united opposition to the measure. Such a "communion of colonies" he likened to a "communion of churches." He thought that the colonial assemblies should keep in touch with each other so that, in future, if faced with other difficulties with the Mother Country (which, as it turned out, were not long in coming), such a correspondence and united efforts by the colonies through this means might be the only way they could retain their liberties. As it turned out, it was not Otis who put this plan into motion, but Samuel Adams, as will be seen in the next chapter.

---

365 Mayhew's Sermon in Thornton, 103-104.

ANDREW ELIOT'S ELECTION SERMON OF 1765

Another influential, although less known, Pastor was Andrew Eliot (1718-1778) of the North Church in Boston.[366] He, too, was a friend of James Otis, the two Adamses, and John Hancock. Like Mayhew, he was a close student of Locke and Sydney and other writers on civil government. On May 29, 1765, the very day that Patrick Henry made an impassioned speech on the Stamp Act in the Virginia House of Burgesses, Andrew Eliot preached an Election Sermon before the governor and the General Court. Although respectful in tone and expressing admiration for the government of Great Britain, he discussed its constitution as having been achieved by a compact between the king and his people through their representatives. He also described the Massachusetts Charter as a sacred compact between the King and the colony. He spoke of the right of the colonists to resist unjust laws and warned against interfering with their liberties by altering their governments.

STEPHEN JOHNSON ROUSES
RESISTANCE TO THE STAMP ACT

But it was the writings of the Reverend Stephen Johnson, another Lockean thinker, on the Stamp Act (including a Fast Day Sermon on the subject) that made perhaps the greatest impression on readers throughout the colonies. Johnson was not a prominent minister of a major city, but only the pastor of a church in the small Connecticut village of Lyme. He was, however, a powerful thinker and writer. After having perused some papers on the Stamp Act (probably copies of the *Virginia Resolves*), he wrote six articles for the *New London Gazette* which appeared between September 29 and November 1, 1765. These articles were sent to all the other colonies by express riders where they were reprinted and circulated. In true Lockean style, Johnson asserted:

1) That the colonial charters were compacts which, if violated by either party, left the other free of any further obligation.

2) That the constitution of Great Britain ensured [natural] rights that were actually "antecedent to all earthly governments" because they came from "the great Legislator of the universe" and that if the colonists lost these rights it would bring slavery upon their posterity.

---

366 Andrew Eliot, a graduate of Harvard in 1737, was ordained pastor of the New North Church in 1742 where he remained until his death. When Boston was occupied by the British, he helped its suffering inhabitants and ministered to the sick and wounded who were being held prisoners. Although elected president of Harvard, he declined the honor, because he was too attached to his parishioners to leave them. An eloquent speaker, a volume of his sermons was published in 1774.

3) That the people must not be lulled into a false sense of security, but must be ever alert to the dangers to their liberties, and to the necessity of giving specific instruction to their representatives in the case of a future crisis.

Independence being forced on the colonies

His *Fast Day Sermon* was also issued as a pamphlet. It was one of the boldest sermons of the period in which Johnson foresaw the abolition of the colonial charters, and the removal of their governments, all of which would break their connection with Great Britain and which would leave them "absolutely in a state of nature." If this happened he believed they would then be in a position to choose a new government. It was not that the colonists desired independence, he hastened to declare, but that independence might be forced upon them. Such had been the case in the time of Rehoboam (1 Kings 12). Independence had also been forced upon Holland through the despotism of Spain. He believed that if there were a choice between slavery and independence, the colonists would not hesitate to choose independence.

When a state of war existed

He then answered the unspoken question that must have been in the minds of many in his congregation that morning: How could they rightly rebel against the edicts of Great Britain? He declared that they could do so if its edicts were unconstitutional. Referring directly to Locke, he said that any attempt to take away their natural rights constituted a state of war where the people were free to assume their rights and defend them. "May we not ask," he told his congregation, "who is the agressor [sic], he that invades the right of a free people, or they that defend what is only their own?" [367]

"EVERY VILLAGER...COULD TALK LEARNEDLY OF THE REASONS FOR REFUSING TO PAY THE [STAMP] TAX"

Soon other Connecticut pastors joined Johnson in opposing the Stamp Tax and teaching their flocks the reasons why resistance was appropriate.[368] As Miss Baldwin observed of the New England ministers' political education of their congregations at this time: "Every villager who attended

---

367 Stephen Johnson, *Fast Day Sermon*, December 18, 1765, 26.

368 Many other Thanksgiving Sermons were preached after repeal of the Stamp Tax, among them a vigorous one by William A. Patten, of Halifax, Massachusetts. He declared that members of civil society retained all rights they had not agreed to surrender to government, and he cited Locke on the right of the people to decide when their rulers had wronged them. (See Baldwin, 96–97.)

church on the Sabbath day could talk learnedly of the reasons for refusing to pay the tax."[369] What a fitting tribute to these courageous and learned pastors!

NEW ACTS OF TYRANNY

Rejoicing from pulpit and people on the repeal of the Stamp Tax was short lived. They soon learned that when Parliament repealed the tax, it also passed a Declaratory Act stating that Parliament had the authority, power, and right to make laws binding on the colonies, in all cases, whatsoever. This unwelcome declaration was followed in 1767 by the Townshend, or Revenue, Act levying new taxes on the colonies. These new taxes were on paper, glass, painters' colors, sugar—and tea. The tax on tea was low, however, and Lord Townshend may have thought that this would mollify the colonies.

Mercy Otis Warren (1728-1814), the sister of James Otis, Boston lawyer and patriot, wrote in her history of the American Revolution that this "inconsiderable duty on teas finally became an object of high importance and altercation; it was not the sum, but the principle that was contested...."[370] In this and the ensuing events, it is clear that the New England clergy prepared their congregations—and the colonial leaders—to ponder the issue of taxation from the standpoint of principle. That principle was that men should not be deprived of any part of their liberty or property without their own consent exercised through their elected representatives.

PROPERTY AND GOVERNMENT
MUST STAND OR FALL TOGETHER

On January 12, 1768, the Massachusetts Legislature wrote to their agent in London of their determination to seek redress. In the course of their long, impassioned letter, they outlined their political philosophy in very Lockean terms:

> It is the glory of the British constitution that it hath its foundations in the law of God and nature. It is an essential, natural right, that a man shall quietly enjoy, and have the sole disposal of his own property. This right is adopted into the constitution. This natural and constitutional right is so familiar to the American subjects, that it would be difficult, if possible, to convince them, that any

---

369 Baldwin, 104.
370 Mercy Otis Warren, *History of the Rise, Progress, and Termination of the American Revolution*, 2 vols. (Boston, 1805), in Hall, *Christian History of the American Revolution*, 367b.

necessity can render it just, equitable and reasonable, in the nature of things, that the Parliament should impose duties, subsidies, talliages, and taxes upon them internal or external, for the sole purpose of raising a revenue. The reason is obvious; because, they cannot be represented [in Parliament], and therefore, their consent cannot be constitutionally had in Parliament.[371]

The letter went on to declare that "The security of right and property, is the great end of government. Surely, then, such measures as tend to render right and property precarious, tend to destroy both property and government; for these must stand and fall together."[372]

COLONIAL LEGISLATURES DISSOLVED

In 1768, at the suggestion of James Otis, the Massachusetts legislature sent to the speakers of the legislative bodies of the other colonies a circular letter asking for their views on the matter and expressing their own views which were couched in similar terms to their strongly-worded letter to their London agent. When London learned of this letter, Lord Hillsborough, who had replaced Townshend, ordered Massachusetts Governor Bernard to require the House of Representatives to rescind the letter. When they refused to do so, Governor Bernard (1712-1779) dissolved the legislature. (Several other colonial legislatures were dissolved for the same reason.)

A convention of patriots was held in Boston, September 22, giving members of the public time to express themselves on the issue facing them. As a result, the Convention decided to enter into non-importation agreements. This so angered Parliament that they ordered Governor Bernard to send to England the "principal offenders" in the matter to stand trial, and some 4,000 British troops were sent to Boston ostensibly "to aid in the collection of the duties."

THE LEGISLATURE RESISTS A
STANDING ARMY IN TIME OF PEACE

In the spring of 1769, the Legislature answered Governor Bernard's insistent messages as to whether they were prepared to provide for the King's troops by asserting that they would not do so and objecting that Parliament was wrongfully attempting to keep a standing army in their colony in time of peace. It then demanded that the governor order these troops and vessels

---

371 See Letter to Dennys de Berdt, Massachusetts agent in London, dated January 12, 1768, in Hall, *Christian History*, 2:453.

372 Ibid., 455.

"out of this port and the gates of this city...."[373] Governor Bernard, of course, did nothing of the kind. On March 20, he returned to England to explain to Parliament why matters had arrived at such a pass. Parliament grilled him severely, but in the end the King made him a baronet. In Bernard's absence the government was left in the hands of Lieutenant-Governor Thomas Hutchinson (1711–1780), who was as determined as Bernard had been to carry out the British ministry's orders. Feelings continued to run high among Bostonians and, on March 5, 1770, led to the collision between soldiers and citizens known as "the Boston Massacre."

CONTINUED RESISTANCE TO BRITISH OPPRESSION

During these tense times the patriotic Congregational clergy continued to support the resistance to these illegal acts of Parliament. When the Legislature met on Election Day, May 30, 1770, it was not in Boston as was customary, but at Harvard College, Cambridge, where Governor Hutchinson had ordered them to meet. Here they heard Samuel Cooke, pastor of a church in Cambridge, preach a highly significant sermon on "He that ruleth over men must be just, ruling in the fear of God...." 2 Samuel 23:3, 4.

SAMUEL COOKE'S LOCKEAN RÉSUMÉ OF THE ORIGINS OF CIVIL GOVERNMENT

In his election sermon before Governor Hutchinson, Samuel Cooke began by giving a sweeping overview of the history and ends of civil government, grounding it in Revelation and in God's Law of Nature.[374] He gave a very Lockean résumé of the transition from the state of nature to civil government and a full discussion of the natural rights men retain under whatever form of government they choose. True, Cooke does not mention Locke by name, but he probably didn't need to do so, since his hearers were already familiar with "the great Mr. Locke."

Those in authority "are accountable to the society which gave them their political existence"

Cooke discussed how "A society emerging from a state of nature, in respect to authority, are all upon a level, no individual can justly challenge a right to make or execute the laws by which it is to be governed, but only

---

373 See Thornton, 152–53.

374 Dr. Samuel Cooke was a graduate of Harvard and was sixty-two years old at the time he delivered this momentous election sermon.

by the choice or general consent of the community." It is the people who "have a right, under God, to determine who shall exercise this trust for the common interest, and to fix the bounds of their authority." Therefore, as he went on to say, those in authority "are accountable to the society which gave them their political existence."[375] These were bold words, indeed, but bolder were to come:

> This is evidently the natural origin and state of all civil government, the sole end and design of which is, not to ennoble a few and enslave the multitude, but the public benefit, the good of the people; that they may be protected in their persons, and secured in the enjoyment of all their rights, and be enabled to lead quiet and peaceable lives in all godliness and honesty![376]

Rulers are all those in places of power and trust

Lest there be any misunderstanding as to what is meant in the Bible by the term "rulers," Cooke maintained that "By the ruler in the text is intended not only the king as supreme, but also every one in subordinate place of power and trust, whether they act in legislative or executive capacity, or both. In whatever station men act for the public, they are included in this general term, and must direct their conduct by the same upright principles.[377]

Rulers are obliged to rule as ministers of God for the people's good

Perhaps he let his gaze rest upon Lieutenant-Governor Hutchinson at this point, then after a moment to let his words sink in, he continued by warning that "justice" used in the Biblical text was not to be taken in a limited, narrow sense. It was, he said, "a general term, including every quality necessary to be exercised for the public good by those who accept the charge of it. Justice must be tempered with wisdom, prudence, and clemency, otherwise it will degenerate into rigor and oppression." Then, continuing his warning, he declared that "This solemn charge given to rulers is not an arbitrary injunction imposed by God, but is founded in the most obvious laws of nature and reason. Rulers are appointed for this very end—to be ministers of God for good." We can imagine him again fixing his eye upon Hutchinson as he continued by asserting that the people have

---

375 Cooke, *Election Sermon*, May 30, 1770, Boston: Edes and Gill, 1770, in Thornton, 158-59.
376 Ibid., 159.
377 Ibid., 161.

a right to expect that this is how their rulers will govern and, indeed, to require it "as their unquestionable due."[378]

The Constitution must be maintained in its entirety

Cooke also made some acute observations on the nature of the constitution. "A free state will no longer continue so than while the constitution is maintained entire in all its branches and connections." If the legislative powers become entirely independent of each other, he maintained that this would cause "schism in the body politic...." Then he focused on the greatest constitutional concern facing the colonists. He explained that "the effect is the same when the executive is in no degree under the control of the legislative power,—the balance is destroyed, and the execution of the laws left to arbitrary will."

At this point Hutchinson could not have failed to see the drift of the pastor's argument. Like Governor Bernard and the other royal governors before him, Hutchinson believed himself absolutely bound by the instructions he received from the English ministry on all colonial matters, whether or not these instructions violated the English Constitution. Worse, he and Governor Bernard favored—even urged—Great Britain to send troops (foreign troops, at that) to force the colonists to comply with the orders of the ministry in England.

HUTCHINSON VIEWS THE PATRIOT PASTORS AS TROUBLEMAKERS

Although a native of Massachusetts and a distinguished historian of his province, Hutchinson was to side consistently with Great Britain, and viewed the patriot pastors as troublemakers—or worse. He could not understand what Reverend Cooke saw so clearly: that a state in which the executive power cannot be checked by the legislative—when in fact it is completely divorced from the legislative—liberty cannot last. In a vivid image Cooke warned:

> The several branches of civil power, as joint pillars, each bearing its due proportion, are the support, and the only proper support, of a political structure regularly formed. A constitution which cannot support its own weight must fall; it must be supposed essentially defective in its form or administration.[379]

---

378 Ibid., 161-62.
379 Ibid., 165.

Use of the military in time of peace
"a very improper safeguard"

Nor was Cooke reluctant to take up the question of England sending over foreign mercenaries to cow the colonists into submission. "Military aid," said he, "has ever been deemed dangerous to a free civil state, and often has been used as an effectual engine to subvert it." While the military in time of war has been England's "glory and defence," in time of peace it was "a very improper safeguard to a constitution which has liberty, British liberty, for its basis."[380]

Agreement with Locke on the people's reluctance to rebel

To the charge that views such as his encouraged rebellion and anarchy, he pointed out that the people are not so easily moved. Like Locke, he took the view that "The body of a people are disposed to lead quiet and peaceable lives, and it is their highest interest to support the government under which their quietness is ensured. They retain a reverence for their superiors, and seldom foresee or suspect danger till they feel their burdens."[381]

Cooke envisions a government that reaches from sea to sea

As to the quarrel with Great Britain, he insists that "Americans esteem it their greatest infelicity that, through necessity, they are thus led to plead with their parent state…whose interest has always been dear to them, and whose wealth they have increased by their removal [to America] more than their own. They have assisted in fighting her battles, and greatly enlarged her empire, and, God helping, will yet extend it through the boundless desert, until it reach from sea to sea." In a note on this passage, Cooke adds: "Their losses and private expenses, in watches, guards, and garrisons for their defence, and from continual alarms, in all their former wars, have greatly exceeded the public charges."[382] This was an answer to the English view that it needed revenues from America in order to defend it properly.

The colonists' case founded in nature, compact, and their rights as men and as British subjects

He went on to emphasize that the colonists glory in the British constitution and abhor the idea of withdrawing their allegiance from their gracious

---

380 Ibid.

381 Ibid., 167. Locke had written in Chapter XIX of the *Second Treatise*, "For till the mischief be grown general, and the ill designs of the Rulers become visible, or their attempts sensible to the greater part, the People, who are more disposed to suffer, than right themselves by Resistance, are not apt to stir." (See *Second Treatise* in Hall, *Christian History*, par. 230, 1:120.)

382 Ibid., 184.

sovereign and becoming an independent state. They are fully sensible of the mutual benefits of trade with the mother country "and cheerfully submit to regulations of trade productive of the common interest." In his plea that the alarming disputes with the mother country be speedily resolved, he also continued to insist that Americans did not consider their case as "novel, or wantonly made, but founded in nature, in compact, in their rights as men and British subjects....[383]

SIMEON HOWARD'S ARTILLERY-ELECTION SERMON

Another pastor who spoke to the issues facing Boston and all of Massachusetts was Simeon Howard (1733-1804).[384] Although Samuel Cooke did not mention Locke by name in his fine sermon, Simeon Howard did refer specifically to Locke in his Artillery-Election Sermon of June 7, 1773. As we shall see, Reverend Howard's detailed description of the state of nature follows Locke closely, thus belying the notion that Howard (and other pastors) merely used Locke to support whatever position they were taking, with little real knowledge of his ideas.[385]

Howard's definitions of liberty stemming from his Biblical text

Howard took as his text, "Stand fast therefore in the liberty wherewith Christ hath made us free." (Galatians 5:1) After discussing the burdensome Jewish ceremonial laws from which men were freed by Christ, he remarks that "though the words originally refer to that freedom from the Jewish law which the gospel confers on the church of God; yet the reason of the inference holds good in the case of any other real and valuable liberty which men had a right to: So that this observation is plainly deducible from the text: viz. that it is the duty of all men to stand fast in such valuable liberty, as providence has conferred upon them."[386]

He observed that the word liberty is used in different ways, but explained that he intended to dwell mainly on that liberty which is opposed to unjust external force and constraint of men upon each other.

---

383 Ibid., 184-85.

384 See my biography of Howard in Hall, *Christian History of the American Revolution*, 564.

385 It is difficult to see why Bernard Bailyn referred to Howard using Locke to validate his "off hand description of the state of nature," as Howard gave a very accurate and detailed rendering of Lockean ideas in this sermon. Although Bailyn acknowledged that some pastors cited Locke with precision, others (including Howard) he believed referred to him casually "as if he could be relied on to support anything the writers happened to be arguing." (See Bailyn, *The Ideological Origins of the American Revolution*, 28.)

386 Simeon Howard, *Sermon Preached to the Ancient and Honorable Artillery Company*, Boston, 1773, in Hall, *Christian History of the American Revolution*, 193.

Liberty in a State of Nature

"In a state of nature, or where men are under no civil government," Howard reminded the assemblage, "God has given to every one liberty to pursue his own happiness in whatever way, and by whatever means he pleases, without asking the consent or consulting the inclination of any other man, provided he keeps within the bounds of the law of nature. Within these bounds, he may govern his actions, and dispose of his property and person, as he thinks proper."[387] Nor has anyone a right to restrain him in his liberty. But, Howard warns, "This however is not a state of licentiousness, for the law of nature which bounds this liberty forbids all injustice and wickedness; allows no man to injure another in his person or property, or to destroy his own life."[388] But experience soon teaches men that the violent and unruly among them will encroach on the liberty of the others. "This gave birth to civil society, and induced a number of individuals to combine together for mutual defence and security...."[389]

Liberty under Civil Government

Like Locke, Howard also distinguished between liberty in the state of nature and under civil government. "In a state of nature it is all that liberty which is consistent with the law of nature; under civil government, it is all which is consistent with the law of nature, and with such restrictions as they have consented to come under consistently with the law of nature and the end of society...."[390]

Civil liberty ought to be defended

In his discussion concerning the right to resist tyranny and slavery, he insisted that only defensive warfare is just (in this, he was in agreement with the other patriot pastors). But liberty, he averred "is a trust committed to us by heaven: we are accountable for the use we make of it, and ought therefore, to the best of our power, to defend it."[391]

The destruction of civil liberty fatal to religion

Toward the end of his sermon, he reminded the governor, his council, and the assembled House of Representatives of their duty as fathers: "Every man is bound both by the law of nature and revelation, to provide in the best manner he can, for the temporal happiness of his family; and he that

---

387 Ibid., 193-94. (Hall, editor's note: "See Locke on Government," 194a.)
388 Ibid. (See Locke's Second *Treatise*, par. 6.)
389 Ibid., 194. (See Locke, Second *Treatise*, pars. 28, 123.)
390 Ibid., 197. (See similar statement in Locke, *Second Treatise*, par. 22.)
391 Ibid., 202.

neglects this, has, according to the declaration of an inspired apostle, denied the faith, and is worse than an infidel. But in what way can a man be more justly chargeable with this neglect, than by suffering himself to be deprived of his life, liberty, or property, when he might lawfully have preserved them?"[392] He also pointedly asserted that "the destruction of civil liberty is generally fatal to religion. The latter has seldom existed long in any place without the former."[393]

REV. GAD HITCHCOCK'S LOCKEAN SERMONS

As a result of the Boston Tea Party, England named General Thomas Gage to be the new governor of Massachusetts. In the spring of 1774, Rev. Gad Hitchcock (1718-1803) of Pembroke, was asked to give the annual Election Sermon before the Governor, his council and the House of Representatives. "At that time it was not anticipated that General Gage would be governor, still less that he would appear personally at the ceremonies. When it was discovered that Gage did in fact plan to attend, Hitchcock was urged to speak with the utmost discretion. When the day came, however, he spoke out as fearlessly as if the General in all his royal authority had not been facing him and addressed the Governor bluntly.[394]

The people are the only earthly source of civil authority

"The people are the only source of civil authority on earth," Hitchcock declared. As if in warning to General Gage, he went on to say: "Civil authority is the production of combined society—not born with, but delegated to certain individuals for the advancement of the common benefit." Employing Lockean terms, he said that when the power of the government was abused, it was the people's duty to give it into other hands. He also boldly asserted: "If I am mistaken in supposing plans are formed, and executing, subversive of our natural and charter rights...and incompatible with every idea of liberty, all America is mistaken with me."[395]

The Apostle Paul stands fast for his liberty as a Roman citizen. Governor Gage listened to these fearless words with mounting anger as Hitchcock insisted that the danger facing the people of Massachusetts was "not visionary, but real.... Our contention is not about trifles, but about liberty and property; and not ours only, but those of posterity, to the latest generation...." He spoke of the Apostle Paul who was "on all occasions for

---

392 Ibid.
393 Ibid., 203.
394 See my biography of Gad Hitchcock in Hall, *Christian History of the American Revolution*, 563.
395 Ibid.

standing fast not only in the liberties with which Christ had made him free...but also in that liberty, with which the laws of nature, and the Roman state, had made him free from oppression and tyranny." [396]

Although the fuming governor did not walk out on Hitchcock's sermon, many offended Tories did. (Hitchcock later admitted ruefully that it must have been a very moving sermon because so many people got up and left while he was preaching.)

REVEREND HITCHCOCK'S PLYMOUTH ANNIVERSARY SERMON

By the time Hitchcock preached his notable sermon at Plymouth on December 22, memorializing the arrival of the Pilgrim Fathers, the British had closed the Port of Boston (July 1, 1774), an act designed to frighten the other colonies into submission. Instead, there was an outpouring of sympathy for their Massachusetts brothers, and goods came into Massachusetts despite the blockade. Most of all, instead of dividing the colonies, it united them firmly in their resolution to resist the English ministry; nonimportation of English goods was the watchword and the colonies were united in the first Continental Congress.

Reverend Hitchcock spoke with deep feeling of the sufferings the Pilgrims had endured in England which had caused them to flee first to Holland and then to America in search of liberty. He then expounded upon both spiritual and civil liberty. In discussing civil liberty, there were strong echoes from Locke. "Civil liberty is indeed, immediately derived from human compact, and founded on civil government; but it more properly, though remotely, proceeds from nature, as it is the voice of reason that men, for the greater security of their persons and property, and the promotion of their happiness, should form into society, and establish government among them." [397]

Both religious and civil rights depend on liberty

He went on to remind the congregation that both their civil and religious rights depend on liberty. Then, in a sentence that could have been taken from Locke's writings on religious toleration, he made the distinction between the objectives of each. "Matters that pertain to conscience, and the worship and service of God, and the preparation of our Souls for

---

396 Ibid.
397 Gad Hitchcock, *A Sermon Preached at Plymouth*, December 22, 1774, in Hall, *Christian History of the American Revolution*, 32.

another world, are the objects of religious liberty; and those things that relate to our present security and happiness in civil government, are the objects of civil liberty."[398]

Liberty according to "Mr. Locke, that prince of philosophers"

Hitchcock saw many examples in the Old and New Testaments of their friendliness to the cause of liberty, spiritual and civil. He concluded that "no man in [the] community, of any rank or character whatever, can be uninterested in the cause of liberty; or lawfully neglect it; much less make use of his influence in opposing and bearing it down. It is a common cause and a right of nature. Every man that is born into the world, as Mr. Lock [sic], that prince of philosophers hath said, 'is born to it,' and every member of civil and religious society has an unalienable title to, and concern in it; and is bound by the most sacred and indissoluble ties, in a just exertion of his abilities and by every adequate method, to spread the love of it among mankind, and defend it, against tyrants and oppressors."[399]

Liberty a right of nature confirmed by Revelation

Earnestly he contended, "As liberty is the right of nature, confirmed to us by revelation, and essential to our happiness, we ought to be deeply humbled under the tokens of the divine resentments, in suffering so great an adversity to befal [sic] us, as that of being obliged to contend for it in opposition to measures contrived to deprive us of so rich a blessing."[400]

He regretted that there should be contention with the parent state, "Is there any good news from our mother country? Any thing to raise the hopes of our own? Can America entertain expectations from [B]ritish justice or parental sympathy of a deliverance out of her distresses?" He urged that "in the midst of our perplexity and fear, then let us look to God, who is high above all nations; and may we all as one man, break off our sins by repentance, and our iniquities by turning to the Lord...."

Attention to public affairs "a symptom of vital strength in the body politic"

Hitchcock believed that the alarm gone through the land and the great attention to public affairs by all, was "a token for the good, a symptom of vital strength, in the body politic" and that "the firm union and cement of our numerous colonies" and their agreement in the best ways to oppose

---

398 Ibid. Locke also made this point in his *Letter Concerning Toleration*. See *Works*, 6:10-13.
399 Ibid., 41. See par. 55 of Locke's *Second Treatise of Government*.
400 Ibid., 42.

unconstitutional measures showed "the efficacy of the divine influence on the minds of men." Since God works by "means and instruments" in order to accomplish his purposes among men, he earnestly exhorted the congregation not "to expect a deliverance out of our political evils by the immediate exertion of almighty power," but to work themselves, all the while depending on "the divine energy and blessing, and, from the justice of our cause, may we expect that God will work with us and in us, and crown our endeavours with success."[401]

The "much esteemed American Continental Congress"

He believed further that the efforts of the "much esteemed American Continental Congress, whom we voluntarily constitute the guardians of our rights" could bring about a reconciliation with the mother country "and lasting connection with our brethren at home." If not, then he trusted that "we may with firm hope and humble reliance, implore the aids of his providence, who is the almighty avenger of wrongs, with whom is wisdom and strength...."[402]

THE INFLUENCE OF THE CLERGY ON THE POLITICAL LEADERS

The sermons discussed in this chapter are just a few of many on civil government preached by the New England clergy before, during, and after the American Revolution. These sermons educated their congregations and the patriot leaders that emerged to defend colonial liberties, men like James Otis and Samuel Adams. As Alice Baldwin noted, "The clergy were not a class apart. They were the fellow-students, the teachers, and friends of professional and business men and the pastors and guides of less learned farmers. If Mayhew and [Andrew] Eliot read Locke and Sydney and found their teachings deepened and strengthened by the Bible, it is probable that they talked over their convictions with Otis and Thacher and other friends."[403]

John and Samuel Adams and John Hancock were also friendly with Rev. Samuel Cooper, pastor of the Brattle Street Church in Boston and Charles Chauncey of the First Church, as well as Mayhew and Eliot, and often looked to them for counsel. As Baldwin summarized so cogently:

---

401 Ibid.

402 Ibid., 42-43.

403 Baldwin, 169. Mayhew was friendly—and influential—with all the Boston patriot leaders, including John Adams, who admired him greatly.

All through the New England colonies the ministers were helping to spread the theories of the philosophers and to give them
religious sanction. Thus when the trouble with England came to a
head, New Englanders were accustomed to thinking and to arguing
for their rights in terms of natural law, the constitution, government by consent, and the right of resistance, and believed that by
so doing they were following the injunctions of God.[404]

As she also noted, "Old and New Testaments, classic writers, modern
and ancient philosophers and divines and often 'the great Mr. Lock [sic]'
were cited in proof of the duty as well as the right to resist tyranny and
any attack upon the rights of men."[405]

The New England clergy urge defense, not defiance, of law

Here, however, we must interject a cautionary note: The New England
clergy were outspoken in their determination to defend liberty, but this
does not mean that they urged refusal to obey constitutional power. Far
from it. They contended for constitutional law and only against King and
Parliament when these flouted either the constitutional law of England or
the divine Law of Nature. Thus, the New England clergy were the sponsors
of a supremely constructive revolution, one that was in defense of law,
rather than in defiance of it.

> Those who expect to find any thing very satisfactory on
> [the natural rights of colonists] in particular,
> or with regard to the law of nature in general
> in the writings of such authors as Grotius and Pufendorf,
> will find themselves much mistaken.
> It is their constant practice to establish
> the matter of right on the matter of fact....
> The sentiments on this subject have therefore been drawn
> from the purer fountains of one or two of
> our English writers, particularly from Mr. Locke....
>
> (James Otis
> *The Rights of the British Colonies*, 1764)

---

404 Baldwin, 169–170.
405 Baldwin, 129.

CHAPTER EIGHT

Sovereign: King, Parliament, or . . . ?

Mr. Locke says, that security of property is the end for which
men enter into society.... It is certainly more concordant with
the great law of nature and reason...to suppose that the
Colonies are separate, independent and free, than to suppose
that they must be one with Great Britain and slaves. And slaves
they must be...if Great Britain may make all laws whatsoever
binding upon them, especially laws to take from them what portions
of their property she pleases, without and against their consent.

SAMUEL ADAMS
(*Boston Gazette*, January 20, 1772)

IT is certainly true that Englishmen who took Locke's political ideas
with them to America adopted them with even greater thoroughness
than their brothers who stayed at home. This would have gratified Locke
who had become fascinated by the American wilderness in 1669 when he
helped draft *The Constitutions of Carolina* for his patron, Anthony Ashley
Cooper, the future Earl of Shaftesbury. At one time Locke even talked of
emigrating to the colonies. He saw in this vast, undeveloped continent,
peopled by nomadic Indian tribes, the perfect illustration of men living in
"a state of nature" where bargains made "between a *Swiss* and an *Indian* in
the Woods of *America* are binding to them, though they are perfectly in
a state of Nature, in reference to one another. For Truth and keeping of
Faith belong to Men, as Men, and not as Members of Society."[406]

---

406 John Locke, *Second Treatise*, par. 14, in Hall, *Christian History*, 1:61.

"THUS IN THE BEGINNING
ALL THE WORLD WAS AMERICA"

The wilds of America also illustrated to Locke the difference in value between cultivated and uncultivated land. He asked whether in the "uncultivated waste of America, left to Nature without any Improvement, Tillage or Husbandry, a thousand Acres yield the needy and wretched Inhabitants as many Conveniences of Life, as ten Acres of equally fertile Land do in *Devonshire*, where they are well Cultivated?" As Locke surveyed in his mind's eye the virgin wilderness that was the America of his day, he was reminded that "Thus in the Beginning all the World was America...."[407]

His description of the self-reliant life on one's own land did not read like abstract theory to British-American colonists. It was like an account of their own situation in the early days of their colonization when a man's labor on the soil meant the difference between life and death and when the colonial governments of New England were instituted by compact. Here, in America, friends and neighbors became fellow legislators. Increasingly, these stalwart colonials (like Locke) conceived of government, at every level, as existing to protect their natural rights as men as well as their rights as Englishmen. To them, the Lockean ideal of government by consent of the governed was a reality and not a mere philosopher's dream.

Until Great Britain tried to impose an internal tax on the colonists without their consent through their own colonial legislatures, his Majesty's subjects in America were, by and large, willing to allow Parliament to control their foreign trade and even to prohibit their manufactures as part of England's colonial policy. Merchants might grumble at being forbidden to trade with other nations than England or to be forced to sell their raw materials to England (at her price) and buy finished products from her (again at her price). But until the Stamp Act of 1765, there was no focus for their discontent. In the decade following England's attempt to impose the Stamp Tax on the colonists without their consent through their own legislatures, colonial leaders argued vehemently with Parliament for their constitutional rights as Englishmen.

So it was that during the years between 1764 and 1772 the political views of the colonists changed radically. In 1764, two great political leaders emerged in Massachusetts. One of them was Boston lawyer James Otis (1725–1783). The other was Samuel Adams (1722–1803), second cousin

---

407 Ibid., par. 49, 1:70.

of John Adams. Both men wrote papers on the rights of the colonists, Otis in 1764 and Adams in 1772. Both cited John Locke liberally in their papers. The change in the relationship with Great Britain that occurred between these two dates is reflected in the writing of Otis, whose demands for colonial self-government were limited by the admissions he made of parliamentary power over the colonies. On the other hand, Samuel Adams, writing in 1772, asserts unequivocally the natural rights of the colonists. Whatever degree of parliamentary power Adams may have accepted earlier, by 1772 he looked forward resolutely to independence.

JAMES OTIS' PAPER CRITICIZED BY OPPOSING POLITICAL CAMPS

When James Otis published his eloquent plea for colonial self-government, *The Rights of the Colonies Asserted and Proved* (1764), it was criticized by opposing political camps; the Tories found it much too assertive of colonial liberties while some American Whigs thought it too compliant with Parliament's assertions of power over the colonies. Otis was a strong advocate of colonial rights, but he also believed that Great Britain had a right to regulate American trade (although he objected to the English policy forbidding the colonies to trade with each other). As Otis saw it, the colonies were part of the great British Empire. Therefore, the Mother Country had the right to govern all *external* matters such as trade and war and peace. When it came to local self-government, however—particularly in the matter of taxation—he drew the line.

THE FIRST FAINT OUTLINES OF THE FEDERAL THEORY

What Otis outlined in his paper has often been described as "dominion status," but actually showed, as I have written elsewhere, "the first faint outlines of what was to develop in the future as American *federal theory*." What he described pointed toward two coordinate systems of government—the state and the federal—each supreme in its own sphere. In conceiving of the possibility of such a dual governmental relationship between the colonies and the Mother Country, Otis was in advance of his time.[408] He saw that relationship as including a full measure of local self-government for the colonies. He summarizes it in these words:

---

408 See Mary-Elaine Swanson in *Study Guide to The Christian History of the Constitution of the United States of America*, Vol. 2: *Christian Self-Government with Union*, Compiled by Verna M. Hall, Palo Cedro, California: American Christian History Institute, 1988, 42.

That no parts of His Majesty's dominions can be taxed without their consent: That every part has a right to be represented in the supreme or some subordinate legislature: That the refusal of this would seem to be a contradiction in practice to the theory of the constitution: That the colonies are subordinate dominions, and are now in such a state, as to make it best for the good of the whole, that they should not only be continued in the enjoyment of subordinate legislation, but be also represented in some proportion to their number and estates, in the grand legislature of the nation: That this would firmly unite all parts of the British empire, in the greatest peace and prosperity; and render it invulnerable and perpetual.[409]

STRONG COLONIAL SENTIMENT FOR
LOCAL SELF-GOVERNMENT

Had Great Britain continued to allow a generous amount of local self-government between 1764 and 1776, independence might have been delayed for many years. It was inevitable, though, that at some point Great Britain's thirteen colonies along the Atlantic seaboard would claim the liberty and local self-government that had become so important to them. We must remember that, as seen in the previous chapter, the colonists were also led to discern the importance of these political ideas through listening to the Congregationalist clergymen of New England whose sermons and pamphlets thoroughly nurtured these sentiments.

PARLIAMENT'S PRESUMED POWER
OVER THE COLONIES

The idea that the colonists had a right to local self-government, however, was the farthest thing from the minds of most leaders in Parliament during the long struggle for liberty and local self-government that began with the Stamp Tax in 1765. At the time Otis wrote his paper on the rights of the colonies, most colonists still thought in terms of the way the home government had worked in the past when it was balanced (albeit precariously) between the power of the king and the power of Parliament. It was the Glorious Revolution of 1689 that began the great change in favor of parliamentary power. Certain words in William and Mary's coronation oath are a significant indication of what was to come. They promised to govern the people of Great Britain and "the dominions thereunto belonging *according*

---

409 James Otis, *The Rights of the British Colonies*, in Hall, *Christian History*, 2:391.

to the Statutes in Parliament agreed on."[410] Over time, this phrase was to give Parliament increasing power over both Great Britain and her colonies.

In the beginning, however, the Mother Country took very little interest in the struggling North American colonies. Later, of course, this was all to change. Jedidiah Morse, in his *Annals of the American Revolution* (1824) relates the extent of British control over North American colonial trade:

> During a century and a half, from their first emigration, the colonists were left to tax themselves,...Great Britain, however, restrained and regulated their trade. She named the ports and nations to which only their merchandise might be carried, and with whom only they might trade. She obligated them to carry to her all their raw materials which might be wrought up for her emolument, and their other productions which she needed, or which might increase her wealth. She prohibited their manufacturing any articles among themselves, which might injure her manufactures or commerce, and their procuring manufactures from any other part of the globe, or even the products of European countries which were her rivals, until they were first brought into her ports.[411]

THE COLONIES PROVIDE
A READY MARKET FOR ENGLISH GOODS

As the colonies prospered, the Mother Country began to see in them an excellent source of raw materials and a ready market for England's manufactured goods—if the economy of the colonies were controlled to England's advantage. The Dominions, which belonged to the Crown through their charters, gradually became viewed as within the purview of Parliament, which finally decided to assert its full authority over the American colonies by imposing an internal tax.

AN UNFORESEEN PROBLEM

There was, however, a problem Parliament did not foresee: For too long the colonies had been allowed to develop their own self-governing institutions. English colonials, like James Otis, felt themselves in some sense a part of the British Empire but only in external matters, such as trade, were they inclined to let England retain control. In *internal* matters relating to their own colonial assemblies, through which they had a substantial degree of local self-government, they were increasingly disinclined to acknowledge

---

410 Coronation Oath. Emphasis added.
411 Jedidiah Morse, in Hall, *Christian History*, 2:351.

the power of the English Parliament in which they had no representation.[412] In their eyes—well-taught as they were by their pastors and legislators— internal taxation without their consent contravened the rights accorded Englishmen under the English Constitution. These were sacred rights that Englishmen at home had struggled long to attain and which "the great Mr. Locke" had so ably defended. "No taxation without representation!" became the rallying cry of the patriots. In their view, as Friedrich von Gentz related, "...the British Parliament was no more entitled to exercise the right of taxation over them, than over the people of Ireland."[413]

As it happened, however, Parliament had asserted just such a right in relation to the Irish. As early as 1641 the Irish had challenged Great Britain in their Rebellion, which took place precisely because of the English Parliament's attempt to enforce its rule over Ireland. Shortly after, in 1644, a Declaration by an anonymous author was widely read. It was a sweeping denial of Parliament's right to legislate for Ireland. In 1698, William Molyneux, who was, it will be remembered, a close friend of John Locke's, followed up this Declaration with a work of his own expanding the view set forth by the earlier Irish author.[414] Molyneux was a Protestant member of the Irish Parliament and shared Locke's political views. He had the courage to reject the English Parliament's pretended authority over Ireland.

It is safe to say that Locke shared his sentiments, since the claims of the English Parliament clearly usurped rights Locke had vigorously asserted, i.e., the rights of a people to be self-governing and to elect their own representatives to a legislative body which would truly represent them. Molyneux's book caused a furor in England and was investigated by a Parliamentary committee which found (of course) "that the said Book was of dangerous consequence to the crown and people of England, by denying the authority of the king and parliament of England, to bind the kingdom and people of Ireland, and the subordination and dependence that Ireland has, and ought to have upon England, as being united and annexed to the imperial crown of this realm."[415] Fortunately, Molyneux escaped prosecution.[416]

---

412 See Friedrich von Gentz, *The French and American Revolutions Compared*, translated by John Quincy Adams and published by him in 1810, reprinted in *Three Revolutions* published by Henry Regnery Company, 1959, page 40, for an interesting discussion by this astute foreign observer on the viewpoint of the colonists with respect to the Mother Country's authority over them.

413 Gentz, 16.

414 An interesting account of Molyneux and his work is found in Charles Howard McIlwain's *The American Revolution* (Ithaca, New York: Cornell University Press, 1961), 45-50.

415 McIlwain, 46.

416 In April of 1698, he wrote to Locke about the paper he had written titled *The Case of Ireland's Being*

WILLIAM PITT ASSERTS PARLIAMENT'S SOVEREIGN AUTHORITY OVER THE COLONIES

It is not surprising then that when the eighteenth century colonists in the New World began to assert the same ideas, they were met with the same resistance. Even the great William Pitt generally supported the Declaratory Act of 1766 asserting England's sovereignty over the colonies:

> Let the sovereign authority of this country over the colonies be asserted in as strong terms as can be assigned and be made to extend to every point of legislation whatsoever. That we may bind their trade, confine their manufactures, and exercise every power whatsoever, except that of taking money out of their pockets without their own consent."[417]

At least, Pitt was wise enough to see the injustice of the last-mentioned act, although not of the former. He was ahead of the other members of Parliament who, in the main, were stubbornly opposed to according even the latter right of consent to internal taxation. The important thing to note here is that even the most staunch English Whigs, although imbued with the Lockean idea as it pertained to the supremacy of the legislative branch of government, stopped short at the basic issue of the individual's right to self-government. Once admitted, however, the right of the individual to be self-governing could only find its just political development through local self-governing bodies.

JAMES OTIS AND HIS RIGHTS OF THE BRITISH COLONIES

Although James Otis may have seemed to hamper himself by attempting to reconcile parliamentary authority with colonial self-government, the tension between the two areas of authority led him to feel his way toward a new idea—the federal principle—that was eventually to play such a prominent role in creating the unique American federal union. *The Rights of the British Colonies* is permeated with Lockean logic, and Otis quotes liberally

---

Bound by Acts of Parliament in England Stated and said he would send him a copy, as he desired to know his opinion of its contents. The next letter from Molyneux in the correspondence, however, does not mention the work, but only thanks Locke for his hospitality during his recent visit to England. Clearly, any discussion regarding the matter would have occurred during his visit. It was not long afterward that Molyneux died.

417 McIlwain, 150-151. As McIlwain shows on pages 50-51, this Declaratory Act for the American colonies is almost the same as the Declaratory Act of 1719 in which Parliament declared its sovereignty over Ireland.

from Locke's *Second Treatise Of Civil Government*.[418] His pamphlet proved highly influential in the colonies and was even published in London where it received sympathetic attention in the press.[419] This is perhaps surprising, since his Lockean-inspired words were bold and blunt:

> The Colonists being men, have a right to be considered as equally entitled to all the rights of nature with the Europeans, and they are not to be restrained in the exercise of any of these rights, but for the evident good of the whole community.
>
> By being or becoming members of society, they have not renounced their natural liberty in any greater degree than other good citizens, and if 'tis taken from them without their consent, they are so far enslaved.[420]

Otis went on to develop his theme from the Law of Nature which, in Lockean fashion, he declared "was not of man's making, nor is it in his power to mend it, or alter its course. He can only perform and keep it, or disobey and break it."[421] Still, he accepted the power of Parliament over the colonies when he admitted as "one of the first principles" from which he deduced the rights of the colonies, "that all of them are subject

---

418 James Otis was born in West Barnstable, Massachusetts in 1725 and became a prominent lawyer in Boston. In 1760 he was made advocate general. The year 1761 saw him elected to the Massachusetts Assembly. In 1764, he published his eloquent pamphlet, *The Rights of the British Colonists Asserted and Proved*. From this time until 1769 he took a large part in the resistance to unjust taxation by Great Britain. In the latter year he was savagely beaten by one John Robinson, a customs officer, and two others during a dispute in a public room. His sister, historian Mercy Otis Warren, related the incident as occurring because of a paper her brother wrote condemning the conduct of the commissioners of the customs. She viewed the beating as an attempt to assassinate Otis. (See her account in Mercy Otis Warren, *History of the Rise, Progress, and Termination of the American Revolution*, 1805, in Hall, *Christian History of the American Revolution*, 380.) From the time of the beating his reason steadily declined into insanity, occasionally interrupted by sane periods. In 1770, John Adams wrote with alarm of the mental decline he observed in Otis. "In short I never saw such an Object of Admiration, Reverence, Contempt, and Compassion all at once as this. I fear, I tremble, I mourn for the Man, and for his Country. Many others mourne over him with Tears in their Eyes." (Diary entry of John Adams, January 16, 1770. See *John Adams: A Biography in His Own Words*, 2 vols., ed. by James Bishop Peabody, New York: Newsweek Book Division, 1973, 1:106.) In 1783, Otis died in an extraordinary way while standing at the window of a friend's house. His sister relates: "...as if in consequence of his own prayers, his great soul was instantly set free by a flash of lightning." (in Hall, *Christian History of the American Revolution*, 380.) Death came in the same year that the peace treaty was signed between Great Britain and America acknowledging America's independence.

419 American historian Richard Frothingham wrote: "This pamphlet was advertised in the *Boston Gazette*.... It was reprinted in London by Almon; and in the *Gazette* of April 8, 1765, is the following, copied from a London paper: "As the ministry propose to tax the Americans, this excellent treatise, which was lately published in the colonies and universally approved of there, is highly necessary for the perusal of the members of both Houses, and of such who choose to make themselves masters of an argument so little understood, but of so great consequence to every British subject and lover of constitutional liberty." See Hall, *Christian History*, 2:368.

420 James Otis, *The Rights of the British Asserted and Proved*, (1764) in Hall, *Christian History*, 2:384.

421 Ibid.

to, and dependent on Great Britain; and that therefore as over subordinate governments, the parliament of Great Britain has an undoubted power of lawful authority to make acts *for the general good*, that by naming them, shall and ought to be equally binding, as upon the subjects of Great Britain within the realm." [422] He discerned, however, that the political and civil rights of the colonies rested not only upon acts of Parliament, but also on English common law. "Upon these grand pillars of liberty shall my defence be rested." [423] Thus, even if Parliament tried to annul all their charters, the colonists would still be British subjects and so, he confidently stated, "No act of parliament can deprive them of the liberties of such. . . ." [424]

BOUNDS OF THE LEGISLATIVE POWER DEFINED

In summarizing the bounds of the legislative power "which by God and nature are fixed," he turned to Locke's four bounds of a legitimate legislature:

> 1. To govern by stated laws. 2. Those laws should have no other end ultimately, but the good of the people. 3. Taxes are not to be laid on the people, but by their consent in person, or by deputation. 4. Their whole power is not transferable.

"These," Otis proclaims, "are the first principles of law and justice and the great barriers of a free state, and of the British Constitution in particular." [425] These bounds "which by God and nature are fixed," he declared, "hitherto have they [the parliament] a right to come, and no further." [426] Therefore, the imposition of internal taxes by Parliament is "absolutely irreconcilable with the rights of the Colonists as British subjects, and as men. I say men, for in a state of nature no man can take my property from me, without my consent. If he does, he deprives me of my liberty, and makes me a slave. If such a proceeding is a breach of the law of nature, no law of society can make it just." [427] In words that again echo Locke, Otis concluded: "For what one civil right is worth a rush, after a man's property is subject to be taken from him at pleasure, without his consent." [428] From this passage it is clear that while Otis bowed to Parliament, in certain respects, it was with the understanding of that body's strictly limited powers—based on the

---

422 Ibid., Otis, 2:386. Emphasis added.
423 Ibid.
424 Ibid., 2:386.
425 Ibid., 2:387.
426 Ibid.
427 Ibid., 2:388.
428 Ibid.

Law of Nature as elucidated by Locke. "To say Parliament is absolute and arbitrary is a contradiction. The Parliament cannot make 2 + 2 = 5...."[429]

The Supremacy of Divine Authority

Otis explained that for Parliament merely to declare a law does not necessarily make that law valid:

> There must be in every instance, a higher authority, viz. God. Should an act of parliament be against any of his natural laws, which are immutably true, their declaration would be contrary to eternal truth, equity, and justice, and consequently void....[430]

But, Otis confidently assured his readers, such unjust laws would be adjudged so "by the Parliament itself, when convinced of their mistake."[431] It was his position that it was up to the colonies to show the members of Parliament their error, so that they would then repeal any unjust laws such as the Stamp Act.

The Stamp Act drove the colonies together and, at the urging of the Massachusetts House of Representatives, a general congress of all the colonies was held in New York in October 1765. James Otis was sent as one of the delegates. Here he counseled remonstrance rather than resistance. Even after the British sent soldiers to Boston in 1768, Otis continued to counsel against resistance. By this time, however, Samuel Adams and others were beginning to believe that it was unlikely Great Britain would yield without firm resistance and that, in the end, independence might well be inevitable.

Whig Views on Parliamentary Supremacy

At the time of the Stamp Act, however, the Whig doctrine on both sides of the Atlantic was a doctrine of parliamentary supremacy. As historian Charles McIlwain has noted,

> By their creed, the British Empire was one commonwealth and Parliament was its master. Such a theory imposed no checks on any abuses of Parliaments' power; it was sovereign and *legibus solutum*."[432]

---

429 Ibid., Otis.
430 Ibid., 2:388-389.
431 Ibid., 2:389.
432 McIlwain, 157-58.

As the repeated remonstrances and petitions of the colonies were as repeatedly rejected by Parliament, it gradually dawned upon British America that this Whig doctrine "offered no more remedy against an oppressive parliament than the theory of divine right had offered against a despotic King, and that was only 'sighs and tears.'"[433]

Up to about 1768 America was still Whig in the British sense, but from then on British Whig doctrine declined rapidly. By 1774, it was all but eclipsed by the much broader and higher view of God's Law of Nature as the basis for resistance. This view held that local self-government accords more with God's will for man than the "omnipotency" of a distant government. Despite his deference toward Parliament, revealed in his paper on colonial rights, James Otis affirmed the Lockean idea that laws Parliament made were illegitimate and, hence, void if they went against the divine Law of Nature or the English Constitution. Thus, as we have seen, Otis also affirmed that under the Law of Nature and the Constitution of England, the colonists had the right to local self-government through their colonial assemblies. These ideas, already made familiar by the sermons of their ministers, took root in public thought and steadily and inevitably moved the colonies toward independence.

SAMUEL ADAMS:
FATHER OF
THE AMERICAN REVOLUTION

In Massachusetts, Samuel Adams became its boldest spokesman. He has been rightly called "the father of the American Revolution."[434] No man worked more assiduously for liberty and local self-government than did he. On the eve of revolution, Jefferson wrote that Samuel Adams was constantly holding caucuses of distinguished men in order to determine the consensus of opinion on measures to be taken. He ascribed great influence to Samuel Adams in promoting the cause of American independence. His labors in the cause had been for years so unremitting, that it may be justly said of him, 'His feet were ever in the stirrup, his

---

433 McIlwain, 158.

434 Samuel Adams was born on September 27, 1722 in Boston, Massachusetts. He became politically prominent beginning with the Stamp Act crisis and worked assiduously to mold public opinion and to strengthen his fellow colonists in their determination to stand for their political rights. He arranged town meetings, wrote Boston's protest against the Stamp Tax, led in the debates, and over time became so strong a foe to the British ministry's attempts to exert absolute sovereignty over the colonies that attempts were made to buy him off, which he curtly rebuffed. He was a member of the Continental Congress, a signer of the Declaration of Independence and, after the American Revolution, was elected governor of Massachusetts. He died on October 3, 1803.

lance ever in its rest.'"[435] John Adams spoke of his cousin Samuel in the same vein. "Adams is zealous, ardent and keen in the Cause, is always for Softness, and Delicacy, and Prudence where they will do, but is staunch and stiff and strict and rigid and inflexible, in the Cause...."[436]

A RABBLE ROUSER AND AN "INCENDIARY"?

This description of Samuel Adams belies the oft-heard assertion today that he was a rabble-rouser and incendiary. Ironically, those who repeat these unflattering estimates of his character are actually quoting the remarks of prominent and angry Tories of the time! It was Massachusetts Governor Thomas Hutchinson who described him in a letter as "the Grand Incendiary of the Province" and probably blamed him for the angry mob who tore his house down.[437] But Samuel Adams did not condone lawless violence. He was always for proceeding from a firm foundation of natural and constitutional law. He worked assiduously to educate public opinion through the well-reasoned newspaper articles he wrote. He was a man of acute intellectual character and discernment. John Adams gives this estimate of Cousin Samuel's intellect and character:

> Adams I believe has the most thorough Understanding of Liberty, and her Resources, in the Temper and Character of the People...as well as the most habitual, radical Love of it, of any of them—as well as the most correct, genteel and artful Pen. He is a Man of refined Policy, stedfast [sic] Integrity, exquisite Humanity, genteel Erudition, obliging, engaging Manners, real as well as professed Piety, and a universal good Character, unless it should be admitted that he is too attentive to the Public and not enough so, to himself and his family.[438]

ADAMS ENDOWED WITH
A CLEAR AND LOGICAL MIND

American historian George Bancroft described Samuel Adams as:

> a provincial statesman of a clear and logical mind, which, throughout a long life, imparted consistency to his public conduct. His will resembled well-tempered steel, which may ply, but will not

---

435 Thomas Jefferson, cited by Richard Frothingham in *The Rise of the Republic*, (1890), in Hall, *Christian History*, 1:351.

436 John Adams, diary entry for 1765, December 23, in *John Adams: A Biography in His Own Words*, 1:109.

437 See C. V. Wells, *Life of Samuel Adams* (1865), in Hall, *Christian History*, 1:364.

438 John Adams, diary entry for December 23, 1765, in *A Biography in His Own Words*, 1:109.

break. Bred as a Calvinist of the strictest sect, his riper judgment confirmed him in his creed. On church government he adhered to the Congregational form, as most friendly to civil and religious liberty; was a member of the church; and the austere purity of his life witnessed the sincerity of his profession. Evening and morning his house was a house of prayer, and no one more revered the Christian Sabbath. He was a tender husband, an affectionate parent, and could vividly enjoy conversation with friends; but the wall of his modest mansion never witnessed anything inconsistent with the discipline of the man whose desire for his birthplace was that "Boston might become a Christian Sparta."[439]

Writing as *Valerious Poplicola* in the *Boston Gazette* of October 28, 1771, Sam Adams criticized the view (expressed by Thomas Hutchinson in his *History of Massachusetts*) that the colonies should be "subject to the controul of the parent state." In refuting Governor Hutchinson's position, Adams cited Locke:

> Mr. Locke, in his treatise on government discovers the weakness of this position. That every man is born a subject to his Prince, and therefore is under the perpetual tie of subjection and allegiance; and he shows that express consent alone makes any one a member of any commonwealth. He holds that submission to the laws of any country, and living quietly and enjoying privileges and protection under them, does not make a man a member of that society, or a perpetual subject of that commonwealth, any more than it would make a man subject to another, in whose family he found it convenient to abide for some time, tho' while he continued under it, he were obliged to comply with the laws, and submit to the government he found there. Every man was born naturally free; nothing can make a man a subject of any commonwealth, but his actually entering into it by positive engagement, and express promise and compact.
>
> If the sentiments of this great man [Locke] are well grounded, our historian before he asserted so peremptorily that the ancestors of this country as colonists were subject to the controul of the parent state, should have first made it appear that by positive engagement, or express promise or contract, they had thus bound themselves.[440]

---

439 George Bancroft, *History of the United States*, New York, 1886, in Hall, *Christian History*, 2:361.

440 Samuel Adams, *Boston Gazette*, 28 October 1771, in Hall, *Christian History*, 2:470. The Locke discussion on express consent that Adams refers to is in the *Second Treatise*, par. 122.

It was clear to Adams that the colonists had never given "the parent state" any authority to make laws for them.

> No body can have any power to make laws over a free people, but by their own consent, and by authority receiv'd from them: It follows then, either that the people of this province have consented and given authority to the parent state to make laws over them, or that she has no such authority.... If they are a separate body politick, and are free, they have a right equal to that of the people of Great Britain to make laws for themselves, and are no more than they, subject to the controul of any legislature not their own.[441]

Adams observed tartly that the author whose views he was criticizing (Governor Hutchinson) maintained that "'the people of Ireland were under the same mistake' with our ancestors; that is in thinking themselves exempt from the controul of English acts of Parliament." With biting irony Adams brings up the views of both Locke and his friend, Molyneux, on this subject:

> Our historian tells his readers by way of consolation, that "it may serve as some excuse for our ancestors, but they were not alone in their mistaken apprehensions of the nature of their subjection"; and he appears to be mighty glad that "so sensible a man as Mr. Molineux, the friend of Mr. Locke, engag'd in the cause." But we want no excuse for any supposed mistakes of our ancestors. Let us first see it prov'd that they were mistakes.
>
> "'Till then," he concluded, "we must hold ourselves obliged to them for sentiments transmitted to us so worthy of their character, and so important to our security: And we shall esteem the arguments of so sensible, and it might justly be added, so learned a gentleman as Mr. Molineux, especially as they had the approbation of his friend Mr. Locke to be valid, while we see nothing to oppose them, but the unsupported opinion of Mr. Hutchinson."[442]

---

441 Ibid. Here he quotes from Hooker's *Ecclesiastical Politie*, I.1, Sect. 10, as quoted in Locke's *Second Treatise* as a footnote to par. 134, as follows: "*The lawful power of making Laws to Command whole Politick Societies of Men, belongs so properly unto the same intire* [sic] *Societies, that for any Prince or Potentate of what kind soever upon Earth to exercise the same of himself, and not by express Commission immediately and personally received from God, or else from authority deriv'd at the first from their Consent, upon whose persons they impose laws, is no better than mere* Tyranny. *Laws they are not therefore which publick approbation hath not made so.*"

442 Ibid., 473.

SAMUEL ADAMS—
THE RIGHTS OF THE COLONISTS

Perhaps the most masterly summary of the development of American political thought was given by Samuel Adams in 1772 in his *The Rights of the Colonists as Men, as Christians, and as Subjects*. It might be more precise to say that he presented the whole argument—not so much as a development, but as three parallel lines of thought: 1) the natural rights of the colonists as men; 2) their rights as Christians; and 3) their rights as subjects under the English Constitution. Nevertheless, the order in which he states them is significant. He did not begin, as might have been expected, with constitutional rights, followed by Christian rights, and concluding with natural rights. He began in reverse order, beginning with natural rights.

The Natural Rights of the Colonists

Adams outlines the colonists' natural rights in Lockean fashion: "First, a right to Life; Secondly, to Liberty; Thirdly, to Property; together with the right to support and defend them in the best manner they can. These are evident branches of, rather than deductions from, the duty of self-preservation, commonly called the first law of nature."[443] Then follows a distillation of Locke's argument for when and how men enter political society:

> When men enter into society, it is by voluntary consent; and they have a right to demand and insist upon the performance of such conditions and previous limitations as form an equitable original compact. Every natural right not expressly given up, or, from the nature of a social compact, necessarily ceded, remains. All positive and civil laws should conform, as far as possible, to the law of natural reason and equity.[444]

Religious Freedom as a Natural Right

Religious freedom, declares Adams, is both a natural and civil right. "As neither reason requires nor religion permits the contrary, every man living in or out of a state of civil society has a right peaceably and quietly to worship God according to the dictates of his conscience." Quoting from the Preface to Locke's *Letter on Toleration*, he continues: " 'Just and true liberty, equal and impartial liberty,' in matters spiritual and temporal, is a thing that all men are clearly entitled to by the eternal and immutable laws

---

443 Samuel Adams, *The Rights of the Colonists as Men, as Christians, and as Subjects*, in Hall, *Christian History*, 1:365. On self-preservation, see Locke, *Second Treatise*, par. 6. Initial caps added for emphasis.
444 Ibid.

of God and nature, as well as by the law of nations and all well-grounded municipal laws, which must have their foundation in the former." [445] Adams urges full toleration of differing modes of worship as consistent with civil society, asserting that "... it is now generally agreed among Christians that this spirit of toleration, in the fullest extent consistent with the being of civil society, is the chief characteristical mark of the true Church. Insomuch that Mr. Locke has asserted and proved, beyond the possibility of contradiction on any solid ground, that such toleration ought to be extended to all whose doctrines are not subversive of society." [446]

Adams notes that Locke would exclude from toleration those religions that "teach doctrines subversive of the civil government under which they live." [447] Under this heading are listed the Roman Catholic Church because of that church's doctrines which declared that, as Adams explains, "princes excommunicated may be deposed, and those that they call heretics may be destroyed without mercy." He also mentions the absolute government of the Pope in all Christian countries dominated by Roman Catholicism, so as to introduce a government within a government, "leading directly to the worst anarchy and confusion, civil discord, war, and bloodshed." [448] Here Adams remarks that these rights "may be best understood by reading and carefully studying the institutes of the great Law Giver and Head of the Christian Church, which are to be found clearly written and promulgated in the New Testament." He reminds his readers that "By the act of the British Parliament, commonly called the Toleration Act, every subject in England, except Papists, &., was restored to, and re-established in his natural right to worship God according to the dictates of his conscience." [449] Nor was this all, for the charter of the province of Massachusetts "granted, ordained, and established that there shall be liberty of conscience for all Christians in the province (again, with the exception of Roman

---

445 Ibid. The quote "Just and true liberty, equal and impartial liberty," from Locke's *Letter Concerning Toleration* (1714. ed.) in Hall, *Christian History*, 2:45, is from the preface entitled "To the Reader," written by the translator of the work from the original Latin presumably with Locke's approval. See John Locke, *Works*, 6:4.

446 Here Adams inserts a star and below the remark "See Locke's "Letters of Toleration." He may have been thinking of such passages from Locke as: "If the Gospel and the apostles may be credited, no man can be a Christian without charity, and without that faith which works, not by force, but by love," (*Works*, 6:6). "The toleration of those that differ from others in matters of religion, is so agreeable to the Gospel of Jesus Christ, and to the genuine reason of mankind, that it seems monstrous for men to be so blind, as not to perceive the necessity and advantage of it, in so clear a light," (Ibid., 6:9).

447 Samuel Adams, *Rights of the Colonists...*, in Hall, *Christian History*, 1:366.

448 Ibid.

449 Ibid., 367.

Catholics).[450] It is not surprising that Adams should lay great weight on the right to worship God according to one's conscience. As a Congregationalist, he was mindful that this dissenting faith had been fiercely persecuted in England by the Anglican Church and that the Pilgrim Fathers were imprisoned and driven out of the country. How precious then must be the religious liberty they had at last achieved in the New World which the English Toleration Act had also guaranteed from the reign of William and Mary.[451]

As Samuel Adams saw it, the right of the colonists as subjects came first of all from their rights as men and as Christians. "All persons born in the British American Colonies are, by the laws of God and nature and by the common law of England...declared to be entitled to all the natural, essential, inherent, and inseparable rights, liberties, and privileges of subjects born in Great Britain or within the realm."[452] The rights Adams lists as primary are the same ones Otis had listed earlier. In listing them, he quotes, in part, directly from Locke, just as Otis did:

> First, "The *first and fundamental, positive Law* of all Commonwealths of states *is the establishing the Legislative Power*; as the *first and fundamental natural Law*, also, which is to govern even the Legislative [power] itself, *is the preservation of the Society*."[453]

> Secondly, the Legislative has no right to absolute, arbitrary power over the lives and fortunes of the people; nor can mortals assume a prerogative not only too high for men, but for angels, and therefore

---

450 It should be noted once again that the objection to according religious freedom to Roman Catholics was political rather than theological. It was the reputation of the Catholic Church at that time as a persecutor of Protestants and a political force against Protestant nations that concerned Adams.

451 Although he was a Calvinist, Samuel Adams did not take a prejudiced attitude against other Christian denominations. When he was a delegate to the First Continental Congress in 1774 and word came that the British were bombarding Boston, prayer was needed, but the members were concerned as to whom to ask to give prayers since there was a great diversity of religious opinion among the delegates. American historian Richard Frothingham relates that: "On this day Samuel Adams, in answer to the objection to opening the sessions with prayer, said that he could hear a prayer from a man of piety and virtue, who was a friend to the country, and moved that Mr. Duche, an Episcopalian, might be desired to read prayers to the congress on the following morning. The motion prevailed...." (From Frothingham's *The Rise of the Republic of the United States*, in Hall, *Christian History*, 2:576.) The Reverend Duche read Psalm 35 which begins "Plead Thou my cause, O Lord, with them that strive with me, and fight Thou against them that fight against me...." and then, as John Adams observed, he "unexpectedly to anybody struck out into an extemporary prayer for America, for the congress, for Massachusetts, and especially for Boston, which was so fervent that it filled the bosom of every man present." Samuel Adams' gracious suggestion at this time of great tension and anxiety was providentially used to provide just the right minister with the right message they all needed to hear.

452 Samuel Adams, *The Rights of the Colonists...*, in Hall, *Christian History*, 1:368.

453 Ibid., quoting from Locke, *Second Treatise*, par. 134.

reserved for the Deity alone.[454]

The Legislative cannot justly assume to itself a power to rule by extempore arbitrary decrees; but is bound to see that justice is dispensed, and that the rights of the subjects be decided by promulgated, standing, and known laws, and authorized "independent judges"; that is, independent as far as possible, of Prince and people.[455]

There should be one rule of justice for rich and poor, for the favorite at court, and the countryman at the plough.[456]

Thirdly, "The supreme power cannot justly take from any man any part of his property, without his consent in person or by his representative."[457]

"What liberty can there be when property is taken away without consent?"

After enumerating these "first principles of natural law and justice and the great barriers of all free states and of the British Constitution in particular," Adams declared that "It is utterly irreconcilable to these principles and to many other fundamental maxims of the common law, common sense, and reason, that a British House of Commons should have a right at pleasure to give and grant the property of the Colonists."[458] And he asks: "Now what liberty can there be where property is taken away without consent? Can it be said...that this continent...has the least voice, vote, or influence in the British Parliament?" Not that he would have it so. Indeed he declares that "it would only be hurtful; as, from their local situation and circumstances, it is impossible they should ever be truly and properly represented there."[459]

Samuel Adams Foresees Great Population Growth

There was another reason that the far-sighted mind of Samuel Adams grasped. "The inhabitants of this country, in all probability, in a few years, will be more numerous than those of Great Britain and Ireland together; yet it is absurdly expected by the promoters of the present measures that these, with their posterity to all generations, should be easy, while their

---

454 Ibid., Samuel Adams. For Locke's exact wording, see *Second Treatise*, par. 135.
455 See Locke, par. 136.
456 These words are slightly paraphrased from Locke, in par. 142.
457 See Locke, par. 138.
458 Samuel Adams, *The Rights of the Colonists...*, in Hall, *Christian History*, 1:368.
459 Ibid., 368–69.

property shall be disposed of by a House of Commons at three thousand miles' distance from them, and who cannot be supposed to have the least care or concern for their real interest. . . ."[460] He bluntly noted that "The Colonists have been branded with the odious names of traitors and rebels only for complaining of their grievances. How long such treatment will or ought to be borne, is submitted."[461] Clearly, Samuel Adams was ready for independence.

SAMUEL ADAMS PUBLICIZES
LOCKE'S SECOND TREATISE

In 1773, Edes and Gill, of Boston, published Locke's *Second Treatise of Government* alone rather than along with the *First Treatise* that refuted the monarchist political ideas of Sir Robert Filmer. Samuel Adams explained in his review in the *Boston Gazette* of March 1, 1773, that "the latter Part only is now republish[ed] here, which has also rendered it much cheaper than if incumbered with the prolix Confutation of Filmer and his Disciples, few of which are yet to be found in this Country."[462] Nevertheless, Adams gave a terse summary of Locke's "first discourse" which he admitted "has also been of great Use, as it is a most thorough Refutation of the Errors of Sir Robert Filmer, and his Followers, viz. — 'That all the kings of the Earth derive their Titles from God thro' King Adam'"—and 'that Adam's eldest Male heir, wherever and whatever he be, has a right to be recogniz'd as the first Monarch of the Globe in Point of Rank,' etc. But where he is to be found, or to find his Kingdom, even Filmer could never tell." He concludes that "These Vagaries have to all appearance long since been pretty generally exploded."[463]

Adams characterized the present situation in the colonies as "very alarming." He was referring to the fateful decision of the British ministry to pay the salaries of the colonial judges making them dependent upon Great Britain and thus independent of colonial legislatures. Although Parliament had backed down and rescinded the Townshend Act's taxes, it had adroitly retained the innocuous tea tax as a symbol of the right of Parliament to tax the colonies and legislate for them. It was in this dark and foreboding

---

460 Ibid., 370.
461 Ibid.
462 Samuel Adams, reviewing and quoting from Locke's *Essay Concerning the Extent and End Of Civil Government*, on the front page of *Boston Gazette and Country Journal* for Monday, March 1, 1773, photostatic copy reproduced, in Hall, *Christian History*, 2:69.
463 Ibid.

atmosphere that Samuel Adams now urgently recommended a close study of Locke's essay on government.

> Every honest and good Man in America must be under a very sensible Concern for himself and for his Posterity. — Perhaps there never was a Time since the Discovery of this new World, when People of all Ranks every where show'd so eager a Spirit of Inquiry into the Nature of their Rights and Privileges, as at this Day. — This at all Times is a laudable Spirit, and ought to be encouraged. — It has therefore been judged very seasonable and proper to put it in the Power of every free Man on this Continent to furnish himself at so easy a Rate with the noble Essay just now republished.[464]

Adams was zealous to educate his readers and stressed the value of this Essay for the "intelligent Reader" in order to gain a better view of "the Rights of Men and of Englishmen and a clearer insight into the Principles of the British Constitution than all the Discourses of Government." As noted in Chapter 6, he recommended that it be "early and carefully explained by every Father to his Son, by every Preceptor in our public and private Schools to his Pupils, and by every Mother to her Daughter."[465]

THE MANY POLITICAL CONTRIBUTIONS OF SAMUEL ADAMS

The many contributions Samuel Adams made to the Revolutionary cause were remarkable. They earned him the title, "Father of the American Revolution." Discreet and mild-mannered, Adams was a great listener and had perhaps even keener political instincts than his more famous cousin. He certainly had greater diplomacy than prickly Cousin John. It was because of Samuel Adams' far-sighted view of the future that the colonies were helped to band together and hold the first Continental Congress of 1774. Samuel Adams also put to work an idea that Reverend Jonathan Mayhew had first suggested during the Stamp Act crisis: Committees of Correspondence, first within the towns and counties of Massachusetts; then, when Virginia adopted the idea, as a device for uniting the patriots throughout all the colonies.

---

464 Ibid., right-hand column. For the complete text of this passage see Hall, *Christian History*, 2:69.
465 Ibid.

PURITAN JOHN LOCKE SPEAKS
TO PURITAN SAMUEL ADAMS

As a devout Puritan, Adams appreciated in the works of John Locke the religious and political insights of a fellow Puritan. He obviously had read not only the first and second treatises on government, but also the *Letter Concerning Toleration* to which he referred approvingly in his *Rights of the Colonists*. Certainly Samuel Adams was one of the most consistently Lockean political thinkers in the colonies. The next chapter shows how Samuel Adams and Cousin John both worked to ground the patriot case for liberty, not merely on the English Constitution, but on God's Law of Nature as they had learned it from John Locke.

In their quest for the rights of the colonists to local self-government, both Samuel Adams and James Otis before him were led repeatedly to consult "the great Mr. Locke" in order to see what he had to say on the subject. Through their work, it became increasingly clear to the people who followed their arguments for political liberty that sovereignty over the colonies did not reside in either king or parliament. But if not with them, where *did* sovereignty properly reside? It was a question soon to be answered.

The First Continental Congress declares:

"That the inhabitants of the English Colonies in North America,
by the immutable laws of nature,
the principles of the English Constitution,
and the several charters or compacts,
have the following Rights:
"1. That they are entitled to life, liberty, and property,
and they have never ceded to any sovereign power whatever,
a right to dispose of either without
their consent...."

A Declaration of Rights, 1774[466]

"A DECLARATION OF RIGHTS
made by the Representatives of the good people of VIRGINIA...
which rights do pertain to them and their posterity,
as the basis and foundation of Government.

1. That all men are by nature equally free and independent,
and have certain inherent rights,
of which, when they enter into a state of society,
they cannot, by any compact, deprive or divest their posterity;
namely, the enjoyment of life and liberty,
with the means of acquiring and possessing property,
and pursuing and obtaining
happiness and safety."

The Virginia Declaration of Rights,
12 June 1776[467]

---

466 A Declaration of Rights of the First Continental Congress as Philadelphia, 14 October 1774, from *The Journal of the Continental Congress 1774-1789*, in Hall, *Christian History*, 2:586.

467 *The Virginia Declaration of Rights*, from the final draft, in Helen Hill Miller's *George Mason: Gentleman Revolutionary* (Chapel Hill, North Carolina: The University of North Carolina Press, 1975), 339-40.

CHAPTER NINE

Three Lockean Declarations

"We hold these Truths to be self-evident, that all Men are created equal, that they are endowed by their Creator with certain unalienable Rights, that among these are Life, Liberty, and the Pursuit of Happiness. That to secure these Rights, Governments are instituted among Men, deriving their just Powers from the Consent of the Governed...."

THE DECLARATION OF INDEPENDENCE
July 4, 1776

THREE revolutionary documents reveal how much the Founding Fathers were influenced by the political philosophy of John Locke: the Declaration of Rights of 1774 produced by the First Continental Congress; George Mason's Virginia Declaration of Rights of June 1776 (which acted as the model for the state declarations that followed it); and, finally, the American Declaration of Independence written by Thomas Jefferson and amended by the Congress of 1776. It was certainly no accident that the writers of these documents used Lockean ideas and even specific Lockean phraseology. The founding generation had been born and bred to Locke, just as they had been raised on the Bible. One author says of this period: "Most Americans had absorbed Locke's works as a kind of political gospel and the Declaration [of Independence], in its form, in its phraseology, follows closely certain sentences in Locke's second treatise on government...."[468]

The aristocratic Founding Fathers of the South, unlike their New

---

468 Carl Becker, *The Declaration of Independence: A Study in the History of Political Ideas* (New York: Alfred A. Knopf. 1960), 27. Becker insists that prior to 1776, the Founding Fathers were not influenced by many French writers. On the contrary, most of the writers who influenced them were English, especially Locke (see 27). Although Becker has some useful insights, his view of Locke as introducing a new secular kind of compact which ignored divine Revelation is incorrect. A much better study is *Defending the Declaration* by Gary Amos, referred to earlier.

England brethren, usually did not receive their Lockean ideas from ministers of their Anglican churches, but rather from their own reading of
Locke.[469] His works were staples in the libraries of English gentlemen,
particularly the *Essay on Human Understanding*. They also were intimately
acquainted with his treatises on government. So pervasive was Locke's
influence in the South that Mrs. Charles Carroll of Carrollton, Maryland,
whose husband was one of the signers of the Declaration of Independence,
was painted holding Locke's book on education, its title and author clearly
seen in the picture. Like her husband, she too admired the works of Locke
and, to a wife and mother, his work on education was particularly appropriate for use in the painting.[470]

THE FIRST CONTINENTAL CONGRESS CONVENES IN 1774

When the First Continental Congress convened at Carpenter's Hall in
Philadelphia on September 5, 1774, its fifty-five delegates came from twelve
states (Georgia declined to send any delegates, but promised to follow the
consensus of opinion of the other colonies in their quest for redress of their
grievances). The delegates had been elected by their colonial assemblies or,
in some cases, by revolutionary conventions held in their colonies.

Character of the Delegates

As American historian Richard Frothingham observed, all the delegates
were "men of uncommon ability, who had taken a prominent part in the
political action of their several localities, had won public confidence,
and were fair exponents of the aims, feelings, and political ideas of the
country."[471] They represented "the ability, culture, political intelligence,
and wisdom" of their colonies. Eight had attended the Stamp Act Congress
of 1765, but most of them had never met before.

In addition to a knowledge of John Locke's political writings, the

---

469 There were exceptions. In 1750, Becker notes, a volume was published in Boston of twenty sermons
dealing with natural rights and natural law as preached in the parish church at Charleston, S.C.
by the Reverend Samuel Quincy.

470 I am indebted to Robert H. Hurwitz for his account concerning Mrs. Carroll and the painting.
He writes that Professor Ann Diamond brought it to his attention and Ms. Ann Van Devanter,
Guest Curator of the Baltimore Museum of Art, gave him further background information on Mrs.
Carroll and the painting. (See Hurwitz, "John Locke and the Preservation of Liberty...." in *The
Moral Foundations of the American Republic*, third edition, Robert H. Hurwitz, ed., Charlottesville:
University Press of Virginia, 1986, note 11, on 142.) Charles Carroll (1737-1832) was a prominent
Maryland Roman Catholic who became a member of Congress in 1776. He outlived the other
signers of the Declaration of Independence, dying when he was 95 years old.

471 Richard Frothingham, *The Rise of the Republic of the United States* (1890) in Hall, *Christian History*,
2:574.

delegates all knew the history of their Mother Country. They knew how important to that history was the English Declaration of Rights of 1689. (It will be recalled that John Locke had an influence on that earlier revolution through his friend Sir John Somers, the major drafter of the Declaration of Rights of 1689.)

An Alliance between the Two Parent Colonies

Particularly helpful at the convention of 1774 was the alliance that developed between the two parent colonies, Massachusetts and Virginia, which became the leaders of the move toward independence. A close and lifelong friendship developed between Samuel Adams and Richard Henry Lee of Virginia. Both were influenced by Lockean political ideals, and both were farsighted in their efforts to achieve liberty and self-government in their colonies. As early as 1764 Lee had written to a friend in London that:

> the free possession of property, the right to be governed by our representatives, and the illegality of taxation without consent, are such essential principles of the British constitution that it is a matter of wonder how men, who have almost imbibed them in their mother's milk, whose very atmosphere is charged with them, should be of opinion that the people of America were to be taxed without consulting their representatives....[472]

The Virginia delegates arrived in Philadelphia on September 2, five days after the Massachusetts men arrived. John Adams was impressed favorably by the Virginians. He wrote that they seemed to him to be "the most spirited and consistent of any."[473] Later Adams appraised Richard Henry Lee as "a masterly man."[474] He was that, indeed.

---

472 Cited by John Carter Matthews in *Richard Henry Lee* (Williamsburg, Virginia: Virginia Independence Bicentennial Commission, 1978), 4. Richard Henry Lee (1732-1794) was from an influential Virginia family distinguished for their tireless political activity in the cause of liberty. Educated in England, he returned to Virginia when he was nineteen years old. He was elected to the House of Burgesses when he was only twenty years old and for his first speech chose to come out boldly in opposition to slavery, proposing a heavy tax on future importation of slaves. He was an outspoken opponent of the Stamp Tax in 1764, and was asked to prepare an address to the King and a Memorial to the House of Lords. These are considered to be among the best state papers of that period. He took a leading role at the First Continental Congress where he impressed his fellow delegates with his political knowledge and the "fire and splendor" of his oratory in defense of colonial liberties. As a member of Congress in 1776, he introduced the resolution calling for independence from Great Britain and continued to serve in Congress until 1780. He was also a member of the Virginia Convention which ratified the Constitution of the United States. He became one of the first U.S. senators under the Constitution and it was he who proposed the Tenth Amendment which sets specific limits on federal power over the states. He retired from public life in 1792.

473 Cited by John Carter Matthews, 23.

474 Ibid.

Richard Henry Lee: An Effective Bridge between North and South

Although little mentioned today in comparison with Jefferson, Madison and Washington, Richard Henry Lee was a most important member of this Congress and those that followed. He was wise and, though often bold, was thoroughly capable of the fine art of diplomacy. Lee acted as a providential bridge between the plain spoken, sober-suited New Englanders and the elegant aristocrats of the South, many of whom were not impressed with men such as Samuel and John Adams and thought them too radical. Lee, on the other hand, was a southern aristocrat, educated in England and a fine orator. As a plantation owner, he was also a man of substance and was of an old and respected family. Although Lee, too, was somewhat radical in Southern eyes, he was able to articulate colonial grievances and convictions with clarity, polish, and grace. With the urgency of his dynamic rhetoric, he awakened the minds and hearts of many of the delegates to the necessity of demanding a redress of grievances from Parliament—and from the King. John Carter Matthews, in his biography of Lee, noted that: Lee's twenty years in the House of Burgesses taught him how to oppose measures without angering his opponents.[475] Samuel Adams must have thought him an instrument of Divine Providence. Both John and Samuel Adams were very willing to let Lee—and any other delegates sensitive to the plight of blockaded Boston—speak for them.

A Committee on Rights Appointed

After Congress assembled on September 5, Peyton Randolph was elected as its chairman. The delegates lost no time in forming a committee on rights, infringements, and remedies. According to John Adams, two delegates from each colony were appointed to the committee which began its meetings in Philadelphia on September 8 at Carpenters Hall. We know that both John and Samuel Adams were anxious to ground colonial rights on the Law of Nature as they had learned it from Locke. In Richard Henry Lee of Virginia they found a strong ally. According to Adams, Lee stressed that colonial rights were built on "a fourfold foundation—on Nature, on the [B]ritish Constitution, on Charters, and on immemorial usage...." Lee maintained, however, that "we should lay our Rights on the broadest Bottom, the Ground of Nature...." He pointed out that their ancestors had found no government here and, continuing in Lockean terms, he asserted that "Life and Liberty, which is necessary for the Security of Life, cannot

---

475 See Matthews, 24.

be given up when we enter into Society."[476]

John Adams related in his diary that Lee was "for making the Repeal of every Revenue Law, the Boston Port Bill…and the Removal of all the Troops, the end of the Congress, and an abstinence from all Dutied Articles…Rum, Molasses, Sugar, Tea, Wine, Fruits, etc." an urgent priority. If Americans abstained from the articles and stated their rights firmly in a series of resolutions, Lee told Adams, he was "absolutely certain that the same Ship which carries home the Resolution will bring back the Redress."[477]

Lee was supported by the rest of the Virginia Delegation, in his desire to declare illegal both the Boston Port Bill that blockaded Boston and the alterations in the government of Massachusetts designed to shift legal and political power from the colonies to England. Not only should these acts be declared illegal, but Lee declared that Congress should demand their repeal as well as repeal of the Quebec Act extending the boundaries of that province to the Ohio River, thus taking territory away from Virginia. Lee also made the point that in the Quebec Act the British Ministry also acknowledged the Roman Catholic Church in Quebec as the established church, and with the stroke of a pen, Great Britain had also abolished English law in Quebec. This was tantamount to "erecting a tyranny" in the province of Quebec which would be a constant threat to freedom in the other Protestant colonies.

Paul Revere Arrives with the Suffolk Resolves

The New Englanders were acutely conscious that English General Gage was busy fortifying occupied Boston. It was a tense time for them as days passed in debate. Then, on September 17, an express rider from Massachusetts—none other than Paul Revere—unexpectedly turned up bringing with him bold resolutions from the towns comprising Suffolk County, Massachusetts. Soon known as the Suffolk Resolves, they had been drafted by Massachusetts physician and patriot, Dr. Joseph Warren, and they roundly condemned Parliaments' latest acts.[478]

These Resolves were a clarion call to action and reinforced Lee's arguments for action. The first resolution declared that they acknowledged

---

476 Ibid.

477 John Adams, cited by Matthews, 23.

478 Dr. Joseph Warren (1741-1775) American physician and patriot. He was born at Roxbury, Mass., graduated from Harvard in 1759 and became a physician in Boston in 1764. In 1774, he was a member of the Massachusetts Provincial Congress and its president in 1775. He was killed fighting for American liberty at the Battle of Bunker Hill on June 17, 1775.

George III as the rightful successor to the throne of England who as such was "entitled to the allegiance of the British realm, and agreeable to compact, of the English colonies in America" and that "said covenant is the tenure and claim on which are founded our allegiance and submission." The second resolve then boldly claimed the civil and religious rights bequeathed to them by their forefathers, eloquently declaring:

> THAT it is an indispensable duty which we owe to God, our country, ourselves, and posterity, by all lawful ways and means in our power to maintain, defend, and preserve those civil and religious rights and liberties, for which many of our fathers fought, bled, and died, and to hand them down entire to future generations.

Surely John Locke would have approved of the clear-eyed, bold determination of these colonial Englishmen to defend their civil and religious rights, just as their fathers had done in his day. The third and fourth resolves were blunt and direct—and also very Lockean:

> THAT the late acts of the British parliament for blocking up the harbour of Boston, for altering the established form of government in this colony, and for screening the most flagitious violators of the laws of the province from a legal trial, are gross infractions of those rights to which we are justly entitled by the laws of nature, the British constitution, and the charter of the province.

> THAT no obedience is due from this province to either or any part of the acts above-mentioned, but that they be rejected as the attempts of a wicked administration to enslave America.[479]

The Suffolk Resolves went on to urge all the colonies—"to withhold all commercial intercourse with Great Britain, Ireland, and the West Indies...." until colonial rights were restored. Another important resolve was that "this county, confiding in the wisdom and integrity of the [C]ontinental Congress, now sitting at Philadelphia, pay all due respect and submission to such measures as may be recommended by them to the colonies, for the restoration and establishment of our rights, civil, and religious, and for renewing that harmony and union between Great-Britain and the colonies, so earnestly wished for by all good men."[480]

A most important and eloquent resolve demonstrated the determination of the patriots not to allow or condone attempts at mob rule. It urged

---

479 Suffolk Resolves, from the *Journals of the Continental Congress* 1774-1789 in Hall, *Christian History*, 2:578.
480 Ibid., 581.

upon all "not to engage in any routs, riots, or licentious attacks upon the properties of any person whatsoever, as being subversive of all order and government; but, by a steady, manly, uniform, and persevering opposition, to convince our enemies, that in a contest so important, in a cause so solemn, our conduct shall be such as to merit the approbation of the wise, and the admiration of the brave and free of every age and of every country."[481]

Congress Supports and Publishes the Suffolk Resolves

John and Samuel Adams were moved to find that most of the delegates greeted the Suffolk Resolves with hearty support. Richard Henry Lee proposed a resolution that vigorously supported them. His resolution angered and dismayed such men as Joseph Galloway, the Speaker of the Pennsylvania House of Representatives, who thought it treasonous. But the resolution passed and, along with the Suffolk Resolves, was released for publication in the newspapers.

Congress then took up the question of non-importation with Lee opening the debate. Congress readily agreed that no more goods should be accepted from England after a December 1 deadline. They then moved on to consider the question of non-exportation. Should they prohibit exportation of goods until a July 1775 cut-off date, as Virginia's delegation had been instructed to hold to? Since several colonies had different ideas on the matter, discussion bogged down.

THE DECLARATION OF RIGHTS OF 1774

It was not until almost the end of their proceedings that the First Continental Congress finally passed their own Declaration. During the debates on this document, which was akin to the earlier English *Declaration of Rights* of 1689, the basis of their rights was discussed. Should it be the Law of Nature? Or the British Constitution? Or the colonial Charters? It was decided that, as Richard Henry Lee and the Adamses had suggested, the document be based first, on the Law of Nature, then on the British Constitution, and, lastly on the colonial charters or compacts.

The Preamble to the Declaration stated "That the inhabitants of the English Colonies in North America, by the immutable laws of nature, the principles of the English constitution, and the several charters or compacts, have the following Rights" which are then listed in ten resolutions, of which the first four are perhaps the most significant from the Lockean point of view:

---

481 Ibid.

1) That they are entitled to life, liberty, and property, and they have never ceded to any sovereign power whatever, a right to dispose of either without their consent.

2) That our ancestors, who first settled these colonies, were at the time of their emigration from the mother country, entitled to all the rights, liberties, and immunities of free and natural-born subjects, within the realm of England.

3) That by such emigration they by no means forfeited, surrendered, or lost any of those rights, but that they were, and their descendants now are, entitled to the exercise and enjoyment of all such of them, as their local and other circumstances enable them to exercise and enjoy.

4) That the foundation of English liberty, and of all free government, is a right in the people to participate in their legislative council: and as the English colonists are not represented, and from their local and other circumstances, cannot properly be represented in the British parliament, they are entitled to a free and exclusive power of legislation in their several provincial legislatures, where their right of representation can alone be preserved, in all cases of taxation and internal polity....[482]

American historian Richard Frothingham observed that "the phrase in some instances is similar to that in the Bill of Rights of William and Mary. It presents the colonies as a unit in the vital matters of representation, free discussion, free assemblies, and trial by jury,—in a word, self-government. It was hoped—faintly by some, strongly by others—that the basis laid down in this interesting paper might lead to an act of settlement fixing the terms for a permanent union between America and England."[483]

Would Locke have agreed with this Declaration?

Before proceeding further, it may be well to consider whether or not John Locke would have accepted such sweeping declarations of colonial powers as those contained in this declaration. He probably would not have, if they had come in his century. It would have seemed at that time impracticable for the colonies to have claimed such extensive rights and to have challenged the home government in England to such an extent. But, had Locke lived a century later and been as active in the political affairs

---

482 Declaration and Resolves of the Congress of 1774, October 14, 1774, from *Journals of the Continental Congress*, in Hall, *Christian History*, 2:586.

483 Richard Frothingham, *The Rise of the Republic of the United States* (1890) in Hall, *Christian History*, 2:589.

of the 1760s and 1770s as he had been in the 1680s and 1690s, I believe he would have agreed with William Pitt (now Lord Chatham) who, after reading the papers issued by this congress, declared to the House of Lords:

> When your lordships look at the papers, when you consider their decency, firmness, and wisdom, you cannot but respect their cause and wish to make it your own. For myself, I must declare and avow, that, in all my reading and observation,—and it has been my favorite study: I have read Thucydides, and have studied and admired the master states of the world,—that for solidity of reasoning, force of sagacity, and wisdom of conclusion, under such a complication of circumstances, no nation or body of men can stand in preference to the general congress at Philadelphia.[484]

But would Locke have insisted, like Pitt, that though Parliament should not tax the American colonies without their own consent, it should bind them in all other ways? I think not. Probably Locke would have been among those gentlemen who would have urged conciliation and a large measure of self-government, and he would have applauded these first faint outlines of federal theory, which, if pursued, might have preserved the Empire for many more years. Undoubtedly, he would have sympathized with the insistence on local self-government which his close friend, William Molyneux, had claimed earlier for the Irish Parliament. The issues of the individual's rights to life, liberty, and property, and to consent and compact as the basis of civil government, as well as the right to erect and participate in governmental bodies that protect the individual's natural God-given rights against tyrants were, as we have seen, at the forefront of his political thought. To see his own ideas so well enunciated by this extraordinary congress surely would have been of great satisfaction to him.

AN ASSOCIATION OF ALL THE COLONIES

These Lockean ideas were not only enunciated in the Declaration and Resolves of the First Continental Congress, but also in their *The Association of the United Colonies* that set up a system of commercial non-intercourse with Great Britain. After an enumeration of their grievances, it affirmed that: "To obtain redress of these Grievances, which threaten destruction to the Lives, Liberty, and Property of his Majesty's subjects in North America,

---

[484] For the remarks of William Pitt, the Earl of Chatham, see Frothingham in Hall, *Christian History*, 2:596. In addition to the Declaration, one of the papers Chatham admired, consider also the "Memorial to the Inhabitants of British North America," written by Richard Henry Lee and adopted by Congress on October 21, 1774, and the "Petition to the King" also drafted by Lee.

we are of opinion that a Non-Importation, Non-Consumption, and Non-Exportation Agreement, faithfully adhered to, will prove the most speedy, effectual, and peaceable measure; and, therefore, we do, for ourselves, and the inhabitants of the several Colonies whom we represent, firmly agree and associate, under the sacred ties of Virtue, Honour, and Love of our Country, as follows.... ."

The details were then enumerated in fourteen points, beginning with a provision that a committee be chosen in each county, city, and town from those qualified to vote for representatives in their legislatures. It was to be their duty to see that the Association was being faithfully kept, and, if not, that the matter be publicly revealed in the press. Other headings dealt with such things as a provision that all local manufactures be sold at reasonable prices, "so that no undue advantage be taken of a future scarcity of Goods"; that it was agreed and resolved that there would be no Trade or Commerce with any colony which did not agree to the Association or which violated it, but that they would "hold them as unworthy of the rights of freemen, and as inimical to the liberties of this country." The resolves concluded by asserting that "we do solemnly bind ourselves and our constituents, under the ties aforesaid, to adhere to this Association" until their grievances were redressed.[485]

THE ASSOCIATION AND
THE SENTIMENT OF UNION

Historian Frothingham wisely observed that "The Association has been termed a compact formed for the preservation of American rights...and the commencement of the American Union. It was an embodiment of the sentiment of union, and of the will of the people on the subject of their commercial relations,—the first enactment, substantially, of a general law by America."[486] In his own time, Locke might have opposed the colonies taking charge of their own commercial relations with the Mother Country in such an audacious way. There is evidence that he followed the colonial policies of his own time quite faithfully. But in this later century, he would have come to rethink this position, I believe, and would have desired to allow these English colonists freer trade practices, especially on an inter-colonial basis (for the colonies were even forbidden to trade with each other or to start colonial manufactures that would be in competition with

485 See text in Hall, *Christian History*, 2:590-93.
486 Frothingham in Hall, *Christian History*, 2:590.

English manufactured goods). He would surely have observed that the American colonies were not conquered provinces won by warfare, to be plundered of what they produced, by a conqueror's rights. The inhabitants of these colonies were after all fellow Englishmen. At this point in time, I believe he would have accepted that these intrepid colonial Englishmen were but claiming their natural rights as men—those rights he had so often championed—as well as their rights as Englishmen under the English Constitution, not to mention the rights enumerated in the charters issued to them by English monarchs.

WILLIAM PITT DEFENDS THE COLONIES IN THE HOUSE OF LORDS

When the papers reached London, William Pitt, now Lord Chatham, made valiant efforts to convince Parliament that the colonies should be treated better. On January 20, 1775, he made a motion in the House of Lords that British troops should be removed from Boston. He looked, said one observer, "like an old Roman Senator, rising with the dignity of age, yet speaking with the fire of youth."[487]

In urging that the troops be removed from Boston, Pitt declared he was certain that Massachusetts would never be reconciled if they were not. "What is our right," was his impassioned question, "to persist in such cruel and vindictive measures against that loyal and respectable people?" He declared that they had been abused and misrepresented in Parliament. Yet, under this provocation, how had they behaved? "With unexampled patience, with unparalleled wisdom." It was evident to him that all attempts to establish despotism over such a mighty continental nation must have fatal consequences. "There is," he insisted, "no time to be lost.... Nay, while I am now speaking, the decisive blow may be struck, and millions are involved in the consequence.... Years, perhaps ages, will not heal the wounds."[488]

A few days later (on January 23), the House of Commons received a petition signed by several hundred English merchants, who knew what the American *Association's* ban on buying English goods would mean to their business. It urged Parliament to repeal the "Coercive Acts" concerning

---

487 Cited by Samuel Eliot Morison in *The Oxford History of the American People*, 3 vols. Oxford University Press, 1965, New York: Mentor Books, 1972, 1:279.

488 Morison, 1:279-80. Morison relates that the Duke of Richmond also warned the Lords, "You may spread fire, sword and desolation, but that will not be government...." He also warned them that "No people will ever be made to submit to a form of government they say they will not receive," 280.

which the Americans had complained.[489] It was then that statesman Edmund Burke gave the first of his series of speeches on the need for conciliation with the colonies. The motion to repeal was lost, though, by a wide margin—82, in favor; 197, against.

LORD CHATHAM ON HOW TO SETTLE THE AMERICAN PROBLEM

Although no longer in the House of Commons, Lord Chatham (William Pitt) got a bill introduced there to settle the American problem. If passed, Chatham's bill would have acknowledged the Continental Congress as a legal body, and would have repealed the Coercive Acts, the tea tax, and the Quebec Act. It would also have withdrawn the troops from Boston and would have guaranteed the legal standing of the colonial charters. Samuel Eliot Morison notes that if this bill had been passed, there would have been no war and no Declaration of Independence. But it did not pass. Indeed, it was overwhelmingly defeated.

Lord Chatham was filled with foreboding. On February 1, he warned Parliament in solemn and prophetic words that "Great Britain and America are already in martial array, waiting for the signal to engage in a contest in which...ruin and destruction must be the inevitable consequence to both." His words went unheeded. On February 20, Dr. Joseph Warren wrote to an English friend that while it was still not too late to settle amicably the disputes between the colonies and Great Britain, "if once General Gage should lead his troops into the country, with design to enforce the late Acts of Parliament, Great Britain may take her leave...of all America."[490] General Gage did exactly that, thus precipitating the battles of Lexington and Concord from which there was no turning back.

THE KING REFUSES TO READ "THE OLIVE BRANCH PETITION"

But when Congress convened again in May of 1775, there were still those who believed that the King would be their protector against Parliament. Samuel Eliot Morison writes that only a few delegates, such as Samuel and

---

489 The "Coercive Acts" of 1774, also known as the "Intolerable Acts," included the Boston Port Act blockading Boston; the Massachusetts Government Act altering the government of the province by vesting power previously held by the colonists in the hands of the King; the Administration of Justice Act, authorizing the sending of rebels to England for trial rather than being tried in Massachusetts by a jury of their peers; the Quartering Act ordering the King's troops to be quartered in colonists' homes without their permission and vacant houses and other properties to be requisitioned. (See *Christian History*, 2:347.)

490 Chatham and Warren cited by Morison, 1:281.

John Adams, Benjamin Franklin, the Lees, and Christopher Gadsden of North Carolina thought that independence was the only answer. Even the army that George Washington was chosen to lead was called "the Army of the United Colonies" and the flag contained the British "Union Jack" emblem in one corner.

To explain that they were not at war with the King, but only with his wicked ministers who were abusing their powers, Congress set Thomas Jefferson to work writing *A Declaration on the Causes of Taking Up Arms*. This was done to assure English fellow subjects in other parts of the British Empire that the colonists did not mean to dissolve union with Great Britain. They were fighting for neither glory nor conquest but only in defense of their rights as Englishmen. They hoped that their firm resistance shown at Lexington and Concord would cause the House of Commons to vote Lord North out of office and recall Lord Chatham.

Despite George Washington's amazing feat of bringing together and training 1,000 undisciplined militia into an army at Cambridge where he took command on July 2, 1775, Congress deferred to the wishes of John Dickinson and adopted, on July 8, the "Olive Branch Petition" he had drafted. It expressed profound attachment to the King and begged him to intercede for the colonies to stop the war and repeal the Coercive Acts so that there could be "a happy and permanent reconciliation." Congress recessed on August 2, 1775, until September 5 when they expected they would have news from the King.

What the delegates did not know was that the King was not disposed to protect them from his ministers. He was not misled by wicked counselors, as many Americans had assumed. In fact, he heartily supported all the repressive acts that his ministers had suggested. George III never read the generous, affectionate petition from Congress. He refused to accept it, having long since determined that the Americans were rebels.

THE KING DECLARES THE COLONISTS ARE REBELS

On August 23, 1775, the king proclaimed that a rebellion existed in America "and that it hath been much promoted and encouraged by the traitorous correspondence, counsels, and comfort of divers wicked and desperate persons within this realm." Everyone, he said, was bound by law to help to put down the rebellion and to provide the authorities with information on "traitorous conspiracies."[491] The King also said that the

---

491 Cited by John Carter Matthews in *Richard Henry Lee*, 39.

"utmost endeavors must be taken to suppress such rebellion, and to bring the traitors to justice."[492] New England historian John Wingate Thornton reported that George III's letters to Lord North "show that the war was *his* war." (Thornton also related that after the war, when John Adams was presented at court as the first minister from the United States, the King told him, "I have done nothing in the late contest but what I *thought myself* bound to do.'"[493])

ENGLISH FRIENDS PLEAD FOR AMERICA'S CAUSE

Despite the decided opposition of the King, the friends of America in Parliament continued seeking a way to resolve the dispute between the colonies and the Mother Country. On November 16, 1775, Edmund Burke submitted another conciliatory proposal to the House of Commons. It was rejected by a two to one vote. But Lord Barrington, the Secretary of War, along with Samuel Tucker, who was Dean of Gloucester, and economist Adam Smith all agreed that English troops should not be stationed in the American colonies. The colonies also should be allowed their independence if this was what they wanted, or else they should "state their terms" for remaining in the British Empire.[494] But the King and the overwhelming majority of the members of Parliament chose not to listen to these words of wisdom and moderation. Thus, the die was cast, and the American colonies were forced to move onward to the inevitable formal break with the Mother Country.

The news that the king had summarily rejected the Olive Branch Petition did not arrive in America until November. This was followed by a royal proclamation closing the colonies to all commercial dealings after March 1, 1776. By March, Lord North's Prohibitory Act, passed by Parliament in December, declaring the colonies in rebellion and out of the King's protection had also reached Congress. Richard Henry Lee argued that this called for the abolition of the old colonial governments and he and John Adams introduced a resolution "to the assemblies and conventions of the United Colonies," that:

---

492 George III's proclamation cited by Morison, 1:291. John Wingate Thornton wrote that George III had "an excessive jealousy of ministerial control." It appeared that "he settled questions of state on personal, not on national grounds. Thus, in the midst of the American war, he declared respecting Mr. Pitt..., 'No advantage to my country, nor personal danger to myself, can make me address myself to Lord Chatham, or to any other branch of opposition. Honestly, I would rather lose the crown I now wear than bear the ignominy of possessing it under their shackles.'" (See Thornton in *The Pulpit of the American Revolution*, Boston, 1860, 149.)

493 Thornton, 149.

494 See Morison, 1:291.

[W]here no government sufficient to the exigencies of their affairs have been hitherto established, to adopt such government as shall, in the opinion of the representatives of the people, best conduce to the happiness and safety of their constituents in particular and America in general.[495]

THE VIRGINIA DECLARATION OF RIGHTS

Our attention must now shift to Virginia, because it was here that a model declaration of rights was drawn up by Virginia statesman George Mason. It was widely copied in whole or in part by the other colonies as they became independent states. Robert Rutland in his study of George Mason, says that many of the colonies simply copied the Virginia Declaration, either wholly or in part, as each colony declared itself an independent state.[496] In this way, each colony set about translating Locke's theories of natural rights, compact, and consent into the governments they formed.

George Mason: Planter-Statesman

The author of this splendid declaration of rights was the dean of Virginia's intellectual leaders. Like Locke, this "planter-statesman" of strong scholarly bent yearned for the reflective life of quiet retirement on his plantation, his peace broken only by attending to his duties as a planter. But, like Locke, he found that Divine Providence beckoned him to take an active part in political affairs. The contributions of this "reluctant statesman" are impressive; not only was he the author of the Virginia Declaration of Rights, which stood as a model for the other Colonies to follow, but he was also to write the major part of the new Virginia Constitution.

Because he was the oldest son, his widowed mother had decided not to send him to England to be educated, as was the case with his younger brother, nor did she enroll him in the College of William and Mary. Instead, she trained him to run the plantation which he one day would inherit. As I have written elsewhere:

> This capable woman not only taught George his letters but, as he grew up, she taught him the principles of accounting and estate management. During his boyhood she also paid for tutors and sent him to a small school for a while. But, it was mainly through his own love of learning and the deep interest he developed in the study of English law and Constitutional government, together

---

495 John Carter Matthews, *Richard Henry Lee,* 45.

496 See Robert Rutland, *George Mason: Reluctant Statesman* (Colonial Williamsburg and Holt, Rinehart and Winston, 1961), 67-68.

with his wide reading of the best of literature, that George Mason became an exceptionally well-educated man. Though he never became a lawyer, his neighbors often sought legal advice from him because of his extensive knowledge of the law. Like Benjamin Franklin, George Mason is a prime example of the self-educated man who was in no way inferior to his more conventionally educated neighbors.[497]

Mason certainly studied the law assiduously in his uncle's law library where he undoubtedly read Locke, Sydney, and other English authors who wrote in the same vein. Locke's influence on him is seen by the fact that he knew many passages from Locke by heart including, of course, Locke's writings on "Life, liberty, and property."[498] By 1776, he was well-known for his work in the Virginia Legislature, for his steadfast opposition to the Stamp Act of 1764, which provoked his writing of the Non-Importation Resolutions of 1769 protesting this taxation without representation, and the "Fairfax Resolves" of 1774 eloquently stating the grievances of Virginia against Great Britain. It was not surprising, therefore, that his peers asked him to produce a Declaration of Rights for Virginia enunciating the principles that would underlie the Virginia Constitution. As Gaillard Hunt maintained, these principles were distinctively English. They were found in the Magna Charta, the Petition of Rights, the Acts of the Long Parliament, along with the doctrines of the Revolution of 1688 as explained by Locke."[499]

Lockean Philosophy Firmly in the Foreground

Lockean philosophy is firmly in the foreground of the Virginia Declaration which begins by asserting:

> That all men are by nature equally free and independent, and have certain inherent rights, of which, when they enter into a state of society, they cannot, by any compact, deprive or divest their posterity; namely, the enjoyment of life and liberty, with the means of acquiring and possessing property, and pursuing and obtaining happiness and safety.[500]

---

497 Mary-Elaine Swanson, *The Education of James Madison: A Model for Today.* Montgomery, Alabama: The Hoffman Center, 1994, 113-115.

498 Helen, Hill [Miller], *George Mason: Constitutionalist.* Cambridge, Mass., 1938, 141; cited in editorial note in Robert Rutland, *The Papers of George Mason,* 1725-1792, 3 vols., Chapel Hill, N.C.: University of North Carolina Press, 1970, 1:279.

499 See Gaillard Hunt, *The Life of James Madison,* 1902, New York: Russell & Russell, 1968, 4.

500 See Helen Hill Miller, *George Mason, Gentleman Revolutionary,* 340. The author includes in the appendix to her superb biography of Mason his first draft of the Declaration, as well as the first printed draft, together with the final draft, from which this citation is taken.

Helen Hill Miller, in her biography of Mason, observes that all political thinkers knew Locke's trinity of rights, but that Mason introduced something strikingly new in the use of its third term.[501] Mason emphasized that in addition to life and liberty, no man could be deprived of "the means of acquiring and possessing property, as well as pursuing and obtaining happiness and safety."[502] In England at that time, as Miller implies, the means of acquiring property were limited if one was not already of the propertied class. It was, however, infinitely easier in the New World to carve out for oneself a property in land through one's own labors. It was on this continent in Locke's "state of nature" that the English colonists often endured famine and backbreaking labors in the early days. Still, the land beckoned all around them and those who forsook the old world for the new often did so, not only for political or religious liberty, but also for economic opportunity—even as they still do today. Mason discerned that being free to acquire property was an important natural right.

Lord Kames on Property

Another author admired by George Mason and other Founding Fathers was the Scottish judge, Henry Home, Lord Kames (1696-1782), who was also greatly influenced by Locke. He affirmed Locke's views on property by asserting that this right:

> is established by the constitution of our nature, antecedent to all human conventions. We are led by nature to consider goods acquired by our industry and labor as belonging to us, as our own. We have a sense of feeling of property, and conceive these goods to be our own, just as much as we conceive our hands, our feet, and our other members to be our own; and we have a sense or feeling equally clear of the property of others.[503]

Just so Locke had written that "every Man has a *Property* in his own *Person*. This no Body has a right to but himself. The *Labour* of his Body, and the *Work* of his Hands, we may say, are properly his. Whatsoever then he removes out of the State that Nature hath provided, and left it in, he hath mixed his *Labour* with, and joyned to it something that is his own, and thereby makes it his *Property*."[504]

---

501 Miller, 152.
502 Cited by Miller. Emphasis added.
503 Henry Home, Lord Kames, *Essays on the Principles of Morality and Natural Religion.* Edinburgh: Kincaid and Donaldson, 1751, 108; cited by Miller, 153.
504 Locke, *Second Treatise Of Civil Government*, par. 27. See also par. 32 dealing with land.

Pursuing Happiness and Safety

In addition to the right of acquiring and possessing property, the first clause of Mason's Declaration of Rights also introduces the right of "pursuing and obtaining happiness and safety." Both Mason and, later, Jefferson were to introduce the pursuit of happiness into their declarations. Both may have been influenced by the Swiss author, Jean-Jacques Burlemaqui, whose book *Principles of Natural Law* was published in 1747 and who used this phraseology. The Founders knew, however, that the right to be secure in one's property—of whatever kind—was requisite to ensure happiness. John Dickinson, referring to the connection between property rights and happiness in his seventh *Farmer's Letter to the Inhabitants of the British Colonies* (1767), wrote:

> Let these truths be indelibly impressed on our minds—that we cannot be happy, without being free—that we cannot be free, without being secure in our property—that we cannot be secure in our property, if without our consent, others may, as by right, take it away—that taxes imposed on us by parliament, do thus take it away....[505]

Magistrates as Trustees

The Second Clause of the Declaration of Rights states in unmistakably Lockean terms "That all power is vested in, and consequently derived from, the People; that magistrates are their trustees and servants, and at all times amenable to them." Locke had written in the *Second Treatise*, par. 22, that "the *Liberty of Man, in Society,* is to be under no other Legislative Power, but that established, by consent, in the Common-wealth, nor under the Dominion of any Will, or Restraint of any Law, but what the Legislative shall enact, according to the Trust put in it."

Government Instituted for the Common Benefit

Clause 3 also has a strong Lockean flavor, outlining the reason governments are instituted and the right of the people to alter or abolish them. It begins by asserting that "Government is, or ought to be, instituted for the common benefit, protection, and security of the people, nation, or community;—of all the various modes and forms of Government that is best which is capable of producing the greatest degree of happiness and safety...." And it goes on to state in terms Locke would have approved

---

505 John Dickinson, *Farmer's Letter to the Inhabitants of the British Colonies*, No. 12, Philadelphia, 1767, in Hall, *Christian History*, 2:445.

that "whenever any Government shall be found inadequate or contrary to these purposes, a majority of the community hath an indubitable, unalienable, and indefeasible right, to reform, alter, or abolish it, in such manner as shall be judged most conducive to the publick weal." [506]

Clause 4 states that no man, or set of men, is entitled to exclusive or separate emoluments and privileges from the community, but in consideration of publick services; which, not being descendible, neither ought the offices of Magistrate, Legislator, or Judge to be hereditary.

Mason saw legislators, not as a privileged elite, but as citizens who would go back into private life after serving their countrymen and who would then have to live under the laws they had made and thus would feel, "the burdens of the people." (See Clause 5.)

Clause 6 declares that "elections of members to serve as Representatives of the people, in Assembly, ought to be free" and that members of the community "cannot be taxed or deprived of their property for publick uses without their own consent or that of their Representative so elected, nor bound by any law to which they have not, in like manner, assented, for the public good." (A splendid statement in true Lockean vein.)

Clause 7 declares that all power of suspending laws or their execution without consent of the people's representatives "is injurious to their rights, and ought not to be exercised."

Clauses 8 and 9 dealing with trial by jury and excessive bail or fines and cruel and unusual punishment refers back to the English Bill of Rights, as does Clause 10 dealing with unreasonable searches and seizures. Clause 11 again emphasizes the importance of trial by jury in all cases of suits respecting property and between one person and another. Indeed, Mason says that trial by jury in such cases "ought to be held sacred." [507]

Clause 12 would have struck a special chord with Locke, dealing as it does with freedom of the press which Mason wrote is "one of the greatest bulwarks of liberty, and [one that] can never be restrained but by despotick Governments." Clause 13 declares that standing armies in time of peace "should be avoided as dangerous to liberty; and that, in all cases the military should be under strict subordination to, and governed by, the civil power." Clause 14 simply states that no other government separate from the government of Virginia shall be erected or established within its territories.

Clause 15 is a fine magisterial statement of fundamental principles: "That no free Government, or the blessing of liberty, can be preserved to

---

506 Declaration of Rights in Helen Hill Miller, 340.
507 Ibid.

any people but by a firm adherence to justice, moderation, temperance, frugality, and virtue, and by frequent recurrence to fundamental principles."

Clause 16 which concludes the Declaration is of far-reaching significance. In this statement on religious liberty, Mason was greatly aided by the young James Madison, who was then just getting into politics. It was Madison who suggested a most important change in wording, whereby Mason's language using the Lockean word "toleration" was exchanged for "the free exercise of religion." Now, as we have seen, while Locke spoke of toleration, what he was really describing was religious liberty and, it will be remembered, this was also true of his religious clauses in the *Constitutions of Carolina*. Nevertheless, it is true that the word Locke used in his writings was "toleration." It was probably preferred by Mason who was a staunch member of the Church of England. The important thing to note in this change in wording is that "toleration" implies a concession, while "free exercise" connotes a *right* not a *grant*.

THE VIRGINIA CONSTITUTION

Excellent as the Virginia Declaration was, it did not discuss the character of the structure that would be built upon it. The needed directions for this structure to implement the Declaration's philosophy were soon forthcoming from Mason's pen when he became the principal author of the new Virginia Constitution which took effect on June 29, 1776.

THE DECLARATION OF INDEPENDENCE

The Declaration of Independence followed hard on the heels of Mason's Virginia Declaration of Rights. It was Virginian Richard Henry Lee who proposed the resolution for independence on the floor of Congress on June 7, 1776:

> That these United Colonies are, and of right ought to be free and independent states, that they are absolved from all allegiance to the British crown, and that all political connection between them and the state of Great Britain is, and ought to be totally dissolved.
>
> That it is expedient to take the most effectual measures for forming foreign alliances.
>
> That a plan of confederation be prepared and transmitted to the respective colonies for their consideration and approbation.[508]

---

508 John Carter Matthews, *Richard Henry Lee*, 49.

John Adams seconded these Resolutions, but those who opposed independence mustered a vote to put off debate on them until July 1. On June 11, however, a committee composed of delegates from the different regions of colonial America was appointed to draft a Declaration of Independence. It consisted of John Adams, Massachusetts; Benjamin Franklin, Pennsylvania; Roger Sherman, Connecticut; Robert Livingston, New York; and Thomas Jefferson, Virginia. To Jefferson went the task of the actual writing of the Declaration, as he was already well known as an eloquent political writer.

In Jefferson's original draft his only reference to God was the allusion in the Preamble to "nature's God." The Committee added the phrase, "they are endowed by their Creator with certain inalienable rights." Other changes made by Congress were the addition of the phrase "appealing to the Supreme Judge of the World, for the rectitude of our intention," as well as the closing of the document "with a firm reliance on the protection of divine Providence...."[509] These changes made the Declaration conform more closely to the Christian conscience of most members of this historic congress.[510]

The Lockean Influence

Jefferson's great Declaration is full of Lockean ideas and even phraseology. Some of the wording is almost identical with that of Locke, such as the phrase "mankind are more disposed to suffer while evils are sufferable than to right themselves," which in Locke is "the People, who are more disposed to suffer, than right themselves by Resistance...."[511]

Locke's "But if a long train of Abuses, Prevarications, and Artifices, all tending the same way"[512] becomes in the Declaration of Independence, "But when a long train of abuses and usurpations pursuing invariably the same object...."

---

509 This last phrase has been attributed to Rev. John Witherspoon, Madison's teacher at the College of New Jersey and the only minister serving in Congress at that time.

510 Thomas Jefferson held various religious views throughout his long life, but apparently was never an orthodox Christian. He rejected the divinity of Jesus, but he spoke with great admiration of the moral system of Jesus as "the most benevolent and sublime probably that has ever been taught, and consequently more perfect than those of any of the ancient philosophers...." (Letter of Thomas Jefferson to Joseph Priestley, in 1803, in Swanson, *The Education of James Madison*, 125.) In his *Notes on Virginia* Jefferson asked: "Can the liberties of a nation be thought secure when we have removed their only firm basis, a conviction in the minds of the people that these liberties are the gift of God? That they are not to be violated but with his wrath? I tremble for my country when I reflect that God is just: that his justice cannot sleep forever." (Cited by Cunningham, 62-63.)

511 Par. 230 in Locke's *Second Treatise of Government*.

512 Ibid., par. 225.

Jefferson refers to "the form to which they are accustomed" while Locke says, "in the frame they have been accustomed to."[513] Jefferson accepted Locke's definition of tyranny as "the exercise of power beyond right" which he used in defining George III as a tyrant.[514] All the quotes Jefferson used seem to have been culled from Locke's chapter on the Dissolution of Government, the famous "right of revolution" chapter.

The Declaration of Independence as "an expression of the American mind"

Despite his heavy reliance on Locke, Jefferson claimed that while he was writing the Declaration he had "turned to neither book nor pamphlet." (This comment was in response to Richard Henry Lee who thought that Jefferson had simply copied from Locke's *Second Treatise on Government*.) While Jefferson did not deny that he had read Locke, he insisted that when writing the Declaration he had not been striving for originality. "I did not consider it as any part of my charge to invent new ideas altogether, and to offer no sentiment which had ever been expressed before." On the contrary, his desire was "to place before mankind the common sense of the subject, in terms so plain and firm as to command their assent" and that his document "was intended to be an expression of the American mind."[515]

In this he succeeded brilliantly. His great Declaration admirably stated the philosophical foundation upon which the new government would be erected. After long debate, the Resolution on independence was finally passed on July 2 by 12 to none. (The delegates decided that each colony would have one vote. New York abstained.) On July 3, John Adams wrote prophetically to his wife Abigail:

> The Second Day of July 1776, will be the most memorable Epocha, in the History of America. —I am apt to believe that it will be celebrated, by succeeding Generations, as the great anniversary Festival. It ought to be commemorated, as the Day of Deliverance by solemn Acts of Devotion to God Almighty. It ought to be solemnized with Pomp and Parade, with Shews, Games, Sports,

---

513 Ibid., par. 223.

514 The Declaration states that "The history of the present King of Great Britain is a history of repeated injuries and usurpations all having in direct object the establishment of an absolute Tyranny over these states.... A Prince, whose character is thus marked by every act which may define a Tyrant, is unfit to be the ruler of a free people."

515 Letter of Thomas Jefferson to Henry Lee, dated May 8, 1825 cited by Noble Cunningham, Jr., in *In Pursuit of Reason: The Life of Thomas Jefferson*, 48.

Guns, Bells, Bonfires, and Illuminations from one End of this Continent to the other from this Time forward forever more.[516]

Although John Adams thought that July 2 would be the great day of celebration for Americans, it turned out to be July 4, the day that Congress approved the Declaration of Independence after it had been amended. A large portion of the work chastising George III for his tyrannical acts toward colonial America was dropped from the Declaration, much to Jefferson's disappointment. But the work stands all the stronger today for omitting most of Jefferson's diatribe against the king, thereby emphasizing the lofty principles underlying our American system of government.

Like Mason's Declaration of Rights, this foundational document also awaited the structure that would be placed upon it by the Constitution of the United States. As will be seen in the next chapter, this great document also owes much to the political ideas of John Locke and of the Glorious Revolution that he had championed.

---

516 *The Book of Abigail and John—Selected Letters of the Adams Family* (1762–1784), edited by L.H. Butterfield, Mark Friedlaender and Mary-Jo Kline (Cambridge, Mass. and London England: Harvard University Press, 1975), 142.

CHAPTER TEN

Locke's Influence on the State and National Constitutions

It is certainly very material that the true doctrines of liberty,
as exemplified in our political systems,
should be inculcated on those who are to sustain
and may administer it....
Sidney and Locke are admirably calculated to impress on young
minds the right of nations to establish their own governments,
and to inspire a love of free ones....

JAMES MADISON
to Thomas Jefferson (1825)[517]

IN recent times, it has been said that the influence of John Locke on the formation of the United States Constitution was minimal. Donald Lutz of the University of Houston, for instance, takes this stance. After assessing the relative influence of various writers on the Founding Fathers from the 1760s to 1805, he asserts that while references to Locke are frequent in the 1770s, they decline in the 1780s at the time when the states were busy writing their constitutions. At this point, references to Montesquieu, with his discussion of forms of government and the separation of powers become much more frequent. Lutz believes that this should not be surprising. His reason for saying this, however, is very surprising. He acknowledges that Locke was profound in discussing the proper basis for government and for how to oppose tyranny, but believes that Locke had little to say about how

---

517 Letter of James Madison to Thomas Jefferson, February 8, 1825, in *James Madison: A Biography in His Own Words*, 2:383.

government should be designed. Therefore, Lutz maintains that Locke's influence was only felt in justifying the American Revolution and the right Americans had to write their own state constitutions as well as the national constitution. He asserts that Locke's influence in regard to the design of either state or national constitutions has been greatly exaggerated and that finding him "hidden" in passages in the United States Constitution is not supported by evidence to support this assertion.[518]

LOCKE ON INSTITUTIONAL DESIGN

But is this true? It seems quite odd to say that Locke had little to say about institutional design. True, he did not give the Founders everything they needed, for they were about to design something quite new: A federal republic uniting thirteen fledgling states into one nation. Certainly, the Founders found help in their reading of Montesquieu with his emphasis on the separation of powers into legislative, executive, and judicial. (Locke's division, it should be recalled, was between legislative, executive, and federative.) But we have seen that Locke had a good deal to say about the design of government, notably on the proper role of the executive, the primary importance of the legislative branch, the limits of its power, and the rules that should govern it. Locke also discussed, though briefly, the various forms of a commonwealth. Chapters IX through XIII of the *Second Treatise* are particularly rich in analysis of the powers of civil government and their proper relationship to each other.

It would seem that those who crafted the state constitutions, as well as the Constitution of the United States, were keenly aware of the wisdom of many of Locke's recommendations. By the time of constitution-making, however, there was little need to cite Locke directly, since everyone long ago had absorbed the arguments in his *Two Treatises of Government*. When they came to deal with the great issue of what form of government should be adopted by the union, the principles they invoked were essentially the same Lockean ones outlined in the Declaration of Independence and in the state declarations of right. Nor is it easy to understand why "finding him [Locke] hidden in passages of the U.S. Constitution is an exercise that requires more evidence than has hitherto ever been provided." First of all, the passages one can trace to Locke's influence are not "hidden." It is not therefore necessary to launch forth on a sea of speculation to find Locke's influence. The evidence is already there.

---

518 See Donald S. Lutz, "The Relative Influence of European Writers on Late Eighteenth-Century American Political Thought," in *The American Political Science Review* 78 (1984): 192-93.

LOCKE AND THE STATE CONSTITUTIONS

But before considering Locke's influence on the Constitution of the United States, it would be well to start with the state constitutions. Locke may not have been mentioned as often by name in the arguments at the various state constitutional conventions as in the revolutionary period, but Lockean ideas were still very much present at these conventions as the delegates sought to protect the individual against arbitrary government, always a great concern of Locke's.

It was Alice Baldwin who, writing of New England, said that "the constitutional convention and the written constitution were the children of the pulpit."[519] Almost all the members of the New England clergy were well-educated men who, as we have seen, were accustomed to preaching to their congregations on governmental matters. Their views were highly respected by their congregations. New England ministers, particularly in Massachusetts and New Hampshire, were in the forefront of the discussions on constitution-making and often served in provincial congresses and conventions.[520] As Baldwin relates, they were vigilant in insisting that when the colonists had broken away from the Mother Country, they had put themselves in a State of Nature; a new government could only be formed by a compact among the people through representatives elected by them to serve in a special constitutional convention.

This echoes Locke who had written that when a government is dissolved because of tyranny by the governing power, "the People are at liberty to provide for themselves, by erecting a new Legislative, differing from the other, by the change of Persons, or Form, or both as they shall find it for their safety and good."[521] These New England pastors also were intent on having a declaration of rights included in their new state constitutions—again, in order to protect the individual from arbitrary government. "When a constitution was presented to them," wrote Alice Baldwin, "that had not been formed in this fashion they led their townspeople to reject it, proceeded to give their reasons, and continued their demands upon the Assembly."[522] Their actions underscore once again how well these ministers understood what they had learned from the Holy Scriptures and also from

---

519 Baldwin, *The New England Clergy and the American Revolution*, 134.

520 Ibid., 135. Connecticut and Rhode Island adopted their old charters as the basis of their new state governments. Thus, observes Baldwin, "there was no need for any new application of the theories of government."

521 John Locke, *Second Treatise*, par. 220.

522 Baldwin, 136.

Locke which they saw illustrated in the history of the Glorious Revolution in England—a revolution that had engrossed Locke's thoughts and energies while he was advising its leaders.

REVEREND JONAS CLARK —CONSTITUTION MAKER

Notable among these clergymen was Reverend Jonas Clark, of Lexington, who had been an active supporter of the War of Independence and who had written a stirring account of the Battle of Lexington* which he had observed from his church nearby. The following biographical note on Clark reveals that he not only served the town of Lexington as its minister but also drew up many of the town's important papers beginning at the time of the Stamp Act. As E. L. Magoon relates:

> In 1765, the citizens vindicated the popular movement in respect to the Stamp-Act. In 1767, they unanimously concurred with the resolution of Boston, to prevent the consumption of foreign commodities. In 1768, they argued with great force against the right of Great Britain to tax America. In 1772, they resolved, in most thrilling terms, to seek redress for daily increasing wrongs; and in 1774, they took measures to supply themselves with ammunition, arms, and other requisites for military defence. What hero drew those masterly papers, defended their principles, and fired the people at all hazards to defend them? History has recorded the fact, the Reverend Jonas Clark was their author and chief defence. He was one of the many patriotic clergy of New England, who instructed their beloved flock in peace, and guarded them amid the dread necessities of war.[523]

Reverend Clark's service to his country did not end with the War of Independence. He became equally active in proclaiming the need for a state constitutional convention in order to draw up a constitution for the new state of Massachusetts. When, in 1778, the state Assembly drafted a constitution and presented it to the people, he was quick to object that the work had not been done by a special convention convened for that purpose alone nor did it include a declaration of rights. In June 1778, Jonas Clark was called upon once again by the town of Lexington to present the town's views

---

* See Jonas Clark, *The Battle of Lexington: Sermon and Eyewitness Narrative*, Nordskog Publishing Inc., 2007.

523 E. L. Magoon, *Orators of the American Revolution* in Rosalie J. Slater, *Teaching and Learning America's Christian History: The Principle Approach*, San Francisco: Foundation for American Christian Education, 1965, 49.

of why it could not accept the constitution presented by the Assembly.[524] His reasons for rejecting the 1778 document are distinctly Lockean:

> It may be observed that it appears to us that in emerging from a state of nature into a state of well-regulated society, mankind gave up some of their natural rights in order that others of greater importance to their well-being, safety and happiness, both as societies and individuals, might be the better enjoyed, secured, and defended. That a civil Constitution or form of government is of the nature of a most sacred covenant or contract entered into by the individuals which form the society, for which such Constitution or form of government is intended, whereby they mutually and solemnly engage to support and defend each other in the enjoyment of those rights which they mean to retain.[525]

"THE MAIN AND GREAT END OF…ANY CONSTITUTION…."

He then declared that it was absolutely necessary to have these fundamental retained rights stated explicitly in a Declaration of Rights, "so that Government and persons in authority might know the limits of their powers and that all members of society might know when their rights were violated or infringed."[526] Four other areas in the proposed constitution particularly concerned him.

> FIRST, he was convinced that equality of representation was vital to the preservation of the people's liberties and to their peace and safety. He believed that the distribution of representation in the assembly's document was inadequate and that it would leave the small towns at the mercy of corrupt and "designing men," which he said had been a frequent occurrence in England.[527]

---

524 Other distinguished Massachusetts clergymen who opposed the 1778 Constitution produced by the Assembly included: Boston patriot Samuel Cooper; Habijah Weld of Attleborough; Joseph Willard of Beverly; Peter Thacher of Malden; and Thomas Allen and Valentine Rathbun, of Pittsfield. (See Baldwin, 137.)

525 Lexington Town Records, 1778–1791, Record of June 15, 1778, cited by Baldwin, 138.

526 See Baldwin's summary, 138.

527 Locke commented on the injustice of the inequality of representation that occurred in Great Britain where some towns which had disappeared still had representatives in Parliament despite an extinct population. "Things of this World are in so constant a Flux, that nothing remains long in the same State. Thus…flourishing, mighty Cities come to ruine, and prove in time neglected and desolate Corners, whilst other unfrequented places grow into populous Countries, fill'd with Wealth and Inhabitants. But things not changing equally, and private interest often keeping up Customs and Privilege, when the reasons of them are ceased, it often comes to pass…that in tract of time this Representation becomes very unequal…. [W]e see the bare Name of a Town, of which there remains not so much as the ruines…or more Inhabitants than a Shepherd is to be found, [which] sends as many representatives to the grand Assembly of Law-makers, as a whole County numerous

SECOND, rotation in office was vital, and so he advocated a limita-tion on eligibility to serve.[528]

THIRD, he believed that the legislative and executive branches ought not to be blended, as appeared to be the case in the proposed constitution.[529]

FOURTH and last, he believed strongly that better provisions for amendment by the people ought to be included in the constitution.[530]

Alice Baldwin sums up eloquently this extraordinary minister's influence on the constitutional proceedings of his state:

> This minister, who held his people in the hollow of his hand and who was the friend and counsellor of statesmen, had, through years of meditation and study, worked out in fine detail the theories of government, and he greatly desired to see his state put them into effect. That his people appreciated his peculiar ability is evidenced by their choosing him in 1779 to serve as their representative in the Constitutional Convention.[531]

PASTORS WHO SERVED AT THE CONSTITUTIONAL CONVENTION

At least thirteen pastors represented their towns at the Massachusetts Constitutional Convention of 1779-1780. Jonas Clark was among the most influential ministers, who included the Reverend Gad Hitchcock of Pembroke, the Reverend Peter Thacher of Malden, the Reverend Henry Cummings of Billerica, and the Reverend Samuel West of Dartmouth.

---

in People, and powerful in riches.... [I]t being the interest, as well as intention of the People, to have a fair and equal Representative: whoever brings it nearest to that is an undoubted Friend to, and establisher of the Government and cannot miss the Consent and Approbation of the Com-munity." (John Locke, *Second Treatise*, extracts from pars. 157, 158).

528 Locke wrote that if the legislative power was vested in those who served for a time and then returned "into the ordinary state of subjects," they must then be replaced by new representatives chosen by the people. He does not discuss, however, whether he thought frequent rotation of power was necessary.

529 Locke advanced the same view that the Legislative and Executive Power should be "in distinct hands, (as they are in all moderated Monarchies, and well-framed Governments)...." *Second Treatise*, par. 159.

530 Amending the English Constitution can be done at any time by Parliament. Wisely, our forefathers chose another method: Under the U.S. Constitution, Article 5: "The Congress, whenever two thirds of both Houses shall deem it necessary, shall propose Amendments to this Constitution, or, on the Application of the Legislatures of two thirds of the several States, shall call a Convention for proposing Amendments, which, in either Case, shall be valid to all Intents and Purposes, as Part of this Constitution, when ratified by the Legislatures of three fourths of the several States, or by Conventions in three fourths thereof, as the one or the other Mode of Ratification may be proposed by the Congress...."

531 Baldwin, 138-39.

Hitchcock and West served on the committee to draw up the Constitution and West was asked to write an address to the people regarding the Constitution. In addition to the contributions of these Congregational ministers at the Constitutional Convention, Baptist preachers Isaac Backus and Hezekiah Smith fought in the press for complete religious toleration in Massachusetts. Their newspaper articles and addresses to the Assembly created strong opposition to paying the salaries of Congregational ministers. The arguments used by these pastors, along with those of sympathetic Congregational clergymen, resulted in greater tolerance under the eventual constitution of 1780 than known under the old provincial laws. "The arguments used were those of natural, constitutional, and Christian rights, and there was much quoting of Locke and comparison of the religious with the political situation."[532]

JONAS CLARK'S ELECTION SERMON

Jonas Clark was chosen to preach the election sermon under the new government established by the Massachusetts Constitution. In that election sermon delivered in 1781, this minister who had so faithfully served the people of Lexington as both religious and political educator, declared— again in Lockean terms:

> It is in compact, and in *compact alone*, that all just government is founded. The first steps in entering into society, and towards the establishment of civil government among a people, is the forming, agreeing to, and ratifying an original compact for the regulation of the state—describing and determining the mode, departments, and powers of the government, and the rights, privileges, and duties of the subjects....[533]

Clark asserted that while this compact existed, "a sacred regard ought to be paid to it." No person, body, party, or order had any right to change or violate it. Furthermore, as Clark pointed out, changes or amendments to the constitution should only be done by common consent of the people or their representatives.

> It remains, however, with the community, state, or nation, as a public, political body, at any time, at pleasure, to change, alter, or totally dissolve the constitution, and return to a state of nature, or to form a new government as to them may seem meet.[534]

---

532 Baldwin, 139.
533 Jonas Clark, *Massachusetts Election Sermon of 1781*, cited by Baldwin on 180.
534 Ibid.

"Equality and independence," he proclaimed, "are the just claim—the indefeasible birthright of men. In a state of nature, as individuals, in society, as states or nations, nothing short of these ever did or ever will satisfy a man or a people truly free—truly brave."[535]

BILLS OF RIGHTS
IN THE OTHER STATE CONSTITUTIONS

Of course, the New England states were not the only ones to emphasize the need for a bill of rights to precede their constitutions. Indeed, as George Mason, principal author of the Virginia Declaration of Rights of 1776, maintained, the Virginia Declaration "was afterwards closely imitated by the other United States."[536] Thus, eight of the thirteen original states adopted constitutions with separate Declarations of Rights—Virginia, Pennsylvania, Maryland, Delaware, North Carolina, Connecticut, Massachusetts, and New Hampshire (and later Vermont). New Jersey, Georgia, New York, and South Carolina included statements of rights within the body of their constitutions.[537]

LOCKE ON GOVERNMENT AS THE PEOPLE'S TRUSTEE

It is clear that this emphasis on protecting individual rights against invasion by governmental power echoes Locke who always insisted on the fiduciary power of government, that government was only the people's trustee with no arbitrary power to deprive the people of their inherent rights which antecede civil government. As Locke pointed out, "the Legislative being only a Fiduciary Power to act for certain ends, there remains still *in the People a Supream Power to remove or alter the Legislative*, when they find the *Legislative* act contrary to the trust reposed in them."[538] It was evident to the authors of the state constitutions that there was no better way to make this clear than to precede or include in their constitutions a statement of the fundamental rights which the people retained and which government could not legally invade. It must be made clear that abuse of power is a breach of trust which can result in a new government being formed.

It will be recalled that the great Virginia Declaration of Rights of 1776 was the first of these state declarations and that its author, George Mason, was a confirmed Lockean in his convictions regarding the law of nature,

---

535 Ibid., 180–81.
536 Cited by Helen Hill Miller, *George Mason: Gentleman Revolutionary*, 153.
537 Ibid., 154.
538 Locke, *Second Treatise*, par. 149, in Hall, *Christian History*, 1:98.

the right of the individual to his life, liberty, and property, and the proper role of civil government. Thus, Lockean principles were embedded in the state constitutions first, then in the United States Constitution.

FINDING THE SOLUTION TO THE GREAT PROBLEM FACING THE CONSTITUTIONAL CONVENTION AT PHILADELPHIA

The delegates to the convention in Philadelphia were faced with a far more difficult task than those who drew up the state constitutions. They had to deal with much more than the task of establishing a proper relationship between the people and their local governments. Theirs was the complex one of establishing a balanced relationship between the people, their state governments, and a federated government which should not only be representative of the state governments, but of the people themselves. To achieve such a balance was to plow new ground. Previous attempts at federation, both ancient and modern, seemed inadequate to guide them. Locke himself had no advice on such a situation. This is why many years later, James Madison commented on this when he wrote the words at the beginning of this chapter. They are from a letter Madison wrote to Jefferson in response to his proposal of a text book for the Law School at the University of Virginia. The complete quotation reads:

> It is certainly very material that the true doctrines of liberty, as exemplified in our Political System, should be inculcated on those who are to sustain and may administer it. It is, at the same time, not easy to find standard books that will be both guides and guards for the purpose. Sidney and Locke are admirably calculated to impress on young minds the right of Nations to establish their own Governments, and to inspire a love of free ones; but afford no aid in guarding our Republican Charters against constructive violations. The Declaration of Independence, tho' rich in fundamental principles, and saying every thing that could be said in the same number of words, falls nearly under a like observation.[539]

Madison went on to say that what we know today as *The Federalist Papers* "may fairly enough be regarded as the most authentic exposition of the text of the federal Constitution, as understood by the Body which prepared and the Authority which accepted it...."[540] This is certainly the

---

539 Madison, Letter to Jefferson, February 8, 1825, *James Madison: A Biography in His Own Words*, 2:383.
540 Ibid.

case, for when the Constitutional Convention ended its 99 days of labor and presented a constitution to the states and the people for ratification, it was a unique form of government, and one that needed the detailed explications found in *The Federalist*, written by Alexander Hamilton, John Jay, and James Madison. It was something never before achieved: a dual form of government with the national government supreme in its well-delineated and limited sphere and the state governments supreme in their spheres.

It very nearly was not achieved because of the dispute between the large and small states on the question of representation. Without "the Connecticut Compromise," suggested by Oliver Ellsworth and Roger Sherman, the Convention might well have broken up without a constitution. Fortunately, the idea of having the people represented in the House of Representatives by population, but the states represented in the Senate on an equal basis, prevailed. Today, the system still prevails and forms a unique aspect of the dual form of government established by the Constitution of the United States.

Individual Rights and the Constitution

The question of states rights may not seem to have any connection with Lockean political principles until one reflects that the lives of all the individuals inhabiting the less-populated states would have been deeply affected by important national decisions in which their voices would have been drowned out by the voices of their more populous neighbors. This sort of majority rule, however, was not (and is not) in harmony with the underlying doctrine of individual rights of the states and their inhabitants. This was why the battle at the convention between the large and small states was so bitter and, had it not been resolved, might well have caused the country to split apart into competing confederacies. Naturally, the men from the less populous states had no wish to see their freedom absorbed by the men in the more populous states. Why were these men so quick to sense incursions upon their liberty? Surely, it was because they had been raised on Lockean political principles. They were convinced that individuals could not retain their liberties without equal political rights between all of the states. So, too, the establishment of the electoral system, which many today are so blithely, if ignorantly, willing to toss away, was another way of insuring that inhabitants of the smaller states would have a voice in the affairs of the nation.

GEORGE MASON'S OBJECTIONS
TO THE FEDERAL CONSTITUTION

When the work was finally done, some delegates still could not give it their approval. George Mason was one. He had strongly urged his fellow delegates to preface the constitution with a Bill of Rights. He suggested that "with the aid of the State declarations, a bill might be prepared in a few hours." Roger Sherman responded by saying that "the State Declarations of Rights are not repealed by this Constitution; and being in force are sufficient." [541] Mason, however, saw the flaw in Sherman's reasoning and reminded him that "the Laws of the U. S. are to be paramount to State Bills of Rights." [542] Mason was voted down, however, and heading his list of objections to the Constitution was this lack of a Bill of Rights. That it was perilous to rely on unwritten laws, Mason had learned when colonial America had based her appeals to King and Parliament on largely unwritten, or "understood" law—on the "ancient rights of Englishmen." Colonial Americans had found that their view of rights and the view of the distant British Parliament had many differences. Thus, Mason concluded that one could not be too specific in outlining the rights that the citizen expected the government to safeguard. His views on this subject were so strong that they prevented him from signing the constitution and led to his being one of its vigorous opponents at the Virginia Ratifying Convention called upon to ratify the new constitution.

OBJECTIONS AT
THE VIRGINIA RATIFYING CONVENTION

As a delegate to the Virginia Convention, Mason expressed his fears that the new government would convert "what was formerly a confederation, to a consolidated government" and this would mean "to annihilate totally the state governments." Despite his desire for a national union, he expressed his doubts that a national government could handle "so extensive a country." In concluding his remarks on this occasion, he said he wished for "such amendments and such only, as are necessary to secure the dearest rights of the people." [543]

Patrick Henry was another who vigorously opposed the new constitution in its present form. He rose to give a ringing (and very Lockean)

---

541 Cited in Helen Hill Miller, *George Mason*, 262.
542 Ibid.
543 Ibid., 290.

defense of the liberties protected by the Bill of Rights of Virginia:

> The rights of conscience, of trial by jury, liberty of the press...all
> pretentions to human rights and privileges are rendered insecure,
> if not lost, by this change.... Is this tame relinquishment of
> rights worthy of freemen?... It is said eight States have adopted
> this plan. I declare that if twelve States and an half had adopted
> it, I would with manly firmness, and in spite of an erring world,
> reject it. You are not to inquire how your trade may be increased,
> nor how you are to become a great and powerful people, but how
> your liberties can be secured; for liberty ought to be the direct
> end of your government.... Liberty the greatest of all earthly
> blessings—give us that precious jewel, and you may take every-
> thing else:...[544]

On another day, Mason rose again. "That congress should have power
to provide for the general welfare of the union, I grant. But I wish a clause
in the constitution with respect to all powers which are not granted, that
they are retained by the states. Otherwise the power of providing for the
general welfare may be perverted to its destruction." One of Mason's final
speeches at the Virginia Convention dealt with the evils of slavery, "Yet
by this constitution it is to continue for twenty years. As much as I value
a union of all the states, I would not admit the southern states into the
union, unless they agreed to the discontinuance of this disgraceful trade,
because it would bring weakness and not strength to the union." (To this
Madison replied that the south would not have agreed to the constitution
without the clause and that anyway, a twenty-year limit was better than
none, reminding him that the old Articles of Confederation had provided
no limitation whatever.) [545]

Mason also vigorously opposed the judiciary article maintaining that it
would result in the federal government gaining unlimited power. As the
clause-by-clause discussion of the Constitution drew to its close, Helen Hill
Miller relates how, following the lead of Massachusetts, the importance of
drawing up a list of amendments was gaining acceptance and also that
there was a pressing need for a Bill of Rights. All this was largely the
result of Patrick Henry's repeated warnings of how vitally important these
matters were.[546]

---

544 Ibid. Cited by Helen Hill Miller, 290.
545 Ibid., 294.
546 Ibid., 295.

PROPOSED AMENDMENTS
TO THE CONSTITUTION

At last a resolution was approved that the amendments the convention agreed upon would be presented to the first Congress under the new constitution. A five-man committee, which included George Mason and Patrick Henry, drew up a bill of rights consisting of twenty articles. Much of it was from Mason's own Bill of Rights drafted in 1776. Also presented were twenty other amendments, mostly drafted by Henry. All were adopted by the Virginia Ratifying Convention.

James Madison, rightly called "the father of the Constitution," was greatly relieved that his own state had finally ratified the Constitution even though it had appended its long list of proposed amendments to the Federal Constitution. He promised that if he were chosen to represent Virginia as a member of Congress in the new national government, he would push for a bill of rights. Although originally lukewarm about the idea, he had been persuaded by his experience at the Virginia Ratifying Convention and by his friend Thomas Jefferson, that such a bill really was needed. When he took up his post as member of the new federal House of Representatives in May of 1789, Madison soon presented a list of amendments that had been submitted by the states of which a committee selected seventeen proposals. Madison had placed them in the body of the Constitution, but the committee submitted their choice as a separate list of amendments. Ten Amendments survived and constitute the Bill of Rights passed by Congress. It closely follows Mason's Declaration of Rights of 1776 and was agreed to by the states.

JOHN LOCKE AND
THE BILL OF RIGHTS

In these first Ten Amendments may be seen the clearest influence of John Locke on the Federal Constitution. Naturally he had no advice to offer a large country facing the problem of achieving a federation. As one living in a small country, he had never needed to grapple with such a problem. It is certain, however, that if he had been born in Colonial America, he would have ranged himself along with Mason and others who insisted that a Bill of Rights be added to the Federal Constitution. The rights submitted by the various states as in need of federal guarantees were the very rights the Founders had fought a revolution to attain! They were the rights championed by John Locke so eloquently in his *Second Treatise of Government*.

That great champion of religious toleration certainly would have applauded the provision in Article I of the Bill of Rights that "Congress shall make no law respecting an establishment of religion, or prohibiting the free exercise thereof." He who had labored to free the English press from government licensing would have rejoiced that neither would Congress have the power to make any law "abridging the freedom of the press or the right of the people peaceably to assemble, and to petition the Government for a redress of grievances."

Article IV also would have had special meaning for Locke: "The right of the people to be secure in their persons, houses, papers, and effects, against unreasonable searches and seizures, shall not be violated...." Locke, as we have seen, had been forced to write his political thoughts in secret, never knowing, either at home or abroad, when he might be arrested, his manuscripts found and used to destroy him—as had happened to Sir Algernon Sidney.

Article V reiterates the Lockean theme that "No person shall be... deprived of life, liberty, or property, without due process of law; nor shall private property be taken for public use without just compensation." We may also be sure that the great philosopher would have particularly approved the proviso in Articles IX and X:

> IX: The enumeration in the Constitution, of certain rights, shall not be construed to deny or disparage others retained by the people.

> X: The powers not delegated to the United States by the Constitution, nor prohibited by it to the States, are reserved to the States respectively, or to the people.

Locke's (and the Founders') Emphasis on the Legislative Branch

There is also another area of the Constitution where Locke's influence can be seen. This is his emphasis on the legislative branch of government. Locke referred to "the *first and fundamental positive* Law of all Commonwealths" as "*the establishing of the Legislative Power; as the first and fundamental natural Law, which is to govern even the Legislative itself, is the preservation of the Society,* and (as far as will consist with the publick good) of every person in it." Furthermore, "it is not only the *supreme power* of the Commonwealth, but sacred and unalterable in the hands where the community have once placed it." [547]

---

547 John Locke, *Second Treatise*, par. 134.

Because the legislative power is only a delegated power from the people it cannot be passed on to others to whom it has not been delegated. As Locke explained it:

> And when the People have said, we will submit to rules, and be govern'd by *Laws* made by such Men, and in such Forms, no Body else can say other Men shall make *Laws* for them; nor can the people be bound by any *Laws* but such as are Enacted by those, whom they have Chosen, and authorized to make *Laws* for them.[548]

As Locke had seen, so also saw the framers of the United States Constitution, that a clearly-defined legislative branch was of prime importance. Fittingly, the Constitution begins in Article I, Section 1 by establishing the legislative power and defining it precisely: "All legislative powers herein granted shall be vested in a Congress of the United States, which shall consist of a Senate and House of Representatives."

Section 8 sets forth in detail the areas in which Congress shall have power to act. Although to Locke, the legislative power was supreme, the new American system conceived of a balance between the legislative, executive, and judicial powers which, the Founders believed, should be kept separate.[549] Nevertheless, if pressed to say which of the three coordinate powers was of prime importance, the Founding Fathers almost certainly would have named the legislative—because it is the law-making body. Indeed, this is why there was so much debate in regard to the Executive Branch, so much anxiety lest the Executive be given too much power. As for the Judicial branch, its function was simply to interpret the legislation in the light of the Constitution.

Although the framers of the Federal Constitution did their best to work out the wisest possible form of civil government, they recognized that the dual form of government they had devised rested ultimately on the capacity of the individual for self-government. Accordingly the American system, which in so many ways is the fruit of the Christian ethic, demands wide-awake citizens who understand that system to make it work and to keep it in working order.

---

548 Ibid., par. 141.

549 In this they were following Montesquieu's analysis of the earlier English system before it became a Parliamentary one, when the supreme power was divided between King, Lords, and Commons. They thought of the President as corresponding to the King, rather than to the Prime Minister. In reality, the English Constitution did not separate the executive power from the legislative body. Eventually, the monarch became only a figurehead and, in effect, the House of Commons is now supreme, since the House of Lords has been shorn of most of its powers.

James Madison wrote in *The Federalist,*

> that honorable determination which animates every votary of
> freedom, to rest all our political experiments on the capacity of
> mankind for self-government.[550]

REASON AS THE GIFT OF GOD

But this self-government runs to greed and ruin when not supported by
moral law and the conviction, so great in the minds of the New England
pastors we have discussed, that man is only rightly governed when he is
governed by God. They understood that Locke was speaking from within
this framework of thought when he wrote, in the *Second Treatise,* of Reason
or of the Will of God, showing man,

> that being all equal and independent, no one ought to harm an-
> other in his Life, Health, Liberty or Possessions. For Men being all
> the Workmanship of one Omnipotent, and infinitely wise Maker;
> All the Servants of one Sovereign Master, sent into the World
> by his Order and about his business, they are his Property, whose
> Workmanship they are, made to last during his, not one another's
> Pleasure.[551]

Nor is this a negative duty, merely to refrain from harming others. Locke
also saw that "sharing all in one Community of Nature," one ought not
only to preserve himself, but ought "as much as he can to preserve the
rest of Mankind."[552]

Interwoven with all of Locke's political writing is the conviction that
reason itself is the gift of God and that we are indeed His servants because
He is indeed our Sovereign Master, that we are all His workmanship, and
therefore all the property we inherit or produce is but held in trust for
our Maker. His was no self-centered individualist creed of greed for gain
with no concern for others. Locke always believed that, in order to be in
harmony with his Creator, man must recognize that he was put on earth
not to harm others, but to help them. As John Dunn wrote in his book,
The Political Thought of John Locke:

> Whenever he began to sketch out the contours of an ethic and
> searched for the fundamental form which it must take, the touch

---

550 *The Federalist,* No. 39.
551 Locke, *Second Treatise,* par. 6.
552 Ibid.

stone which he set up was always the relation between Creator and created. Somehow all human values were to be elicited from this inexhaustible matrix.[553]

Dunn also observed that "moral experience was, for Locke, a derivative of a religious experience, how wholly lacking in autonomy of value he saw and felt the human condition to be."[554] It was no wonder that the ministers and the Founding Fathers recognized that John Locke was no godless rationalist. They saw him as an earnest Christian like themselves seeking for his fellow man a just and humane government expressive of Christian principles. Had Locke been able to follow these events involving his American cousins, had he seen them struggling with the need to balance individual rights with governmental authority at the state and then at the national level, had he seen how his very words echoed through their bills of right and the national Bill of Rights, he surely would have nodded his head in approval of these, his best and brightest students.

---

553 John Dunn, *The Political Thought of John Locke: An Historical Account of the Argument of the "Two Treatises of Government,"* Cambridge University Press, 1983, 26. Used by permission.
554 Ibid.

PART FOUR

The French Revolution: Locke Abandoned

The high reputation, which he [Locke] deservedly acquired for his enlightened attachment to the mild and tolerating doctrines of [C]hristianity, secured to him the esteem and confidence of those, who were its friends. The same high and deserved reputation inspired others of very different views and characters, with a design to avail themselves of its splendour, and, by that means, to diffuse a fascinating kind of lustre over their own tenets of a dark and sable hue. The consequence has been, that the writings of Mr. Locke, one of the most able, most sincere, and most amiable assertors of [C]hristianity and true philosophy, have been perverted to purposes, which he would have deprecated and prevented, had he discovered or foreseen them.

JAMES WILSON [555]

---

555 James Wilson, "Of the General Principles of Law and Obligation" in *The Works of the Honourable James Wilson, LL.D.*, (Philadelphia, 1804), 1:67-68.

CHAPTER ELEVEN

The Enlightenment Encounters Locke

JAMES WILSON was right. There were those who tried to use Locke to advance their own very different philosophical ideas. Prominent among them were the *philosophes* of eighteenth-century France who grossly misused and perverted Lockean philosophy, all the while hiding behind Locke's illustrious name and attempting to identify him with their philosophical ideas. But their ideas, unlike his, were not rooted in Christianity. They were rooted in either skepticism or, more often, a militant atheism which particularly opposed Christianity. Indeed, it was these men who prepared the ideological ground for the French Revolution. Because of their seeming admiration for "le sage Locke" (as Voltaire called him) and their attempt to blend some Lockean ideas into their own philosophy "of a dark and sable hue," John Locke has been mistakenly identified as a philosopher of the Enlightenment.

ENLIGHTENMENT IDEAS OF
THE LAW OF NATURE
NOT LOCKEAN

Voltaire, Diderot, and Condillac, were fond of expatiating on the joys of man's natural state, governed by "natural law" alone. When they used these terms, however, they were not employing them in a Lockean sense. All that Locke and the French Enlightenment *philosophes* shared was the same terminology—one that had become prevalent in the seventeenth century and which (as we have seen) had become fashionable among both deists and divines. The key words of this terminology—Nature, Natural Law,

Reason—meant different things according to the writer's basic frame of reference. The Enlightenment *philosophes* knew this perfectly well. In their early period (when it was politic to be discreet in expressing anti-Christian sentiments), the language of Natural Law provided a sort of protective coloration. Their radical sentiments could appear perfectly acceptable to Christians—until, upon closer examination, their Christian readers discovered that the basic premise behind the reasoning of these would-be philosophers was, in fact, anti-Christian.[556]

THE *PHILOSOPHES'* MILITANT OPPOSITION TO CHRISTIANITY

Voltaire, whose life span was long (1694–1778), was at the helm of the philosophic movement which aimed at "enlightening" men by destroying their "superstitions"—by which they meant Christianity.[557] Voltaire early conceived a strong hostility toward the Christian faith which, in later years, became an obsession that drove him to sign all his letters to his friends: "*Ecrasez l'infame*," or "Crush out the Infamy." However carefully the *philosophes* wrote in the beginning, hostility to Christianity was as characteristic of their thinking then as it was of the later Enlightenment.[558] Peter Gay, in his remarkable work on the French Enlightenment, *The Rise of Modern Paganism*, observed that this cry, *Ecrasez l'infame*, was directed against Christianity in all its forms.[559]

---

556 A modern example of different usages of the same word is seen in the difference in meaning between the communist interpretation of such a word as "spiritual"—which is a purely humanistic one—and the same word used in its original religious sense.

557 Voltaire was born Francois Marie Arouet on February 20, 1694, at Chatenay, near Paris. He studied in Paris and then in his father's law office, but soon developed a keen interest in literature. In 1717 he was arrested for writing some satirical verses critical of the Regent of France and was imprisoned in the Bastille for a year. After his release he changed his name to Voltaire. He was again imprisoned in 1726 because he had challenged a nobleman to a duel claiming that his opponent had insulted him. Released within a month, he accepted an invitation from Lord Bolingbroke to visit England. In 1729 he returned to France where he lived mainly in Paris. In 1733, he again displeased the authorities with his book *English Letters* which was condemned and burned because in it Voltaire had compared France unfavorably with England in everything in both church and state. Meanwhile, Voltaire was living in the province of Lorraine with Madame du Chatelet. Here he remained for fifteen years until Frederick the Great invited him to the Prussian Court. The visit lasted only three years because Voltaire continually fell into court quarrels and thus fell out of Frederick's favor. France refused him permission to return, so he bought an estate near Geneva, Switzerland where he lived for most of the last twenty years of his life. In February 1778, after the death of Louis XV, he was allowed to return to France. He died in Paris not long after, on May 30, 1778. Among his writings were numerous anonymous attacks on Christianity which appeared in many literary forms. Most of his works were imbued with a hatred of Christianity but, unlike most of the *philosophes*, he was not an atheist.

558 See Peter Gay's eloquent comments in *The Rise of Modern Paganism*, Vol. 1 of *The Enlightenment: An Interpretation*, New York: Alfred Knopf, 1966, 18.

559 Peter Gay, 50.

Voltaire's Efforts to Crush Christianity

As Gay also pointed out, Voltaire never changed his views.[560] By 1760, old and honored, he felt able to discard dissimulation and to attack Christianity openly. At this time he rewrote certain anti-Christian pamphlets he had begun at the court of that kindred spirit, Frederick the Great. He set about methodically to destroy Christianity which he likened to a "beast." As Gay observed:

> To get rid of the beast, Voltaire made himself into the unofficial adviser to the underground army arrayed against it; he began to use the phrase *Ecrasez l'infame*, which gave the army a battle cry and rallied its morale; and he took charge of their tactics: he warned the brethren to conceal their hand, to write simply, to repeat the truth often, to lie if necessary, and to convict the enemy out of his own mouth.[561]

This illuminating passage concludes with the remark that Voltaire was eventually rewarded when his followers acknowledged him as their leader. In 1762, Diderot affectionately saluted him as his "sublime, honorable, and dear anti-Christ."[562] During his last sixteen years Voltaire produced a flood of anti-Christian pamphlets which reiterated by every conceivable means that every man of sense and honor must detest "the Christian sect."[563]

Views of Nature That Ignored God

In addition to Voltaire, other prominent authors opposed Christianity through virulent underground attacks in treatises, poems, and satires. While they appeared to be constructing a system of philosophy which recognized the Law of Nature, their "nature" was a substitute for God. To these philosophers, the Fall of Man was just a myth. Man was naturally good; through education one could make him anything one wanted. Denis Diderot (1713-1784) wrote to his mistress, that humans were not evil by nature. Rather, mankind was corrupted by bad education or bad role models.[564] This was their explanation for man's propensity for evil which

---

560 Peter Gay, 390-91.

561 Ibid.

562 Ibid.

563 See Gay, 390.

564 See Gay, in *The Science of Freedom*, Vol. 2 of *The Enlightenment: An Interpretation*, New York: Alfred A. Knopf, Inc., 1969, 170. Denis Diderot was born at Langres in France. He became well-known for his immensely popular *Encyclopedie* which was subtly larded throughout with anti-Christian propaganda.

they believed could be corrected through "right" education. Because of these views, Voltaire and the other *philosophes* of his persuasion maintained a discreet silence regarding the religious views of the two men whom they professed to admire the most: Isaac Newton and John Locke. They were well aware, however, that both these men were deeply sincere Christians.

Professor Gay points out that although these *philosophes* quoted some of Locke's writings, they never mentioned his *Reasonableness of Christianity*.[565] They simply ignored the Christian foundation of Locke's thought while attempting to borrow from its superstructure. They professed admiration for Locke but then proceeded to dismantle his philosophy of the mind by taking out one of its crucial underpinnings.

LOCKE'S TWO SOURCES OF KNOWLEDGE

It will be recalled that Locke held that man's mind starts out like a blank page on which experience traced its outlines. Locke maintained, however, that what he termed experience was made up of two aspects—two "fountains." But let him speak for himself on the much misunderstood basis of his theory of understanding:

> Let us suppose the mind to be, as we say, white paper, void of all characters, without any ideas; how comes it to be furnished? Whence comes it by that vast store which the busy and boundless fancy of man has painted on it with an endless variety? Whence has it all the materials of reason and knowledge? To this I answer, in one word, from experience: in that all our knowledge is founded, and from that it ultimately derives itself. Our observation employed either about external sensible objects, or about the internal operations of our minds, perceived and reflected on by ourselves, is that which supplies our understandings with all the materials of thinking. These two are the fountains of knowledge, from whence all the ideas we have, or can naturally have, do spring.[566]

These two sources of knowledge Locke called sensation and reflection. It was through sensation, he maintained, that our minds gain knowledge of such things as color, heat, cold, soft, hard, bitter, sweet. The other fountain, he explained, "is the perception of the operations of our own mind within us, as it is employed about the ideas it has got." From this source

---

565 See Gay, in Vol. 1, 321.

566 John Locke, *Of Human Understanding*, Book II, Chapter 1, in *Works*, 1:82-83.

comes "perception, thinking, doubting, believing, reasoning, knowing, willing...."[567]

MAN BORN WITH INNATE FACULTIES

In other words, man was more than a sensible animal, he was a *thinking being* and it was the Creator who had endowed man with the capacity to receive ideas, to compound them, and to judge and sift them in order to know right from wrong. Although not born with innate ideas, man was born with innate faculties with which to evaluate experience, such faculties as those of thinking, willing, judging, memorizing. From the Christian point of view, the most striking thing about Locke's theory of the understanding is his conviction that although man cannot *create* a single "simple idea" with which he is provided through either of the two fountains of knowledge, his mind can *compound* ideas almost indefinitely.[568] God is the Creator and man reflects the Father's creative power in his own creative ability exercised through compounding ideas.

HOW WE KNOW THAT GOD EXISTS

But how do we know that God exists? In Book IV, Chapter X of Locke's work on the human understanding he deals with this question in detail.

> Though God has given us no innate ideas of Himself; though He has stamped no original characters on our minds, wherein we may read His being;...He hath not left Himself without witness: since we have sense, perception, and reason, and cannot want a clear proof of Him, as long as we carry ourselves about us. Nor can we justly complain of our ignorance in this great point, since He has so plentifully provided us with the means to discover and know Him, as far as is necessary to the end of our being, and the great concernment of our happiness.[569]

---

567 Ibid., 1:83.

568 Locke wrote: "When the understanding is once stored with these simple ideas, it has the power to repeat, compare, and unite them, even to an almost infinite variety, and so can make at pleasure new complex ideas. But it is not in the power of the most exalted wit or enlarged understanding, by any quickness or variety of thought, to *invent* or *frame* one new simple idea in the mind, not taken in by the ways afore mentioned [sensation and reflection]; nor can any force of the understanding destroy those that are there; the dominion of man in this little world of his own understanding, being much the same as it is in the great world of visible things; wherein his power, however managed by art and skill, reaches no farther than to compound and divide materials that are made to his hand but can do nothing towards making the least particle of new matter or destroying one atom of what is already in being." Ibid., Book II, Chapter 2, 1:99-102.

569 Ibid., Book IV, Chapter 10, par. 1, 3:55.

How has He "plentifully provided" the means to know that He exists? Locke reasons that, first, man has a clear idea of his own being (self-conscious); second, he knows that nothing cannot produce a being, therefore our being springs from something eternal; third, the eternal Being who created us must be "the source and original of all power; and so this eternal being must be also the most powerful."[570] Next, it is evident that this eternal being is the source of knowledge. There has been a knowing being from eternity. "Thus," Locke says, "from the consideration of ourselves, and what we infallibly find in our own constitutions, our reason leads us to the knowledge of this certain and evident truth, that there is an eternal, most powerful, and most knowing being...."[571] It was plain to Locke that "we have a more certain knowledge of the existence of a God, than of any thing our senses have not immediately discovered to us. Nay, I presume I may say, that we more certainly know that there is a God, than that there is any thing else without [outside of] us."[572] Indeed, such knowledge of God is within our reach, if we will be but apply our minds to it, even as we do to other inquiries.

> For I judge it as certain and clear a truth, as can any where be
> delivered, that the invisible things of God are clearly seen from
> the creation of the world, being understood by the things that are
> made, even his eternal power and Godhead.[573]

FOR ETIENNE DE CONDILLAC
SENSATION WAS ALL

Such ideas, although so clearly expressed in the *Essay on Human Understanding*, were rejected or perverted by the French Enlightenment *philosophes*. Etienne Bonnot de Condillac, for one, was entranced by Locke's idea that men come by ideas through experience, rather than being endowed with a stock of ready-made concepts innately stamped on the mind.[574] To say that at least some ideas came from sensations from without seemed to support his notion that man was only a higher animal. But Locke's other fountain of knowledge—his other branch of experience—the internal operation of

---

570 Ibid., *Works*, Book IV, Chapter 10, par. 4, 3:55.

571 Ibid., 3:57, par. 6.

572 Ibid., 3:58, par. 6.

573 Ibid., 3:58, par. 7. Here, Locke is citing Paul's Epistle to the Romans, Chapter 1, Verse 20.

574 Etienne Bonnot de Mably de Condillac (1715-1780) was born of a noble family in Grenoble. He became a member of the French Academy of Sciences in 1768. Condillac, not John Locke, was the founder of the philosophy of sensationalism which maintains that all man's knowledge comes from his physical senses.

the mind reflecting on its own being, rather than merely responding to external stimuli—did not set so well with him. So Condillac proceeded to revise Locke's philosophy of the mind by expunging this second source of experience, leaving only sensation.

In his *Traite de Sensations* (1754), Condillac also changed the relationship, which existed in Locke, between sensation and reflection. Now reflection did not *follow* sensation, in a time sequence, but was the *result* of sensation, having no life of its own. Sensation was all. Clearly, Condillac's doctrine, named "sensationalism," was critically different from Locke's theory of the mind.[575] Thomas Fowler summed it up well when he wrote of Locke's *Essay on Human Understanding*: "His theory of the origin of knowledge may fairly be called an experiential, but it cannot with any truth be called a sensationalist theory."[576]

THE INSUFFICIENCY OF
MAN'S UNASSISTED REASON

It is not within the province of this work to analyze in detail Locke's *Essay on Human Understanding*. The reader may delve into it for further information on Locke's conclusions. A thoughtful perusal will reveal the important point that (unlike the French *philosophes*) Locke rejected man's "unassisted reason" as an all-sufficient guide. It will be recalled that what prompted him to write his work on the human understanding was in order to discover what God had put within the range of man's comprehension and what, on the other hand, must forever lie beyond it—unless explainable through Divine Revelation. Locke came to the conclusion that:

> [T]hough the comprehension of our understandings comes exceeding short of the vast extent of things; yet we shall have cause enough to magnify the bountiful Author of our being, for that proportion and degree of knowledge He has bestowed on us, so far above all the rest of the inhabitants of this our mansion. Men have reason to be well satisfied with what God hath thought fit for them, since He has given them (as St. Peter says)...whatsoever is necessary for the conveniences of life and information of virtue; and has put within the reach of their discovery the comfortable provision for this life, and the way that leads to a better.[577]

---

575 See Will and Ariel Durant in *The Age of Voltaire*, Vol. IX of *The Story of Civilization*, New York: Simon and Schuster, 1965, 582.

576 Fowler, on *Locke*, 134.

577 John Locke, *Of Human Understanding*, Book I, Chapter 1, par. 5 in *Works*, 1:3-4.

Locke thought it wise for men to be busy with the variety and beauty God had put within their range of understanding and not to "quarrel with their own constitution, and throw away the blessings their hands are filled with, because they are not big enough to grasp everything."[578] What men cannot solve through their "unassisted reason" must remain unanswered unless it can be brought to light by Divine Revelation. Genuine revelation, Locke insists, never goes *against* reason, which is a God-bestowed faculty, although it may go beyond reason. How then can we know when the revelation claimed is genuinely from God?

Locke would have told Condillac that of course it is not enough to believe something is a revelation "only because [we] strongly believe it to be a revelation" for such a "revelation" may not proceed from God, but may only be "the strength of [our] own persuasion" or the "delusions of Satan," who "can transform himself into an angel of light. And they who are led by the son of the morning are as fully satisfied of the illumination, i.e., are as strongly persuaded, that they are enlightened by the spirit of God, as anyone who is so...."[579]

In *The Reasonableness of Christianity*, Locke suggests that we can accept whether a revelation is real upon the credit of the proposer. To him, Jesus clearly appeared in line with prophecy—indeed, as the fulfillment of prophecy—and by His miracles He showed us that He is indeed the long-foretold Messiah. Therefore, we are confronted here with genuine Divine Revelation.

On the other hand, as he discussed in the *Essay on Human Understanding*, there are religious enthusiasts who claim to have heard the voice of God and to be doing God's will, who clearly are not the emissaries of God. Yet, some will believe them simply because they *want* to believe without consulting their reason as to whether this person actually bears the marks of having received a genuine revelation from God.

So how do we know that the voice speaking in our minds is the voice of God? Locke concluded that God has given us reason by which to judge whether a revelation is authentic or not, whether the voice within is from God, from our own minds, or from Satan. One criterion is whether it is accompanied by objective evidence, by some marks that demonstrate it to be divine inspiration, and not mere "enthusiasm."

He warns that:

---

578 Ibid., *Works*, 1:4.
579 Ibid., Book IV, Chapter XIX, pars. 11, 13, 3:154–56.

He therefore that will not give himself up to all of the extravagancies of delusion and error, must bring this guide of his light within to the trial. God, when He makes the prophet, does not unmake the man. He leaves all his faculties in the natural state, to enable him to judge of his inspirations, whether they be of divine original or no. When He illuminates the mind with supernatural light, He does not extinguish that which is natural. If He would have us assent to the truth of any proposition, He either evidences that truth by the usual methods of natural reason, or else makes it known to be a truth which He would have us assent to, by His authority; and convinces us that it is from Him, by some marks which reason cannot be mistaken in.... [I]f reason must not examine their truth by *something extrinsical to the persuasions themselves*, inspirations and delusions, truth and falsehood, will have the same measure, and will not be possible to be distinguished....[580]

The French Enlightenment *philosophes* seized on this idea (that revelation must stand the test of reason) to demolish revelation altogether by their corrupted reason. Men like Diderot and Holbach denied the very existence of God. If they had read Locke closely, they would have learned that he believed firmly that reason, being the gift of God, leads us to a certain knowledge of God and to the reality of Divine Revelation.

HOLBACH'S SYSTEM OF NATURE

Paul Henri d'Holbach (1723-1789), a militant atheist who was better known by his title, the Baron d'Holbach, was another of the French philosophers of this period to devise "a system of nature" which left man's soul out of the picture. He propagandized incessantly against Christianity and, according to Professor Gay, he encouraged bold talk about "the need for strangling the last King in the entrails of the last priest...."[581]

---

580 Ibid., 3:156-57, par. 14. [Italics added for emphasis.] That Locke felt so strongly on this subject was probably because he had seen many instances among the various quarreling religious sects of the Interregnum, claiming to be divinely inspired. Although Quaker leader William Penn was a friend of his, Locke was particularly skeptical about the Friends and their "inner light." Penn, an educated man from a Church of England background, did not abandon Scripture in favor of the Inner Light as did some Quakers who were less educated and prone to what Locke called "religious enthusiasm" or an unreasoning, and to him, excessively emotional approach to religion.

581 Peter Gay, *The Rise of Modern Paganism*, 398. Paraphrased in our time by the American communist leader, Gus Hall, the actual phrase was from a play by the *philosophe* Diderot and read: "...and his hands would twist the entrails of the priest for lack of a rope to strangle the kings." (Et ses main ourdiraient les entrailles du pretre, au defaut d'un cordon pour strangler les rois.) See also Will and Ariel Durant's *The Age of Voltaire*, 666.

Even a glance at his writings justifies the title his contemporaries bestowed on him: "the personal enemy of the Almighty."[582] In Holbach's philosophy there was no place for religion of any kind—neither deism, agnosticism, nor even pantheism were acceptable to him. He utterly repudiated free will and believed man to be only matter, the helpless prisoner of his heredity and his environment. "Soul" was but a part of man's mechanism. In his *Systeme de La Nature*, which Will and Ariel Durant call "the most powerful single volume issued in the campaign [of the *philosophes*] against Christianity," Holbach protested: "To say that the soul will feel, think, enjoy, and suffer after the death of the body is to pretend that a clock shattered into a thousand pieces will continue to strike the hour...."[583]

NATURE NOT
GOD-PRODUCED

Holbach's *System of Nature* did not rest on Nature as Locke had used the term (as God-produced and sustained by God's Law), but simply on the notion that nature was "the great whole that results from the assemblage of matter under its various combinations."[584] From this "great whole," resulting from matter coming together in various ways, Holbach attempted to devise a system of morality resting solely on what Locke had called man's "unassisted reason."

In Holbach's system, governed by material reasoning alone, there is total rejection of even the word God: Holbach rejected all religion which he claimed was "a scourge to the earth."[585] Clearly, his "system" was also a complete repudiation of the philosophical system of John Locke.

HELVETIUS,
THE VOICE OF THE REVOLUTION

Claude Adrien Helvetius (1715-1771)[586] was a member of Holbach's *salon* which included such kindred spirits as Diderot and Jean-Jacques Rousseau. In 1758, he published a work that was destined to have profound effect on French intellectuals. It was titled *De l'Esprit*, or, to give its English title, *On Intelligence*. It created a furor and was the most widely read book of all

---

582 *The Age of Voltaire*, 703.

583 *The Age of Voltaire*, 699. The Holbach quote is on 698.

584 See *The Age of Voltaire*, 701.

585 *The Age of Voltaire*, 704.

586 Claude Adrien Helvetius was born in Paris, in 1715. In his work, *On Intelligence*, he declared that sensation was the source of all mental activity. He visited England in 1764 and in 1765 was the guest of Frederick the Great at Potsdam. He died in 1771.

those who ranted against Christianity.[587] Like Condillac, Helvetius viewed man's mind as the passive recipient of sensation, devoid of any moral sense, since man's only wish was to gratify his own desires. Unpromising as this sounds, Helvetius was convinced that through "education"—or rather, what we today call "social engineering,"—man's thoughts, feelings, and beliefs could be radically altered, so that he would become a "good" man or a "good" citizen (in whatever sense the controlling elite decided the word "good" should be interpreted).

HELVETIUS ADVOCATES A WELFARE STATE

Helvetius followed up his work, *On Intelligence*, with *On Man*, a hardly less radical book in which he advocated a sort of welfare state which would defend the poor against the rich. Will and Ariel Durant further point out in their *Age of Voltaire*, that here was the voice of the Revolution to come.[588]

FALSE VIEWS OF EQUALITY

To Helvetius, not only should men be equal before the law, as Locke acknowledged, but they were born with equal mental capacities. This was an idea Locke had repudiated, recognizing that human beings were born with varying mental capacities.[589] According to Helvetius, however, the only reason we see men who are unequal in mental capacities is solely the effect of chance and the environment.[590] Thus did this French philosopher reject God as the giver of all gifts, as the creative and governing power of the universe. Instead, chance was his god, and environment and circumstance were but the products of chance. Progress depended solely on human knowledge. In order to destroy the seeds of moral evil, one had only to destroy ignorance![591]

A UNIVERSAL RELIGION CONTROLLED BY THE STATE

To promote what he called "natural morality," Helvetius advocated a "universal religion" controlled by the state. Unlike Locke, he sought no balance between reason and Revelation. To him reason was all.[592]

---

587 *The Age of Voltaire*, 682.
588 Ibid.
589 See par. 54 of Locke's *Second Treatise*.
590 See *The Age of Voltaire*, 682.
591 Ibid., 684.
592 Ibid., 686.

This shows his great distance from Locke who, as we have seen, believed that the Divine Revelation in the Holy Scriptures was necessary to guide man's reason aright. Nor did Helvetius believe that the "unhappiness of men and nations" was the result of their separation from God. Instead, it was the result of imperfect laws, and an unequal sharing of wealth.[593] The happiness of the people depended not on religion but on wise legislation alone.[594]

Like the later socialists of nineteenth century France, Helvetius also favored redistribution of the land. He wrote that "When a man's lands exceed a certain number of acres, they should be taxed at a rate exceeding the rent...."[595] The Durants' observation on these two books by Helvetius is particularly cogent. They point out that in them are to be found not only the ideas that caused the French Revolution, but also most of the ideas that "agitate nations today."[596]

THE MARQUIS DE CONDORCET, POLITICAL REFORMER

What Helvetius wanted to do in the field of education, the Marquis de Condorcet (1743-1794) wanted to do in the field of politics and economics.[597] Espousing the prevailing Sensationalist philosophy, he believed that the rights of man can only be discovered by sentient human beings through their ability to reason and therefore arrive at truly moral ideas.[598]

Condorcet also believed that there was no limit to the perfectibility of the human faculties.[599] To Condorcet, it is not God who has the world in His hands and governs it by His wisdom; it is simply a collection of human, impersonal laws that rules the world. Apparently this collection of laws exists without a Lawmaker, an idea that Locke had definitely repudiated.[600]

Thus, through their writings, Voltaire, Diderot, Condillac, Helvetius, Condorcet, and many lesser lights worked toward the overturning of all

---

593 Ibid.

594 Ibid.

595 Ibid., 689.

596 Ibid.

597 The Marquis de Condorcet was a mathematician and was elected to the revolutionary Legislative Assembly of 1791. But he fell from political favor in 1793 and died in prison in 1794.

598 Marquis de Condorcet, "Sketch for a Historical Picture of the Progress of the Human Mind," in *French Philosophers from Descartes to Sartre*, Leonard M. Marsak, editor. Cleveland & New York: Meridien Books, World Publishing Co., 1961, 264-281.

599 Ibid.

600 See Locke's comment on "no law without a Lawmaker" in *Of Ethics in General* printed in King, 1830, 2:122-23.

religious thought and the glorifying of an autonomous "nature." Thus, also did France move steadily toward Revolution and "the Terror" which finally brought its horrors to an end.

JOHN ADAMS
ON THE FRENCH PHILOSOPHES

Most of our Founding Fathers were well aware of what was at work in the writings of the French *philosophes*. John Adams, for example, wrote of them in an ironic vein to Thomas Jefferson:

> No man is more sensible than I am of the service to science and letters, humanity, fraternity, and liberty, that would have been rendered by...Voltaire, D'Alembert, Buffon, Diderot, Rousseau, La Lande, Frederic [the Great], and Catherine [the Great], if they had possessed common sense. But they were totally destitute of it. They seemed to think that all Christendom was convinced, as they were, that all religion was "*visions judaïques*," and that their effulgent lights had illuminated all the world; they seemed to believe that whole nations and continents had been changed in their principles, opinions, habits, and feelings, by the sovereign grace of their almighty philosophy....[601]

Then Adams asked the all-important question: "And what was their philosophy?" He answered: "Atheism—pure, unadulterated atheism. Diderot, D'Alembert, Frederic, De La Lande, and Grimm were indubitable atheists. The universe was master only, and eternal. Spirit was a word without a meaning. Liberty was a word without a meaning. There was no liberty in the universe; liberty was a word void of sense. Every thought, word, passion, sentiment, feeling, all motion and action was necessary. All beings and attributes were of eternal necessity; conscience, morality, were all nothing but fate."

He concluded ironically that, "This was their creed, and this was to perfect human nature, and convert the earth into a paradise of pleasure."[602] Later in the letter he remarked casually: "We all curse Robespierre and Bonaparte; but were they not both such restless, vain, extravagant animals as Diderot and Voltaire?"[603]

---

601 John Adams, Letter to Thomas Jefferson, March 2, 1816, in *"In God We Trust"—The Religious Beliefs and Ideas of the American Founding Fathers*, Norman Cousins, ed., New York: Harper & Brothers, 1958, 269.

602 Ibid., 269–270.

603 Ibid., 270.

JEAN-JACQUES ROUSSEAU

Another writer who was read by the Founding Father generation was the romanticist Jean-Jacques Rousseau. But he did not find many followers among them. In the next chapter, we will see how his political ideas were completely opposite to those of John Locke. His ideas on education—about which he had little practical knowledge—were also very different from Locke's. Nevertheless, Locke and Rousseau are often coupled in learned theses on politics and education as though Rousseau had simply further developed Locke's ideas. This is an extraordinary mistake since his political ideas differed so radically from those of Locke.

Certainly the *philosophes* discussed in this chapter were often happy to use Locke's "high and deserved reputation" as a cloak to conceal their own very different ideas. Unfortunately, too many scholars have believed them, so that the supposed similarities between the ideas of these *philosophes* and those of John Locke seem not to have been examined. Instead, Locke has been conveniently placed in the Enlightenment camp, his name often coupled with those of Helvetius or Condillac, and other proponents of the sensationalist philosophy.

In this chapter, we have seen the great distance between Locke and all the French sensationalist *philosophes*. The following chapter shows what a great distance there also was between the political ideas held by John Locke and those held by Jean-Jacques Rousseau whose influence on the French Revolution was immense and who, tragically, provided a theoretical basis for untrammeled democracy. Indeed, many of his ideas have become influential in modern states—including our own.

CHAPTER TWELVE

Locke and Rousseau – A Study in Contrasts

The Promises and Bargains...between a *Swiss* and an *Indian*,
in the Woods of *America*, are binding to them,
though they are perfectly in a state of Nature,
in reference to one another.
For Truth and keeping of Faith belongs to Men, as Men,
and not as Members of Society.

JOHN LOCKE [604]

The passage from the state of nature to the civil state
produces a very remarkable change in man,
by substituting justice for instinct in his conduct,
and giving to his actions the morality they had formerly lacked.

JEAN-JACQUES ROUSSEAU [605]

NO greater contrast in character, temperament, and philosophy exists than between Jean-Jacques Rousseau (1712-1778) and John Locke (1632-1704). Both men were born and brought up in Calvinist households; both wrote influential treatises on education and on political philosophy; both employed the vocabulary of Natural Law. But here similarity ends and contrast begins.

The sentence from Locke quoted above is the epitome of his personal philosophy of life. No view of Locke's could be more at odds with Rousseau's outlook on life. Rousseau saw man as molded by circumstance, as being initially good and faithful, but afterwards corrupted by society. Then, paradoxically, it fell to government to redeem man and give him moral standards. Locke saw individuals not as opposed to society but as the

---

604 John Locke, *Of Civil Government*, Book II, par. 14, in Hall, *Christian History*, 1:61.
605 Jean-Jacques Rousseau, *The Social Contract*, 1762, in *The Social Contract and Discourses*, translator, G. D. H. Cole, New York: E. P. Dutton and Company, Inc., 1950, 18.

essential building blocks of society. Far from being an inevitable corrupting influence on the individual, society simply reflected the character of the individuals who composed it—the character of individuals and their moral convictions and then man and man. Keeping of faith, or keeping of covenants (as his Puritan teachers taught him), belonged first of all to a man as an individual. Locke surely learned from the Puritan preachers of his boyhood that the Old Testament is replete with instances of God offering a covenant to individuals, such as His covenants with Moses, Abraham, and David. Locke saw the patriarchs and their families as forming the nucleus of a God-ordained society.[606]

CHARACTER CONTRASTS

When we turn to the personal characters of Rousseau and Locke, we find again great contrasts. Rousseau's character was weak and vacillating. Sadly lacking in personal ethics, he was often a faithless friend.[607] He always had an excuse, however, for his unfaithful behavior: It was circumstances that had pushed him to do the wrong thing. On the other hand, we have seen how John Locke throughout his life displayed strength of character, resolve, morality, honesty, and faithfulness in friendship.

Rousseau was unable to hold a position, although he tried several different professions, and was found either incompetent or unwilling to fulfill their requirements. Locke was steady and reliable in his undertakings and loyal to his long-time engagement as secretary and physician to the Earl of Shaftesbury and as tutor to his son and grandson. When he was secretary to the ambassador to Venice, Rousseau evidently believed that his position was too menial. (This was often his complaint when serving as secretary or tutor.) Although Locke's position with Shaftesbury also verged at times on the menial, he never complained.[608] Rousseau quarreled with nearly all of his friends and was unable to command the respect of those whom he served. Locke was a faithful friend and commanded his patron's complete respect and trust, as well as the respect and trust of many prominent scholars and statesmen of his time.

---

606 Locke frequently discussed Abraham in the *First Treatise Of Government* in connection with the growth of society under the patriarchs, pointing out that not one of them was given absolute authority over the others as an heir of Adam, as Sir Robert Filmer supposed. See, for example pars. 132-33; 135-36; 160.

607 Perhaps the worst instance of his indifference to others was his desertion of his music teacher when the latter collapsed in an epileptic fit in the strange city they were visiting. (See Rousseau's *Confessions*, New York: Alfred A. Knopf, 1923, 158.)

608 Fowler relates that Locke dined at the stewards table, and when Shaftesbury rode out in state, he accompanied the coach on foot. See Fowler, 24-25.

ROUSSEAU AND RELIGION

Rousseau entertained a passionate belief in god, but his was not the god of the Christian; rather, it was a vague presence behind nature. This vague deistic view he apparently acquired through his association with some members of the coterie of *philosophes* he met in Paris. Thus, he came to disparage Biblical revelation. Locke, as we have seen, was a firm Christian who turned to the Bible as his authority on the nature of God. Rousseau changed his faith from Protestant to Roman Catholic and back to Protestant as circumstances dictated the advantage; Locke remained a life-long Protestant.

DELUSIONS OF PERSECUTION VS. MENTAL EQUILIBRIUM

Over time Rousseau developed a persecution complex which, in late life culminated in delusions—all this, despite the fact that he was often treated with great kindness by influential admirers and was supported by them from time to time (an aid he seldom appreciated for long). Although "wanted" by the English authorities and moving often from place to place in his years of exile in Holland, Locke maintained his mental equilibrium, not railing against fortune or the "machinations" of others.

SELFISH ABANDONMENT VS. NURTURING LOVE

In addition to their governmental writings, both men wrote famous treatises on the education of children, but Rousseau forced his mistress to abandon all of their five children, although he knew the chances were poor that these babes would survive the rigors of a foundling home. Locke, on the other hand, substantially aided his young cousin, Peter King, bestowing love, thought, care and all possible aid to him in his career, all of which were decisive in forming his character and turning this grocer's son into a member of Parliament and finally Chancellor of England. Locke genuinely loved children and young people and was, in turned loved by them.

Rousseau was a failure as tutor precisely because he had so little love for children. (Indeed, he seems to have been one of those men whose love for "mankind" is so great that there is little left over for individual men and women.) Because of Locke's love of children, he was a highly successful tutor, despite some rather unpromising material in Shaftesbury's dull son, who must have tried the patience of the brilliant scholar; yet there is no hint of this in his writings or in contemporary reports of his attitudes. Locke was not only a great theoretician in the field of education, but a practical educator, who painstakingly carried out his own theories in the education of Lord Shaftesbury's son and grandson.[609]

BENEVOLENCE VS. INDIFFERENCE

As alluded to earlier, Rousseau repeatedly displayed the most callous indifference to others (which, of course, he always rationalized). When his former mistress begged him for financial help in a time of great need, he gave little to her and what he did give he gave reluctantly. In his biography of Rousseau, Lester Crocker observes that he must have given the money to her very ungraciously, because she never asked for help again even when she became desperately poor and Rousseau could have helped her.[610] Locke, as we have learned, showed his care for the feelings of others through his courtesy and kindness. We have seen, too, his practical efforts to help the poor through his personal benevolences.

Rousseau's death was a pitiable one; pursued by imaginary persecutors, he believed he was imprisoned in the country estate where he was staying. Actually, his benefactor had put it at his disposal out of pity for his poor health and lack of money. The circumstances surrounding Rousseau's death indicates that he may have committed suicide.

Locke, like Rousseau, battled against illness all his life but kept his good cheer and died at Sir Francis and Lady Masham's estate where he had lived as a "paying guest" during his last years. He died a Christian, at peace with God and man, while Lady Masham was reading to him from the Psalms.

THE CAUSE OF ROUSSEAU'S POOR CHARACTER

Rousseau was a truly pitiable man, but it would be a mistake to lay the blame for his neuroses on his Calvinist upbringing. In actuality, Rousseau suffered more from a too lax religious upbringing. The family was only nominally Calvinist. Absent was a strengthening spiritual education. This is surely more to blame for Rousseau's weakness of character than his father's undisciplined life, although in the absence of a strong Christian background, his father's character failings probably had some effect on him.

---

609 Locke's *Thoughts on Education* (1693) was a compilation and amplification of an extensive correspondence with his friends Edward and Mary Clarke regarding the education of their children.

610 See Lester G. Crocker, *Jean-Jacques Rousseau: The Quest, 1712–1758*, Vol. 1 of 2, New York: The Macmillan Company, 1968, 1:345.

Locke, like Rousseau, lost his mother early in life. It will be recalled that he was raised by his father, a severe gentleman who kept his son in awe of him when John was a boy. However, as he grew up his father gradually admitted him to a close relationship. Judged by today's standards, this stern attitude toward a small boy would seem to be more promotive of childhood neurosis than the indulgence and affection Rousseau received in his childhood. Yet Rousseau was the neurotic while Locke developed into a sensible, well-balanced adult, apparently unharmed by his father's severity and even speaking of it with approval.

CONTRASTING POLITICAL PHILOSOPHIES

As political philosophers, the contrast between Locke and Rousseau is equally striking. Despite their use of the Natural Law vocabulary, they stand at opposite poles philosophically. At the heart of this divergence is the difference in their basic concepts of the nature of man. As Rousseau realized, how you define man's nature determines your view of Natural Law and Natural Right.[611] In his *Discourse on the Origin of Inequality*, which is at the base of his political philosophy, he expressed the view that the first man, Adam, was not in a state of nature because he received his commandments directly from God. He also asserted that if men are unequal it was only because religion had made them believe that God willed it when He took mankind out of the state of nature immediately after creating them.[612] (Rousseau does not mention the Fall of Man as the explanation for his flawed and unequal abilities.) Instead, he suggests that religion had not forbidden from considering what might have happened to mankind *"if it had been left to itself."*[613] From this deistic assumption he then outlines an evolutionary concept of life with the "original man" beginning as an animal without any rationality.[614] This savage man he saw as functioning like an animal only able to see and feel like other animals.[615] True, the "human machine" differed from that of other animals in its ability to choose courses of action. For Rousseau this ability was a kind of free will.

---

611 See Rousseau's "Discourse on the Origin of Inequality" where he quotes Burlemaqui as saying that the idea of right "and more particularly that of natural right, are ideas manifestly relative to the nature of man." (Discourse in *The Social Contract and Discourses*, 191.)

612 Ibid., 197-98.

613 Ibid., 198, emphasis added.

614 Ibid., 210.

615 Ibid., 209.

ROUSSEAU'S VIEW OF REASON

Unlike Locke, Rousseau did not recognize reason as a fundamental, God-given quality distinguishing natural man from animals. Rather, he viewed reason, as well as the faculty of moral sense, as evolving and resulting from natural man's freedom and ability to choose. Commenting on this in a keenly perceptive passage from his biography of Rousseau, Professor Crocker notes that Rousseau seemed unable to admit that man has a superior understanding to that of the animal kingdom. Nor could Rousseau admit that the reason man was free from mere instinct was because he was endowed with a superior mental ability that enabled him to do so!! [616]

REASON AN INTRUDER IN EDEN

According to Rousseau, it is not reason but feeling that characterizes man. Rousseau believed that man was naturally good and compassionate but that when his reason developed, he became depraved.[617] This is an extraordinarily bold statement and one that shows his immense distance from Locke's view of man's natural state in which reason and reflection were fundamental, God-given qualities identifying man and distinguishing him from the animal world.

In Rousseau's view, reason was an intruder into Eden causing men to notice their differences, especially with regard to those who excelled in any art. He believed that this was the first step toward inequality and also toward vice.[618]

LOCKE'S CHRISTIAN VIEWS OF NATURE AND REASON

It is easy to see how very different from Locke's ideas are the views of Rousseau in regard to the role of reason—its nature, development, and results in the life of man. Although, as we have seen, Locke gave some consideration to man's natural state as a primitive being, he is not usually discussing what may have been true historically, but, rather, what is true philosophically. Hence, his references to the State of Nature in *Of Civil Government* are so often in the present tense. Locke's primary use of the term "State of Nature" is as he defines it in his *Second Treatise*:

---

616 Crocker, 1:257-58.
617 See *Discourse on Inequality*, 204.
618 Ibid., 241.

To understand political Power right, and derive it from its Original, we must consider, what State all Men are naturally in, and that is, a *State of perfect Freedom* to order their Actions, and dispose of their Possessions, and Persons as they think fit, within the bounds of the Law of Nature, without asking leave, or depending upon the Will of any other Man.[619]

Clearly, Locke's "State of Perfect Freedom" is a rational state. Nowhere does Locke discuss man as evolving from an animal without intelligence into an intelligent being, as does Rousseau. As a Biblical Christian, Locke viewed man as a created being, endowed with reason by his Creator. This is clearly and eloquently stated in the Introduction to *Of Human Understanding*:

For, though the comprehension of our understandings comes exceeding short of the vast extent of things; yet we shall have cause enough to magnify the bountiful Author of our being, for that proportion and degree of knowledge He has bestowed on us, so far above all the rest of the inhabitants of this our mansion. Men have reason to be well satisfied with what God hath thought fit for them, since He hath given them (as St. Peter says)…whatsoever is necessary for the conveniences of life and information of virtue; and has put within the reach of their discovery the comfortable provision for this life, and the way that leads to a better.

How short soever their knowledge may come of a universal or perfect comprehension of whatsoever is, it yet secures their great concernments, that they have light enough to lead them to the knowledge of their Maker, and the sight of their own duties.[620]

In the *Second Treatise Of Civil Government* Locke calls reason "that measure God has set to the actions of Men, for their mutual Security."[621] Reason, in Lockean terminology, is a moral faculty, an ability to discern in some measure, what is God's will; indeed, man's reason is the offspring of that Reason which Locke called the Will of God, or the Law of Nature.

GOD-GIVEN LIBERTY VS. PRIMITIVE NATURAL FREEDOM

This God-given, hence supremely constructive state of liberty, governed by God's Law of Nature, contrasts sharply with Rousseau's primitive natural

---

619 Locke, *Second Treatise*, Of the State of Nature, par. 4, in Hall, *Christian History*, 1:58.
620 Locke, *Of Human Understanding*, par. 5, in *Works*, 1:3-4.
621 Locke, *Second Treatise*, Of the State of Nature, par. 8, in Hall, *Christian History*, 1:59.

freedom governed only by physical laws. Because of the materialistic basis of his reasoning concerning man's nature, Rousseau could not make a distinction between what the Christian calls "right reason" and "depraved reason." His view of reason was completely dark. He saw it only as a faculty evolved by nature which tended to divide and disrupt men's relationships with each other. He could not conceive that it could unite and uplift mankind. Rousseau believed that society had corrupted man and brought evil into the world.[622] Because of his conviction that man was naturally good but that society demoralized him and took away his natural goodness, he felt that another kind of society needed to be created.[623]

JOHN LOCKE ON
THE BEGINNINGS OF SOCIETY

It is with relief that we turn to John Locke for a better evaluation of the beginnings of political society. Here we find a very different view from Rousseau's on the nature of man. Individualist though he is, Locke is also a Christian. Therefore, he does not present the individual as autonomous and in opposition to society, or as one whom society must inevitably corrupt. Speaking of the injustice and confusion he believed occurs in a State of Nature, where *"every one has the Executive Power of the Law of Nature,"* Locke concluded that "therefore God hath certainly appointed Government to restrain the partiality and violence of Men."[624]

Unlike Rousseau, Locke disbelieved in man's self-sufficiency. He quoted with approval these words of the English churchman, Richard Hooker, on man in the State of Nature:

> ...*for as much as we are not by our selves sufficient to furnish our selves with competent store of things, needful for such a Life, as our Nature doth desire, a Life fit for the Dignity of Men; therefore to supply those Defects and Imperfections which are in us, as living single and solely by our selves, we are naturally induced to seek Communion and Fellowship with others, this was the Cause of Men's uniting themselves at first in Politick Societies.*[625]

Locke also defined man's state in the following passage which has a strongly Biblical flavor: "God having made Man such a Creature, that, in His own Judgment, it was not good for him to be alone, put him under

---

622 Crocker, 1:259-60.
623 Ibid.
624 See *Of Civil Government,* in *Second Treatise,* par. 13, in Hall, *Christian History,* 1:60.
625 Ibid., 1:61.

strong Obligations of Necessity, Convenience, and Inclination to drive him into *Society* as well as fitted him with Understanding and Language to continue to enjoy it." [626]

MUTUAL COOPERATION OR "THE BONDS OF SERVITUDE"?

Locke believed that men were drawn together by the Creator with the intent of their mutual cooperation; Rousseau believed man could only be free if he were completely self-sufficient. Rousseau did not see cooperation resulting from men's association with each other. Rather, it was "the bonds of servitude" which occur because of men having to depend on each other. Slavery results from being in a position where he must have the help of others. On the other hand, Rousseau confidently asserts that this does not occur in the state of nature, for here men are independent of each other. Each is his own master. [627]

That the "law of the strongest is of no effect" in the State of Nature, is precisely what Locke found unacceptable. To him, one of the "inconveniences" of the State of Nature was precisely that man's enjoyment of his liberty and the fruit of his labors must have been "very uncertain and constantly exposed to the Invasion of others." To Locke it was evident that "the enjoyment of the Property he has in this State is very unsafe, very unsecure." [628] It was for this reason, Locke argued, that men were willing to leave such a hazardous life for the blessings of living together under laws that would protect their lives, liberties, and possessions.

ROUSSEAU'S ROMANTIC VIEW OF PRIMITIVE MAN

Rousseau, however, takes a very romantic view of primitive man in his solitary state. Primitive man was naturally good and compassionate. It was only as his faculties developed that a state of inequality also appeared. [629]

Rousseau believed that this was because some men excelled in various skills and others did not. The first step toward inequality and vice came as men became aware of these differences. As primitive society developed, primitive man lost his "goodness" and could not cope with the new conditions. What Rousseau called "morality" (in contrast to primitive

---

626 Ibid., 1:78.
627 See Jean-Jacques Rousseau, *Discourse on the Origin of Inequality*, 233.
628 John Locke, *Of Civil Government*, in *Second Treatise*, par. 123, in Hall, *Christian History*, 1:91.
629 See Rousseau, "Discourse on the Origin of Inequality," 242.

"goodness") was the fruit of the developing society he envisioned. What was suitable in the pure state of nature was no longer proper in the new-born state of society.[630]

THE PERFECTION OF THE INDIVIDUAL OR THE DECREPITUDE OF SOCIETY?

The innocent pastoral life that Rousseau imagined had existed in the State of Nature, he believed no longer existed when men entered society. Now there were more opportunities for offense resulting from the increase of inequality that occurred as society developed. Punishments for these offenses had to become more and more severe. Therefore, Rousseau saw primitive men as losing some of "their natural compassion." He believed, though, that this semi-civilized state was one of happiness and stability. In fact, he was sure it was the ideal state for men where they were meant to remain. It was "the youth of the world." Subsequent advances toward "*the perfection of the individual,*" *actually led to the* "*decrepitude of the species.*"[631]

VIRTUE: CONFORMING TO THE GENERAL WILL OR TO THE WILL OF GOD?

This was an *Idee fixe* of Rousseau's: that as individuals developed, society was not improved but, instead, became depraved. In fact, the species as a whole suffered in the ratio that the individual developed. Rousseau's ideal society sank the individual into subordination to the whole. This idea was expressed in his concept of a "*moi commun*" or "collective self." In his *Discourse on Political Economy*, he defined virtue as nothing more than the conformity of each individual will to the general will.[632]

Locke, on the other hand, would say that virtue lies in conformity to the Will of God. He saw virtue as a God-given quality which created society but was not the fruit of society. As he wrote: "For Truth and keeping of faith belong to Men as Men, and not as Members of Society."[633] Locke saw reason as a God-given quality which helped man to fulfill his duties as a human being, but he saw "that human Reason unassisted, failed Men in its great and proper business of Morality." And he reminded his readers that:

> It never from unquestionable Principles, by clear Deductions, made out an entire Body of the Law of Nature. And he that shall collect

---

630 Ibid., Rousseau, 242.

631 Ibid., 243

632 See Jean-Jacques Rousseau, "Discourse on Political Economy" in the *Social Contract and Discourses*, 298.

633 John Locke, *Of Civil Government* in *Second Treatise*, par. 14, in Hall, *Christian History*, 1:61.

all the moral Rules of the Philosophers, and compare them with those contained in the New Testament, will find them to come short of the Morality delivered by our Saviour, and taught by His Apostles; a College made up for the most part of ignorant, but inspired Fishermen.[634]

PROPERTY: A NATURAL OR CONVENTIONAL RIGHT?

In their ideas on the origins of society, there is no greater contrast between Locke and Rousseau than their attitudes toward property. We have seen that to Locke "the great and *chief end...* of Men's uniting into Commonwealths, and putting themselves under Government, *is the Preservation of their Property.* To which in the state of Nature there are many things wanting."[635] As we have also seen, Locke's concept of property was an all-embracing one meaning men's "Lives, Liberties, and Estates, which I call by the general Name, *Property.*"[636] So, to Locke, man's fundamental rights are three: Life, Liberty, and Property.

To Rousseau, man's fundamental rights were two: Life and Liberty. How man can sustain either of these without the third element—the right to the fruits of his labors—seems not to have occurred to him. He asserts, in *The Discourse on the Origin of Inequality,* that the right to property was only a convention of human institution; and that they could dispose of their property in whatever way they wanted. But this was not the case with the "essential gifts of nature," which he identifies as "life and liberty."[637] In *The Social Contract* Rousseau also differentiated between "possession" which he defined as the effect of force or the supposed "right of the first occupier." But the right to property, he declared, should only be founded on "a positive title."[638]

In fact, as Professor Crocker observed, property was "the arch-villain among Rousseau's villains."[639] In the ideal state Rousseau outlines in *The Social Contract,* citizens are only allowed to hold private property as "depositaries of the public good."[640] In the *Discourse on the Origin of*

---

634 John Locke, *The Reasonableness of Christianity,* in Hall, *Christian History,* 2:87.

635 John Locke, *Of Civil Government,* in *Second Treatise,* par. 124, in Hall, *Christian History,* 1:91.

636 Ibid., par. 123.

637 Jean-Jacques Rousseau, "Discourse on the Origin of Inequality" (1755), in *The Social Contract and Discourses,* 259.

638 Jean-Jacques Rousseau, "The Social Contract," Chapter VIII in *The Social Contract and Discourses,* 19.

639 Lester Crocker, 263.

640 Jean-Jacques Rousseau, "The Social Contract," Chapter IX in *The Social Contract and Discourses,* 21.

Inequality, Rousseau utterly rejects the idea of private property in highly-colored terms later echoed by Karl Marx and other apostles of twentieth-century communism.

Rousseau passionately believed that the first man who enclosed a piece of ground and called it his own was the real founder of civil society. How many crimes and misfortunes might have been averted, he claimed, by "pulling up the stakes, or filling the ditch" and crying out to his neighbors, "Don't listen to this imposer because the fruits of the earth belong to us all, and the earth itself to no one."[641]

Clearly, Rousseau rejected Locke's idea that property results from the individual's labors. Nowhere does he recognize, as Locke did, that by improving property, by subduing and cultivating the earth, man adds something to it that comes from his own labor and so imparts to it a new value that it did not have before. Indeed, Locke believed that every man has the foundation of property *in his own person.*

According to Rousseau, it was wrong to say "I built this well," or "I have this place because I worked for it." Why? Because what right did such a man have to demand to be paid for doing what his fellows did not ask him to do?[642] Rousseau maintained that such a man should have gotten the *express* and *universal* consent of mankind, before taking more of the common subsistence than he needed for himself.[643]

Even making allowances for the extravagance and impracticality implicit in his language ("express and universal consent of all mankind"), the tenor is clear: the individual's productivity is to be at the disposal of the society. The question naturally arises: *How* is this to be decided? In condemning the man who put his time and energy into digging a well, because it was without the permission of everyone else, Rousseau condemned necessary productivity. Furthermore, to wait on society's permission to support one's life is to invite starvation.

If he had read Locke a little more closely, Rousseau would have discovered that the great English philosopher had already pointed out the folly of such notions:

> By making an explicit consent of every Commoner, necessary to any one's appropriating to himself any part of what is given in common, Children or Servants could not cut the Meat which

---

641 Ibid., Rousseau, "Discourse on the Origin of Inequality," 234-35.
642 Ibid., 250.
643 Ibid. Emphasis added.

their Father or Mother had provided for them in common, without assigning to every one his peculiar part. Though the water running in the Fountain be everyone's, yet who can doubt, but that in the Pitcher is his only who drew it out? His Labour hath taken it out of the hands of Nature where it was common, and belong'd equally to all her Children, and hath thereby appropriated it to himself.[644]

THE ORIGIN OF MAN'S
TITLE TO PROPERTY

Locke was willing to grant that originally "God gave the World to Men in Common," but he was also convinced that because "he gave it to them for their Benefit, and the greatest conveniences of Life they were capable to draw from it, it cannot be supposed he meant it should always remain common and uncultivated." On the contrary, Locke advanced the view that "God gave the World . . . to the use of the industrious and rational, (and *Labour* was to be *his Title* to it;) not to the Fancy or Covetousness of the Quarrelsom [sic] and Contentious."[645]

Rousseau saw things differently: property ownership was not a natural right, but only a civil one. He did not see it as the effect of the efforts of industrious and rational individuals. Nor was it something produced by individual efforts from the raw materials provided by nature. Rousseau's view of property was essentially a negative non-creative one. He did not recognize, as did John Locke, that "he who appropriates Land to himself by his Labour, does not lessen but increase the common stock of Mankind." As Locke realized, "the Provisions serving to the support of human Life, produced by one acre of Inclosed and Cultivated Land are (to speak much within compass) ten times more than those which are yielded by an Acre of Land of an equal richness lying waste in Common."[646]

Rousseau took a more romantic view of nature, assuming (mistakenly) that the earth brought forth all its fruits spontaneously, so that man had only to pluck them off the vine. To him, appropriating any part of this spontaneous abundance for oneself (beyond "subsistence") was a usurpation of the "right" of all other men to live off generous Mother Nature. The idea that labor is what authenticates the right to property was foreign to Rousseau's psychology. He seemed unable to make a living and was consumed with bitterness and jealousy toward the wealthy. Yet he did not

---

644 John Locke, *Of Civil Government*, in *Second Treatise*, par. 29, in Hall, *Christian History*, 1:64.
645 Ibid., par. 34, 1:65-66.
646 Ibid., 1:67.

hesitate to live off wealthy patrons, even while pretending to disdain their patronage. Rousseau's nature appears to have been essentially weak and parasitical. Out of his individual nature and character came his concept of property and the ideal government, even as Locke's views of property and civil government were determined by his individual character.

THE FOUNDATION OF ROUSSEAU'S IDEAL GOVERNMENT

Upon what basis did Rousseau's ideal government rest? It rested upon "the total alienation of each associate, together with all his rights, to the whole community...."[647] Indeed, he wrote that these clauses of the social contract were reducible to this single point.[648] According to Rousseau, the "total alienation" of the individual and his rights to the community, would confer, upon the collective body thus formed, unlimited power over the individual. Later, to justify such a sweeping abrogation of rights, he draws this dangerous and simplistic analogy: Because nature gives to each man absolute power over all his members, the social contract also gives to the political world absolute power over all its members.[649] Is such an "absolute power" for the purpose of ensuring the individual's right to life, liberty, and property? Are there ground rules by which the Sovereign power is limited? By no means!

According to Rousseau, each man gives up, by the social contract, only that portion of his power, possessions, and liberty "as it is important for the community to control," and it must also be granted that "the Sovereign is the sole judge of what is important"![650]

ROUSSEAU'S DEMOCRATIC ABSOLUTISM VS. HUMAN RIGHTS

Particularly worth noting in this passage is Rousseau's stress on the absolute power of the Sovereign (that is, the "public person...formed by the union of all other persons") to judge what is important to the community. Here is an introduction to "democratic absolutism," by an elite governmental corps

---

647 Jean-Jacques Rousseau, "The Social Contract," Book I, Chapter VI, in *The Social Contract and Discourses*, 14.

648 Ibid. In Rousseau's *Discourse on Political Economy*, he also suggests that the people "should be early accustomed to regard their individuality only in its relation to the body of the State, and to be aware...of their own existence merely as a part of that of the State." (See in *The Social Contract and Discourses*, 307.)

649 "The Social Contract," Book II, Chapter IV, in *The Social Contract and Discourses*, 28.

650 Ibid.

ruling absolutely in the name of the people! So, in the end, Rousseau's "sovereignty of the people" turns out to be "sovereignty in the name of the people."

John Locke rejected any form of absolute and arbitrary government. In the *Second Treatise*, he declared that "Absolute Arbitrary Power, or governing without *settled standing Laws*, can neither of them consist with the ends of Society and Government.... It cannot be supposed that [men] should intend...to give to any one, or more, an *absolute Arbitrary Power* over their Persons and Estates, and put a force into the Magistrate's hand to execute his unlimited Will arbitrarily upon them: This were to put themselves into a worse condition than the state of Nature, wherein they had a Liberty to defend their Right against the Injuries of others...."[651]

THE INDIVIDUAL
NOTHING APART FROM THE WHOLE?

To Rousseau, however—and to the revolutionaries who followed him and are with us still—what constitutes "good" government is the collective good only.

> ➤ To Locke, the individual was the primary building block of good government; his happiness was found in being able to enjoy his life, liberty, and the fruits of his labors.

> ➤ To Rousseau, man's happiness was to be found in obeying the "general will." By "general will," in contradistinction to an aggregate of individual wills, or "the will of all," Rousseau seemed to mean that men, as individuals, have their own particular wills, but as "good citizens," they have a general will for the common good (which to him meant viewing oneself as subordinate to the whole).[652]

LIFE:
THE GIFT OF GOD
OR THE GIFT OF THE STATE?

Locke saw life as the gift of God and men as His workmanship; Rousseau insisted that life is a mere "bounty of nature" and that the state has the

---

651 *Second Treatise*, par. 137, in Hall, Christian History, 1:94-95.

652 Rousseau says in Book II, Chapter III, 28, of "The Social Contract," "There is frequently much difference between the will of all and the general will. The latter regards only the common interest; the former regards private interest, and is indeed but a sum of private wills."

right to decide whether a citizen shall live or die on the basis of what is expedient for the state. He wrote: "…when the prince [that is, the state or government] says to him, 'It is expedient for the State that you should die,' he ought to die, because it is only on that condition that he has been living in security up to the present, and because his life is no longer a mere bounty of nature, but a *gift made conditionally by the State*."[653]

How far this is from Locke's view that when the individual compacts with others to form civil government, he does not give up his God-given gift of life and his other God-given rights to the State; he only delegates power over these rights to the civil government. Indeed, as we have learned, Locke was convinced that because man's life is a gift from his Creator, it is not his own to give away.

> For a Man, not having the Power of his own Life, *cannot*, by compact, or his own Consent, *enslave himself* to any one, nor put himself under the absolute, arbitrary Power of another, to take away his Life, when he pleases. No body can give more Power than he has himself; and he that cannot take away his own Life, cannot give another Power over it.[654]

THE PURPOSE OF DELEGATED POWER

Furthermore, as Locke also indicated, the power men delegate to the state is for the sole purpose of preserving their lives, liberties, and fortunes. In his chapter "Of the Ends of Political Society" in the *Second Treatise*, he makes it clear that men give to society many of the powers they possessed in the State of Nature, "yet it being only with an intention in every one the better to preserve himself, his Liberty, and Property…the Power of the Society, or *Legislative* constituted by them, can *never be suppos'd to extend farther than the common good*; but is obliged to secure every one's Property…."[655] Thus in regard to the "*Supream or Legislative Power*" or any extent of the legislative power, "the preservation of Property being the end of Government, and that for which Men enter into Society," Locke declared that for men to lose what they had entered into society to protect and preserve was "too gross an absurdity" for anyone to accept.[656]

---

653 Jean-Jacques Rousseau, "The Social Contract," Book II, Chapter V, in *The Social Contract and Discourses*, 32. Emphasis added.

654 John Locke, *Of Civil Government*, in *Second Treatise*, par. 23, in Hall, *Christian History*, 1:63.

655 Ibid., par. 131, 1:92.

656 Ibid., par. 138, 1:95.

THE PROPER ROLE OF GOVERNMENT: TO EQUALIZE CITIZENS OR TO PROTECT THEIR RIGHTS?

Locke and Rousseau were also at opposite poles in regard to the state's role in regard to equality. In Rousseau's egalitarian view of the ideal society, the proper role of civil government is to equalize men, while in Locke's view, the proper role of civil government is to protect all men in their natural rights to their lives, liberties, and possessions. Locke maintained that although there was a sense in which all men were equal, they were not equal in all ways: age, virtue, talents, and merit often placed men above the common level. Yet all this exists along with the equal condition men were in respecting jurisdiction or dominion over each other. In fact, by equality he meant *"that equal Right* that every Man hath, to his Natural *Freedom,* without being subjected to the Will or Authority of any other Man."[657]

ROUSSEAU'S REJECTION OF FUNDAMENTAL LAW

Perhaps the most dangerous element in Rousseau's philosophy was his rejection of fundamental law. He made it very clear that the state had "no fundamental law that could not be revoked" and that this even included the social contract![658]

On the other hand, John Locke based his political ideas on the assumption that fundamental law was a fact, appearing first through either the natural or revealed laws of God and, secondly, in the fundamental laws of just societies.

REMAKING HUMAN NATURE

But Rousseau denied that there can be any fundamental pre-existing law, or any law of the land which cannot be contravened by the sovereign power. He also believed that the Sovereign (meaning the elite that ruled in the name of the people) had the duty to remake society by remaking human nature, abolishing man as he is in order to recast him along more "desirable" lines. This audacious theme is defended in the *The Social Contract,* where he asserts that any one who wants to change mankind's institutions must first change the nature of human beings, must separate them from their own resources and give them new ones which they cannot

---

657 Ibid., 1:71, par. 54.
658 Jean-Jacques Rousseau, "The Social Contract," Book III, Chapter XVIII, in *The Social Contract and Discourses,* 101.

use, however, without the help of other people. This is not all: Individual resources must be destroyed so that each person can do nothing by himself without help from others.[659]

In his *Discourse on Political Economy*, Rousseau gives an even more chilling example of "social engineering," in an idea that came to be known in the twentieth century as "brain-washing." He writes that it is fine to work with men as they are, but it is better to make them what they ought to be. He concludes with the dogmatic declaration that in the end, "all peoples become in the long run what the government makes them...."[660] These statements make it hard to see the essence of Rousseau's philosophy as anything other than totalitarian. The state is not, as it was with Locke, man's servant. Instead, it is his god, having the awful power not only to constrain him physically but to condition and control him mentally. Examples easily come to mind of such techniques in use in modem times by which individuals are controlled mentally and often without their knowing what is happening to them.[661]

Passing from the world of Rousseau's "thought control" to Locke's straightforward view of the end and purpose of law and the duty of law-makers is like going from a dark room into the light of day. Unlike Rousseau, Locke was not interested in remaking man in his own image. He would have laughed at the notion that man, by playing God, could remake the fundamental nature and character of his fellow man. He saw all men as being "the Workmanship of one Omnipotent, and infinitely wise Maker: All the servants of one Sovereign Master, sent into the World by his Order, and about his Business...."[662] He certainly would not have agreed with Rousseau that the business of governmental elites was to attempt to remake men in their own limited and often warped image. But then Locke was a Christian philosopher and Rousseau was not.

ROUSSEAU REJECTED REVELATION

Of course, Rousseau excluded fundamental law from his version of "natural religion." He claimed that it was only because states sought to give

---

659 Jean-Jacques Rousseau, "The Social Contract," Book II, Chapter VII, in *The Social Contract and Discourses*, 38.

660 Jean-Jaques Rousseau, "Discourse on Political Economy," in *The Social Contract and Discourses*, 297.

661 Lester G. Crocker notes Rousseau's totalitarian tendencies and cites a similar statement by China's Chou En-Lai as being typical of others by communist leaders in China and in the old Soviet Union, all reflecting Rousseau's idea of remaking an entire people in the image desired by the elite leaders. See Crocker, *Jean-Jacques Rousseau: The Quest*, 1:280.

662 John Locke, *Of Civil Government*, in *Second Treatise*, par. 6, in Hall, *Christian History*, 1:58.

authority to their laws that the makers of nations claimed that their own wisdom was the wisdom of the gods.[663] Rather than receiving the written Revelation of God in the Bible, he ridiculed it in an ironic allusion to the Law of Moses: He said that anyone can engrave words on stone tablets, or claim secret dealings with a god, or indulge in some other deception so as to deceive the people.[664] There was no need for Revelation.

CHRISTIANITY DESTROYS THE UNITY OF THE STATE?

For Rousseau, Christianity was just one among many religions. While with one breath he praises Christianity, with the next he affirms that it destroys the unity of the state because it is not concerned with the things of this world. Although Rousseau asserted that all states were established on some kind of religious basis, he was convinced that the law of Christianity weakens men and does not strengthen the constitution of the state. He also believed that the spiritual kingdom that Jesus wanted to bring to the world separates theology from politics and so destroys "the unity of the state."[665] He also believed that "Jesus came to set up on earth a spiritual kingdom, which, by separating the theological from the political system, made the State no longer one...."[666] He cited Thomas Hobbes with approval because Hobbes argued for the supremacy of the secular over the religious power.

It appears that Rousseau had not read any of Locke's letters on toleration which supported the idea of two powers so as to preserve and enlarge religious liberty: One (the political power) deals with man's civil concerns, and the other (the Church) deals with his spiritual needs. Each had its own sphere and each was complementary to the other. Toward the end of his first *Letter Concerning Toleration*, Locke wrote:

> These things being thus explained, it is easie [sic] to understand to what end the legislative power ought to be directed, and by what measures regulated, and that is the temporal good and outward prosperity of the society; which is the sole reason of men entering into society, and the only thing they seek and aim at in it; and it is also evident what liberty remains to men in reference to their eternal salvation, and that is, that every one should do what his conscience is persuaded to be acceptable to the Almighty,

663 Jean-Jacques Rousseau, "The Social Contract," Book II, Chapter VII, in *The Social Contract and Discourses*, 40-41.

664 Ibid., 41.

665 Ibid., Book IV, Chapter VIII, 131.

666 Ibid., 131.

on whose good pleasure and acceptance depends their eternal happiness; for obedience is due in the first place to God, and afterwards to the laws.[667]

Rousseau, however, was not concerned about religious liberty. He did believe it impossible, however, to have a state without a religious basis of some kind. So he advocated a "civil religion" for his ideal state: Although it could not force any one to believe the doctrines of the state, it could banish whoever would not believe them, not because of impiety, but because of being anti-social![668]

Rousseau concludes by suggesting that if anyone, after publicly assenting to these dogmas of the state, then acts as though he does not believe them, he should be punished by death. What are Rousseau's dogmas for his civil religion? To do him justice, they consist of belief in "a mighty, intelligent, and beneficent Divinity, possessed of foresight and providence, the life to come, the happiness of the just, the punishment of the wicked, the sanctity of the social contract, and the laws...."[669] But who is this Divinity? Who are the just, and who are the wicked? What are good and evil according to Rousseau? Obviously, something very different from the definitions of a Christian philosopher like John Locke.

Locke's position, as we have seen, was that civil government had no business meddling in matters of conscience. As a Christian, Locke believed that God alone has authority over men's consciences, whereas Rousseau, as a totalitarian, believed the State had full authority over men's consciences and their religious activities. Locke believed that neither church nor state had a right to compel the conscience of the individual with civil penalties. In his view, the most severe penalty a church could exercise would be to expel a member of its body. That person would be free, however, to seek spiritual sustenance elsewhere, and a church could never confiscate his property.

To summarize the contrasting political ideas of Locke and Rousseau, we may say that:

Rousseau's political views were collectivist, egalitarian, and totalitarian.

Locke's political views were based on the sanctity of the individual as God's creation and the need for civil government to protect his natural rights to life, liberty, and property.

---

667 John Locke, *A Letter Concerning Toleration*, in *Works*, 6:43.
668 Jean-Jacques Rousseau, "The Social Contract," Book IV, Chapter VIII, in *The Social Contract and Discourses*, 139.
669 Ibid.

To Rousseau, liberty was primarily the independence or sovereignty of the State to whom the individual gave up all his natural rights.

To Locke, individuals only delegated their sovereign power to civil government to be exercised on their behalf provisionally.

To Rousseau, the individual utterly relinquished his right of self-government to the state which then had complete authority over him. To this mystic entity man even owed his very life

In Locke's system, all just human laws must proceed from fundamental law, i.e., the Law of God expressed either in revelation and/or in God's Law of Nature.

To Rousseau, government was a one-sided agreement in which the individual renounced all that he had to a government which then granted him only what it chose to give him.

To Locke, civil government was instituted by men as a compact to preserve their natural rights to life, liberty, and property. Government was a trust, and the trustees were accountable to the people whose interest they represented.

To Rousseau the right to property was not a natural right but one created by government.

To Locke the right to property was a natural right along with life and liberty.

THE TRAGEDY OF FRANCE

The tragedy of the French Revolution was that it followed Rousseau, rather than Locke. The soil of the Revolution had been well prepared by Voltaire, Diderot, Holbach, Condillac, and all the other "enlightenment" *philosophes;* but Rousseau subsequently was even more influential than Voltaire and his stable of propagandists. When the French Revolution finally came, it was to Rousseau, not Locke, that its radical leaders turned for political guidance in the forming of their "ideal state." What came forth was not the romantic panacea that Rousseau had envisioned, but a fearsome, devouring monster from whom no one was safe.

Rousseau had reduced religion to the level of the socially convenient. As will be seen in the following chapter, the leaders of the French Revolution actually put into place their version of Rousseau's civil religion, but along the way they abandoned God totally and turned churches into Temples of Reason. However much some of the progenitors of the French Revolution claimed to admire Locke, it was Rousseau's vision that the revolutionaries followed. His vision was also the model for the many subsequent revolutions that have followed into our own times. Indeed, it is our tragedy that we modern Americans have chosen increasingly to follow Rousseau's vision of a democracy untrammeled by the limits of fundamental law, one in which constitutions mean only what the court says they mean, and whatever society's current norms are become enshrined in the laws of the land.

The French Revolution ought to have served as a sufficient cautionary tale to prevent the slide into this abyss. But most politicians have forgotten what happened in the French Revolution. Revisiting this revolution will show us that, in the end, it was not a father of civil liberty, but of the modern totalitarian state. The battle lines are still drawn between Rousseau as the preeminent philosopher of the French Revolution, a revolution that produced spiritual and civil tyranny—and John Locke as the preeminent philosopher of the American Revolution, a revolution that produced genuine civil and religious liberty.

CHAPTER THIRTEEN

From Lafayette and the Constitutionalists To Robespierre and the Radicals

Every man is born with inalienable and imprescriptible rights;
these are the freedom of his opinions, the care for his honour
and his life, the right of property, the entire disposition
of his person, his industry, and all his faculties,
the communication of his thoughts by every possible means,
the pursuit of well-being, and resistance to oppression.

LAFAYETTE
(Declaration of the Rights of Man and of Citizens, 1789)[670]

Property is the right of each and every citizen to enjoy and
to dispose of the portion of goods that is guaranteed to him by law.

ROBESPIERRE
(Declaration of Rights, 1793)[671]

As the Lockean revolution in America produced a government where the individual under God was considered the basic unit of sovereignty, so the revolution in France (following Rousseau rather than Locke) produced a government where the people as a whole were theoretically sovereign. Ironically, though, the result of this supposed "Sovereignty of the People" was an all-powerful state such as Rousseau had outlined in

---

670 Reprinted in Andreas Latzko's *Lafayette: A Life*. Translated from the German by E. W. Dickes, New York: The Literary Guild, 1936, 146. Lafayette's Declaration was later amended by the National Assembly before its final adoption on August 26, 1789. See Appendix A for final version.

671 Maximilian Robespierre's proposed Declaration of Rights of 1793. See George Rudé's *Robespierre*, Englewood Cliffs, N. J.: Prentice-Hall, Inc., 1967, 53.

his *Social Contract*, which totally absorbed the power of the people. For the radical revolutionaries, led by Maximilian Robespierre (1758-1794), the state—as interpreted by them—was omnipotent.

THE REFORMERS
VERSUS THE REVOLUTIONARIES

But this is not how the French Revolution began. In the beginning, the Marquis de Lafayette (1757-1834) and those who followed his views wanted to reform the state and limit the power of kings through a written constitution. They wanted to follow the lead of England in establishing a constitutional monarchy and the lead of America (and that meant the lead of John Locke) in acknowledging the rights of every citizen to life, liberty, and property. How did this happen? What fired Lafayette's ardor for liberty? What led him to go against his king's orders, risking his all to support the American colonists in their fight against another king? It would seem that the seeds of a desire for liberty and justice for all men was planted early in his life. Born in 1757 in a moldering ancestral chateau in Auvergne, young Gilbert du Motier, Marquis de Lafayette, spent his early years there, raised by his grandmother and his aunt. The Parish priest taught him to pray, to read and write, and the basics of Latin grammar. (Lafayette's father, an army officer, had died in battle before Gilbert was born, and his mother returned to Paris soon after his birth to look after family interests at the Court of Louis XV.) Here in the Auvergne, far from the Court, Lafayette early developed sympathy for the wretchedly poor peasants in this region of unyielding soil. The simplicity of Gilbert's own life in the home of impoverished aristocrats did not prepare him for life at Court.

LAFAYETTE SHOCKED
BY THE FRENCH COURT

But to Court he went at the age of eleven when his mother summoned him to Paris to attend an elite school for young noblemen. When the young marquis began attending Court functions he was shocked and angry at the pleasure-loving nobility who were endlessly searching for lucrative positions at Court and were totally uninterested in the plight of the wretchedly poor populace surrounding them. He was even more incensed when he learned how the grain prices were being kept artificially high in order to fill the pockets of the noble landowners. The price of grain was so high that the poor could scarcely buy a loaf of bread. Desperate for food, the people of Paris often rioted, but their protests were put down ruthlessly.

MARRIAGE AND UNEXPECTED WEALTH

Suddenly, at the age of fourteen, two important events occurred in Gilbert du Motier's life that were to change its course. In the same week, he lost both his mother and her father, the wealthy Marquis de La Riviere (not an unusual occurrence in a time when disease often felled even the most wealthy). The impoverished young aristocrat was now very rich from the inheritance of his grandfather's estates. From being considered by the Court as a rawboned provincial, a hot-tempered redhead, awkward on the dance floor, and ineligible as a suitor, he was now eligible to marry into any of the "best" families.

The Duke d'Ayen-Noailles lost no time in persuading him to marry his daughter Adrienne. Since Lafayette was only fourteen years old and the bride-to-be was only twelve, the marriage was postponed for two years. They were married just ten days before Louis XV died. Their marriage was a very happy one, and Adrienne was always supportive of her husband's decisions even when they took him away from her for long periods of time. When troubles came later, she fought to defend his interests and showed great heroism during the French Revolution.

A PROVIDENTIAL EVENT?

Lafayette's father-in-law got him a post in his regiment which was sent to Metz where the garrison was under the military rule of the Duc de Broglie, an old comrade-in-arms of Lafayette's father. De Broglie greeted the son warmly and insisted he sit at his table that night, rather than at his regimental commander's table. This seems to have been a providential event, for a special banquet was being given that night to honor a visit from the English King George III's brother, the Duke of Gloucester.

At dinner, Gloucester spoke with astonishing frankness on what he viewed as his brother's mishandling of the American colonists. According to Andreas Latzko's admirable biography of Lafayette, the duke insisted that it did not take more than common sense to see that the uprising in Boston could have been prevented without a single shot being fired. But, instead, George III had refused to honor the rights possessed by all English subjects to pay taxes only when they had been voted into law by their own duly elected representatives.[672] The Duke went on to claim confidently that a few seats in the Parliament of their Mother Country would satisfy the colonists. Instead, his brother's arrogance had rebelled

---

672 Andreas Latzko, *Lafayette: A Life*, 25.

against the colonists and any sort of Parliamentary advice that would have moderated his position.

Lafayette was enthralled by Gloucester's account and was filled with indignation when Gloucester said that England was hiring foreign mercenaries from German princes to help put down the American rebellion. Here were these colonial farmers defending themselves with their own rifles against the raw power of mercenary forces! Lafayette thought that it would be a great thing to use his sword to help these liberty-loving people.

THE DECLARATION OF INDEPENDENCE ENROLLS LAFAYETTE IN THE COLONIAL CAUSE

This momentous event was followed by an even more momentous one. It happened the next day when the Duke of Gloucester was inspecting the fortifications at Metz. He was accompanied by the garrison's officers including Lafayette. They were interrupted by a courier who brought Gloucester important mail from England. The duke opened the dispatch and then read aloud to the officers the Declaration of Independence that Congress had just published. Here was Lafayette's first encounter with Lockean political ideas, and he was transported by them. Some ten years later, Lafayette described it in detail in his *Mémoires de ma main*. He wrote that the Duke of Gloucester's first reading of the Declaration of Independence "Enrolled my heart (*mon coeur fut enrôlé*)."[673]

LAFAYETTE ESCAPES TO AMERICA

Lafayette yearned to take ship at once for the New World and to fight alongside the American colonists. Nor was this the momentary emotional allegiance of a boy of seventeen. He forged ahead and bought a sea-going sailing vessel and named it *Victoire*. He recruited other young nobles with an itch for adventure if not always the same idealistic enthusiasm of their leader. When word reached Louis XVI of Lafayette's intentions, he issued an order to stop him. But on April 17, 1777, after a series of elusive stratagems, Lafayette and his companions finally set sail for America from a small port in Spain where the *Victoire* had been secretly berthed.

"THE HERO OF TWO WORLDS"

The scope of this book cannot follow in detail Lafayette's arrival in America and his heroic service under General Washington, nor can it discuss in

---

673 Ibid, Latzko.

depth the close friendship that developed between the young stripling and the general who became like a father to him; indeed, Washington came to look upon him as the son he had never had.[674] It is certain that during Lafayette's time in America, he learned much about American political ideas which, as we have learned, were closely derived from John Locke's writings. So convinced of the rightness of the American cause was he, that he spent thousands of French *livres* equipping American soldiers for battle as well as fighting valiantly beside them.

It was a joyful time for Lafayette, when, in the summer of 1778, France sent to America an army of 6,000 men under the command of General Rochambeau. The fleet, led by Comte d'Estaing (a distant cousin of Lafayette's), blockaded the English in New York. Since France was now at war with England, Lafayette felt that he was needed at home and he returned to France in the autumn of 1778. He had arrived in America as a teenager with no battle experience and now at twenty-one years old, he returned as an experienced general in the Continental army headed by George Washington. On his triumphant return home, Louis XVI forgave him for being absent without leave and only penalized him with a week's house arrest with his family! Marie Antoinette graciously called him "the hero of two worlds."[675]

In 1781, he persuaded Louis XVI to send a fleet to America carrying 4,000 troops under the command of Admiral de Grasse. He joyfully returned to America in time to participate in the victorious conclusion of the war at Yorktown. Lafayette could not know that soon he would face another Revolution in his own country. But when it came, he would be armed with American ideas and with a Lockean vision of government to offer to his own people.

---

674 At his own wish, Lafayette fought without pay in General Washington's army, distinguishing himself in the Battle of Brandywine where he was wounded in the thigh and bedridden for several weeks. Not yet fully healed, he persuaded Washington to let him join General Green's brigade selected to stop the duke of General Hesse-Cassel's push from Canada to join General Howe's troops. Lafayette and his 300 men came upon the advance guard of 350 Hessian mercenaries. He took the enemy by surprise in the dark cutting down part of their forces with the remainder surrendering. Washington then gave him command of a brigade of his choice. He chose a Virginian brigade which he was shocked to discover were shabbily dressed and often without boots. Lafayette then paid for uniforms for the 1,200 men and even paid the arrears in their pay.

675 Word had already reached France from Gérard de Rayneval, the French minister in America, to the Comte de Vergennes at Versailles, of Lafayette's "discernment and ability" in regard to some differences between Admiral d'Estaing and the American General Sullivan. He gave the most "salutary advice," Rayneval said. He added that Lafayette's conduct which was "prudent, courageous, and amiable" had made him very popular with Congress, as well as with the army and, indeed, with all Americans. Rayneval concluded by observing that Lafayette's military abilities were rated very highly by the Americans. See Andreas Latzko's *Lafayette: A Life*, 25.

THE FRENCH MONARCHY
AND TAXATION

It was in 1787 that the first opportunity for reform unexpectedly appeared. Lafayette eagerly grasped it as a chance to begin achieving his goals for France. The French people had long groaned under the absolute rule of their monarchs who had taxed them unmercifully and then squandered the money they raised while a sycophant aristocracy—which was exempt from taxation—jockeyed for prestige and largesse at the royal court. Provincial assemblies were long dead. All government was centralized in the person of the king and his representatives throughout the provinces. When Louis XVI (1754-1793) was facing national bankruptcy resulting from the reckless spending of previous monarchs and the enormous debts of his Queen, Marie Antoinette (1755-1793), he was urged to convene an "assembly of notables" to help him stave off imminent financial disaster.

THE ASSEMBLY OF NOTABLES

Lafayette became a member of The Assembly of Notables which was convened February 22, 1787.[676] Proposals were discussed for provincial assemblies as a means to collect taxes more efficiently and were agreed to by most of the notables including Lafayette. He also seized an opportunity to champion the cause of Protestants whose rights had been severely curtailed since the revocation in 1685 of the Edict of Nantes of 1598 that had given Protestants the liberty to practice their religion. Religious liberty was a cause dear to Lafayette's heart. Shortly after his return to France in 1785, he wrote to George Washington about the persecution of Protestants in his country:

> Protestants in France are under intolerable despotism.... Marriages are not legal among them; their wills have no force of law; their children are to be bastards; their persons to be hanged. I have put it into my head to be a leader in that affair, and to have their situation changed.... [W]hen in the course of the fall, or winter, you hear of something that way, I wanted you to know I had a hand in it.[677]

---

676 Of the 144 members of this Assembly of Notables, there were seven princes, fourteen archbishops and bishops, thirty-six dukes and peers, marshals of France, and noblemen; twelve counselors of state and Masters of Requests; thirty-eight magistrates of sovereign courts; twelve deputies of States-districts, and twenty-five municipal officers of large towns. See M. Guizot and Madame Guizot De Witt, *France*. New York: Peter Fenelon Collier, MDCCCXCVIII, 5:453.

677 Cited by Andreas Latzko in *Lafayette: A Life*, 116.

It was Lafayette who led the support in the Assembly of Notables for revising these afflictive laws. Though many of the delegates were sympathetic, the most they were willing to do was to appeal to the king to rectify "a regimen of proscription equally opposed to the general interest of religion, to good morals, to population, to national industry, and to all the principles of morality and policy."[678]

Lafayette also boldly attacked the abuses of the tax collectors who extracted large sums of money for themselves from the taxes they collected. He asked the king for an investigation of these abuses. But little came in the way of revising the system of taxation. The notables were unwilling to take any actions that might subject themselves to taxation. They were shocked, however, at the extent of the deficit and also were confused by the contradictory figures given them. In the end, they simply turned these matters back to the King. "We leave it to the king's wisdom," they said. "He shall himself decide what taxes will offer the least inconveniences, if the requirements of the State make it necessary to impose new sacrifices upon the people."[679] Lafayette did not concur. He entered the following petition in the minutes of the assembly:

> We humbly beg His Majesty now to fix a date when he will him-
> self assume control of all operations, and assure a happy re-
> sult thereof for all time, through the convocation of a National
> Assembly.[680]

In making this request, Lafayette was resurrecting an old institution not summoned since 1614 (probably because French monarchs like Louis XIV preferred a policy of royal absolutism). Originally known as the States-General, this body had been summoned by kings whenever they were in desperate need of funds. It had been made up of the nation's Three Estates: the clergy, the nobility, and the middle class. When the King's brother, the Count d'Artois, asked Lafayette if he was actually requesting a revival of this ancient body, he replied enigmatically: "Yes, monseigneur, and perhaps even something better."[681]

Elated when the provincial assemblies were revived, Lafayette visit-ed his home territory of Auvergne where he was rapturously received by the people and elected to their assembly. Lafayette was proud to tell

---

678 See Guizot, 346-347.
679 Guizot, 350.
680 Latzko, 126.
681 Ibid.

Washington that this assembly was one of a few that did not vote for an increase in their taxes.[682] To the King and the royal party, Lafayette was now considered an agitator whose democratic reforms ran counter to the desires of king and court. Even before the Assembly of Notables concluded on May 25, 1787, Lafayette wrote to Washington: "The King, his family, and the high personages of his entourage, with the exception of a few friends, do not forgive the liberty I have taken. But it is above all my popularity among the other classes of the nation that they grudge me."[683] Nevertheless, Lafayette wrote optimistically to Washington that France would come

> Little by little, without a great convulsion, to an independent representation and, consequently, to a diminution of the royal authority. But it is a matter of time, and will proceed the more slowly [because] the interest of powerful men will clog the wheels.[684]

FRANCE UNPREPARED
FOR SELF-GOVERNMENT

Lafayette did not seem to realize that the great mass of the people in France were illiterate and had neither experience nor understanding of the duties of self-government. Nor could he foresee the enormous difficulties that faced him and his fellow reformers. George Washington, however, had more foresight. When word reached him of the increasing political tensions in France, he tactfully warned his young friend that "but little irritation would be necessary to blow up the spark of discontent into a flame, that might not easily be quenched. If I were to advise, I should say that great moderation should be used on both sides. Let it not, my dear Marquis, be considered as a derogation from the good opinion, that I entertain of your prudence, when I caution you, as an individual desirous of signalizing yourself in the cause of your country and freedom, against running into extremes and prejudicing your cause."[685]

---

682 In a letter dated January 1, 1788, Lafayette wrote: "I am returned from the Provincial Assembly of Auvergne wherein I had the happiness to please the people and the misfortune to displease government to a very great degree. The Ministry asked for an increase of our revenue. Our province was among the few who gave nothing...." (Cited by Rosalie J. Slater, in "Washington and Lafayette," *The Journal of the Foundation for American Christian Education,* Vol. VI (1994-1995), 122, quoting from *The Letters of Lafayette to Washington, 1777-1799,* ed. Louis Gottschalk. Privately printed by Helen Fahnestock Hubbard, New York, 1944, 337-338.)

683 Latzko, Letter of the Marquis de Lafayette to George Washington, May 5, 1787, 127.

684 Ibid., 128.

685 Letter of George Washington to the Marquis de Lafayette, June 18, 1788, in *The Washington Papers,* edited and with an introduction by Saul K. Padover, New York: Harper & Brothers, 1955, 248.

THOMAS JEFFERSON'S ENTHUSIASM FOR THE FRENCH REVOLUTION

Thomas Jefferson, who had been sent to Paris in 1785 to replace Benjamin Franklin as the United States' Minister to France, watched the coming revolution with an enthusiasm and optimism equal to Lafayette's. Washington Irving, in his biography of George Washington, wrote of Jefferson at this period:

> Carrying with him his republican principles and zeal, his house became the resort of Lafayette and others of the French officers who had served in the American Revolution. Politics became the theme of all societies, male and female, and a very zealous party was formed which acquired the appellation of the Patriot Party, who, sensible of the abuses of the government under which they lived, sighed for occasions of reforming it.... By this party Jefferson was considered high authority from his republican principles and experience, and his advice was continuously sought in the great effort for political reform which was daily growing stronger and stronger.[686]

Jefferson watched the Assembly of Notables with great interest and believed that the convening of provincial assemblies that emerged from this assembly would become "the instrument for circumscribing the power of the crown and raising the people into consideration."[687]

A NATIONAL ASSEMBLY REPLACES THE OLD STATES-GENERAL

Lafayette's desire for a real national assembly was finally fulfilled when the States-General met in Versailles on May 5, 1789. The king wanted the three estates to vote as separate bodies which had been the custom in the past. But this would have buried the will of the members of the Third Estate, two to one. Therefore, the Third Estate, which had the largest number of delegates, insisted on a single assembly to govern the deliberations, each delegate to have a vote. When the other two orders disagreed, the Third Estate, on June 17, 1789, proclaimed itself a National Assembly and swore not to adjourn until it had given France a constitution. Lafayette joined the Third Estate on the advice of Jefferson who had come to believe that

---

686 Washington Irving, *Life of Washington*. Chicago, New York and San Francisco: Belford, Clark and Company, n.d., 3:277. (A note by Irving in this volume is dated 1856.)

687 Cited by Noble Cunningham, Jr. in *In Pursuit of Reason: The Life of Thomas Jefferson*. Baton Rouge and London: Louisiana State University Press, 1987, 119.

the aristocracy could not be relied upon to support reform.[688] By June 27, Louis XVI reluctantly allowed the Three Estates to meet as one assembly, since the minor nobility and the clergy were already joining the Third Estate in the newly formed National Assembly. Marie Antoinette, however, was utterly opposed to the National Assembly and thought that troops should be assembled to close it down and also to punish the unruly populace in Paris which ardently supported it.

LAFAYETTE'S DECLARATION OF THE RIGHTS OF MAN

Just at this time when an alarmed king was surrounding Versailles and Paris with a ring of mercenary troops that frightened many of the members of the National Assembly into silence, Lafayette rose and read to the Assembly his "Declaration of the Rights of Man." The date was July 11, 1789, just three days before the Paris populace rose and stormed that symbol of royal tyranny, the infamous prison known as The Bastille.[689]

Lafayette's declaration was modeled after the state declarations of right in the new United States, particularly that of Virginia, as well as the American Declaration of Independence.[690] Noble E. Cunningham writes that "Lafayette consulted closely with Jefferson in drafting a declaration of rights to submit to the National Assembly." According to James Morton Smith, a copy exists of Lafayette's declaration with Jefferson's annotations in the margins.[691] Given Jefferson's love of Locke's writings on government, it is no surprise that Lafayette's Declaration of Rights has a distinctly Lockean flavor. Lafayette also asked Jefferson to send him a copy of the United States Bill of Rights with his notes on it. Jefferson obliged.

Lafayette's proposed Declaration of Rights contained much good

---

688 See Cunningham, 124.

689 Through *lettres de cachet* distributed by the King to almost anyone around him who asked, innocent men and women were thrown into the Bastille there to languish for years in conditions of wretched degradation without recourse to the law until a merciful death released them. Troublesome husbands or wives could be thrown into the Bastille by their vengeful spouses, or a person against whom the holder of the *lettre de cachet* held a personal grudge could also be arrested and without trial thrown into this foul prison.

690 Lafayette had already written to Washington in 1788 to praise the proposed Constitution for the United States, but he also expressed concern that there was no Declaration of Rights. See his letter reproduced in Rosalie J. Slater's article in *The Journal of the Foundation for American Christian Education*, VI:121-22.

691 Cunningham, 126. See also *The Republic of Letters, The Correspondence between Thomas Jefferson and James Madison 1776-1826*, James Morton Smith, ed., 3 vols. New York & London: W. W. Norton & Company, 1:631, note 35. Smith cites several sources regarding the annotations that Jefferson made on a draft copy of Lafayette's text for the Declaration of Rights shortly before its presentation at the National Assembly on July 11, 1789.

material, such as the statement that "every man is born with inalienable and imprescriptible rights" among which Lafayette included the right to life, property, industry, and free expression of opinions, and the right to resist oppression. The Declaration also insisted that "no man may be made subject to laws other than those agreed to by him or his representatives, promulgated in advance, and legally applied." It also asserted that the legislative, executive, and judiciary powers be distinct and defined, that judges be impartial and that "the laws must be clear, precise, and uniform for all citizens."

This has quite a Lockean ring. But the statements that "The principle of all sovereignty resides in the nation" and that "No corporation and no individual can have an authority which does not expressly emanate therefrom" gives one pause. This would seem to be quite different from the Lockean emphasis on governmental authority as emanating from a society of individuals who have come together to create civil government as a trust answerable to them. Was France to become the new sovereign taking to itself the omnipotent powers hitherto exercised by the monarch? Surely, such was not Lafayette's intention, but the phrase is capable of this interpretation.

AMENDMENTS TO LAFAYETTE'S DECLARATION OF RIGHTS

The Declaration was debated by the Assembly, and other statements regarding the rights of man were inserted. A preamble asserted that "the National Assembly recognizes and proclaims, in the presence and under the auspices of the Supreme Being, the following rights of man and of the citizen." There followed Lafayette's text as amended and amplified with additional statements among which were that:

➤ The natural rights of each man are unlimited except those which assure to other members the enjoyment of the same rights.

➤ Law is the expression of the general will and every citizen has a right to participate personally, or through his representative, in its foundation;

➤ Law must be the same for all;

➤ All citizens are equal in the sight of the law and therefore are equally eligible to fill public offices;

➤ No person is to be accused, arrested, or imprisoned except according to the law and anyone attempting to execute an arbitrary order will be punished;

➤ All persons are to be held innocent until proved guilty;

➤ No one shall be disquieted on account of his opinions, including his religious views, provided their manifestation does not disturb the public order established by law.

➤ One of the most precious rights of man is the free communication of ideas.

The document also declared that no longer was the aristocracy to be exempt from taxation, nor was the Catholic Church, which owned vast tracts of land and had long levied its own taxes.

Property was acknowledged as "an inviolable, sacred right," and it was declared that no one shall be deprived of his property except where public necessity dictated and then "only on condition that the owner shall have been previously and equitably indemnified."[692]

JEFFERSON ATTENDS
DEBATES OF THE NATIONAL ASSEMBLY

Jefferson attended many of the debates of the National Assembly and urged his reforming friends to seek a compromise with the government on what it was willing to yield, leaving until later what was still lacking. On July 11, he wrote with great enthusiasm of the Assembly's accomplishments thus far and asserted that "they have prostrated the old government, and are now beginning to build one from the foundation."[693] Alexander Hamilton, too, wrote a warmly congratulatory note to Lafayette expressing, however, his concern for the difficulties that must still lie ahead, such as keeping the "vehement character" of the people under proper control and warning of the possible unwillingness of the nobility to make the necessary sacrifices.[694]

---

692 Even before adoption of the Declaration of Rights, the National Assembly, on August 4, "witnessed a long procession of nobles and churchmen, who, fired by a noble impulse of enthusiasm and renunciation, had come of their own accord to abdicate their feudal rights, and to receive in return a promise of pecuniary indemnity." (See Andre Lebon's *Modern France: 1789-1895*. New York: G. P. Putnam's Sons, 1898, 15.) Later, under the first French Constitution of September 3, 1791, every institution of the Old Regime in conflict with "the principle of equality" was abolished. Titles of nobility, feudal rights, hereditary offices bought with money; all these were swept away. Lafayette concurred and never again used the title of Marquis, preferring to be known simply as General Lafayette.

693 Cited by Washington Irving in his *Life of Washington*, III:280.

694 See Irving, 3:282.

Despite Lafayette's courageous acts at the Assembly of Notables and the States-General and his courageous contributions to the National Assembly, there were those in the radical clubs that were quickly forming who tried to undermine the people's love for Lafayette. They believed him to be too favorable to the King and Queen. After all, he was an aristocrat, was he not? On the other hand Louis XVI and Marie Antoinette were deeply angered by Lafayette's Declaration of Rights and his espousal of democratic principles that they thought would radically restrict, if not abolish, the monarchy. Thus, he was attacked and undermined from both sides. After Louis XVI, on September 4, 1791, finally accepted the Constitution crafted by the National Assembly and swore to uphold it, Lafayette decided it was time to resign his position as the commander of the Paris Guard. On October 8, after the National Assembly had dissolved, he formally handed in his resignation to the Mayor of Paris. He intended to retire from public life and looked forward to living quietly in the country with his beloved wife.

But this was not to be. Hardly had he started in on repairs to the old chateau than word reached him that his country had declared war on Austria because they had discovered that Marie Antoinette had been trying to get Austria, which was led by her brother the Emperor Leopold, to come and liberate them from the new government and the Constitution which she despised. Finally, the Emperor Leopold decided to form an offensive alliance with Sweden against France. Lafayette was called upon to lead one of three armies to defend France from invasion. Lafayette found himself once again with the army installed at Metz.

THE RADICALS OPPOSE "THE ENGLISH PARTY"

The radicals in the National Assembly knew Lafayette to be of the constitutional or "English party," who held up English constitutional monarchy as the ideal to follow. These radicals, who were mostly followers of Rousseau, had scant respect for the constitutionalists. They incited the people to action. A mob attacked the Tuileries Palace in Paris on August 10, 1792 and massacred the royal family's Swiss Guards. Louis XVI and Marie Antoinette fled for safety to the National Assembly only to be stripped of royal authority. As Washington Irving wrote:

> It was at once the overthrow of the monarchy, the annihilation of the constitutional party, and the commencement of the reign of

terror. Lafayette, who was the head of the constitutionalists, was involved in their downfall.[695]

Lafayette, who had protested an earlier attempt (in June 1792) on the lives of the king and queen, was now denounced in the National Assembly as a traitor unworthy to be commander in the army. A decree was issued for his arrest, and he was forced to flee for his life to neutral Belgium which transferred him to the Austrians who believed him to be an enemy of their own Marie Antoinette. They promptly imprisoned him in a fortress at Olmütz.[696] Here he remained for five years. Meanwhile, the radicals who had taken control of France executed their King on January 21, 1793, and declared France a republic. France was already at war with Austria and Prussia and in March and April of 1794, the fledgling republic, knowing the plans of the crowned heads of Europe to repress its new government, declared war on England, Holland, and Spain.

AMERICAN REACTIONS TO THE FRENCH REVOLUTION

When word reached America of the execution of Louis XVI, some three months after the event, the reaction was mixed. Some Americans, already elated by the news in 1792 that France was now a republic (like their own they supposed), thought the United States should go to her aid. Others, shocked by the summary execution of Louis XVI who had aided our Revolution, opposed aiding the new republic. Some believed that if America should go to war, it should not be on the side of France—but on England's side.

Although Thomas Jefferson did not want the United States to enter the war, he remained intensely sympathetic to the Revolution going on in France. It should be remembered, however, that he was not in France at that time of Louis XVI's execution and so did not see the Terror that followed. He had returned to America and was in Washington's cabinet as Secretary of State.

As early as September 10, Gouverneur Morris (1752-1816), who became American minister to the French court in 1792, wrote a letter to Jefferson

---

695 Irving, 3:347.

696 George Washington wrote (unsuccessfully) to the Austrian authorities, asking for Lafayette's release, but it was only through the wary cooperation of an ambitious young general whose star was rising—General Napoleon Bonaparte—that Lafayette was finally freed on September 19, 1797. But Lafayette, a republican to the core, was uneasy about Napoleon long before he made himself Emperor of France in 1804, thus destroying the last vestiges of the republic of which Lafayette had dreamed.

relating some of the despicable acts of the radicals. "We have had one week of unchecked murders in which some thousands have perished in this city. It began with between two and three hundred of the clergy, who had been shot because they would not take the oaths prescribed by the law, and which they said were contrary to their conscience."[697] This was only the beginning of "the Terror." Jefferson, however, took a sanguine view of the matter. He believed that

> ...in the struggle which was necessary [to found the republic], many guilty persons fell without the forms of trial, and with them, some innocent. These I deplore as much as anybody, and shall deplore them to the day of my death. But I deplore them as I should have done had they fallen in battle.... My own affection has been deeply wounded by some of the martyrs to this cause, but rather than it should have failed, I would have seen half the earth desolated; were there but an Adam and Eve left in every country, and left free, it would be better than as it is now.[698]

NO INTERMEDDLING IN
THE AFFAIRS OF FRANCE OR ENGLAND

Alexander Hamilton, also in Washington's cabinet as Secretary of the Treasury, took an opposing view regarding the French Revolution. He recognized that it was not akin to ours. He opposed "intermeddling" in the affairs of either England or France. In a newspaper article dated February 8, 1794 and signed "Americanus" he wrote,

> To defend its own rights, to vindicate its own honor, there are occasions when a nation ought to hazard even its existence.... But let us at least have the consolation of not having rashly courted misfortune.... If there can be any danger to us, it must arise from our voluntarily thrusting ourselves into the war [between France and England].... The most violent resentment, as before intimated, would no doubt in such a case be kindled against us, for what would be called a wanton and presumptuous intermeddling on our part....[699]

Sickened by the violent turn the French Revolution had taken, he warned: "But let us not corrupt ourselves by false comparisons or glosses,

---

697 Gouverneur Morris, Letter to Thomas Jefferson, dated September 10, 1792, in Irving's *Life of Washington*, 3:347-48.

698 Thomas Jefferson, Letter to William Short, in Irving, 3:348.

699 Alexander Hamilton, *Americanus*, February 8, 1794, reprinted in Hall, *Christian History*, 2:17-18.

nor shut our eyes to the true nature of transactions which ought to grieve and warn us...."[700]

GEORGE WASHINGTON'S DECLARATION OF NEUTRALITY

George Washington was deeply shocked by the execution of Louis XVI and the increasing arrests and executions of aristocrats (just because they were aristocrats) by the radicals now in control of the French government.[701] His proclamation of neutrality between the warring parties was a wise step. But many sympathizers with the French Revolution viewed the proclamation as pro-British, perhaps even pro-monarchy. Though supported by some of the press, Washington was reviled by democratic republican newspapers that ardently supported the revolution in France. It was a shock to Washington to see a large segment of the public so easily swayed against him. Although it hurt and angered him, he stood firm. He was convinced that America should not become entangled in European politics.

THE RADICALS AND THEIR REVERED ROUSSEAU

Meanwhile, in France, the radicals who had banished Lafayette turned to the inversion of Lockean ideas found in their revered Rousseau, whose writings permeated the thinking of all classes of Frenchmen. One eyewitness wrote:

> He alone inoculated the French with the doctrine of the sovereignty of the people and with its extremist consequences. It would be difficult to cite a single revolutionist who was not transported over these anarchical theories and who did not burn with ardor to realize them.[702]

---

700 Ibid.

701 Concerned for Madame Lafayette, Washington deposited some two hundred guineas with a banker in Holland on her behalf. He wrote: "The uncertainty of your situation, after all the inquiries I have made, has occasioned a delay in this address and remittance; and even now the measure adopted is more the effect of a desire to find where you are, than from any knowledge I have obtained of your residence" (Irving, 3:239). He did not know that she was already in prison and that she was to see her grandmother, her mother, and her sister executed. She herself was only spared through the stern warnings of Gouverneur Morris that as the wife of America's great friend, General Lafayette, and innocent of any acts against the republic, she should be spared. Morris was able to prevent her execution, but not to liberate her. That task was left to James Monroe who succeeded him as American Minister to France. It was not until the Terror had ended that she was freed on January 22, 1795. Ever the devoted wife, she and her daughters then voluntarily joined Lafayette in his Austrian prison.

702 Hippolyte Adolphe Taine, *The Ancient Regime*, translated by John Durand. New York: Henry Holt & Company, 1891, 2:182.

The same eye-witness also contended that Rousseau's *Social Contract* became nothing less than "the Koran of the Jacobins of 1790 [and] of the republicans of 1791...." He claimed he heard a revolutionary read from it to "a street corner crowd in 1788."[703] John Morley, the author of a classic biography of Rousseau, written from the English standpoint, also asserts that *The Social Contract* was closely followed by the Jacobins.[704] The French historian Taine refers to it as "a catechism in every hand."[705] A kind of mystical force in Rousseau's emotional prose exercised a strong influence over the many revolutionaries. (The same quasi-religious fervor in our time also applied to the followers of Karl Marx, such as Chairman Mao and his "little red book" designed to change the character of the Chinese people.)

Morley was convinced that the actions taken by this predominant party early in 1794 can only be understood when we learn that they were the result of directly applying Rousseau's political ideas.[706]

"THE STATE MUST LAY HOLD ON EVERY HUMAN BEING AT HIS BIRTH...."

As an example of Rousseau's influence, Morley quotes from a Decree of the Committee of Public Safety, dated April 20, 1794. It paraphrased Rousseau in the same way that the American revolutionaries' writings paraphrased Locke:

> You must entirely refashion a people whom you wish to make free—destroy its prejudices, alter its habits, limit its necessities, root up its vices, purify its desires. The state therefore must lay hold on every human being at his birth and direct his education.[707]

Like Rousseau, the hard-core revolutionaries wanted not only to reform society, but to re-form men after their own image. The revolutionaries had replaced the Lockean views of Lafayette and his fellow constitutionalists, with their own radical ideas.

---

703 Ibid.

704 See John Morley, *Rousseau and His Era*, 2 vols. New York: MacMillan & Co., 1923, 2:182. The reference is to the revolutionary club that met in the Rue Jacob in Paris.

705 Taine, *The Ancient Regime*, 318.

706 Morley, *Rousseau and His Era*, 2:182-83.

707 Ibid., 132-33. See Rousseau's *Social Contract*, Book II, Chapter VII, "Of the Legislator."

THE DESTRUCTIVE GENIUS
OF THE MEN OF THE TERROR

The men of the Terror were obsessed by the kind of destructive genius with which Locke had had little patience. He disliked those whose main efforts were to destroy, rather than to create, knowing that destruction is quick and easy, but building is slow and difficult. Regarding such men, he once commented:

> A building displeases them. They find great faults in it; let them demolish it, and welcome, provided they endeavor to raise another in its place if it be possible.[708]

This destructive determination of the radicals, resulted in the abandonment of due process of law and in the travesty of justice seen in the so-called trials of the Revolutionary Tribunal, trials which denied right of counsel to the accused who were judged on the most emotional and least judicial basis imaginable.

How different was the American Revolution, fought in defense of law, from the French Revolution, fought in defiance of it. Friedrich Von Gentz put it well when he wrote:

> Never in the whole course of the American Revolution, were the rights of man appealed to for the destruction of the rights of a citizen; never was the sovereignty of the people used as a pretext to undermine the respect due to the laws....[709]

THE RADICAL REVOLUTIONARIES
PLAY GOD TO THEIR FELLOW MEN

Having cast off the restraints of religion, the French revolutionaries now became intoxicated with their fancied new freedom. They imagined they could play god to their fellow men, that they could give legality to any system of government they chose to devise, absolutely without reference to the laws of God whom many of them rejected as mere superstition to be eradicated from the human consciousness as quickly as possible. Even though they mouthed natural law, as interpreted by Rousseau, their tyranny soon became apparent.

---

708 Pierre Coste, *The Character of Mr. Locke* (1704), in Locke's *Works*, 1823 ed., 10:171.

709 Friedrich von Gentz, *The French and American Revolutions Compared* (1810), as translated by John Quincy Adams, and reprinted in *Three Revolutions*, including reflections on the Russian Revolution by Stephen T. Possony. Chicago: Henry Regnery Company, 1959, 71.

More and more individuals from all walks of life were hauled before the Revolutionary Tribunal on vague charges of "sympathizing" with the "aristos," and many of these unfortunate people also received the verdict of death, along with the aristocrats with whom they may, or may not, have been sympathetic. The Guillotine, that terrible new weapon, was also used to liquidate the life of fellow revolutionaries who were believed to have deviated from acceptable revolutionary standards.

MAXIMILIAN ROBESPIERRE
—DISCIPLE OF ROUSSEAU

In a work devoted to the impact of John Locke's political ideas at different times and places, it is obviously impossible to deal with the French Revolution comprehensively, as, for instance, to discuss the many shades of opinion and the many prominent personalities involved in this struggle for power. One personality, however, stands out more strongly than that of the other radical leaders of the Revolution; one person, more than all others, most completely represents the ideology of the French Revolution after Lafayette and the constitutionalists were swept aside. That individual was Maximilian Robespierre (1758-1794), a country attorney, who rose to be the leader of the radical revolutionaries. It was he who condemned Lafayette as a traitor and who created what history now knows as The Terror.[710] As it happens, Robespierre was a devoted disciple of Jean-Jacques Rousseau and such words as these by Rousseau rang in his ears: "All articles of the social contract, when clearly understood, will be found reducible to this single point—the total alienation of each associate, and all his rights, to the whole community." [711] The Lockean or "English ideas" of the rights of

---

710 Robespierre, Maximilian Marie Isidore de, was born May 6, 1758 in the town of Arras, France. After studies at the local college, he attended the College of Louis Le Grand in Paris. After finishing his legal studies, he returned to his home town to practice the law. His first taste of the political world was when he was elected one of the deputies to attend the States-General held in Versailles in 1789. His bearing and serious manner of speaking attracted attention. Of austere manner and dress, he was uninterested in money and became known as "the incorruptible," but was not above political maneuvers that his enemies would not have so named. In 1791, he proposed and got a decree passed prohibiting members of the current assembly from sitting in the next assembly—which resulted in the power of the Jacobins, with him as their leader, becoming supreme. He was one of the deputies sitting in the national convention called in 1792. As chief of the radicals, his was the main voice calling for the execution of Louis XVI, who was guillotined on January 21, 1793. In the following year he sent many of his enemies to the guillotine during "the reign of terror." Marie Antoinette and the Duke of Orleans were the first to go; then Robespierre's political rivals Danton and Camille Desmoulins and others. Paris saw the slaughter of thousands in the coming months. Finally, his rivals and enemies, wondering who among them would be next to mount the steps to the guillotine, denounced Robespierre on the floor of the revolutionary convention. He was arrested and executed by the same guillotine to which he had sent so many others.

711 Jean-Jacques Rousseau, "The Social Contract," Book I, Chapter VI, "Of the Social Contract," 14.

the individual were foreign to him. As the prime political figure during the Terror, Robespierre was the impassioned defender of the new revolutionary government which swept aside all individual rights and enforced a rigid, all-encompassing dictatorship, the likes of which France was not to see again until the German Occupation of France during World War II. All this was for the avowed purpose of defending the state from a supposed vast "conspiracy" which threatened at any time to destroy it.

THOUSANDS SENT TO THE GUILLOTINE

Just six days after Robespierre took office as President of the Revolutionary Convention, on June 4, 1794, the Convention suspended all guarantees of justice, and an "enemy of the people" was defined so loosely that almost anyone could be arrested on such a charge. From June 10 to July 27 some 1,285 persons were sent to the guillotine. This pre-eminent champion of the Terror (like Hitler, Stalin, Mao Tse Tung, and all other political fanatics before and since who have defaced political and religious history) was a desperately sincere man who believed unswervingly in the ideal state he saw in his mind's eye. Not only did he believe in it, he was determined to impose it upon his fellow citizens no matter the cost.

ROBESPIERRE'S IDEAL STATE

His ideal state was cut almost whole cloth from *The Social Contract*. Alfred Cobban declares in his book *Aspects of the French Revolution* that Rousseau was the writer Robespierre cited most often in his speeches and writings.[712] George Rudé, editor of *Robespierre*, writes that Robespierre was saturated with Rousseau's political ideas, so much so that he slept with a copy of *The Social Contract* in his bedroom.

It was from Rousseau that Robespierre got his conviction that a "civil religion" could be socially useful, provided it was stripped of all "superstition." Like Rousseau, he was also convinced that the people were basically good, but that they could be misled at times by a perversion of the "general will."

VIRTUE SEEN AS
LOVE OF EQUALITY

Although Robespierre insisted on "virtue," it was not the Christian quality Locke referred to when he wrote: "Truth and keeping of Faith belongs to

---

712 See Alfred Cobban, *Aspects of the French Revolution*, New York: George Braziller, Inc., 1968, 51.

Men as Men, and not as Members of Society."[713] Rather, Robespierre (like Rousseau) followed Montesquieu's definition of virtue in a republic as love of equality. Montesquieu wrote: "What I call virtue in a republic is love of country, that is to say, love of equality. It is neither a moral nor a Christian virtue," Montesquieu insisted. "It is a political virtue...."[714]

REPRESENTATIVE GOVERNMENT
SEEN AS A NECESSARY EVIL

Robespierre defined "la Patrie" as "the land where one is a citizen and a member of the sovereign." This phrase "member of the sovereign" was Rousseau's way of expressing what was to him the *indivisible sovereignty* of the people. Since the people *as a whole*, were sovereign, this whole could not logically be represented. Therefore, to Robespierre, representative government was just a necessary evil. Again, this was Rousseau's idea and was completely opposite to John Locke's theory of representative government where individuals were represented by other individuals. This idea of the indivisible sovereignty of the people as a whole was perhaps the most pernicious political idea that Robespierre passionately advanced. Since he disliked the word representative, he used "mandataire" or mandatory. He had to admit that it was not practically possible for all the people, as one great whole, to transact all public business. Still, he insisted that assembled political bodies should not be considered as representative bodies. They were simply made up of the "mandataries" of the people; a curious semantic twist. To get around the problem of representative government which, in his view, threatened "the sovereignty of the people," he suggested such cumbersome devices as large assemblies (supposedly to avoid factionalism) and the holding of legislative meetings in huge arenas accommodating 10,000 to 12,000 spectators. It never seems to have occurred to him that such a Roman Circus approach to government could only result in mob rule and the consequent rise of demagogues eager to manipulate the mob. Perhaps it never occurred to him because he was just such a demagogue himself.

Robespierre's proclamation of "the sovereignty of the people" and their innate "virtue" were ideas that Parisian working men liked. For them, "sovereignty of the people" meant the right of assemblies to pass legislation,

---

713 John Locke, *Of Civil Government*, in Hall, *Christian History*, 1:61.
714 Charles de Secondat, Baron de Montesquieu, *The Spirit of the Laws*, 1748. New York: The Colonial Press, 1900, xxxv.

to control the national deputies and even to dismiss them, to supervise public officials, and even to start insurrections.[715]

Although Robespierre passionately believed in the goodness of the people, taken as a whole, he paradoxically did not believe virtue resided in individuals. He declared: "Morality which has disappeared in most individuals can only be found again in the mass of the people and in the general interest."[716] Cobban observed shrewdly that Robespierre did not think of man, the individual, as having the principles of virtue. No, it was "the people" whose goodness he was always praising."[717] Clearly, Robespierre's view of man was an abstraction. One senses that he was continually outraged by the reality of individuals who fell short of his abstract ideal. It is significant that Robespierre seldom mentions natural man in his writings, an omission that was not lost on Cobban, who pointed out how significant this was because it showed the decline of the political ideas of John Locke which were firmly grounded on the individual. Instead, the idea of "the people" or "the nation" prevailed.[718]

TWO BASIC TENETS:
SOVEREIGNTY OF THE PEOPLE
AND ABSOLUTE EQUALITY

In order to bring all individuals in line with his indivisible idea of sovereignty, Robespierre (like Rousseau before him) leaned heavily on the concept of equality as a basic tenet of his political philosophy. Cobban makes the point that Robespierre closely connected the sovereignty of the nation with equality of rights. This is seen in his statement that the Declaration of Rights could be reduced to these two principles: Sovereignty of the nation and equality of rights.[719]

Robespierre was by no means alone in his emphasis on the sovereignty of the people and its concomitant, their absolute equality. This was the prevailing view of the hard-core revolutionaries who supported the Terror. Further, this emphasis on equality struck a responsive chord in the

---

715 See Francois Furet and Denis Richet, in *The French Revolution*. New York: The Macmillan Company, 1970, translated by Stephen Hardman, 190. The authors explain that these radicals also got rid of unlimited ownership of property and replaced it with "equality of possession," and this right was restricted to the "extent of physical needs." One wonders how they interpreted these needs!

716 See Cobban, *Aspects of the French Revolution*, 139. I have translated the citation from Robespierre which Cobban gave in the original French.

717 Ibid., 138-39.

718 Ibid., 138. The idea of nationhood is not, of course, incompatible with individualism, unless it is believed that the whole is primary and the parts secondary.

719 Ibid., 141.

French mind. The people had suffered for so long from such grossly unjust inequalities, that it is easy to understand how equality became "the ruling passion of the times," as Alexis De Toqueville put it. The solution that the revolutionary leaders offered was to attempt to create a new society where men were as uniform and as equal as possible considering the differences that were bound to exist between individuals.[720] Locke's idea of equality was much more complex than Rousseau's and far truer to reality. In the chapter on Paternal Power in the *Second Treatise*, Locke explained:

> Though I have said above, Chapt. II, *That all Men by Nature are equal*, I cannot be supposed to understand all sorts of *Equality*: *Age* or *Virtue* may give Men a just Precedency: *Excellency of Parts and Merit* may place others above the common Level: *Birth* may subject some, and *Alliance* or *Benefits* others, to pay an Observance to others to whom Nature, Gratitude, or other respects may have made it due; and yet all this consists with the *Equality*, which all Men are in, in respect of Jurisdiction or Dominion one over another; which was the *Equality* I there spoke of, as proper to the Business in hand, being that *equal Right*, that every Man hath *to his natural Freedom*, without being subjected to the Will or Authority of any other Man.[721]

This view is very far from the kind of absolute equality advocated by Rousseau and Robespierre, an equality enforced by the government and calling itself "the Sovereignty of the People."

TWO RULING FRENCH PASSIONS: EQUALITY AND LIBERTY

In the early days of the French Revolution there was another ruling passion which was apparently "less deeply rooted." This was the desire for liberty. According to De Tocqueville, it was the desire not only to be equal but also to be free.[722] The "also" is important here because, *first* of all, it was equality that the people wanted, and *then* "also" to be free. Unhappily, liberty and absolute equality (which means enforced equality) are mutually exclusive. Remarking on these two "ruling passions" of the time, De Tocqueville observed sadly that the idea of and the desire for full political liberty were the last to appear and, sadly, were the first to disappear.[723]

---

720 See Alexis De Tocqueville, *The Old Regime and the French Revolution*, 1856, translated by Stuart Gilbert. Garden City, New York: Doubleday Anchor Books, 1955, 208.

721 John Locke, *Second Treatise*, par. 54, in Hall, *Christian History*, 1:71.

722 See De Tocqueville, *The Old Regime and the French Revolution*, 208.

723 Ibid., De Tocqueville, 157.

De Tocqueville's analysis of his countryman's thoughts points up the fundamental difference between the French and American Revolutions: The American War for Independence was fought to secure liberty; the French Revolution was fought mainly to attain equality. This is illustrated in the development of Robespierre's political thought. His first zeal for liberty rapidly passed away in favor of a desire for an authoritarian elite—ruling, of course, for the good of the people! What would this elite do? It would enforce equality.

ROBESPIERRE AS ARCHITECT OF THE MODERN WELFARE STATE

Unhappily, we can hear echoes of his political ideas in today's modern state. J. M. Thompson in his *Robespierre and the French Revolution*, goes as far as to call Robespierre a prophet and designer of the modern Welfare State.[724] The state Robespierre envisioned certainly was a strongly interventionist and socialist one intent on eroding individual rights. By contrast, in the early days of the Revolution, when it was in the hands of the constitutionalists, property rights of the individual were acknowledged and even specifically guaranteed in Lafayette's Declaration of Rights of 1789. Here it was stated in true Lockean vein: "Property is a sacred and inviolable right." Therefore, the Declaration did nothing to restrict the individual's right to property. After the fall of the monarchy and the rise of the radicals to power, however, Robespierre challenged the Lockean concept of the "sacred and inviolable" nature of property.

In 1793, a new Constitution was drawn up to replace the constitution of 1791. On April 24, 1793, Robespierre addressed the Convention assigned this task and bluntly set forth his political agenda. He proposed a progressive income tax and urged that the new Constitution distinguish clearly between property rights that were "just" and those that were "unjust." (Later Robespierre recommended confiscating the property of "enemies of the people" and redistributing it to the poor. But this proposal was never put into effect.)

PROPERTY NOT A NATURAL RIGHT BUT ONLY A SOCIAL INSTITUTION?

In this speech before the Convention of 1793, Robespierre quoted with seeming approbation the passage in the earlier 1791 Declaration of Rights

---

724 See J. M. Thompson, *Robespierre and the French Revolution*, New York: Collier Books, 1969, 143-144.

which speaks of liberty as "the most valuable property of man, the most sacred of the rights that he holds from nature." In the next breath, he undermined this Lockean thought by defining property, not as a natural right, but (following Rousseau) as a "social institution." He boldly challenged the Convention by declaring that although they had drafted many articles assuring property rights, they had never defined them nor had they explained their legitimacy. He believed, therefore, that their declaration was not made for the average man but for "capitalists, profiteers, speculators, and tyrants." [725] How often we have heard similar words today mouthed by radicals still intent on obliterating property rights by asserting that those who exercise these rights are all "greedy capitalists."

As an attorney, Robespierre was especially clever in the wording of his revolutionary ideas so that they would sound reasonable rather than revolutionary. In his proposals regarding property, he said that it was the right of all citizens to possess and to dispose of *that portion of goods guaranteed to him by law.*" [726] A nice-sounding phrase until one analyzes the second part of the sentence where one begins to see property rights rapidly evaporating!

Robespierre's proposed Declaration of Rights contained another interesting proposal in Point 14 which concerned aiding those who lacked necessities and affirming this as a debt to be paid by anyone who had a surplus of goods. But then it continued by saying that it belonged to the law to decide the way this debt would be paid! [727] The sentiment that begins this sentence is one with which Christians (among them John Locke) and other religious people would concur. The second part unhappily vests the state with unlimited power to define "surplus" and to determine how much of it shall be taken from one taxpayer to give to another. Fortunately, the statement on property that was finally used in the French Constitution of 1793 was: "Property is the right to dispose at will of the fruits of one's industry." [728]

THE GUIDANCE AND COERCION OF AN ALL-POWERFUL STATE

Despite his talk of the virtue of the people, it is clear that Robespierre did not trust them to manage their own affairs in a moral fashion without

---

725 Cited by George Rudé, in *Robespierre*, 53.

726 Ibid. Emphasis added.

727 Ibid., 55.

728 Ibid., 59.

the guidance and coercion of an all-powerful state elite. Robespierre did not believe that revolutionaries should "rest all [their] experiments on the capacity of mankind for self-government," as did James Madison (see *The Federalist Papers*, No. 39). Indeed, Robespierre believed that "virtue [as he defined it], if it did not emerge spontaneously from below, had to be enforced from above." [729]

ROBESPIERRE ENFORCES ARBITRARY GOVERNMENT

As the sovereignty of the people became increasingly equated in Robespierre's mind with the rule of the virtuous, it was also increasingly equated with his own definition of virtue and with his growing belief that he alone really knew what political virtue meant. Those around him who thought they were part of the new ruling elite soon discovered that if they opposed Robespierre's doctrines, they would be sent to the guillotine. Cobban shrewdly observes that it became more and more difficult to tell the difference between the will of the people and Robespierre's will! [730]

Arbitrary arrest and summary execution (Robespierre called these "revolutionary measures"), if in a "good" cause (as defined by Robespierre) were patriotic acts, but in support of "despotism" they were "instruments of oppression." [731] In his drafting of decrees, ostensibly to protect the people against their "enemies," he abandoned the due process of law. Consequently, the trials held by the Revolutionary Tribunal were mere travesties of law. Any criticism of the Revolution's aims and methods as outlined in Robespierre's gospel was, to him, evidence of counter-revolutionary activity. That is no wonder, since he had rejected the Lockean ideals Lafayette had presented to the people in the early days of the Revolution!

LOCKE'S DENUNCIATION OF ARBITRARY GOVERNMENT

John Locke, who had long protested against arbitrary government or government by extemporaneous decrees, would have been shocked at the capricious nature of the revolutionary government driven by Robespierre.

---

729 See Cobban, *Aspects of the French Revolution*, 186.

730 Ibid., 188.

731 Ibid., 164. Robespierre wrote: "When the Revolution is effected by despotism against the people, revolutionary measures, in these hands, are only instruments of cruelty and oppression: but, in those of the people overturning despotism and the aristocracy, revolutionary measures are only salutary and are acts of universal benevolence." (My translation from the quotation cited by Cobban in the original French.)

Recollect what Locke had to say about arbitrary government and extemporaneous decrees:

> Though the *Legislative* [power]…be the *Supream* Power in every Common-wealth; yet
>
> *First*, it is *not*, nor can possibly be absolutely *Arbitrary* over the Lives and Fortunes of the People…. For no Body can transfer to another more Power than he has in himself; and no Body has an absolute Arbitrary Power over himself, or over any other, to destroy his own Life, or take away the Life or Property of another…. The Rules that they [the legislative power] make for other Men's Actions, must, as well as their own…be conformable to the Law of Nature, i.e., to the Will of God, of which that is a Declaration, and the *fundamental Law of Nature being the Preservation of Mankind,* no Human Sanction can be good, or valid against it.
>
> *Secondly*, The *Legislative*, or supreme Authority cannot assume to its self a Power to Rule by Extemporary Arbitrary Decrees, but *is bound to dispense Justice,* and decide the Rights of the Subject *by promulgated standing Laws, and known Authoris'd Judges.*[732]

THE TERROR ENDS

But the Will of God did not enter into Robespierre's conception of government; for him it was only "the will of the people" that mattered, and he believed he was doing their will. It was right to him that anyone could seize another citizen on mere suspicion of being a "conspirator" against the Revolution. A citizen's denunciation was sufficient for a "trial" before the Revolutionary Tribunal. Defense counsel was forbidden to the unfortunate defendant who was left to the mercies of the "patriotic" jury which was instructed to render one of two verdicts: acquittal—or death.

Such fanaticism began to fill many of Robespierre's fellow revolutionaries with fear for their own lives. As Robespierre drew the net tighter, and his dark declamations continued against the "enemies of the people," no one knew who would be next in the tumbrels bound for the guillotine. Finally, the inevitable revolt was mounted against him. Robespierre was denounced as an enemy of the people and was summarily guillotined. So ended the Terror.

---

732 John Locke, *Second Treatise of Government*, pars. 135-36, in Hall, *Christian History*, 1:93-96.

ROBESPIERRE'S GOD

We have called Robespierre a desperately sincere man, and so he was; like Rousseau, he had a vision of a bright new world of honor and virtue and plenty. But it was a vague, abstract vision without firm underpinnings. Since he had turned his back on his Christian faith, religion had no existential reality for Robespierre. His political ideas, like his religion, also were abstractions. His God—to the extent that he still believed in God—was not a transforming, immanent power, but only the vague impersonal force of Deism which left man to find his way alone.

To be fair, however, it must be noted that Robespierre was not an atheist. In fact, he opposed the atheistic trend of his colleagues at the Convention of 1793 and disapproved of the excesses of the de-Christianization movement they assiduously promoted. Through establishment of a "Cult of the Supreme Being," Robespierre hoped to undergird the new state with authority and an aura of legitimacy which he knew it would not have without the support of religion. The reasons Robespierre gave for the adoption of the Cult of the Supreme Being are certainly utilitarian: "To the legislator everything that is useful and good is truth. The idea of the Supreme Being and the immortality of the soul is a constant reminder of justice; that idea is therefore social and republican." [733] Some historians take the position that he viewed his Cult of the Supreme Being as just a political convenience. Certainly, like Rousseau's Civil Religion, it was not meant to be a new form of Christianity but rather a substitute for Christianity.

DE-CHRISTIANIZING FRANCE

Under the new calendar the revolutionaries drew up to supplant the Christian calendar, every tenth day, the "decadi," was the new day of rest, replacing the Christian Sunday. The people were discouraged from observing the Sabbath. Instead, the inhabitants of each town were asked to assemble on the "decadi" around an altar dedicated to "La Patrie." Here the laws of the Republic were read aloud and a "sermon" preached on some civic virtue. All this was done in a religious manner with organ music and hymn singing—except that the hymns were patriotic songs.

This was how the radical revolutionaries put the State in the place of God and tried to make men believe in the old pagan idea that they lived for and at the permission of the state. There were attempts to convert church

---

733 See Furet and Richet, *The French Revolution*, 374.

buildings into "Temples of Reason." Catholic priests were only tolerated if they swore to uphold the revolutionary government. By their oath of allegiance to the Revolution, they became its employees and were bound to act under official instructions—very much as the official churches of the old Soviet Union operated in the late twentieth century. In this way the radical leaders of the French Revolution attempted to weld together civil government and religion under the supreme power of the state.

LOCKE ON GIVING THE STATE POWER OVER RELIGION

John Locke's analysis of the evil results stemming from state domination over religion are discussed in his *Letter Concerning Toleration*. Here, it will be recalled, Locke made the case that "He jumbles heaven and earth together, the things most remote and opposite, who mixes these two societies, which are, in their original, end, business, and in everything, perfectly distinct, and infinitely different from each other." [734] He saw that the civil magistrate had no right to dictate to the citizen in regard to his religious persuasion, because "...the care of souls is not committed to the civil magistrate any more than to other men. It is not committed unto him, I say, by God, because it appears not that God has ever given any such authority to one man over another, as to compel anyone to his religion." [735] Why no compulsion? Locke replies: "All the life and power of true religion consists in the inward and full persuasion of the mind; and faith is not faith without believing." [736]

EQUALITY IN ALL THINGS?

The Lockean ideas of individual rights held by Lafayette and the early French revolutionaries ultimately were superseded by another desire—for equality in all things. This desire could not help ending in a demand for an authority to enforce equality. The desire for equality, rather than liberty, periodically has caused great political upheavals in France ever since Robespierre seized the reins of the French Revolution. Each time a new revolution took place, there were calls for "a strong man" to take charge. For a long time, France oscillated between monarchy and republicanism.

---

734 John Locke, *Works*, 6:21.

735 Ibid., 6:10.

736 Ibid., 6:10-11.

Alexis De Tocqueville was acutely aware of this phenomenon. He was convinced that France had had so many abortive attempts to establish a free political system—always reverting to authoritarianism of some kind—because Frenchmen were trying to graft the idea of liberty onto institutions inimical to it.[737]

It was hard for Lafayette to understand the difference between the English political system, which was more decentralized with more areas of local self-government, and the French political system, which was almost completely centralized in, and controlled by, the monarch. In France, as we have seen, the nobility all flocked to Versailles for the King's favors. In England, most of the aristocracy spent much more time on their country estates. There was not the same wretched and ignorant peasantry that existed in France. Through the influence of Protestants in England, the people had gradually learned to read—so that they could understand the Bible for themselves. This led them to reason Biblically concerning civil government. Nothing like this appears to have happened in France where the common people in Lafayette's time were wretchedly ignorant with no concept of self-government.

When Lafayette was finally allowed to participate in French politics once again, he had observed many political upheavals in the republic under its Directorate with Napoleon as First Consul, then the Empire under Napoleon, followed by the return of the monarchy under the Bourbon kings. Despite the bad rule of Louis XVIII and Charles X, Lafayette clung to his conviction that France could be better governed by a constitutional monarchy. In 1830, after the revolution that caused Charles X to abdicate, the Duke d'Orleans was next to seek to become King Louis-Phillipe.[738] But Lafayette was to be as bitterly disappointed in Louis-Phillipe as he had been in the two Bourbon kings who had preceded him. He continued, however, to fight for the people's constitutional rights in the Chamber of Deputies where he served from 1818 to 1824 and again between 1825 and 1830.

In 1824, at the invitation of Congress, Lafayette visited the United States and was voted a gift of $200,000. It came from a grateful nation mindful of all that Lafayette's help had meant to the United Colonies as they struggled for their right to self-government. This money was a Godsend for Lafayette who on his return to France from the Austrian prison at Olmütz

---

737 See De Tocqueville, *The Old Regime and the French Revolution*, 167.
738 See Olivier Bernier's, *Lafayette, Hero of Two Worlds*. New York: E. P. Dutton, 1983, 310.

had found himself virtually penniless except for funds Gouverneur Morris had loaned to his wife. It had been a constant struggle to keep financially afloat and continue paying his debts. Now, his financial worries were over. Lafayette did not live to see France finally become a lasting republic (that was not until 1875, and he died in 1834), but his Declaration of Rights is now the Preamble of the Constitution of the Republic of France.[739]

Whether under a monarchy or a republic, Frenchmen continued for many years to seek a better life through mighty efforts for governmental reforms. Toward the end of an illuminating chapter on "How the Desire for Reforms Took Precedence over the Desire for Freedom," in his book, *The Old Regime and the French Revolution*, De Tocqueville made a statement of profound political significance: "The man who asks of freedom anything other than itself is born to be a slave."[740] Locke would have added that "where there is no Law, there is no Freedom. For Liberty is to be free from the Restraint and Violence of others...."[741] For Locke, Law was necessary in order to perpetuate man's God-given liberty.

In this chapter, we have seen the great difference between the American and French Revolutions that lay in their underlying philosophies — one placing God and human liberty first, and the other placing the State and absolute human equality first. And we can see that the sharp differences in these two political viewpoints are at the root of many of today's political conflicts in the United States and elsewhere in the free world. Shall we follow Locke — or Rousseau? Shall America remain free and a beacon light to nations who have not yet discovered the value of liberty, or shall freedom gradually die out and be replaced by the all-powerful state envisioned by Rousseau? These are questions that loom larger every day, demanding an answer. Certainly, a people's understanding of the basis of law is critical to the direction their government will take.

The next chapter of this book discusses how in the nineteenth and twentieth centuries eminent jurists and teachers in universities and law schools in the United States took a deliberate turn away from the Law

---

739 Each year, on July 4, Lafayette's descendants assemble at his grave in a small Paris cemetery on the Rue de Picpus for official ceremonies honoring "the hero of two worlds" who was buried in American soil sent to France. The United States Ambassador and his staff attend the event. The American flag flies over Lafayette's grave as it has done (by his wish) ever since his death in 1834. In fact, it was the only American flag to fly anywhere in occupied Europe during World War II. (*Los Angeles Times* article, n.d. from Paris reporter, Nino Lo Bello.) See also Slater, Rosalie, "Two Men, Two Revolutions: George Washington and the Marquis de Lafayette" for an illustrated story of Lafayette including a photo of his grave, *Journal of the Foundation for American Christian Education*, Vol. VI, 103-153.

740 See De Tocqueville, *The Old Regime and the French Revolution*, 169.

741 John Locke, *Works*, 5:370.

of Nature accepted by John Locke and our Founding Fathers as basic to good government, and adopted a pragmatic view of law as whatever the people want. The results have been devastating to judicial interpretation of the Constitution and to the parameters of power set by our Founding Fathers for our protection.

The twentieth century also saw the rise of Marxist philosophy based on Karl Marx's misinterpretation of Lockean ideas of law and liberty as arising from the philosophy of sensationalism. As will be seen, Marx derived many of his ideas from the French Sensationalist interpretation of Locke—and, of course, from Rousseau. Those ideas are still with us, such ideas as liberty *from* religion, liberty *from* property rights, and liberty *from* "bourgeois morality." Today, religion, property rights, and morality are all under attack.

PART FIVE

The Modern Secular State: Locke Repudiated

[O]ur political theory of the nature of the judicial function is unsound....
In its origin it is a fiction,
born in periods of absolute and unchangeable law....
Today, when all recognize...that legal principles are not absolute,
but are relative to time and place, and that juridical idealism
may go no further than the ideals of an epoch,
the fiction should be discarded....
In their origin equity and natural law are also general fictions....

JUSTICE ROSCOE POUND
(*The Spirit of the Common Law*, 1931) [742]

---

742 Roscoe Pound, *The Spirit of the Common Law*, 1921. Boston: Beacon Press, 1963, 171-72.

CHAPTER FOURTEEN

Challenges to Natural and Constitutional Law

The Communist Revolution is the most radical rupture
with traditional property-relations; no wonder that its development
involves the most radical rupture with traditional ideas....
The proletariat will use its political supremacy to wrest,
by degrees, all capital from the bourgeoisie,
to centralize all instruments of production in the hands of the State,
i.e., of the proletariat organized as the ruling class;
and to increase the total of productive forces as rapidly as possible.

KARL MARX
(*The Communist Manifesto*) [743]

BEGINNING in the middle of the nineteenth century, American law
schools began to reject the Law of Nature as fundamental to a proper
understanding of the intentions of the drafters of the Constitution of the
United States, who often referred to the importance of the Law of Nature
as one of their "first principles." [744] American law schools began to adopt
an evolving view of law as constantly changing according to whatever the
people want. This resulted in a vast change in constitutional law and the
kind of decisions that now come from the Supreme Court of the United
States. On the heels of these sweeping changes in the field of jurisprudence,

---

743 Karl Marx, *The Communist Manifesto* (1848), with an Introduction by Stefan T. Possony. Chicago: Henry Regnery Company, 1954, 53-54.

744 See James Madison in *The Federalist*, No. 43, under point 9, where he speaks of "the transcendent law of nature and of nature's God, which declares that the safety and happiness of society are the objects at which all political institutions aim...."

which began in the mid-nineteenth century, came the political philosophy of Karl Marx (1818-1883), which began to eat away at the foundations of freedom in the field of politics.

DARWIN'S THEORY OF EVOLUTION PENETRATES LAW SCHOOLS

The dangerous and radically new approach to constitutional interpretation was rooted in Charles Darwin's theory of evolution. It was to have far-reaching results. Humanist Julian Huxley wrote that evolutionary theory should not be limited to human evolution, but that it should include religion and law so that the universal nature of evolution would be discerned as an "all pervading process."[745] All pervading it certainly has become. In religion, it has resulted in casting aside the moral teachings of the Bible in favor of the changing norms of society. In the *Encyclopaedia Britannica* (Vol. 20), Huxley also wrote of transforming the studies of History, Law, and Political Economy and creating new studies such as Social Psychology, Anthropology, Comparative Religion, Criminology, and Social Geography![746]

When and where did this momentous change begin in American law schools? It can be traced to the 1870s at Harvard, when Christopher Langdell, Dean of the Harvard Law School, began to apply Charles Darwin's theory of evolution to the law. Constitutional lawyer John W. Whitehead writes that Langdell's "real impact on law education was his belief that the basic principles and doctrines of the law were the products of an evolving and growing process over many years."[747] At first lawyers and teachers in other law schools were highly critical of Langdell's notions. Soon, however, his students became lawyers and professors at these same law schools, thus transforming their curriculum.

BLACKSTONE'S COMMENTARIES OUSTED AS A LEGAL MODEL

Eventually ousted as a model was Sir William Blackstone's (1723-1780) *Commentaries on the Laws of England* (1754-1769), the legal volume so influential among the Founding Fathers. Why? Because it taught, as had

---

745 Julian Huxley, "Evolution and Genetics," in *What Is Science?* ed. J. R. Newman. New York: Simon and Schuster, 1955, 272-78, cited by constitutional lawyer John W. Whitehead in *The Second American Revolution*. Elgin and Weston, Illinois: David C. Cook Publishing Co., 1982, 46.

746 Cited by Whitehead, 46.

747 Ibid.

John Locke before him, that all law was based on the law of God revealed through the Bible or through God's Law of Nature. Blackstone wrote about the Law of Nature and God's law revealed in the Scriptures in terms remarkably like John Locke's:

> This law of nature, being coeval with mankind and dictated by God Himself, is of course superior in obligation to any other. It is binding over all the globe, in all countries, and at all times: no human laws are of any validity if contrary to this; and such of them as are valid derive all their force and all their authority, mediately or immediately, from this original.[748]

Recollect that Locke wrote of God's Law of Nature:

> The Law of Nature stands as an Eternal Rule to all Men, *Legislators* as well as others. The *Rules* that they make for other Men's Actions, must, as well as their own and Other Men's Actions, be conformable to the Law of Nature, i.e., the Will of God, of which that is a Declaration, and the *fundamental Law of Nature being the preservation of Mankind,* no Human Sanction can be good, or valid against it.[749]

Blackstone, like Locke, knew that man's reason was unable fully to understand the Law of Nature without the divine Revelation God gave to men in the Scriptures. Of the Revealed Law Blackstone wrote:

> This has given manifold occasion for the benign interposition of divine providence; which in compassion to the frailty, the imperfection, and the blindness of human reason, hath been pleased...to discover and enforce its laws by an immediate and direct revelation. The doctrines thus delivered we call the revealed or divine law, and they are to be found only in the Holy Scriptures. These precepts, when revealed, are found upon comparison to be really a part of the original law of nature, as they tend in all their consequences to man's felicity. But we are not from thence to conclude that the knowledge of these truths was attainable by reason, in its present corrupted state...[U]ndoubtedly the revealed law is of infinitely more authenticity than that moral system, which is framed by ethical writers, and denominated the natural law.[750]

---

748 William Blackstone, *Commentaries on the Laws of England,* Oxford: Clarendon Press, 1765, in Hall, *Christian History,* 1:142.

749 John Locke, *Second Treatise Of Civil Government,* par. 135, in Hall, *Christian History,* 1:94.

750 Blackstone's *Commentaries,* 1765, in Hall, *Christian History,* 1:142-43.

As we have learned, Locke had addressed this dual nature of God's Law in *The Reasonableness of Christianity*. What were the limits of human reason in studying the Law of Nature? He wrote that it had proved "too hard a Task for unassisted Reason, to establish Morality in all its Parts upon its true Foundation, with a clear and convincing Light.... We see how unsuccessful in this, the Attempts of Philosophers were before our Saviour's time. How short their several Systems came of the perfection of a true and compleat Morality is very visible."[751] Indeed, he continued,

> 'tis plain in Fact, that human Reason unassisted, failed Men in its great and proper business of Morality. It never from unquestionable Principles, by clear Deductions, made out an entire Body of the Law of Nature. And he that shall collect all the moral Rules of the Philosophers, and compare them with those contained in the New Testament, will find them to come short of the Morality delivered by our Saviour, and taught by his Apostles; a College made up for the most part of ignorant, but inspired Fishermen.... But such a Body of Ethicks proved to be the Law of Nature, from Principles of Reason, and reaching all the Duties of Life; I think no Body will say the World had before our Saviour's time.... Such a Law of Morality Jesus Christ hath given us in the New Testament; but by the latter of these ways, by Revelation.... Here Morality has a sure Standard, that Revelation vouches, and Reason cannot gainsay, nor question; but both together witness to come from God the great Law maker.[752]

THE LAW OF NATURE
AND THE LAW OF REVELATION

Locke, and after him, Blackstone, saw the need to understand the Law of Nature and the Law of Revelation as the two foundations of God's Law which should undergird all human laws. Blackstone wrote that: "Upon these two foundations, the law of nature and the law of revelation, depend all human laws; that is to say, no human laws should be suffered to contradict these."[753] So for both Blackstone and Locke civil law was grounded in Divine Law as expressed in the Bible and the Law of Nature. This was the firm ground they trod. But in nineteenth century America

---

751 John Locke, *The Reasonableness of Christianity*, 1714 edition, in Hall, *Christian History*, 2:86-87.
752 Ibid., 2:87-90.
753 Blackstone's *Commentaries*, in Hall, *Christian History*, 1:143.

the new evolutionary theories of government were causing that ground to crumble away. The absolutes proclaimed by Locke and Blackstone were being discarded.

JUSTICE HOLMES
REJECTS MORAL ABSOLUTES

Oliver Wendell Holmes, Jr. (1841-1935), a Justice of the Supreme Court of the United States from 1902-1932, was an influential voice for the new sociological conceptions of law. He expressed views which were not merely skeptical of any absolutes underlying law, but which completely rejected them. Following Darwinian notions, as he interpreted them, Holmes declared that he saw no reason for viewing man as differing in importance from "a baboon or a grain of sand."[754] Whitehead's comments on this startling passage provide an illuminating reminder of the end consequences of Holmes' train of thought:

> The logical conclusion of man's significance being no greater than "a baboon or a grain of sand" found its expression in the Supreme Court's decision in *Roe v. Wade*, which upheld the right to abortion-on-demand. To the Supreme Court, the unborn child, as a nonperson, had little significance.[755]

What then did Holmes believe was the nature of law? He contended that it was whatever expressed the purposes of a society at a certain point in its particular history![756] According to Holmes, the important question was: What do the most powerful forces in a community want to do—and are they willing to cast aside any "inhibitions" that would prevent them?[757] Such thinking as this was to have great effect on the way many Supreme Court justices began to view the Constitution. Some seemed to believe that the Constitution of the United States was merely something to get around rather than to uphold.

---

754 See quote in Richard Hertz, *Chance and Symbol*, Chicago: University of Chicago Press, 1948, 107, cited by Whitehead, 52.

755 Whitehead, 52.

756 See G. Edward White, *The American Judicial Tradition*, New York: Oxford University Press, 1976, 157, cited by Whitehead, 50. This makes one think of the letter written by President Franklin Delano Roosevelt on July 5, 1935, to Representative Samuel B. Hill, chairman of a sub-committee considering a bill for regulation of the coal industry, in which Roosevelt said: "I hope your committee will not permit doubts as to constitutionality, however reasonable, to block the suggested legislation." Letter cited by Felix Morley in *Freedom and Federalism*, Chicago: Henry Regnery Co., 1959, 121.

757 Letter from Oliver Wendell Holmes, Jr., to John C. H. Yu, August 26, 1926, published in Harry C. Shriver, ed., *Justice Oliver Wendell Holmes: His Book Notices and Uncollected Letters and Papers*, New York: Da Capo Press, 1973, 187, cited by Whitehead, 51.

The Constitution Is
Whatever the Judges Say It Is?

For example, another follower of Langdell, Charles Evans Hughes, who was later appointed Chief Justice of the United States Supreme Court, declared as early as 1907 that "the Constitution is what the judges say it is."[758] Be it noted, not what the Constitution says. Whitehead notes that Hughes' statement "was representative of a clear break with the American legal past."[759] That past, as we have seen, was based on Divine Law as revealed in the Bible and God's Law of Nature. To the Founding Fathers, human laws had to square with divine law, coming to man through Reason and Revelation.

Justice Pound
Champions Sociological Law

Roscoe Pound, who succeeded Christopher Langdell as the Dean of the Harvard Law School, made the new views clear when he noted that to those who are under the influence of evolution, the word "nature" does not mean what it did in former times.[760] Justice Pound's writing has become extremely influential. Indeed, Justice Arthur J. Goldberg, in his preface to the 1966 edition of Pound's *The Spirit of the Common Law*, observed that no man then living had such a great influence on the legal community as had Pound. He referred to the work as containing the very essence of contemporary "sociological jurisprudence."[761]

Throughout *The Spirit of the Common Law*, there is a constant tension between Justice Pound's conscientious relating of the history of the common law, natural law, and natural right, and his desire to see law less focused on the individual and more on society's needs. His thoughts on natural law and natural right are important, because they show that for him these ideas had seen their day and were no more.

The main stumbling block for him in natural law, as seen by our Puritan forebears, was its emphasis on the rights of the individual. To Justice

---

758 See David J. Danielski and Joseph S. Tulchin, eds., *The Autobiographical Notes of Charles Evans Hughes*, Cambridge: Harvard University Press, 1973, 143, as quoted by Perry Miller, *The Life of the Mind in America*, London: Victor Gallancz, 1966, 115; cited by Whitehead, 20.

759 Whitehead, 20.

760 Roscoe Pound, *Introduction to the Philosophy of Law*, 1922. Republication: New Haven, Connecticut: Yale University Press, 1959, 31, cited by Whitehead, 48.

761 See Arthur J. Goldberg, Preface to *The Spirit of the Common Law* by Roscoe Pound, 1921, Boston: Beacon Press, 1963, paperback ed., first page (unnumbered).

Pound, these rights placed too many restraints on the law and stood in the way of social action. He also wrote disparagingly of the custom of legal interpretation of laws based on unchangeable, fundamental, God-given law, because, in his view, this turned judges into "mere automatons." He insisted that legal principles are not absolute but are merely relative to their time and place. He also claimed that equity and natural law must now be viewed as "legal fictions."[762]

Justice Pound's great interest was in the good of society, rather than in the natural rights of individuals. He believed that he was answering the desires of society in addressing what he took to be one of the main concerns of the people of his day. He claimed that people are not asking to be permitted to attain welfare by their own efforts, but that they want society to do this for them.[763]

A RADICALLY DIFFERENT VIEW OF SOCIETY AND GOVERNMENT

This statement led to a vast change in constitutional interpretation based on a so-called "living Constitution," one that the Founders had supposedly left purposely vague and incomplete, with the blanks to be filled in by the all-mighty wisdom of the Supreme Court. On the contrary, the Constitution provided for change through its amending process, *not by reinterpreting the clear intentions of the Constitution*. But these new legal minds found the amending process too cumbersome, too liable to failure. The men who were enamoured of Darwin's theories and (in the case of Justice Holmes) had discarded their religious convictions on the importance of the individual, were eager to shape the government and so give life to their new sociological theories.[764] What better way than "the living Constitution"? Lawrence Tribe, a Harvard Law professor and influential spokesman for the evolutionary view of the Constitution who is often asked by the media for

---

762 See Roscoe Pound, *The Spirit of The Common Law*, 1921, Boston: Beacon Press, 1963, 172.

763 See Pound, 109.

764 Justice Pound, however, seems to have tried to retain some power for the individual. He wrote, somewhat uneasily, in *The Spirit of the Common Law*, 111, that there was "a danger now that certain social interests will be unduly emphasized and that governmental maternalism will become an end rather than a means...." (That, of course, is the problem; the more power a government has, the more it will take.) He continued by warning that "even if we grant that ultimately all interests, individual and public, are secured and maintained because of a social interest in so doing, this does not mean that individual interests are to be ignored.... Although we think socially, we must still think of individual interests, and of that greatest of all claims which a human being may make, the claim to assert his individuality, to exercise freely the will and the reason which God has given him." He was struggling between two radically different viewpoints without being fully aware of the conflict, or else he offered this passage as a prudent concession to individual rights.

commentary on various judicial cases, insists that, in his view, the highest mission of the Supreme Court is "to form a more perfect union" between what is right and the rights enunciated in the Constitution's "necessarily evolutionary design."[765]

Harry V. Jaffa, the leading scholar today on Abraham Lincoln and a firm proponent of following the original intent of the founding Fathers, as embodied in the Constitution, does not spare even conservative justices on the Supreme Court who have been influenced by the "living Constitution" myth. He cites the following words from Chief Justice William Rehnquist's essay on "the Notion of a Living Constitution,"

> If such a [democratic] society adopts a constitution and incorporates in that constitution safeguards for individual liberty, these safeguards do indeed take on a generalized moral rightness or goodness. They assume a general social acceptance neither because of any intrinsic worth nor because of any unique origins in someone's idea of natural justice, but instead simply because they have been incorporated in a constitution by a people.[766]

Jaffa is understandably amazed at this instance of "the complete alienation of conservative jurisprudence from the principles of the American founding and of Abraham Lincoln."

> The contemptuous reference to "someone's idea of natural justice" is all the consideration he [Rehnquist] gives to the Constitution of Madison, Jefferson, Marshall, and Lincoln!... Consider the implications of what the Chief Justice has asserted. If safeguards for individual liberty do not have "*any* intrinsic worth," then neither does individual liberty, nor individual life. This is pure nihilism. The illusion of morality—and it is here regarded only as an illusion—has as its cause nothing but the will of the people who have adopted it.[767]

Jaffa goes on to point out that the popular will has—or should have—its bounds. Our Founders gave their consent, "not to the powers of government, but to the *just* powers of government.... Chief Justice Rehnquist's idea of unbounded popular will is perfectly consistent with the plebiscite,

765 See Lawrence Tribe, *American Constitutional Law*, Mineola, New York: Foundations, 1978, iv. Cited by Whitehead, 48.

766 Harry V. Jaffa, "Our Embattled Constitution," in *Imprimis*, June 2004, Vol. 33, No. 6, 5. Reprinted by permission from *Imprimis*, the national speech digest of Hillsdale College, www.hillsdale.edu.

767 Ibid., 5-6.

which has been the instrument of 'legitimacy' for tyrants from Napoleon to Hitler and Stalin." [768]

THE "LIVING CONSTITUTION" AND TRANSNATIONALISM

Where does all this leave the Constitution of the United States? It would appear that it leaves it largely in limbo. Certain members of today's court not only desire a completely fluid Constitution, but they are now looking to other countries for legal precedents! John Leo in a column titled "Creeping Transnationalism" in *U.S. News & World Report* for July 21, 2003, writes that "Justice Breyer is perhaps the court's most zealous advocate of finding legal answers abroad. In a case focusing on allowable delays of execution (*Knight v. Florida*), he said he found 'useful' court decisions on the matter in India, Jamaica, and Zimbabwe." Leo asks incredulously: "We're taking our legal cues from Zimbabwe?" Leo also relates that on "ABC's *This Week*, Supreme Court Justice Breyer said a challenge for the next generation will be 'whether our Constitution [fits] and how it fits into the government documents of other nations.'" Leo was alarmed at "the suggestion that the U.S. Constitution may have to be adapted to foreign governing documents."

Surely John Leo was rightly alarmed at this suggestion, for our constitutional and legal systems, with their strong Christian moorings, are the best the world has ever known. Trying to dilute them with ideas and philosophies of governments foreign to our own is the height of folly. Certainly, the members of the United States Supreme Court are obliged by their oaths to uphold the United States Constitution. Leo's article also pointed out that in his argument regarding the Texas sodomy case, Justice Anthony Kennedy "also referred to a brief arguing that America must bring itself into line with modern western thought." In his dissent, Justice Scalia, pointed out that "It isn't the Supreme Court's job to 'impose foreign moods, fads, or fashions on Americans'."

A FALSE VIEW OF INTERNATIONAL RELATIONS

If more of the justices had seriously studied Locke and Blackstone and really knew the roots of the American system, they would not be wandering

---

768 Ibid., 6. Nor does Professor Jaffa spare conservative Justice Antonin Scalia whom he cites as writing that "The whole theory of democracy...is that the majority rules; that is the whole theory of it. You protect minorities only because the majority determines that there are certain minority positions that deserve protection." But, asks Jaffa, "What if the majority does not elect to protect minority positions? Or what if some minorities are protected but not others?"

off to foreign fields in search of answers to American legal questions. It is certainly not any part of the duties of the justices to suggest that we merge our system of government into the other governments of the rest of the world, many of which have little or no understanding of our legal system and are often hostile to it. Yet, the false view of international relations is taking hold in our legal system. How did the Law of Nations, which respected national sovereignty, change into the idea of a supra world government and a World Court, whose aim is to have its rules become binding on all nations? We may trace this evil seed back to Rousseau as implemented by Karl Marx.

THE IMPORTANT DIFFERENCE
BETWEEN SOCIETY AND THE STATE

We have already learned that Rousseau's ideal government was totalitarian, that is, it was supposed to rule every aspect of the individual's life. Rousseau made no distinction between the voluntary activities of society and the coercive power of the state, whereas John Locke did so.[769] Felix Morley in his thoughtful study, *Freedom and Federalism*, expressed his conviction that "Locke's great influence on the founding fathers goes far to explain why the difference between society and state is generally recognized on this side of the Atlantic."[770] He correctly noted that "*society is the voluntary collective action of individuals in areas where the state is not concerned,*" and also that "If the state is concerned whenever people gather for any purpose, as Rousseau implies, then of course the *state absorbs society* and the latter has no independent existence."[771] America has gone far down this road. But in the early republic, Alexis De Tocqueville, that perceptive French observer of American life, marveled that Americans were constantly forming associations of many different kinds—from those embracing religious and moral concerns to the building of inns, hospitals, prisons, and schools. He concluded by observing that whereas in France you find the government

---

769 In his *Second Treatise Of Civil Government* Locke discussed the first society as that between man and wife. Other components of society he identified as relations between parents and children, and between masters and servants (today, we would say employers and employees). As Locke noted, however, "each of these, or all together, came short of Political Society...if we consider the different Ends, Tyes, and Bounds of each of these." Political societies arise when "any number of Men are so united, as to quit every one his Executive Power of the Law of Nature, and to resign it to the publick, there and there only is a Political, or Civil Society." But, as Locke repeatedly cautioned, people only agree to put themselves under government in order to protect their natural rights to "life, liberty, and property." See Chapter 7, pars. 77, 84, 85 in *Of Civil Government* in Hall, *Christian History*, 1:78-79.

770 Felix Morley, *Freedom and Federalism*, Chicago: Henry Regnery Company, 1959, 30.

771 Ibid. Emphasis added.

at the head of new undertakings, and in England some titled person, in the United States it is associations of citizens who form societies to address needs as they arise. In these associations, people of different ages and backgrounds are represented.[772] He also wrote that he admired the great skill with which Americans propose some project and find so many people ready to come forward and join with them to pursue it *voluntarily*.

THE TENDENCY OF THE STATE
TO ABSORB SOCIETY

Americans still form associations and foundations dedicated to religious, charitable, educational, medical, and many other areas of life. All these emanate from and are a part of society as distinct from the state. Nowadays, though, many worthy voluntary organizations accept help from the state— a mistake. Why? It is a mistake because whenever the tendrils of the federal government embrace a private venture, they suffocate it with a myriad of rules and regulations and oblige the recipient to bow to its edicts whether or not they reflect the ideas and ideals of the association. In other words, as Felix Morley wrote, the state absorbs society until it has no independent existence.

This comes about because there is not a clear distinction in men's minds between society and the state. This blurring can be traced to an infatuation with the ideas of Rousseau, who not only blurred, but obliterated any such distinction. In 1955, Felix Morley wrote that "Rousseau's refusal to admit any such distinction has been widely accepted in Europe, and is indeed a tenet of European socialistic as well as communistic thought." But he pointed out that, "American political thinking has preferred to follow the lead of John Locke...."[773] This was still true at the time Morley wrote. Since the 1950s, however, American academics also have progressively succumbed to the blurring of these two distinctively different areas of mankind's life—society and the state. But traditionally, society has been considered as that area of life where individuals voluntarily act with other individuals in all matters that do not harm others. The state existed merely to guarantee protection for the individual from the predatory acts of others. This greatly limited governmental power. Unfortunately, there are always those—whether called emperors, kings, or commissars—who wish to have unlimited control over mankind.

---

772 See Alexis De Tocqueville, *Democracy in America*, 2 vols., 1835-1840, New York: Vintage Books, 1955, 2:114.
773 Felix Morley, *Freedom and Federalism*, 30.

Rousseau could only conceive of a totalitarian government which would supervise the people in *all* aspects of their lives. The distinction between private and public concerns was obliterated in his philosophy. He was also hostile to the idea of long-lasting constitutions, presumably because this would limit the sovereignty of the people. At the convening of every public assembly, he said that it should always be asked if it pleased "the Sovereign" [i.e., the people] to retain their present form of government?[774] Who made Rousseau's ideas so popular in the twentieth century, even when people did not know the author of these ideas by name? The answer is Karl Marx, who built upon Rousseau's theories. In so doing, he gave them new life.

Karl Marx and the Pagan State

For the better part of the twentieth century the forces of liberty and the natural rights of individuals were arrayed against what came to be known as "the age of Marx." For a time Marxism constituted the government of nearly half of the world's population. Where it did not overtly rule, its covert influence was at work to undermine the foundations of freedom. Unlike Rousseau, Marx was no dreamy idealist, but a man determined to implement Rousseau's egalitarian theories.[775] It was from his father that he imbibed Rousseau's ideas, along with those of other so-called "Enlightenment philosophers."[776]

Marx based his political philosophy on the supposed need to dispossess the individual of his property. Just how this would usher in a Golden Age of freedom, Marx was never able to explain because, in fact, abolition of private property leads to tyranny and want, not to liberty and abundance. Biographer Robert Payne asked the key question: If all property becomes the property of the state, then who will protect men from the state?[777]

Marx's views on property rights were, of course, completely at odds with Lockean philosophy, based as the latter was on the natural right of the individual to possess property. Let us always remember that Locke viewed "Property" as triune, comprising the individual's life, liberty, and

---

774 Jean Jacques Rousseau, *The Social Contract*, 1791, in *The Social Contract and Discourses*, 101.

775 See the intriguing chapter on "Marx Implements Rousseau" in Felix Morley's *Freedom and Federalism*, Chicago: Henry Regnery Company, 1959, 37-46.

776 See David McClellan, *Marx Before Marxism*, New York: Harper & Row, 1970, 71.

777 See Robert Payne, *Marx, A Biography*. New York: Simon and Schuster, 1968, 109.

possessions. Let us also remember that Locke recognized the responsibility accompanying that right: to be good stewards of what, in reality, belongs to God.

MARX'S MISINTERPRETATION
OF LOCKE

Marx's comments on Locke indicate the same basic misinterpretation of the English philosopher's ideas that had been propagated by the French Enlightenment. Marx simply accepted Helvetius' evaluation of himself as a disciple of Locke.[778]

Of course, as we have already seen, the views of Helvetius and the other Enlightenment *philosophes* were in direct opposition to Locke. But, like Helvetius (and Condillac) who wrongly claimed kinship with Locke, Marx followed their materialistic interpretation of the great English philosopher. He apparently knew only one "fountain" of Locke's teaching regarding the source of the ideas in the human mind. That fountain, "sensation," was the one expounded by the Enlightenment as the sole source of men's ideas. The French *philosophes* chose not to deal with Locke's second "fountain" of knowledge which was "reflection." So Marx concluded that if man gets all his knowledge from sensation, he will be easily shaped by his surroundings.[779]

This view certainly reflects the reasoning of the French Sensationalist School. But however much the adherents of that school attempted to lay it at Locke's door, it is a misreading of Locke's philosophy of the mind. The way man experiences what it means to be human is not through manipulation of his environment by social engineers, nor through conditioning by other men playing God to him. It is through the God-given *reflective* capacity of his mind, through its ability to reason in accord with conscience and the divine Law of Nature, that man becomes "really human."

John Locke discerned that it is consciousness which shapes the raw materials of sensory experience into a world of its own choice. Man is not *made* human by his surroundings. He is made so by virtue of his God-given capacity, not only to receive sensations, but to think and to reflect.

But this line of reasoning was lost on Marx. He taught that consciousness does not determine man's being but, rather, it is his "social being"

---

778 See *The Essential Writings of Karl Marx*, David Caute, ed., New York: The MacMillan Company, 1967, 29.
779 See Ibid., 30.

which determines his consciousness.[780] Marx showed his distance from Locke in his views of the Law of Nature and right reason, when he wrote that, although earlier philosophers had based their ideas of Law as coming from reason, the view of modern philosophers is that it comes from *"the idea of the whole."*[781]

THE STATE AS "THE GREAT ORGANISM"

Starting with the "whole" and with the state as "the great organism," all-embracing and all-powerful, man obeys the laws of the state and in doing so is obeying "his own reason—human reason," as Marx emphasized.

Conversely, Locke started with the individual and saw the state as the product of the interaction of individuals in a society structured to conform to God's Law of Nature.

But for Marx, the individual and his conscious being were simply formed by "the great organism" of the state.

Through his miscategorization of Lockean philosophy as materialist and sensationalist, Marx believed that Locke, the expositor of a philosophy of law based on Reason and Revelation and individual rights under the Law of God, was actually a materialist and the progenitor of socialism. Marx thought he saw "two trends in French materialism," one having its origin in Descartes, and the other in Locke's philosophy as developed by the French, and that it led to socialism![782]

Accepting as authentic the French materialist adaptation of Locke, it is no wonder Marx declared that when Locke's essay crossed the channel, "it was welcomed enthusiastically like a long-awaited guest."[783] This did indeed happen, but it was only *after* the French *philosophes* changed the Christian basis of Locke's philosophy by removing one of its two "fountains" of understanding: the mind's ability to reflect upon its contents. But all of this eighteenth-century intrigue was lost on the nineteenth-century radical, Karl Marx, who evidently had only a superficial and derivative knowledge of Locke's writings, or else he might have had the wit to see that Locke was never in the materialist/sensationalist camp.

---

780 See Karl Marx and Friedrich Engels, Preface to *A Contribution to the Critique of Political Economy*, cited by Caute, 49.

781 See Caute, 90. Emphasis added.

782 Ibid., 26.

783 Ibid.

NO TRANSCENDENT ETHIC

As an atheist, Marx had no transcendent ethic to turn to for guidance, no objective standards beyond his own theories. Both Marx and Engels advocated murder and violence in order to effect their revolutionary aims—even as today's terrorists continue to do.[784]

Locke placed the individual, "not the whole," in the center of his political system. It was clear to him that because God created men as individuals, he evidently meant them to function as such, applying their power of choice to the making of their lives and their world. Individual liberty was essential to the individual's development, as well as to the preservation of his life and the fruits of his labor. Liberty was also essential to a flourishing society and needed to be protected by civil government—not hampered or destroyed.

Marx, however, placed the "organism" of the state, i.e., the proletariat, at the center of his philosophy, the state to be under the control, not of the whole, as Rousseau had envisioned, but of only a *part* of the whole, i.e., the proletariat or working-man. Class warfare was an inevitable result of this reasoning. So great were the powers of the state envisioned by Marx that not even the proletariat could retain liberty for long. Marx always thought of an intellectual elite standing behind the scenes and pulling the strings of a puppet population, manipulating them, as in his advice to promise the peasants land in order to get their support, then to dispossess them when the revolution was successful.[785] Indeed, Marx advocated the total "abolition of private property"!

Locke, of course, saw the state as obligated to protect private property and strongly objected to taking away any part of a man's property without his consent. In his famous *Manifesto*, Marx advocated a "heavy, graduated income tax" as a method of eliminating the middle class. He never succeeded, however, in explaining how eliminating this most productive, stable element of society (which Aristotle had viewed as its most vital constituent) would result in abundance. In the long run, it does not. Individuals who are increasingly deprived by burdensome taxation of the fruits of their labor usually get discouraged and produce not more, but less.

---

784 In their *Blueprint for Revolution: A Plan Against Democracy*, Marx and Engels urged: "Far from opposing the so-called excesses, those examples of popular vengeance against hated individuals or public buildings which have acquired hateful memories, we must not only condone these examples but lend them a guiding hand." Cited by Payne, 240.

785 This became the strategy used by the communists in both Russia and China. In Western nations this confiscation of private property by the state is often referred to as "nationalization."

RIGHTS OF INHERITANCE?

Nevertheless, Marx did not foresee this and so all rights of inheritance of property were also to be abolished.[786] In Lockean theory, men are free to enjoy the fruits of their own voluntary labor, reaping whatever they sow. They are also free to bequeath their property to their children. Marx also advocated forced labor.[787] In the old Soviet Union forced labor was used, and this still appears to be the case in communist China.

THE LAW OF NATURE OR EVOLUTIONARY SOCIETAL LAW?

Locke accepted law as pre-existing, as of God: "The law of Nature is the Will of God." He saw the law of God as the yardstick by which all "municipal laws" are to be judged. To Marx, law was simply the result of social and economic evolution, the result of the "class struggle." Thus Marx was an adherent of "the social good" theory of justice.[788] This is a humanistic, relativistic theory, while natural law adherents view law as stemming from an absolute, pre-existing power apart from man: the Law of God written on the heart.

LIBERATED FROM OR LIBERATED TO?

The ideas of Marx and the evolutionary political theorists are still alive and kicking today, tearing away at the fabric of constitutional government. Another most disquieting idea inherited from Marx is shown in his complaint that in "the Old Society" man had the liberty *to* worship God, *to* hold property, *to* engage in business, all positive values.[789] This was the Old Society that Marx wanted to replace with totally negative ideas—Liberty *from* religion, the very cement of Western Civilization; liberty *from* the right to hold property and accumulate capital, which, in America, has produced unparalleled affluence for the people; liberty *from* the "egoism

---

786 See Point 2 in *The Communist Manifesto.*

787 See Point 8 in the *Manifesto.*

788 See Professor Otto A. Bird, *The Idea of Justice*, New York: Frederick A. Praeger, 1967. This is an illuminating work, in which Bird also discusses the "positive law" theory, championed by Thomas Hobbes. In this view of justice, it is conformity to the law; law is determined and characterized by the law-making power, whatever that may be. This view is at one with the "social good" theory, in that adherents of both schools believe men can decide on a norm of justice quite independently of reference to any pre-existing, fundamental law, such as the Law of God or the Law of Nature. To both the "positive law" theorist and the "social good" advocate, there is no objective standard of right: Justice is what the reigning power or social utility decrees.

789 See Karl Marx, cited by Caute, 174.

of business," which provides work and self-respect for those who otherwise would be idle, unfruitful, and unsatisfied.

ABSOLUTE EQUALITY: THE GREAT VIRTUE?

Marx could not see the positive side of liberty; he could only see the capitalist as an exploiter, not as a provider of jobs and a higher standard of living. Nor could he see the need for capital in order to produce abundance. In his economic theology, profits were the new devil. Absolute equality was the great virtue. Like so many revolutionaries, Marx was not so much interested in the creation of a new society as in the destruction of the old. Marx, like Voltaire, hated Christianity and the Lockean role of the individual as paramount to society. Hatred is on every page of *The Communist Manifesto*. What a contrast can be clearly seen between Marx, the destructive revolutionary, and Locke, the constructive reformer!

We are still living with the ideas of Rousseau and Marx and now also with the advocates of a "living Constitution" to be amended by the simple expedient of reinterpretation by the judges of the United States Supreme Court. In both the political and legal areas fundamental principles have been swept aside as unneeded and unwelcome in an age dubbed "post-Christian." But are these principles really outmoded? Are they not firmly supported in the Constitution of the United States? The next and final chapter of this book answers these and other vital questions facing us today.

CHAPTER FIFTEEN

Recovering Our Lockean Political Roots

The Framers of our Constitution explicitly sought to put into motion
the principles enunciated in the Declaration of Independence,
a document which they believed derived its authority from
the "Laws of Nature and Nature's God...."
Thus the Constitution cannot be understood
primarily as an historical document;
it must be understood as a document embodying
the natural law teachings of the Declaration....

EDWARD J. ERLER[790]

PROFESSOR ERLER'S words quoted above are a concise expression of
the conclusions reached by some wiser members of academia today
who have become thoroughly fed up with the notion held by the prevailing
school of constitutional law that the Constitution of the United States is
not a document of principles, but merely one of procedures. In this view, the
Declaration's statements of principles and its veneration for natural rights
are simply the work of a now vanished culture and outdated moment in history. As we have seen in the preceding chapter, the prevailing view in law
schools today is that the Constitution must be viewed as a "living" document
and that "an important step in its evolution has been its escape from the
confinements of natural law thinking which characterized the Founders."[791]

---

790 Edward J. Erler, "The Constitution of Principle" in *Still the Law of the Land? Essays on Changing Interpretations of the Constitution*, Hillsdale, Michigan: Hillsdale College Press, 1987, 29-30.
791 See Thomas F. Payne's Introduction to *Still the Law of the Land?*, xiv.

"OUR PECULIAR SECURITY
IS IN ... A WRITTEN CONSTITUTION"

Thomas Jefferson wrote in 1803 that "Our peculiar security is in possession of a written constitution. Let us not make it a blank paper by construction."[792] Nevertheless, this is what the Supreme Court has been doing for years: cutting the Constitution off from its supposedly outmoded moorings in fundamental, eternal principles—in God's Law of Nature—recognized by conscience and by reason. As a result, the rulings of the Court have run increasingly counter to the views of the majority of Americans. Recent polls (and discussion by media pundits) have revealed the great chasm that exists between the views of most Americans and those of the Supreme Court on abortion, prayer in schools, display of the Ten Commandments, and other social issues which are of great importance to Christians.

Prominent among these other issues facing the courts was the removal of a granite monument etched with the Ten Commandments which Alabama Chief Justice Roy Moore had put on display in Montgomery's state judicial building. This removal was ordered by the Alabama Supreme Court which also removed Chief Justice Moore from the Court because he had refused to remove the alleged offensive granite monument. That Court's arrogant act ignores the fact that the east pediment of the United States Supreme Court Building contains a marble relief entitled "Justice, the guardian of Liberty," the central figure of which is Moses holding a tablet in each hand containing the Ten Commandments. But this is not all! To enter the Supreme Court's chamber from the foyer, one must go through two great doors on which the Ten Commandments are engraved on the two lower panels. In the courtroom, above the heads of the justices, is a marble relief with two central figures representing "The Power of Government" and "The Majesty of the Law." Between these two figures, very prominently displayed, are the Ten Commandments. The figure representing "The Power of Government" has his arm resting upon the tablet.

The Supreme Court Building was erected in 1935, but it was still a time when Americans knew their heritage of liberty, knew that the Ten Commandments were fundamental to American law. In fact, they were the Biblical statement of the moral law God had established originally in the Law of Nature, but which were being cast aside by mortals. So what were these Alabama Supreme Court justices thinking when they made

---

792 Letter of Thomas Jefferson to William Cary Nicholas, September 7, 1803.

this ruling? Many people knelt on the steps of the judicial building praying that this ruling would be rescinded. But, of course, it was not. These Alabama Supreme Court justices were determined to make their decision the law even though it went against history, reason, and the will of the people.

COLLISION OF THE
LEGISLATIVE AND JUDICIAL BRANCHES

Our legislators are duty bound to see that the American people have the opportunity to engage in a debate on social issues that are of great concern to them and to see to it that the courts do not preempt the decision-making power of state legislatures and the Congress of the United States. "Government by consent of the governed" was a vital component of our forefathers' political system, one which they had learned well from reading John Locke's great work on civil government. The question, of course, is whether Locke's views and those of our Founders are pertinent today or are merely of antiquarian interest.

In this connection, Dr. Thomas F. Payne of the political science department at Hillsdale College asked some very pertinent questions in his introduction to a series of cogent essays, *The Constitution: Still the Law of the Land?*

> If the Constitution is to be understood as consistent with human liberty and dignity, must it also be understood as grounded in immutable principle, or must the natural-right framework of interpretation be discarded as outmoded and unduly restrictive? If the Framers were wrong, should we take steps to reform the Constitution? If they were right and still present superior claims to understanding constitutionalism and the rule of law, then should steps be taken *to restore the original understanding of their work?* [793]

Critical to restoring the original understanding of the Framers' work is a proper understanding of the Law of Nature as the Law of God, as John Locke saw it. This is vital because Locke's views on the subject were widely accepted by the Framers of the Constitution and were embodied in the Declaration of Independence. Only as we restore an understanding of the framers' reasoning can we decide whether their views are still pertinent today.

---

[793] Thomas F. Payne, Introduction to *Still the Law of the Land?*, xiv-xv. Emphasis added.

WHY THE CONFUSION REGARDING
NATURAL LAW AND NATURAL RIGHT?

There is considerable confusion today about what Locke meant by the Law of Nature. It has been the aim of this book to clear up the many misconceptions currently prevalent among many scholars. Although Locke strongly—and repeatedly—expressed his conviction that the Law of Nature is the Law of God, many Protestant Christian legal scholars are sufficiently confused about Lockean political ideas to believe that Locke "secularized" natural law and was a rationalist who disbelieved in divine revelation. Catholic scholars still accept natural law, but only as presented by Thomas Aquinas, Aristotle, Plato, and other ancient philosophers. To them, too, Locke is viewed as a secularizer of natural law. The facts about Locke's view of the Law of Nature reveal the error of this view. They show that:

1) Locke clearly defined the Law of Nature as the Law of God revealed through God-given reason and intuition.

2) Locke acknowledged the need for Scriptural Revelation to correct men's limited and flawed understandings.

3) Locke recognized the Law of Nature as the Will of God revealed to men subjectively, while Revelation was God's will revealed objectively in the Holy Scriptures. Indeed, as we have seen, Locke's deep conviction was that the Scriptures confirmed and completed the Law of Nature, giving it authority as the Law of God.[794]

WHY NOT RELY EXCLUSIVELY
ON BIBLICAL LAW?

The next important question is: If Locke was a Christian, why did he not build his political system exclusively on Biblical law? This was a popular idea in the seventeenth century and is again popular today among those who believe that natural law theories, whether those of Aquinas or Locke, lead away from Biblical law.

It would seem that the reason Locke relied heavily on the Law of Nature

---

794 See Chapter Six of this book, titled "The Law of Nature in John Locke's Writings," for a full discussion of Locke's views on the Law of Nature. See also Chapter Seven on Locke's *Two Treatises
Of Government* and the writings of Founding Fathers for Locke's views on natural rights. Also see
Chapter 10. For Locke's influence on the American declarations of rights and the Declaration of
Independence, see Chapter 11. For his influence on the Constitution, see Chapter 12. However we
understand Locke on this point, it is important to remember that the objective Law is needed to
make appropriate use of any subjective Law of Nature.

and natural rights in his political writing was, quite simply, because he had seen the often misguided efforts of the members of Parliament after the execution of Charles I during the period known as "the Interregnum." Right before his eyes Locke saw the sad results of parliamentary debates between contending religious groups, each claiming to have the "right" interpretation of Biblical law but often citing it outside the Biblical context. One member of Parliament, Sir Harry Vane (1613-1662),[795] sometime governor of the Massachusetts Bay Colony, had already witnessed (and tried to arbitrate) the endless disputes in New England over what a particular Biblical citation meant. He witnessed the same thing in Parliament.[796]

CONTENDING VIEWS ON BIBLICAL LAW

The Word of God was hurled back and forth by contending political parties. A harsh, persecuting influence was at work in Parliament. According to their adversaries, those who advanced the "wrong" interpretation of the Bible should be excluded from Parliament and also punished. There was great discussion on whether there should be a state church to replace the Anglican one of the English kings. If so, what would be its requirements? The Presbyterians were certain that power should only be in the hands of the "saved." But the Army, which generally favored establishing a republic, was largely made up of Independents who wanted religious liberty. Another group wanted a government based largely on Old Testament law represented only by "the elect." The waters were constantly roiled by contention among these various religious groups, each wishing to impose their interpretation of Biblical law on the others through the power of civil government.

·On the other hand, John Lillburne (1614-1657), the "Leveller" leader of a group of democratic republicans, believed that God had created all men equal and had endowed them with reason, which he believed could enable them to set up a government that would be just and fair to all. Lillburne, who coined the phrase "freeborn rights," strongly believed that God's grace was given to all if they would but accept it.

---

795 See J. H. Adamson and H. F. Folland in their admirable biography, *Sir Harry Vane: His Life and Times 1613-1662.* Boston: Gambit, 1973, 199.

796 Refer to Part One, Chapter One of this book for more details on this subject. As the Law of Nature is part of God's Law as revealed in Scripture, it is abundantly clear that Christians will continue to debate and ultimately resolve application of the Scriptures to questions of civil polity as their most sure foundation, hopefully now without the political polarity of Locke's time.

These religious conflicts during the Interregnum must have had an influence on Locke's later political writing, even though in both of his *Two Treatises of Government* Locke uses Biblical citations to confirm his theory of government. Let us recollect, too, that in *The Reasonableness of Christianity* Locke brought out in even greater detail his conviction of the necessity of Revelation to guide and correct reason. Locke was certain that Jesus, as the long awaited Saviour, brought the perfect moral system, one that far exceeded all the efforts of the pagan ancients. It ought to be relatively easy to see how Locke's political ideas, thus based, could unite Christians in support of a truly constructive body politic that accorded with the moral principles brought to the world by Jesus Christ.

John Calvin's Views on Natural Law

Nevertheless, some prominent Reformed scholars today vigorously oppose natural law doctrines from whatever source. This is difficult to understand when we read what John Calvin has to say about natural law in his *Institutes of the Christian Religion*. Here he writes: "It is a fact that the law of God which we call the moral law is nothing else than a testimony of natural law and of that conscience which God has engraved upon the minds of men."[797] Calvin also wrote:

> Now that inward law, which we have above described as written, even engraved, upon the hearts of all, in a sense asserts the very same things that are to be learned from the Two Tables. For our conscience does not allow us to sleep a perpetual insensible sleep without being an inner witness and monitor for what we owe God, without holding before us the difference between good and evil and thus accusing us when we fail in our duty. But man is so shrouded in the darkness of errors that he hardly begins to grasp through this natural law what worship is acceptable to God.... Accordingly (because it is necessary both for our dullness and for our arrogance), the Lord has provided us with a written law to give us a clearer witness of what was too obscure in the natural law, shake off our listlessness, and strike more vigorously our mind and memory.[798]

---

797 John Calvin, *Institutes of the Christian Religion*, 2 vols. Library of Christian Classics, Vols. XX and XXI, ed. John T. McNeill; trans. by Ford Lewis Battles, Philadelphia: Westminster Press, 1977, 2:1504. Note: The completed and final edition of the *Institutes* was published in 1559.

798 John Calvin, *Institutes*, I:367-368.

EVANGELICAL SUPPORT
OF NATURAL LAW

But what about the diverse religious groups that make up American society today?

Can the Law of Nature bring together people from various religious backgrounds in matters that concern justice and morality in the civil realm? Certain American Evangelicals think this can be done. Charles Colson, for example, maintains that natural law is the appropriate basis from which to support moral dialogue in the civil realm.[799] Norman Geisler, too, argues in favor of what he calls "the natural moral law" as the basis for ethical decision-making in the realm of civil government.[800]

Alan F. Johnson, in "Is There a Biblical Warrant for Natural-Law Theories?" also supports the view that the "natural moral law" can play an important role in "the evangelical ethic" which he identifies as "a fully Christian ethic." Johnson believes "that there are two chief sources of ethical knowledge that must be incorporated dialogically into any serious evangelical Christian ethic...."[801] The two ethical sources which should be included in Evangelical Christian ethics are natural law and Biblical law.[802] These are the two elements that John Locke referred to as "Reason and Revelation."

David Jones, too, emphasizes the importance of appealing to natural law because here is found "common ground" for both Christians and non-Christians to promote justice and morality. Therefore, he maintains that Christians should appeal to the sense of justice held by all "who bear God's image."[803]

A CAUTIONARY NOTE

But there is a flaw in the idea of using the Law of Nature in dialogue with non-Christians. This is because human reason is not an adequate guide apart from the Divine Revelation in the Holy Scriptures. That is why Locke referred to reason as only "the candle of the Lord," and why he

---

799 See Colson's comments in "Self-Evident Truth," in *Jubilee*, February, 1992.

800 See Norman L. Geisler, "Natural Right," in *In Search of a National Morality*, ed. William Bentley Ball, Grand Rapids: Baker Book House, 1992, 114-119.

801 Alan F. Johnson, "Is There a Biblical Warrant for Natural-Law Theories?" in *Journal of the Evangelical Theological Society*, Vol. 25, No. 2, June 1982, 197.

802 We would say, as we have established in this work, that the Law of Nature is essentially the Law of God, that ultimately there is but one Law to which all will eventually appeal.

803 See David Jones, "Neither Warfare nor Withdrawal," in *In Covenant*, Volume 10, No. 2, Spring 1995, 6.

urged close reading and study of the Bible. The Law of Nature apart from its Christian context cannot be rightly understood by the non-believer. Such a conflict between Scriptural law and natural law did not occur in the world of our forefathers, saturated as that world was with Christian ethics on which there was broad agreement. Today, any revival of natural law theories as they pertain to civil government might well be besieged by new secular theories of what is "natural" which would not be in harmony with the Founding Fathers' interpretation of the Law of Nature.

NATURAL LAW
"MAKES NO SENSE WITHOUT GOD"

We must always remember that to the Founding Fathers all law was seen as coming from God, the great Lawgiver. Today, Catholic scholar Charles Rice points out that every law has a lawgiver and that natural law makes no sense unless we understand that God is its author.[804]

Darwinism, Marxism, and post-modernism have now largely effaced Locke's understanding of the Law of Nature in the hearts and minds of those upon whom a popular civil order depends. As we noted in the history of the French Revolution, a people unprepared in character and wisdom regarding civil liberty cannot sustain freedom.

Another approach toward once more mainstreaming Lockean thinking is to emulate America's patriot pastorate. The American clergy taught the people the fundamentals of applied Biblical principles in Lockean terms. If Locke's ideas are to find receptive soil, they will be in people who once more generally understand and appreciate the Bible in the same way Locke did. Thus, we might propose that the contemporary Biblical Christian relearn the underlying Biblical principles upon which Locke based his ideas of right and wrong, justice, right to property, and liberty.

THE DECLARATION
FOUNDATIONAL TO THE CONSTITUTION

Today it is important for Christians also to understand that the fundamental natural law principles stated in the Declaration of Independence were foundational to the Constitution and were so understood as late as the 1860s.[805] Indeed, at the Reconstruction Congress meeting in 1866,

---

804 See Charles Rice, *50 Questions on the Natural Law*, San Francisco: Ignatius Press, 1995, 28–29.
805 James Madison wanted a statement of these principles to appear in the Constitution but was persuaded that it was not needed because the state constitutions did have such declarations.

Thaddeus Stevens, in urging adoption of the Fourteenth Amendment to the Constitution, declared:

> It cannot be denied that this terrible struggle [of the Civil War] sprang from the vicious principles incorporated into the institutions of our country [i.e., slavery]. Our Fathers had been compelled to postpone the principles of their great Declaration, and wait for their full establishment till a more propitious time. That time ought to be present now.[806]

Professor Erler, quoted at the beginning of this chapter, points out that references to the Declaration as law were so frequent in these debates that it is clear that the Reconstruction Congress was ratifying "a refounding of the regime" in the Constitution that had occurred after the victory in the Civil War. He believes that the Civil War was, in a sense, "the last battle of the Revolutionary War," because it was only the Reconstruction Amendments that brought the Constitution into line with the principles of the Declaration of Independence.[807]

PRINCIPLES AND PROCEDURES

If it is in the Constitution that one finds the procedures our Founders thought necessary to perpetuate the Law of Nature, life, liberty, and property rights, and the consent of the governed, it is in the Declaration of Independence that we find these guiding principles clearly stated. They are also stated throughout the writings of the Founding Fathers. In *The Federalist*, No. 43, James Madison refers "to the transcendent law of nature and nature's God, which declares that the safety and happiness of society are the objects at which all political institutions aim...."[808] Alexander Hamilton declared that "the sacred rights of mankind...are written, as with a sunbeam, in the whole *volume* of human nature, by the Hand of the Divinity itself; and can never be erased or obscured by mortal power."[809]

In its insistence on viewing the Constitution as merely one of procedures, divorced from fundamental principles, the Supreme Court of the

---

806 See Edward J. Erler, *Equality, Natural Rights, and the Rule of Law: The View from the American Founding*, Bicentennial Essay No. 4, Claremont, California: Claremont Institute, 1984, 31.

807 See Edward J. Erler, "The Constitution of Principle," in *Still the Law of the Land?*, 31-32. The importance of the principles of the Declaration to the Framers of the Constitution has usually been accepted, but more recent jurisprudence has denied that the Declaration is a part of our organic law. The views given above would seem to make it clear that this was not the case in 1866.

808 James Madison, *The Federalist*, No. 43. The comment occurs in a discussion on ratification of the Constitution by nine states instead of by unanimous consent of all thirteen.

809 Alexander Hamilton, in a pamphlet published February 5, 1775 and titled "The Farmer Refuted."

United States has stripped the Constitution of all philosophical content. This makes it easy for the Court to substitute the notions of its members, which are in many cases very much the product of secular, ever-changing theories of right and wrong.

THE JUDICIAL BRANCH
—THE WEAKEST?

The Framers of the Constitution would be amazed at the vast powers now claimed by the Supreme Court to determine public policy. Why then did most of the Framers of the Constitution of the United States believe that the judiciary would be the weakest branch of the three? Could the answer lie in the *limited powers* that the Framers conceived for the judiciary? It appears clear that most of the men attending the Constitutional Convention in Philadelphia believed that the powers of the judiciary should be confined to the cases that came before it and that the Court's rulings were to be binding only "upon the parties to a suit, as to the object of that suit." In other words, the Supreme Court was to adjudicate specific cases, but not to set public policy, for that was the prerogative of the Congress and the Chief Executive.

The intentions of the Framers become even clearer when we discover that a proposed Council of Revision, which would have given the federal judiciary a part in policy-making power, was rejected by the Constitutional Convention. In debates on this subject, Elbridge Gerry protested that the Council of Revision "was making statesmen of the judges, and setting them up as guardians of the rights of the people, as the guardians of their rights and interests. It was making the expositors of the laws the legislators, which ought never to be done...."[810]

Many other delegates opposed involving the judges in policy-making. John Dickinson of Delaware pointed out that the "Justiciary of Aragon became by degrees the law-giver." Roger Sherman of Connecticut "disapproved of judges meddling in politics and parties." Hugh Williamson of North Carolina also opposed "admitting the judges into the business of legislation."[811] That the judiciary should have no part in the legislative process was made abundantly clear when their possible role in the proposed Council of Revision was conclusively rejected.

---

810 "Debates in the Federal Convention of 1787 as Reported by James Madison" in *The Making of the American Republic: The Great Documents, 1774-1789*, edited by Charles Callan Tansill, New Rochelle, New York: Arlington House, n.d., 424.

811 Ibid., June 6, August 15, and July 21.

Ironically, James Madison had at first favored the inclusion of the judiciary in the Council because, thinking of it as the weakest branch, he believed it ought to have "an additional opportunity of defending itself against legislative encroachments." This shows once again that Madison, in the company of many of the Framers, saw the legislative branch as the most dangerous, having had in the states, Madison believed, a tendency "to absorb all power."[812] In 1788, however, after the Constitution was finished—but before its final adoption—Madison wrote of his concern regarding the judiciary:

> In the state constitutions and, indeed, in the federal one also, no provision is made for the case of a disagreement in expounding them [the laws]; and as the courts are generally the last in making the decision, it results to them, by refusing or not refusing to execute a law, to stamp it with its final character. This makes the Judiciary Department paramount in fact to the Legislature, *which was never intended and can never be proper.*[813]

HOW FINAL
ARE THE DECISIONS OF
THE SUPREME COURT?

In regard to the Supreme Court's expanded use of judicial power today, Edward S. Corwin, a leading scholar on constitutional law in the twentieth century, was convinced that what threatens the influence of the people on the Supreme Court is that the Court's readings of the Constitution are considered as final, at least for every part of the government excepting the Court. This finality in construing the Constitution, he believed, should only be applied to the particular individual cases decided.[814]

This view coincides with a cogent statement by Abraham Lincoln during the Lincoln/Douglas debates when he said that the doctrine of judicial supremacy would lead to the "despotism of an oligarchy." In his First Inaugural Address Lincoln also stated clearly his views on the judicial power:

> I do not forget the position, assumed by some, that constitutional questions are to be decided by the Supreme Court; nor do I deny

---

812 Ibid. Drafting the Federal Constitution, Madison's words on July 21.

813 *The Writings of James Madison*, 9 vols., ed. Gaillard Hunt, New York: G. P. Putnam's Sons, 1900-1910, 5:294. Emphasis added.

814 See Edward S. Corwin's, "Curbing the Court," in *The Annals of the American Academy of Political and Social Science*, 185, May 1936, 55.

that any such decisions must be binding, in any case, *upon the parties to a suit, as to the object of that suit*, while they are also entitled to a very high respect and consideration in all parallel cases by all other departments of the government. And while it is obviously possible that decisions may be erroneous in any given case, still the evil effect following it, *being limited to that particular case*, with the chance that it may be overruled and never become a precedent for other cases, can better be borne than could the evils of a different practice.[815]

Lincoln went on to point out that

at the same time, the candid citizen must confess that if the policy of the government, upon vital questions affecting the whole people, is to be irrevocably fixed by decisions of the Supreme Court, the instant they are made, in ordinary litigation between parties in personal actions, *the people will have ceased to be their own rulers,* having to that extent practically resigned their government into the hands of that eminent tribunal.[816]

Lincoln, of course, had in mind the Dred Scott decision of the Supreme Court denying citizenship to blacks because they were deemed to be property rather than persons. Let us remember, however, that on June 19, 1862, Congress simply ignored this ruling and prohibited slavery in the territories. Harry V. Jaffa, the leading scholar of Abraham Lincoln in our time, remarked recently on the modern scholarly views of Lincoln's attitude toward slavery prior to 1946 (when Jaffa's first book on Lincoln, *The Crisis of the House Divided,* appeared) that "Lincoln, by insisting that the moral condemnation of slavery had to be the basis of all public policy concerning it, was held to be a herald of unreason, of passion, and of war." Jaffa defended Lincoln on his own ground:

I did so by taking the self-evident truths of the Declaration of Independence—as did Lincoln—as assertions of right reason, and not of opinion merely. And I have maintained with Lincoln that right reason, no less than Scripture, is the voice of God. According to Lincoln, those who would deny freedom to others could not, under a just God, long remain in possession of their own. When Lincoln said that as he would not be a slave, so he would not be a master, he was saying neither more nor less than Jesus when

---

815 Abraham Lincoln, *First Inaugural Address* (1861). Emphasis added.
816 Ibid. Emphasis added.

he said, "Whatsoever you would that others do unto you, do you unto them." Prophecy was with us then. It is with us yet, if we would hear it.[817]

President Lincoln's definition of the constitutional limitations on the Supreme Court clearly accords with the intentions of the Framers of the Constitution. Yet, the paucity of definition and commentary in the Constitution in regard to the role of the judiciary is surprising. This may have been because it was such a "given" in the Framers' minds that what Montesquieu wrote about the judiciary was true: "Of the three powers above mentioned [executive, legislative, and judicial], the judiciary is in some measure next to nothing...."[818] But why was this the case? Clearly, it was because the only way the judiciary could claim larger powers than to adjudicate specific cases brought before it was by invading either the executive or legislative powers.

This is why Montesquieu also wrote: "Again, there is no liberty, if the judiciary power be not separated from the legislative and executive. *Were it joined with the legislative, the life and liberty of the subject would be exposed to arbitrary control; for the judge would then be the legislator.*"[819] Also significant is his definition of the three powers which follows on the heels of the above remarks:

> There would be an end of everything, were the same man or the same body...to exercise those three powers, that of enacting laws, that of executing the public resolutions, and *of trying the causes of individuals.*[820]

This shows Montesquieu's view of the province of the judiciary—that it should try the causes of individuals and have nothing to do with legislation or public policy. An editorial note on these passages in one edition of Montesquieu's *Spirit of Laws*, says: "The greater part of the principles produced in this chapter by Montesquieu is derived from Locke's 'Treatise upon Civil Government,' xii."[821]

---

817 Harry V. Jaffa, "Our Embattled Constitution," in *Imprimis*, June 2004, Volume 33, No. 6, 5-7. Reprinted by permission from *Imprimis*, the national speech digest of Hillsdale College, www.hillsdale.edu.

818 Baron de Montesquieu, *The Spirit of Laws*, 2 vols., ed. Frederic R. Coudert, Section 6, "Of the Constitution of England," New York: The Colonial Press, 1900, I:156. See also in Hall, *Christian History*, 1:134-38 for extended extracts from *The Spirit of Laws*.

819 Ibid., 152. Emphasis added.

820 Ibid. Emphasis added.

821 Ibid., 156, see editorial note.

Who Has the Right
to Interpret the Constitution?

Now, the judiciary does in fact have the right and duty to determine the meaning of the Constitution in regard to specific cases that come before it. Does this mean that their decisions are written in stone and may not be reversed by the legislature? Madison declared in the House of Representatives in 1789 that "nothing has yet been offered to invalidate the doctrine that the meaning of the Constitution may as well be ascertained by the legislature as by the judicial authority." [822] In response to an argument that whenever the meaning of the Constitution is doubtful, it must be left to the judiciary to decide its meaning, Congressman Madison contended strongly that the legislature had as much right to do this as the judiciary "...but I beg to know upon what principle it can be contended that any one department draws from the Constitution greater powers than another, in marking out the limits of the powers of the several departments."

The Constitution as
the Charter of the People

Madison went on to remind the legislators that *"The Constitution is the charter of the people in the government, it specifies certain great powers as absolutely granted, and marks out the departments to exercise them. If the constitutional boundary of either be brought into question, I do not see that any of these independent departments has more right than another to declare their sentiments on that point."* [823]

Legislative Primacy Paramount

Clearly, in a republican or representative form of government the legislature as the law-making body is paramount, even in a government of separation of powers. Legislative primacy was a given in the minds of the Founding Fathers, as necessary in a republic. Otherwise, if unelected judges with lifetime appointments succeeded in also taking over legislative functions, there would be government by an oligarchy as Jefferson wrote in 1820 to a Mr. Jarvis:

> You seem to consider the judges as the ultimate arbiters of all constitutional questions; a very dangerous doctrine, indeed, and one

---

822 James Madison, *The Debates in the Several State Conventions on the Adoption of the Federal Constitution*, Jonathan Elliott, ed., 5 vols., New York: Burt Franklin, 1888, 4:399.
823 Ibid., 4:382.

which would place us under the despotism of an oligarchy.... The Constitution has erected no such single tribunal, knowing that to whatever hands confided, with the corruption of time and party, its members would become despots. It has more wisely made all the departments coequal and cosovereign within themselves... the Constitution in keeping the three departments distinct and independent, *restrains the authority of the judges to judiciary organs*, as it does the executive and the legislative to executive and legislative organs.... I know *no safe depositary of the ultimate powers of society but the people themselves; and if we think them not altogether enlightened enough to exercise their control with wholesome discretion, the remedy is not to take it from them but to inform their discretion by education.*[824]

THE REMEDY FOR JUDICIAL USURPATION

What Madison and Jefferson feared has indeed happened. We are now faced with a judiciary which claims supremacy over the other branches of government. What is the remedy? There are several possible solutions. Most of them, however, have a downside.

1) The most popular one—that of appointing strict constructionist judges to the Supreme Court and other federal courts—is extremely difficult to achieve given the extreme antagonism of the opposition party to such judges.

2) A second proposed solution is to change the indefinite appointment of the justices to a definite period of time, but such a change would involve a constitutional amendment.

Proponents of these proposals have argued that they are necessary in order to make the court accountable for its action. They argue that if the Supreme Court is going to continue to rule on social issues of great importance to the people, it should be accountable to the people and their representatives.

Opponents have objected on the grounds that these proposals encroach on the independence of the Court which the Framers of the Constitution wanted and that these proposals would violate the separation of powers established by the Framers. There remains, however, a third possibility

---

824 *The Writings of Thomas Jefferson*, 9 vols., Washington edition, 1853–1854, 12:178–79. Emphasis added.

which, given the current disconnect between the Supreme Court and the people, might now be possible.

This third possibility is to invoke the specific language already in the Constitution regarding the powers to be exercised by the Supreme Court. Article III, Section 2 of the Constitution states that: "the Supreme Court shall have appellate jurisdiction, both as to Law and Fact, *with such exceptions, and under such Regulations as the Congress shall make.*"[825]

A SIGNIFICANT SUGGESTION

As early as 1805, during impeachment proceedings against Justice Samuel Chase, Chief Justice Marshall suggested that "the modern doctrine of impeachment should yield to an appellate jurisdiction in the legislature." Justice Marshall was in favor of reversing those legal opinions that the legislature deemed unsound.[826]

There have been many attempts to do just this. In the year 1981 there were some twenty-five bills in Congress to remove the Supreme Court's appellate jurisdiction over cases bearing on social issues such as abortion and school prayer. None passed. Yet, this is probably the best method to curb the Court from interfering with the legislative branch of government. Because it is written in the Constitution, it would not require a constitutional amendment.

Perhaps the time has come when the people's obvious disapproval of the Court's actions on many social issues finally may make it possible to curb the Supreme Court from imposing unconstitutional rulings on an unwilling people. But to accomplish this, we need courageous and persistent legislators.

As John Locke wisely observed, "we have reason to conclude, that all peaceful beginnings of *Government* have been *laid in the Consent of the People.*"[827] In a republic, such as ours, this is particularly true. At the founding of our nation the people's representatives alone had the right to make public policy on their behalf. They still have this right, if they will exercise it. This means that they can curb an activist Supreme Court bent on forcing legislators to conform to its unconstitutional rulings. Such a bruising task will not be politically popular, but unless this is courageously undertaken, the self-governing Americans have taken for granted will

---

825 The term appellate refers to appeals to a higher court having the power to review and affirm, reverse, or modify the decision of a lower court. Emphasis added.

826 See Albert J. Beveridge, in *The Life of John Marshall*, 4 vols., Boston: Houghton Mifflin, 1929, 3:177.

827 John Locke, *Second Treatise Of Civil Government*, par. 112, in Hall, *Christian History*, 1:88.

go on being eroded until there is no turning back from government by a judicial oligarchy answerable to no one.[828]

CURBING POWER UNDER THE ENGLISH CONSTITUTION

In John Locke's time, it was the power of kings that had to be curbed if subjects were to have their rights under the Great Charter of England. With the growth of the English system, Parliament became supreme. The judicial power, once so closely linked to the king, became independent but could not—and cannot now—vaunt itself above the lawmaking body. Indeed Locke saw that the first and fundamental duty of all commonwealths is to establish the legislative power as the supreme power of the commonwealth. He was also careful to state that this supreme power must not be arbitrary; it must govern by settled, standing laws. It cannot take from anyone any part of his property without his consent in person or through his legislators. Locke insisted that the legislative power is only in order to preserve and never "to destroy, enslave, or designedly to impoverish the Subjects."[829]

Finally, Locke reminds us that "the Obligations of the Law of Nature, cease not in Society, but only in many Cases are drawn closer, and have by human Laws known Penalties annexed to them, to inforce their Observation. Thus the Law of Nature stands as an Eternal Rule to all Men, legislators as well as others. The *Rules* that they make for other Men's Actions, must, as well as their own, and other Men's Actions, be conformable to the Law of Nature, i.e., to the Will of God, of which that is a Declaration, and the *fundamental Law of Nature being the preservation of Mankind*, no Human Sanction can be good, or valid against it."[830]

Locke concluded this chapter, on "The Extent of the Legislative Power," with a recapitulation of the duties of the legislative branch, which is as cogent today as when it came from the pen of "the great Mr. Locke":

---

828 The conservative Heritage Foundation in March 2004 informed their supporters of the most recent grabs at legislative power by federal judges. The Ninth Circuit U.S. Court of Appeals has declared it unconstitutional to consider "decency and respect" for American values when the National Endowment for the Arts uses our tax dollars. This means that American taxpayers are forced to support obscene and offensive art; the Ninth Circuit Court of Appeals also ruled last year that because of the "offensive" words "under God," it is now unconstitutional to recite the Pledge of Allegiance in public schools. A federal judge in San Francisco issued an injunction to stop the U.S. Navy from deploying its new high-volume, low-frequency active sonar—one of our best protections against enemy submarines. The Court's grounds for this serious decision? That this important component of our national security might "harass" marine mammals.

829 See par. 135 of the *Second Treatise Of Civil Government*.

830 Ibid.

1) The legislative body must govern by established laws the same for all, not one law for the rich and another for the poor, not one "for the Favourite at Court" and another "for the Country Man at Plough."

2) Laws must be designed for no other end than the good of the people.

3) Legislators must not raise taxes on the people's property without their consent, "given by themselves, or their Deputies."

4) The legislature must not transfer the power of making laws to any other body than where the people have placed it.

As detailed earlier, this last point is one that our legislators today need to ponder seriously. To allow the courts to usurp the constitutional authority of the legislature, when a clear remedy lies within the reach of Congress through the language in Section 2 of Article III which states that "the Supreme Court shall have appellate Jurisdiction...*with such Exceptions, and under such Regulations as the Congress shall make*" [*emphasis added*] is to refuse to face up to their duty. One answer is to use this wording to remove social issues from the appellate jurisdiction of the Court.

PROPERTY TODAY:
A NATURAL RIGHT?

Throughout this book, much has been said about the Law of Nature and natural rights[831] as seen by John Locke. As we arrive at our conclusion, it would seem prudent to remind the reader of Locke's great contribution to the natural right theory seen in his view of "life, liberty, and property" as *not three separate rights* but intrinsically *one* great right which he called "Property." It began—and indeed still begins—with the life of the individual, then his liberty which is essential to his productivity, followed by the right to enjoy the fruits of his labors without fear that the government will confiscate his property or control it to his detriment. Locke insisted that those who govern, "can never have a Power to take to themselves the whole, or any part of the Subjects' *Property*, without their own Consent. For this would be in effect to leave them no *Property* at all."[832]

So where does taxation fit into this picture? The key words are, of course, "without their own Consent." Locke readily admits that:

---

831 With the understanding that natural is synonymous with God-given.
832 See John Locke, *Second Treatise*, par. 139, in Hall, *Christian History*, 1:95.

'Tis true, Governments cannot be supported without great Charge, and 'tis fit every one who enjoys his share of the Protection, should pay out of his Estate his proportion for the maintenance of it. But still it must be with his own Consent, i.e., the Consent of the Majority, giving it either by themselves, or their Representatives chosen by them.[833]

He warned that "the *Legislative* can have no Power to transfer their Authority of making Laws, and place it in other hands. For what Property have I in that, which another may by right take, when he pleases to himself?" He might also have said: Nor can any other power claim the right belonging to legislators to tax the people without their own consent.

This is what happened in Missouri, where a judge ordered a tax hike of $1.8 billion in taxes for improvements to the school system, such as swimming pools and a new planetarium. Clearly, this was a legislative matter for the people's representatives to decide. But here a judge usurped the right of the legislature to levy taxes.[834]

It was Locke's insistence that the people could not be compelled to pay taxes without their own consent which struck a responsive chord throughout the American colonies and helped precipitate their war with the Mother Country. Locke—and our Founders—would surely be distressed to see the many violations of property rights today such as judges usurping the legislative branch of government and also the growing power of governmental agencies and commissions which often decide the fate of the citizen's property, quite apart from the legislative process. Constantly increasing rules and regulations at all levels of government inform an owner what he can or cannot do with his property. How has this bureaucratic tangle come about?

For much of the twentieth century, American radicals followed the Soviet line that property was not a legitimate human right. There was a constant drum-beat *against* property ownership, pitting it against human rights, rather than seeing it as a necessary part of human rights without which the individual could not defend his life and liberty.

At the local level, this has resulted in severe restrictions by city and county governments on what kind of design the home owner can use and even how the house has to be sited and what landscaping plan can be

---

833 Ibid., par. 140, 96.
834 The Heritage Foundation in March 2004 informed the public of this court action in Missouri.

used.[835] On a larger scale, extreme environmentalists bring suits against property owners all over the country who have wetlands on their property where there may be endangered species, such as the snail darter. This often results in property owners suddenly being told they cannot develop their property but must leave it undeveloped. Harassment of individuals and small business by environmental agencies of the Federal Government has become commonplace. Three different versions of Federal wetland laws further complicate the matter. Various states have come up with their own definitions in which, in some cases, neither water nor wet soil need to be present!

The U.S. Forest service informed a rancher in Nevada, that he could not clear brush from his irrigation ditch—something that ranchers had done for generations. When he tried to get clarification from the U.S. Court in Reno, the Forest Service promptly filed criminal charges against him in a U.S. Court in Las Vegas which convicted the rancher of tampering with the "wetlands" on his property. In another case, an environmental agency in Los Angeles slapped a lien on a trophy shop owner's bank account (with which he paid his employees). The agency claimed that the ozone filter on his desktop laser printer was faulty and that the lien was necessary to see to it that he paid the hefty fine the agency demanded. These are but two of numerous such examples of arrogant behavior by unelected functionaries working for various governmental agencies.[836]

When we look at these abuses of natural rights, it becomes clear that the ideas of John Locke on the Law of Nature, natural rights, and the indivisibility of the individual's "life, liberty, and property" are as vital to free societies today as they were in Great Britain's "Glorious Revolution" of 1688 and our own American Revolution of 1776. Let us remember that the rights extolled by John Locke were enshrined in our Declaration of Independence and further embodied in the Constitution of the United States. The Founders did not expect later generations to sweep these rights aside as no longer needed. There are signs that only the radical left, the so-called "progressives," wish to do this. The recent election in 2010 shows, however, that they are on a collision course with the vast majority of Americans.

---

835 The author is indebted to a landscape architect friend for these details. This architect expressed increasing frustration at the constant interference of city and/or county bodies with house and garden designs.

836 See, for example, Robert J. Ernst, III, "The Real Environmental Crisis: Environmental Law," *Imprimis*, Vol. 23, No. 5, Hillsdale, Michigan: Hillsdale College, May 1994:3. Reprinted by permission from *Imprimis*, the national speech digest of Hillsdale College, www.hillsdale.edu.

WHY THE 'PROGRESSIVES'
DISREGARD CONSTITUTIONAL RIGHTS

We owe an arrogant disregard of Constitutional rights to the rise of the Progressive movement which began to follow the ideas of Darwin discussed in the previous chapter, as well as to "historicism" which taught that all ideas are only relative to their own time and must change as time moves on. This view became prominent in Germany in the 1880s.[837] These ideas of evolution and change undermined the idea of God-given natural law and natural rights as immutable. Soon these ideas found their way into American politics.

One of the first to embrace the new "progressive" ideas was Theodore Roosevelt who, running in 1901 as a Republican, became the twenty-sixth president of the United States. In 1916 he wrote:

> I do not for one moment believe that the Americanism of today should be a mere submission to the American ideals of the period of the Declaration of Independence. Such action would be not only to stand still but to go back.... I have actively fought in favor of grafting on our social life, no less than on our industrial life, many of the German ideals.[838]

In 1912, Roosevelt ran again for the presidency (but unsuccessfully) as the candidate of the Progressive Party.

Woodrow Wilson, who was the winner in the 1912 race for the presidency, was also an unabashed supporter of the new ideas. In a speech titled "What is Progress?" he declared that "Some citizens of this country have never got beyond the Declaration of Independence." He went on to assert that he thought "that document is of no consequence to us."

The reasons he gave for this statement were amazing:

> Government is not a machine. It falls not under the theory of the universe, but under the theory of organic life. It is accountable to Darwin, not to Newton.... Living political constitutions must be Darwinian in structure and in practice....
>
> All that progressives ask or desire is permission—in an era when "development," "evolution," are the scientific words—to interpret

---

837 See D. W. Bebbington's *Patterns in History*, Downer's Grove, Ill., 1979, 92-116.

838 Cited by Matthew Spalding in his excellent book *We Still Hold These Truths: Rediscovering Our Principles, Reclaiming our Future*, Wilmington, Delaware: Intercollegiate Studies Institute, 2009, 195.

the Constitution according to the Darwinian principle; all they ask is recognition of the fact that a nation is a living thing and not a machine.[839]

These ideas of evolution and expanding government appear again in the Franklin Delano Roosevelt presidency: In his Annual Message to Congress of 1944, he first said:

> This republic had its beginning, and grew to its present strength, under the protection of certain inalienable political rights—among them the right of free speech, free press, free worship, trial by jury, freedom from unreasonable searches and seizures. They were our rights to life and liberty.[840]

But then he went on in a very different vein declaring that "As our nation has grown in size and stature, however—as our industrial economy expanded—these political rights proved inadequate to assure us equality in the pursuit of happiness." Finally, he comes to the heart of the matter:

> We have come to a true realization of the fact that true individual freedom cannot exist without economic security and independence....
>
> In our day, these economic truths have become accepted as self-evident. We have accepted, so to speak, a second Bill of Rights under which a new basis of security and prosperity can be established for all regardless of station, race, or creed.[841]

The next day Roosevelt was chastised in a *Wall Street Journal* editorial for referring to the Bill of Rights in the past tense. But in 1944 Roosevelt had a long list of new "rights" that he believed government should guarantee to the citizen, all of which involved increasing dependence upon the federal government. This was exactly what the Founding Fathers wished to avoid. They envisioned free Americans prospering under a variety of private institutions, not hobbled by reliance on the state, which inevitably entails a gradual loss of liberty and self-government.

---

839 Cited by Spalding in *We Still Hold These Truths*, 195–96.

840 Cited by Spalding, 200.

841 Cited by Spalding, 201.

THE RESULTS OF
GOVERNMENT EXPANSION AND CONTROL

Today we see the results of years of government expansion and control over the lives of Americans, as seen in the previous chapter. Now, with the Obama administration we are faced with a more rapid and radical expansion of the power of the federal government and an unprecedented spending program that has produced a huge crippling debt such as this nation has never seen before. J. D. Foster, a policy analyst for the Heritage Foundation, writes that the massive new taxes President Obama proposed for an already ailing economy "come in many different forms, but each of them will eventually affect every American."

LAND OF THE "MOSTLY FREE"?

Amanda J. Reinecker notes in a Heritage Foundation paper on January 20, 2010, that the Foundation had just released its 2010 Index of economic freedom which reveals some alarming news on America's ranking among the world's free economies. She writes that "For the first time, America ranks as only 'mostly free'—behind countries like Canada, Ireland, and Switzerland." She also notes that "Americans are not happy about this. More and more of them are voicing their disapproval of big government policies which give way to more taxes and less freedom."[842]

WHEN CONGRESS IS DOMINATED
BY THE CHIEF EXECUTIVE

During the time that the legislative branches of our government in both House and Senate were dominated by one party, they pushed through President Obama's program that has saddled the nation with a staggering national debt—made all the worse because of the lingering economic recession. It has also resulted in a sharply increased centralization of power in the central government.

Also from The Heritage Foundation, that respected organization reports that the 2012 Obama budget proposes to:

➤ Add 43 different tax hikes.

---

842 The Index is a joint project of the *Wall Street Journal* and the Heritage Foundation and has been published for the past sixteen years. It analyzes the economic freedom of 179 countries with scores in three categories: 1) government burdens upon businesses and entrepreneurs; 2) intrusiveness of government; and 3) the fundamental societal characteristics that support today's most prosperous economies. http://dancingczars.wordpress.com/2010/01/20/

➤ Add $1.5 trillion to the American tax burden, or $12,000 per household, over the next decade.

➤ Spend almost 23 percent of the American gross domestic product from 2012 through 2021.

➤ Increase the top tax rate by 4.6% to 39.6%.

➤ Increase capital gains tax from 15% to 20% for high-income earners.

➤ Raise the death tax to 45% and reduce the exemption amount to $3.5 million from $5 million.

➤ Raise middle-income families tax burden through the alternative minimum tax (AMT). Limiting middle-income deductions would increase the tax bill by $321 billion over ten years—a permanent tax hike.

➤ Increase miscellaneous business taxes which will add more than $207 billion over ten years.[843]

But when citizens began to notice the abuses of the Constitutional rights of the citizen going on under the Obama administration, many networked and participated in grass roots activities including peaceful gatherings under the T.E.A. ("taxed enough already") party and other banners, and they voted in droves for Republicans or Independents in the 2010 elections. Let us hope it will become even more clear that the ideas of John Locke on the indivisibility of the individual's God-given rights to "life, liberty, and property" are as *vital to free societies today* as they were in the American Revolution of 1776. Having seen what happened in England's Parliament under its kings, Locke stressed the independence of the legislative branch over the powers of the chief Executive (in his day, the King). In his *Second Treatise on Government* he wrote:

> The great end of Men's entering into Society, being the Enjoyment of their properties in Peace and Safety, and the great instrument and means of that being the Laws establish'd in that Society; *the first and fundamental positive Law* of all Commonwealths, *is the establishing of the Legislative Power*; as the *first and fundamental natural Law*, which is to govern even the Legislative itself, *is the preservation of the Society*, and (as far as will consist with the publick good)

---

843 [NOTE: Editor has substituted later statistics to update what the author had provided.] From "Obama's 2012: Higher Taxes, Slower Growth" by Curtis Dubay, March 21, 2011: http://www.heritage.org/research/reports/2011/03/obamas-2012-budget-higher-taxes-slower-growth.

of every person in it. This *Legislative* is not only *the supream Power* of the Commonwealth, but sacred and unalterable in the hands where the Community has once placed it; nor can any edict of any Body else, in what form soever conceived, or by what Power soever backed, have the force and obligation of a *Law*, which has not its *Sanction from* that *Legislative*, which the publick has chosen and appointed. For without this the Law could not have that, which is absolutely necessary to its being a *Law, the consent of the society,* over whom no Body can have a Power to make Laws, but by their own Consent, and by Authority received from them.[844]

Our new Congress in 2011, with the help of the free expression of private citizens as well as the individual sovereign states, needs to stiffen their backs against domination by the Chief Executive. Meanwhile, we all need to remember that the rights extolled by John Locke were embedded in our Declaration of Independence and further embodied in the Constitution of the United States. It is to be hoped that the right to "life, liberty, and property" will endure because of our recovering vigilance, remembering that Locke's term "Property" means "the lives, liberties, and estates" of the people, "which I call by the general Name, PROPERTY." Let us also heed the words of James Madison, the "Father of the Constitution," and an admirer of John Locke, who wrote:

PROPERTY.... In the former sense, a man's land, or merchandise, or money, is called his property. In the latter sense, a man has a property in his opinions and the free communication of them. He has a property of peculiar value in his religious opinions, and in the profession and free use of his faculties, and free choice of the objects on which to employ them. In a word, as man is said to have a right to his property, he may be equally said to have a property in his rights. Where an excess of power prevails, property of no sort is duly respected. No man is safe in his opinions, his person, his faculties, or his possessions.... Government is instituted to protect property of every sort....

Conscience is the most sacred property.[845]

---

844 John Locke, *Second Treatise Of Civil Government*, Chapter XI. "Of the Extent of the Legislative Power," reproduced from the 1714 edition, which was printed from "a copy corrected by himself," in Hall, *Christian History*, 1966 rev. ed., 1:93. (This photostatic reproduction from the 1714 edition is so important because it shows us Locke thinking through each sentence and then deciding on the typography to be used to follow his thoughts. The passage, though long, is clear as we follow particularly his italics!)

845 James Madison, in his essay, "Property," 1792, in *Letters and Other Writings of James Madison*, 4 vols., Philadelphia: J. B. Lippincott & Co., 1867, 4:478-480, and cited in Hall, *Christian History*, 1:248a.

THE NEED FOR A
CONSTITUTIONAL EDUCATION

An urgent need still confronts us. Because most of our young people are not being adequately educated in American history, they are growing up not knowing the significance of the system of government the Founders gave us. Therefore, as long as this continues, they cannot possibly understand how to protect their lives, liberties, and property. As seen in the preceding chapter, for many years schools have followed Julian Huxley's objective of transforming the educational system in favor of Darwinian ideas. Today, instead of history, our children are being taught Social Studies which, so far as our history is concerned, seem only to pick the mistakes and errors in our history. On the other hand, when teaching American history as a cohesive whole, as a long chain of cause and effect, we can see what our Founders saw: the hand of divine Providence in the affairs of men. Bits and pieces of history, taken out of context, are a great disservice to young Americans who then grow up not knowing the treasures entrusted to them in their heritage and particularly in the Declaration of Independence and the Constitution of the United States. It is no wonder that they fall easy prey to specious arguments in favor of socialistic policies, instead of understanding and perpetuating the great heritage left by their forefathers.

It is important for Americans to know the ideas behind the Declaration of Independence and the Constitution. Whose ideas were influential with the Founding Fathers? What better place to start than with John Locke's *Two Treatises of Government?* The first *Treatise* demolished the idea of absolute monarchy and the second provided our Founding Fathers with a blueprint for establishing a system of government that would ensure the citizen's "life, liberty, and property." Let us hope that no longer will these rights be neglected, but will be understood and protected by a grateful people as necessary to their future liberty as citizens of these United States.

The End

APPENDIX

APPENDIX A

The Virginia Declaration of Rights

(June 1776)

A DECLARATION OF RIGHTS made by the Representatives of the good people of VIRGINIA, assembled in full and free Convention; which rights do pertain to them and their posterity, as the basis and foundation of Government.

1. That all men are by nature equally free and independent, and have certain inherent rights, of which, when they enter into a state of society, they cannot, by any compact, deprive or divest their posterity; namely, the enjoyment of life and liberty, with the means of acquiring and possessing property, and pursuing and obtaining happiness and safety.

2. That all power is vested in, and consequently derived from, the People; that magistrates are their trustees and servants, and at all times amenable to them.

3. That Government is, or ought to be, instituted for the common benefit, protection, and security, of the people, nation or community, — of all the various modes and forms of Government that is best which is capable of producing the greatest degree of happiness and safety, and is most effectually secured against the danger of mal-administration;—and that whenever any Government shall be found inadequate or contrary to these purposes, a majority of the community hath an indubitable, unalienable, and indefeasible right, to reform, alter, or abolish it, in such manner as shall be judged most conducive to the publick Weal.

4. That no man, or set of men, are entitled to exclusive or separate emoluments and privileges from the community, but in consideration of

publick services, which, not being descendible, neither ought the offices of Magistrate, Legislator, or Judge to be hereditary.

5. That the Legislative and Executive powers of the State should be separate and distinct from the Judicative; and, that the members of the two first may be restrained from oppression, by feeling and participating the burdens of the people, they should, at fixed periods, be reduced to a private station, return into that body from which they were originally taken, and the vacancies be supplied by frequent, certain, and regular elections, in which all, or any part of the former members, to be again eligible, or ineligible, as the laws shall direct.

6. That elections of members to serve as Representatives of the people, in Assembly, ought to be free; and that all men, having sufficient evidence of permanent common interest with, and attachment to, the community, have the right of suffrage, and cannot be taxed or deprived of their property for publick uses without their own concent [sic] or that of their Representative so elected, nor bound by any law of which they have not, in like manner, assented, for the publick good.

7. That all power of suspending laws, or the execution of laws, by any authority, without consent of the Representatives of the people, is injurious to their rights, and ought not to be exercised.

8. That in all capital or criminal prosecutions a man hath a right to demand the cause and nature of his accusation, to be confronted with the accusers and witnesses, to call for evidence in his favour, and to a speedy trial by an impartial jury of his vicinage, without whose unanimous consent he cannot be found guilty, nor can he be compelled to give evidence against himself; that no man be deprived of his liberty except by the law of the land, or the judgment of his peers.

9. That excessive bail ought not to be required, nor excessive fines imposed, nor cruel and unusual punishments inflicted.

10. That general warrants, whereby any officer or messenger may be commanded to search suspected places without evidence of a fact committed, or to seize any person or persons not named, or whose offence is

not particularly described and supported by evidence, are grievous and oppressive, and ought not to be granted.

11. That in controversies respecting property, and in suits between man and man, the ancient trial by Jury is preferable to any other, and ought to be held sacred.

12. That the freedom of the Press is one of the great bulwarks of liberty, and can never be restrained but by despotick Governments.

13. That a well-regulated Militia, composed of the body of the people, trained to arms, is the proper, natural, and safe defence of a free State; that Standing Armies, in time of peace, should be avoided, as dangerous to liberty; and that, in all cases, the military should be under strict subordination to, and governed by, the civil power.

14. That the people have a right to uniform Government; and therefore, that no Government separate from, or independent of, the Government of Virginia, ought to be erected or established within the limits thereof.

15. That no free Government, or the blessing of liberty, can be preserved to any people but by a firm adherence to justice, moderation, temperance, frugality, and virtue, and by frequent recurrence to fundamental principles.

16. That Religion, or the duty which we owe to our Creator, and the manner of discharging it, can be directed only by reason and conviction, not by force or violence; and therefore, all men are equally entitled to the free exercise of religion, according to the dictates of conscience; and that it is the mutual duty of all to practise Christian forbearance, love, and charity, towards each other.

(Text taken from Helen Hill Miller's *George Mason: Gentleman Revolutionary,* Chapel Hill: The University of North Carolina Press, 1975, 339-340.)

APPENDIX B

The Declaration of Independence

IN CONGRESS, JULY 4, 1776
THE UNANIMOUS DECLARATION
OF THE THIRTEEN UNITED STATES OF AMERICA

WHEN IN THE COURSE OF HUMAN EVENTS, it becomes necessary for one people to dissolve the political bands which have connected them with another, and to assume among the powers of the earth, the separate and equal station to which the Laws of Nature and of Nature's God entitle them, a decent respect to the opinions of mankind requires that they should declare the causes which impel them to the Separation.

WE hold these truths to be self-evident, that all men are created equal, that they are endowed by their Creator with certain unalienable Rights, that among these are Life, Liberty, and the pursuit of Happiness. That to secure these rights, Governments are instituted among Men, deriving their just powers from the consent of the governed. That whenever any Form of Government becomes destructive of these ends, it is the Right of the People to alter or to abolish it, and to institute new Government, laying its foundation on such principles and organizing its powers in such form, as to them shall seem most likely to effect their Safety and Happiness. Prudence, indeed, will dictate that Governments long established should not be changed for light and transient causes; and accordingly all experience hath shown, that mankind are more disposed to suffer, while evils are sufferable, than to right themselves by abolishing the forms to which they are accustomed. But when a long train of abuses and usurpations, pursuing invariably the same Object evinces a design to reduce them under absolute Despotism, it is their right, it is their duty, to throw off such Government, and to provide new Guards for their future security. Such has been the patient sufferance of these Colonies; and such is now the necessity which constrains them to alter their former Systems of Government. The history of the present King of Great Britain is a history of repeated injuries and usurpations, all having in direct object the establishment of an absolute Tyranny over these States. To prove this, let Facts be submitted to a candid world.

He has refused his Assent to Laws, the most wholesome and necessary for the public good.

He has forbidden his Governors to pass Laws of immediate and pressing importance, unless suspended in their operation till his Assent should be obtained; and when so suspended, he has utterly neglected to attend to them.

He has refused to pass other Laws for the accommodation of large districts of people, unless those people would relinquish the right of Representation in the Legislature, a right inestimable to them and formidable to tyrants only.

He has called together legislative bodies at places unusual, uncomfortable, and distant from the depository of their public Records, for the sole purpose of fatiguing them into compliance with his measures.

He has dissolved Representative Houses repeatedly, for opposing with manly firmness his invasions on the rights of the people.

He has refused for a long time, after such dissolutions, to cause others to be elected; whereby the Legislative powers, incapable of Annihilation, have returned to the People at large for their exercise; the State remaining in the mean time exposed to all the dangers of invasion from without, and convulsions within.

He has endeavoured to prevent the population of these States; for that purpose obstructing the Laws for Naturalization of Foreigners; refusing to pass others to encourage their migration hither, and raising the conditions of new Appropriations of Lands.

He has obstructed the Administration of Justice by refusing his Assent to Laws for establishing Judiciary powers.

He has made Judges dependent on his Will alone, for the tenure of their offices, and the amount and payment of their salaries.

He has erected a multitude of New Offices, and sent hither swarms of Officers to harrass our people, and eat out their substance.

HE has kept among us, in Times of Peace, Standing Armies, without the Consent of our legislatures.

HE has affected to render the Military independent of and superior to the Civil power.

HE has combined with others to subject us to a jurisdiction foreign to our constitution, and unacknowledged by our laws; giving his Assent to their Acts of pretended Legislation:

FOR quartering large bodies of armed troops among us: FOR protecting them by a mock Trial, from punishment for any Murders which they should commit on the Inhabitants of these States:

FOR cutting off our Trade with all parts of the world:

FOR imposing Taxes on us without our Consent:

FOR depriving us in many cases, of the benefits of Trial by Jury:

FOR transporting us beyond Seas to be tried for pretended offences:

FOR abolishing the free System of English laws in a neighbouring Province, establishing therein an Arbitrary government, and enlarging its Boundaries so as to render it at once an example and fit instrument for introducing the same absolute rule into these Colonies:.

FOR taking away our Charters, abolishing our most valuable Laws, and altering fundamentally the Forms of our Governments:

FOR suspending our own Legislatures, and declaring themselves invested with power to legislate for us in all cases whatsoever.

HE has abdicated Government here, by declaring us out of His Protection and waging War against us.

HE has plundered our seas, ravaged our Coasts, burnt our towns, and destroyed the lives of our people.

HE is at this time transporting large Armies of foreign Mercenaries to compleat the works of death, desolation, and tyranny, already begun with circumstances of Cruelty & perfidy scarcely paralleled in the most barbarous ages, and totally unworthy the Head of a civilized nation.

HE has constrained our fellow Citizens taken Captive on the high Seas to bear Arms against their Country, to become executioners of their friends and Brethren, or to fall themselves by their Hands.

HE has excited domestic insurrections amongst us, and has endeavoured to bring on the inhabitants of our frontiers, the merciless Indian Savages, whose known rule of warfare, is an undistinguished destruction of all ages, sexes, and conditions.

IN every stage of these Oppressions We have Petitioned for Redress in the most humble terms: Our repeated Petitions have been answered only by repeated injury. A Prince, whose character is thus marked by every act which may define a Tyrant, is unfit to be the ruler of a free people.

NOR have We been wanting in attentions to our Brittish [sic] brethren. We have warned them from time to time of attempts by their legislature to extend an unwarrantable jurisdiction over us. We have reminded them of the circumstances of our emigration and settlement here. We have appealed to their native justice and magnanimity, and we have conjured them by the ties of our common kindred to disavow these usurpations, which, would inevitably interrupt our connections and correspondence. They too have been deaf to the voice of justice and of consanguinity. We must, therefore, acquiesce in the necessity, which denounces our Separation, and hold them, as we hold the rest of mankind, Enemies in War, in Peace Friends.

WE, THEREFORE, the Representatives of the UNITED STATES of AMERICA, in General Congress, Assembled, appealing to the Supreme Judge of the world for the rectitude of our intentions, do, in the Name, and by Authority of the good People of these Colonies, solemnly publish and declare, That these United Colonies are, and of Right ought to be FREE AND INDEPENDENT STATES; that they are Absolved from all Allegiance to the British Crown, and that all political connection between them and the State of Great Britain, is and ought to be totally dissolved; and that as Free and Independent States, they have full Power to levy War, conclude Peace, contract Alliances, establish Commerce, and to do all other Acts and Things which INDEPENDENT States may of right do. AND for the support of this Declaration, with a firm reliance on the protection of Divine Providence, we mutually pledge to each other our Lives, our Fortunes, and our sacred Honor.

(Text reproduced from the original manuscript in the Library of Congress as printed in *The Making of the American Republic*, edited by Charles Callan Tansill, New Rochelle, New York, n.b., except that some paragraphing, not in the original document, has been used.)

APPENDIX C

The Declaration
of the Rights of Man
and the Citizen

The following is the text of the Declaration of the Rights of Man and the Citizen adopted on August 26, 1789:

THE REPRESENTATIVES OF THE FRENCH PEOPLE, constituted as a National Assembly, considering that ignorance, disregard, or contempt of the rights of man are the sole causes of public misfortunes and governmental corruption, have resolved to set forth a solemn declaration of the natural, inalienable, and sacred rights of man: in order that this declaration, by being constantly present to all members of the social body, may keep them at all times aware of their rights and duties; that the acts of both the legislative and executive powers, by being liable at every moment to comparison with the aim of all political institutions, may be the more fully respected; and that demands of the citizens, by being founded henceforward on simple and incontestable principles, may always redound to the maintenance of the constitution and the general welfare.

The Assembly consequently recognizes and declares, in the presence and under the auspices of the Supreme Being, the following rights of man and the citizen:

I. Men are born and remain free and equal in rights. Social distinctions may be based only on common utility.

II. The aim of all political associations is to preserve the natural and imprescriptible rights of man. These rights are liberty, property, security, and resistance to oppression.

III.   The principle of all sovereignty rests essentially in the nation. No body and no individual may exercise authority which does not emanate from the nation expressly.

IV.   Liberty consists in the ability to do whatever does not harm another; hence the exercise of the natural rights of each man has no limits except those which assure to other members of society the enjoyment of the same rights. These limits can only be determined by law.

V.   Law may rightfully prohibit only those actions which are injurious to society. No hindrance should be put in the way of anything not prohibited by law, nor may any man be forced to do what the law does not require.

VI.   Law is the expression of the general will. All citizens have the right to take part, in person or by their representatives, in its formation. It must be the same for all whether it protects or penalizes. All citizens being equal in its eyes are equally admissible to all public dignities, offices and employments, according to their capacity, and with no other distinction than that of their virtues and talents.

VII.   No man may be indicted, arrested, or detained except in cases determined by law and according to the forms which it has prescribed. Those who instigate, expedite, execute, or cause to be executed arbitrary orders should be punished; but any citizen summoned or seized by virtue of the law should obey instantly, and renders himself guilty by resistance.

VIII.   Only strictly necessary punishments may be established by law, and no one may be punished except by virtue of a law established and promulgated before the time of the offense, and legally put into force.

IX.   Every man being presumed innocent until judged guilty, if it is deemed indispensable to keep him under arrest, all rigor not necessary to secure his person should be severely repressed by law.

X.   No one may be disturbed for his opinions, even in religion, provided that their manifestation does not trouble public order as established by law.

XI.   Free communication of thought and opinion is one of the most precious of the rights of man. Every citizen may therefore speak, write, print freely, on his own responsibility for abuse of this liberty in cases determined by law.

XII. Preservation of the rights of man and the citizen requires the existence of public forces. These forces are therefore instituted for the advantage of all, not for the private benefit of those to whom they are entrusted.

XIII. For maintenance of public forces and for expenses of administration common taxation is necessary. It should be apportioned equally among all citizens according to their capacity to pay.

XIV. All citizens have the right, by themselves or through their representatives, to have demonstrated to them the necessity of public taxes, to consent to them freely, to follow the use made of the proceeds, and to determine the shares to be paid, the means of assessment and collection, and the durations.

XV. Society has the right to hold accountable every public agent of administration.

XVI. Any society in which the guarantee of rights is not assured or the separation of powers not determined has no constitution.

XVII. Property being an inviolable and sacred right, no one may be deprived of it except for an obvious requirement of public necessity, certified by law, and then on condition of a just compensation in advance.

(Text reproduced from Georges Lefebvre's *The Coming of the French Revolution*, translated by R.R. Palmer, Princeton, New Jersey: Princeton University Press, 1947, 221-23.)

BIBLIOGRAPHY

Aaron, Richard I. *John Locke*, 1937. Oxford: The Clarendon Press, 1965.

Adams, John. *John Adams: A Biography in His Own Words*, ed. James Bishop Peabody. New York: Newsweek Book Division, 1973.

Adams, Samuel. *The Rights of the Colonists, as Men, as Christians, and as Subjects*, 1772, relating Lockean political ideas to the American colonies. Reprinted in Hall, *Christian History*, Vol. 1.

___. *Boston Gazette*, March 1, 1773. His review of "An Essay Concerning the True Original Extent and End of Civil Government," by John Locke, Esq. Republished in Hall, *Christian History*, Vol. 2.

___. *Boston Gazette*, October 28, 1771 and *Boston Gazette*, January 20, 1772 on the political ideas of John Locke. Republished in Hall, *Christian History*, Vol. 2.

Adamson, J. H. and H. F. Folland. *Sir Harry Vane: His Life and Times*. Boston: Gambit Incorporated, 1973.

Amos, Gary. *Defending the Declaration: How the Bible and Christianity Influenced the Writing of the Declaration of Independence*. Brentwood, Tennessee: Wolgemuth & Hyatt, Publishers, Inc., 1989.

Aristotle. *Aristotle's Politics* in *Aristotle on Man and the Universe*. New York: Walter J. Black, Inc., 1943.

Aristotle. "Nichomachean Ethics," in *Aristotle on Man and the Universe*. New York: Walter J. Black, Inc., 1943.

Ashley, Maurice. *England in the Seventeenth Century*, 1952. Baltimore, Maryland: Penguin Books, 1967.

Ashley, Maurice. *Oliver Cromwell and the Puritan Revolution*, 1958. New York: Collier Books Edition, 1966.

Axtell, James L. *The Educational Writings of John Locke*. Cambridge University Press, 1968.

Bancroft, George, *History of the United States*, New York, 1886.

Bailyn, Bernard. *The Ideological Origins of the American Revolution*. Cambridge, Massachusetts: The Belknap Press of Harvard University Press, 1967.

Baldwin, Alice M. *The New England Clergy and the American Revolution*, 1928. New York: Frederick Ungar Publishing Co., 1958.

Bangs, Carl. *Arminius, A Study in the Dutch Reformation*, 2d ed. Grand Rapids, Michigan: Francis Asbury Press of Zondervan Publishing House, 1985.

Bartlett, Robert Merrill. *The Pilgrim Way*. Philadelphia: Pilgrim Press, 1971.

Becker, Carl. *The Declaration of Independence: A Study in the History of Political Ideas*. New York: Alfred A. Knopf, 1960.

Bernier, Olivier. *Lafayette, Hero of Two Worlds*. New York: E. P. Dutton, 1983.

Bevan, Bryan. *King William III, Prince of Orange: The First European*. London: Rubicon Press, 1997.

Bigongiari, Dino. *The Political Ideas of St. Thomas Aquinas*. New York: Hafner Publishing Co., Inc., 1953.

Bird, Otto A. *The Idea of Justice*. New York: Frederick A. Praeger, 1967.

Blackstone, William. *Commentaries on the Laws of England*, 1765. New York: Oceana Publications, 1966.

Bowen, Catherine Drinker. *The Most Dangersous Man in America: Scenes from the Life of Benjamin Franklin*. Boston and Toronto: Little Brown and Company, 1974.

Brailaford, H. H. *The Levellers and the English Revolution*. Stanford, California: Stanford University Presss, 1961.

Budziszewski, J., Dr. *Written on the Heart: The Case for Natural Law*. Downer's Grove, Illinois: InterVarsity Presss, 1997.

Cicero, Marcus Tullius. *The Treatises of Cicero*. London, 1853, in *The Western Tradition*. Boston: D. C. Heath and Company, 1959.

Clark, Jonas. *The Battle of Lexington: Sermon and Eyewitness Narrative*. Ventura, California: Nordskog Publishing Inc., 2007.

Cobban, Aldred. *Aspects of the French Revolution*. New York: George Braziller, Inc., 1968.

Condorcet, Marquis de. "Sketch for a Historical Picture of the Progress of the Human Mind," in *French Philosophers from Descartes to Sartre*, Leonard M. Marsak, editor. Cleveland & New York: Meridien Books of World Publishing Co., 1961.

Cooke, Samuel, Rev. *Election Sermon, May 30, 1770*. Boston: Edes and Gill, 1770.

Coste, Pierre. "The Character of Mr. Locke," a letter published in the *Nouvelles de la Republiques des Lettres*, February 1705. See John Locke, *Works*, (listed below), Vol. 10.

Cranston, Maurice. *John Locke*. New York: The Macmillan Co., 1957.

Crocker, Lester G. *Jean-Jacques Rousseau, The Quest*. New York: The MacMillan Co., 1968.

____. *Jean-Jacques Rousseau, The Prophetic Voice*. New York: The MacMillan Co., 1973.

Cunningham, Noble E., Jr. *In Pursuit of Reason: The Life of Thomas Jefferson*. Baton Rouge and London: Louisiana State University Press, 1987.

Dickinson, John. Letter No. 7 of his series of "Farmer's Letters to the Inhabitants of the British Colonies," Philadelphia, 1767, in Hall, *Christian History*, Vol. 1.

Dunn, John. *The Political Thought of John Locke: An Historical Account of the Argument of the "Two Treatises of Government."* Cambridge University Press, 1969, 1983.

Durant, Will and Ariel. *The Age of Voltaire*. Vol. IX of *The Story of Civilization*. New York: Simon and Schuster, 1965.

Erler, Edward J. *Equality, Natural Rights, and the Rule of Law: The View from the American Founding*. Claremont, California: Claremont Institute, 1984.

___. "The Constitution of Principle" in *Still the Law of the Land? Essays on Changing Interpretations of the Constitution*, Hillsdale, Michigan: Hillsdale College Press, 1987.

Fiske, John. *The Beginnings of New England*. Boston and New York: Houghton, Mifflin and Company, 1889.

___. *Old Virginia and Her Neighbours*. 2 vols. Boston and New York: Houghton, Mifflin and Company, 1900.

Fowler, Thomas. *Locke*. London: 1888; reprint ed., New York: AMS Press, Inc., 1968.

Frothingham, Richard. *The Rise of the Republic*, 1872.

Furet, Francois and Denis Richet. *The French Revolution*. Translated by Stephen Hardman. New York: The Macmillan Company, 1970.

Gay, Peter. *The Rise of Modern Paganism*, 2 vols. Vol. 1: *The Enlightenment: An Interpretation*. Vol. 2: *The Science of Freedom*. New York: Alfred Knopf, 1966.

Gentz, Friedrich (von). "The French and American Revolutions Compared," 1810. Translated by John Quincy Adams. In *Three Revolutions*, 3-95. Introduction and Reflections on the Russian Revolution by Stefan T. Possony. Chicago: Henry Regnery Company, 1959.

Green, John Richard. *The History of the English People*. Chicago and New York: Belford, Clarke & Co., 1886.

Green, John Richard. *A Short History of the English People*. New York and London: Harper & Brothers, Publishers, 1898.

Guizot, M. and Madame Guizot De Witt. *The History of France*, 6 vols. New York: Peter Fenelon Collier, 1878.

Hall, Verna M., Compiler. *The Christian History of the American Revolution: Consider and Ponder*. San Francisco: Foundation for American Christian Education, 1975; www.face.net.

___. *The Christian History of the Constitution of the United States of America*, Vol. 1: *Christian Self-Government*. San Francisco: Foundation for American Christian Education, 1960; Bicentennial Edition, 1975, www.face.net.

___. *The Christian History of the Constitution of the United States of America*, Vol. 2: *Christian Self-Government with Union*. San Francisco: Foundation for American Christian Education, 1966; 1975; www.face.net.

Hamilton, Alexander. "The Farmer Refuted," February 5, 1775, pamphlet, in *The Basic Ideas of Alexander Hamilton*, ed. Richard B. Morris. New York: The Pocket Library, 1957.

Henry, Patrick. *Speech at the Virginia Convention, March 20, 1775*. In Hall, *Christian History*, Vol. 1.

Hitchcock, Gad. *A Sermon Preached at Plymouth, December 22, 1774*. In Hall, *Christian History of the American Revolution*.

Howard, Simeon. *Sermon Preached to the Ancient and Honorable Artillery Company. Boston, 1773*. In Hall, *Christian History of the American Revolution*.

Hunt, Gaillard. *The Life of James Madison*, 1902; reprint ed., New York: Russell & Russell, 1968.

Hurwitz, Robert H. "John Locke and the Preservation of Liberty..." in *The Moral Foundations of the American Republic*. Editor, Robert H. Lutz. Charlottesville: University of Virginia, 1986.

Hyneman, Charles S. and Donald S. Lutz. *American Political Writing during the Founding Era* (1760-1805), 2 vols. Indianapolis: Liberty Press, 1983.

Irving, Washington. *Life of Washington*. 3 vols. Chicago, New York and San Francisco: Belford, Clarke & Company, n.d.

Johnson, Stephen, Rev. *Fast Day Sermon*, December 28, 1765.

King, Peter, Lord. *The Life of John Locke with Extracts from His Correspondence, Journals and Common-place Books*, 2 vols. London: Henry Colburn, 1829.

Koch, Adrienne. *The Philosophy of Thomas Jefferson*. Gloucester, Massachusetts: Peter Smith, 1957.

Laslett, Peter. *John Locke—Two Treatises of Government. A Critical Edition with an Introduction and Apparatus Criticus*. Cambridge, England: Cambridge University Press, 1960. Mentor Books Edition. New York and Toronto: The New American Library, Inc., 1965.

Latourette, Kenneth Scott. *A History of Christianity*. New York: Harper & Brothers, 1953.

Latzko, Andreas. *Lafayette: A Life*. New York: The Literary Guild, 1946.

Le Bon, Andre. *Modern France: 1789-1895*. New York: G. P. Putnam's Sons, 1898.

Le Clerc, Jean. *The Life and Character of Mr. John Locke*, 1705. Reprinted in *Locke's Essay Concerning Human Understanding*. Chicago: The Open Court Publishing Co., 1905.

Lefebvre, Georges. *The Coming of the French Revolution*. Translator, R. R. Palmer. Princeton, New Jersey: Princeton University Press, 1947.

Locke, John. *The Works of John Locke*, 1714. Germany: Scientia Verlag Aalen, 1963. Reprint of 1823 edition. Ten Volumes.

____. *Essay Concerning Human Understanding*, 1690. In *Works*, Vols. 1-3.

____. *The Fundamental Constitutions of Carolina*. In *Works*, Vol. 10.

____. *Letter Concerning Toleration*, London, 1689. In *Works*, Vol. 6.

____. *Letter to the Reverend Mr. Richard King*, 25 August 1703. In *Works*, Vol. 10.

____. *Memoirs Relating to the Life of Anthony, First Earl of Shaftesbury*. In *Works*, Vol. 9.

____. *Paraphrase and Notes on the Epistles of St. Paul to the Galatians, Corinthians, Romans, Ephesians*, 1705-1707. In *Works*, Vol. 8.

____. *The Reasonableness of Christianity*, 1695. In *Works*, Vol. 7.

____. *The Second Treatise Of Civil-Government*. Photostat copy of 1714 edition. In Hall, *Christian History*, Vol. 1.

___. *A Vindication of The Reasonableness of Christianity,* 1697. In *Works,* Vol. 7.

___. *A Second Vindication of The Reasonableness of Christianity,* 1699. In *Works,* Vol. 7.

___. *Some Thoughts Concerning Education,* 1693. In *Works,* Vol. 3.

___. *Two Treatises of Government,* 1690. In *Works,* Vol. 5.

Loetscher, Lefferts A. *A Brief Hisory of the Presbyterians.* Philadelphia: Westminster Press, 1958.

MacIlwain, Charles Howard. *The American Revolution: A Constitutional Interpretation,* 1923. Ithaca: New York: Cornell University Press, 1958.

McLachlan, H. *The Religious Opinions of Milton, Locke, and Newton.* Manchester: Manchester University Press, 1941.

McLaughlin, Andrew C. *Foundations of American Constitutionalism.* New York University, 1932. Greenwich, Conn.: Fawcett Publications, Inc., 1961.

McLellan, David. *Marx Before Marxism.* New York: Harper & Row, 1971.

Madison, James. *James Madison: A Biography In His Own Words.* 2 vols. ed., Merrill D. Peterson. New York: Newsweek Books, 1974.

___. *Letters and Other Writings of James Madison,* 4 vols. Philadelphia: J. B. Lippincott & Co., 1867.

Martin, W. Stanley. *The Brave Boys of Derry, or No Surrender* (Londonderry, Ireland events of 1688-89). 1900, republished by Nordskog Publishing Inc., 2010.

Marx, Karl. *The Communist Manifesto,* 1848. Gateway Edition. Introduction: Stefan T. Possony. Chicago: Henry Regnery, 1954.

___. *The Essential Writings of Karl Marx.* Editor, David Caute. New York: The Macmillan Company, 1967.

Matthews, John Carter. *Richard Henry Lee.* Williamsburg, Virginia: Virginia Independence Bicentennial Commission, 1978.

Mayhew, Jonathan. *Sermon on Unlimited Submission to the Higher Powers,* 1750. In John Wingate Thornton, *The Pulpit of the American Revolution.* Boston: Gould and Lincoln, 1860.

Miller, Helen Hill. *George Mason: Gentleman Revolutionary.* Chapel Hill, North Carolina: The University of North Carolina Press, 1975.

Montesquieu, Baron de. *The Spirit of the Laws,* 1748. Translated by Thomas Nugent, LL.D. New York: The Colonial Press, 1900.

Morison, Samuel Eliot. *The Oxford History of the American People,* 3 vols. Oxford University Press, 1965. Republished by Mentor Books, New York, 1972.

Morley, Felix. *Freedom and Federalism.* Chicago: Henry Regnery Company, 1959.

Morley, John, Viscount. *Rousseau and His Era,* 1873. 2 vols. New York: MacMillan & Co, 1923.

Otis, James. *The Rights of the British Colonies,* 1764. In Hall, *Christian History,* Vol. 2.

Pangle, Thomas L. *The Spirit of Modern Republicanism: The Moral Vision of the American Founders and the Philosophy of Locke*. Chicago: University of Chicago Press, 1988.

Payne, Robert. *Marx, A Biography*. New York: Simon and Schuster, 1968.

Pound, Roscoe. *The Spirit of the Common Law*, 1921. Boston: Beacon Press, 1963.

Rand, Benjamin, ed. *The Correspondence of John Locke and Edward Clarke*, with a biographical study, 1927. Plainview, New York: Books for Libraries Press, 1975.

Romanell, Patrick, ed. *John Locke: A Letter Concerning Toleration*. New York: The Liberal Arts Press, 2d ed., 1955.

Rousseau, Jean-Jacques. *Confessions*. New York: Alfred A. Knopf, 1923.

____. *The Social Contract and Discourses*. Translated by G. D. H. Cole. New York: E. P. Dutton and Company, Inc.; London: J. M. Dent and Sons, Limited, 1950.

Rudé, George. *Robespierre*. Englewood Cliff, New Jersey: Prentice-Hall, Inc., 1967.

Rutland, Robert. *George Mason: Reluctant Statesman*. Colonial Williamsburg and Holt, Rinehart and Winston, 1961.

Rutland, Robert, ed. *The Papers of George Mason*. Vol. 1: 1725-1792. Chapel Hill: University of North Carolina Press, 1970.

Rushdoony, Rousas J. *The Politics of Guilt and Pity*. Vallecito, California: Ross House Books, 1970.

Slater, Rosalie J. "George Washington and the Marquis de Lafayette: Two Men, Two Revolutions." *The Journal of the Foundation for American Christian Education* Vol. VI (1994-1995): 103-153.

____. *Teaching and learning America's Christian History: The Principle Approach*. San Francisco: Foundation for American Christian Education, 1965; 1975.

Smith, H. Shelton, Robert T. Handy, and Lefferts A. Loetscher. *American Christianity: An Historical Interpretation with Representative Documents*, Vol. 1: 1607-1820. New York: Charles Scribners' Sons, 1960.

Strauss, Leo. *Natural Right and History*. Chicago: University of Chicago Press, 1953.

Swanson, Mary-Elaine. *The Education of James Madison: A Model For Today*. Montgomery, Alabama: The Hoffman Center, 1994.

____. "James Madison and the Presbyterian Idea of Man and Government." In *Religion and Culture in Jefferson's Virginia*, 119-132. Edited by Garrett Ward Sheldon and Daniel L. Dreisbach. Lanham, Maryland: Rowman & Littlefield Publishers, Inc., 2000.

____. "The Law of Nature in John Locke's Writings." *The Journal of the Foundation for American Christian Education*, Vol. VIII (1999-2000): 61-77.

____. *Study Guide to The Christian History of the Constitution of the United States of America*, Vol. 2: *Christian Self-Government With Union*, Compiled by Verna M. Hall. Palo Cedro, California: American Christian History Institute, 1988, 42.

Tansill, Charles Callan, ed. *Debates in the Federal Convention of 1787*, reprinted in *The Making of the American Republic*. New Rochelle, New York: Arlington House, n.d.

Taine, Hippolyte Adolphe. *The Ancient Regime*. Translated by John Durand. 2 vols. New York: Henry Holt & Company, 1891.

Thompson, J. M. *Robespierre and the French Revolution*. New York: Collier Books, 1969.

Thornton, John Wingate. *The Pulpit of the American Revolution*. Boston, 1860.

Tocqueville, Alexis De. *Democracy in America*, 2 vols., 1835 and 1840. Translated by Henry Reeve with revisions by Francis Bowen and Phillips Bradley. New York: Alfred A. Knopf, Inc., 1945. Vintage Books, 1955.

____. *The Old Regime and the French Revolution*, 1835. Translated by Stuart Gilbert. New York: Doubleday Anchor Books, 1955.

Warren, Mercy Otis. *History of the Rise, Progress, and Termination of the American Revolution*, 1805.

Webster, Noah. *An American Dictionary of the English Language*, facsimile 1828 Edition. San Francisco: Foundation for American Christian Education, republished 1967, 1995; www.face.net.

Whitehead, John W. *The Second American Revolution*. Elgin and Weston, Illinois: David C. Cook Publishing Co., 1982; Charlottesville, Virginia: The Rutherford Institute, 2004.

Williams, Elisha, Rev. *Sermon on The Essential Rights and Liberties of Protestants*. In Hall, *The Christian History of the American Revolution*.

Wilson, James. "Of The General Principles of Law and Obligation" Vol. 1, in *The Works of the Honourable James Wilson*, LL.D., Philadelphia, 1804.

Yolton, Jean S., Editor. *A Locke Miscellany. Locke Biography and Criticism for All*. Bristol: Thoemes Antiquarian Books Ltd, 1990.

Yolton, John W. *Locke, An Introduction*. Oxford: Basil Blackwell Ltd., 1985.

GENERAL INDEX

Indexing includes concepts and cross-references to help facilitate research and topical study.

Index to John Locke's Writings

[Dates somewhat approximate as to when written, translated, and published in various editions. This list is not exhaustive.]

KEY: Q=Quotation; P=Paraphrase; C=Commentary/mention

ABOUT THE AUTHOR

Mary-Elaine Swanson (1927-2011), had a distinguished career as a historical researcher, biographer, author, educator, and speaker.

She wrote numerous articles on America's Christian history, and her book *The Education of James Madison: A Model for Today*, 1994, won the Angel Award from Excellence in Media, Los Angeles, and praise from such scholars as Dr. Daniel Dreisbach of American University, Washington, D.C., who wrote: "I can see that you have made a significant contribution to the scholarship on Madison. You have sounded some timely and important themes in this book (themes unfortunately ignored in the standard works on Madison). It is a resource I will draw on to great advantage."

Scholar James McClellan of the Liberty Fund, Indianapolis, Indiana, also praised that book writing that: "Notwithstanding the surge of biographies and interpretive studies on James Madison in recent years, Mary-Elaine Swanson's carefully researched and well-written account of the ideas and education that shaped the thinking of the 'Father of the Constitution' fills an important gap. Particularly noteworthy is her extensive treatment of the influence of the Scottish Enlightenment and Dr. John Witherspoon of

Princeton College on Madison during his formative years, and the author's persuasive argument that Madison's separationist views were not the result of hostility toward Christianity or preference for irreligion over religion, but of a deep-seated concern that all Christian denominations be treated fairly and equally."

Mrs. Swanson wrote over 80 biographies of historians and artists from her original research in primary sources, many of which appear in Verna M. Hall's historic compilations, *The Christian History of the Constitution*, Vol. 1, 1960 and Vol. 2, 1966, *The Christian History of the American Revolution*, 1975, and *George Washington: The Character and Influence of One Man*, 2000.

As Resident Scholar for American Colonial Studies at The Mayflower Institute (now The World History Institute) in Southern California for nearly a decade, she was the co-author with Marshall Foster of the best-selling book and television film, *The American Covenant: The Untold Story*.

Mrs. Swanson subsequently became Vice-President of James B. Rose's American Christian History Institute in Palo Cedro, California, where she produced for parents and teachers a *Study Guide* to Verna Hall's compilation, *Christian History . . .*, Vol. 2: *Christian Self-Government with Union*.

She has spoken at Colonial Williamsburg during their Religion Month. At the Christopher Columbus Quincentenary Symposium sponsored by the Foundation for American Christian Education and co-directed by The Providence Foundation in Virginia, 1992, she presented "The Monroe Doctrine and the Hemisphere of Liberty."

In January 1996 she spoke at a symposium at the University of Virginia, and in 2000, her talk on "James Madison and the Presbyterian Idea of Man and Government" was published in the collection from that symposium, *Religion and Political Culture in Jefferson's Virginia*, edited by Garrett Ward Sheldon and Daniel L. Dreisbach and published by Rowman & Littlefield Publishers, Inc., Lanham, Maryland.

Her cherished, decades-long study of the history of liberty inspired her article "The Law of Nature in John Locke's Writings: A Break with Classic Natural Law," published in *The Journal of the Foundation for American Christian Education*, Volume VIII, 1999-2000.

Nordskog Publishing Inc. is honored to publish posthumously Mary-Elaine Swanson's magnum opus and crowning achievement, **John Locke: Philosopher of American Liberty.**

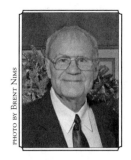

PHOTO BY BRENT NIMS

Publisher's Word

Gerald Christian Nordskog

Why Our Founders Fought for

"Life, Liberty, and Property"

Mary-Elaine Swanson has for many years written from original research innumerable historical biographies and articles and often spoken on America's Christian history and Biblically-based principles of government. I respected and loved Mary-Elaine since the days of the Mayflower Institute meetings where we first met. Now through Nordskog Publishing, I have the privilege of offering to the public her opus *John Locke: Philosopher of American Liberty.*

Writing from and vastly quoting from Locke's original sources, Mrs. Swanson corrects for us the broad misinterpretation and erroneous secularization of his philosophy perpetrated on us by academic collectivism. In her biography of Locke's life, the history of his time is thoroughly presented, showing clearly that he was so much more than a cloistered philosopher. He was actively involved in the major history-changing events of his day, his teaching and writing effective, even instrumental in Parliamentary legislation and the Glorious Revolution which brought William and Mary to the throne, and in the advancement of religious liberty and civil rights in England.

We believe it is vital for Americans to study this now in order to understand how to recover in our generation and perpetuate for our children Biblically-based civil government that has produced the greatest liberty, productivity, and prosperity to the greatest number in the history of the world.

A half a century ago when I was asked to run for public office in California, one of the very first books I read to prepare for that adventure was Frederic Bastiat's *The Law*, a short book but concise and excellent, clarifying what the law should be. Bastiat (1801-1850) was a French economist and statesman, and *The Law*, which is still read over a hundred and fifty years later, was first published as a pamphlet in 1850, the year of his death. He clearly spelled out that it is "Legal Plunder" for rulers and civil governments of any kind to pass laws that take from some and give to others by government decree. It is the same as theft or stealing (according to the Ten Commandments, "Thou shalt not steal"), and socialistic to take property owned by some and mandate redistribution of it to others. Long before, John Locke always affirmed the same principle that required "Life, Liberty, and Property" to be protected and encouraged in a free society founded upon God's Law of Liberty.

Locke's voluminous philosophical writings are all based in the Bible. His (and our founders') reference to Nature's God is always and only to the Creator as we know from His Word and as He was from "In the beginning God" and "Let there be light" before the written Word; and likewise the Laws of Nature and Nature's God is always and only The Law from the Creator and as revealed to us in His Word and in Creation, and the nature of man endowed with God-given capacity for reason to reflect on revealed law. As Mrs. Swanson clearly shows, Locke was not a secular rationalist or sensationist as he has been falsely characterized.

You will see this in the actual writings and reasonings in comparison with the French and other secular-humanist philosophers, but you will see it also as his teaching is applied and effectively walked out in English history and in America—especially when the author examines side-by-side the differences in the French Revolution and the American War for Independence.

Indeed, John Locke penned the "Constitutions for Carolina," and many of the local colonial governments followed Locke's reasoning in drafting their Declarations of Rights. Locke's great contribution to the natural right theory is his view of "life, liberty, and property" as not three separate rights but intrinsically one great right which he called "Property," beginning with the life of the individual. James Madison summed it up in Lockean fashion, "Conscience is the most sacred of all property."

Further, Locke reasoned out from a Biblical basis exactly when men are justified, even impelled, to dissolve corrupt government which violates the legitimate purpose of civil government among men and the inalienable God-given rights it is meant to protect. Some phrases in the American Declaration of Independence read almost as if Jefferson who greatly admired the English philosopher, copied right out of John Locke! Certainly he was well read of Mr. Locke's Biblical stances and utilized some of his verbiage right in our Declaration of Independence.

As Mrs. Swanson observes, Americans, under the laws of England, had uniquely lived out a Biblical culture and practice of local self-government, with the rights of Englishmen. It was England, not the colonies, that forced an overthrow of the existing civil order. Under the imperial monarchy, England imposed intolerable and arbitrary taxes, regulation, and military oppression on the lives of Americans, with none of the representation required by the English Constitution. These impositions intended to undermine and destroy—for the monetary gain of the Mother Country—the legitimate American order. The colonists wrote extensive petitions to the British Parliament and appeals to the king who failed to respond. America's War for Independence, the American Revolution, was a defensive action made necessary to protect the lawful existing order. This unique "revolution" in contrast to many in history that end in tyranny, more closely fit the definition: "a course or motion which brings every point of a surface or periphery of a body back to the place at which it began to move; motion of anything that brings it back to the same point or state." (Noah Webster, *An American Dictionary of the English Language*, facsimile 1828 edition.)

And then those Lockean principles of government were incorporated into the United States Constitution and Bill of Rights. Haven't you wondered just what "the pursuit of happiness" means? and wanted to see clearly what is undermining America and how to effectually overcome it? Well, "Life, Liberty, and Property" (and the "pursuit of happiness") are clearly Lockean, and not just life and liberty but our inalienable right to our personal property is absolutely essential to a free people. We live in a moment of extreme political danger. The contemporary Left hates Locke because he represents an inherent order in the universe. The very language of Christian liberty is nearly lost. Locke through Mrs. Swanson's clear exposition must speak again to our and future generations to arm us with the Biblical principles and reasoning inherent in our foundation and under attack. We, the citizens who are responsible for and have the power to preserve these freedoms our founders fought and died for, need to regain the understanding of the time-proven, Biblical basis of man's rights and liberty and to pass it on to our children.

—Gerald Christian Nordskog, President
Nordskog Publishing, February 22, 2012

Theology Editor's Word

Ronald W. Kirk

The law of the Lord is perfect, converting the soul:
the testimony of the Lord is sure, making wise the simple. (Psalm 19:7)

The spirit of the Lord God is upon me;
because the Lord hath anointed me to preach good tidings unto the meek;
he hath sent me to bind up the brokenhearted, to proclaim liberty to the captives,
and the opening of the prison to them that are bound. (Isaiah 61:1)

Stand fast therefore in the liberty wherewith Christ hath made us free,
and be not entangled again with the yoke of bondage. (Galatians 5:1)

Mary-Elaine Swanson was a great lady and excellent scholar. She aptly and well represents America's Christian history to the present age. Associated with the Christian history movement spearheaded by Verna M. Hall and Rosalie J. Slater of the Foundation for American Christian Education, Mrs. Swanson also conducted research and wrote for Marshall Foster's Mayflower Institute, and later for James B. Rose's American Christian History Institute.

I thank our publisher Gerald Christian Nordskog for the privilege of writing an editor's word to *John Locke*. Mary-Elaine Swanson had tremendous personal influence on me and my family. When I first read the *American Covenant*, co-authored by Mrs. Swanson, my life was changed forever. In 1982, I attended two separate nine-day Leadership Conferences sponsored by James B. Rose, where some of the most accomplished Christian historians and governmental philosophers spoke, including Mr. Rose, Marshall Foster, Charles Hull Wolfe, Paul Jehle, Katherine Dang, Beth Ballenger, Ruth Smith, Ruth's daughter Jeanette, and, of course, Mary-Elaine Swanson. Having committed my own life and studies two years earlier to the cause of Christ and His kingdom, through these conferences I came to recognize the Christian responsibility for stewardship of culture and relational government. Here, sitting at the feet of these leaders, my elementary education in the principles of Biblical liberty began to coalesce with some of the most fundamental and structural elements of applied Biblical Christian faith.

From Mrs. Swanson, I learned of the Biblical roots of American federalism, a corrected form of covenantal civil government first known in Europe during Middle Ages. I learned how the American Founders defined the term we understand today. I learned of the contrasting smothering, paternalistic, and ultimately tyrannical view of government common to Europe, as exemplified by the French Rousseau and Voltaire. I learned of systematic Christian liberty with union, based largely on the philosophical writings of John Locke. Mrs. Swanson spoke on the topic "The Law of Nature—Divine or Human?"

Then there is the personal. In 1984, we providentially moved to a house just four doors from Mary-Elaine and her endearing, personable, and witty husband, Nils. The Swansons invited my wife Christina, our three daughters, and me to tea, and then Mrs. Swanson regaled us with a classical harpsichord concert. How many people do you know who are accomplished on the harpsichord?

In a word, Mary-Elaine Swanson became the dearest of friends as well as mentor. I cannot overstate my gratitude for her contribution to my life and family. (For the same principles of godly, relational government apply—with great success when diligently practiced by faith—from the most intimate spheres of personal relationship to the greatest international ones.)

Our Savior clearly planted His own man John Locke as a singular, strategic, and hugely profound contributor to the history of Christian liberty. As Mary-Elaine Swanson is also a providential figure, her book on John Locke demands reading. Anyone who seeks to understand the difference between godly liberty and the tyranny inherent in humanistic thinking must read this book. Such tyranny was the consistent norm for millennia because of man's inherent sinfulness. If we will recover in our generation the blessings of institutional liberty, we must heed the message of this book.

—Ronald W. Kirk, Theology Editor
Nordskog Publishing, July 4, 2011

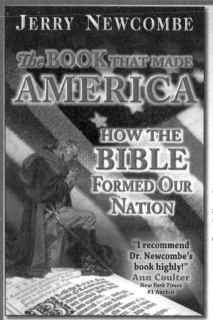

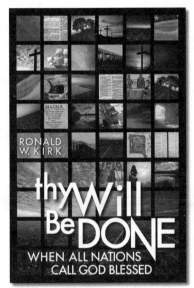

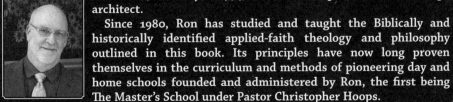

To see all of our exciting titles and
view book contents, and to get ebooks
go to:
www.NordskogPublishing.com

If you like solid and inspiring content,
get our free **eNewsletter,**
The Bell Ringer.
Get it here:
www.NordskogPublishing.com/eNewsletter

We also invite you to browse the
many short articles, poems, and testimonies
by various perceptive writers—
here:
PublishersCorner.NordskogPublishing.com

Ask the publisher about upcoming titles
and e-book versions, and a discount
when you purchase multiple books.